Praise for
When Corporations Rule the World

"*This is a 'must read' book*—a searing indictment of an unjust international economic order, not by a wild-eyed idealistic left-winger, but by a sober scion of the establishment with impeccable credentials. It left me devastated but also very hopeful. Something can be done to create a more just economic order."

Archbishop Desmond M. Tutu
Nobel Peace Laureate

"*Building on the electrifying,* best-selling first edition of *When Corporations Rule the World*, this new edition expands and updates Korten's laser-like analysis of how global corporations dominate people and their governments, and the miserable conditions that result when the few rule the many. Korten then shows practical pathways to a realizable future of more just, prosperous, and sustainable societies. This book will agitate your mind, elevate your soul, and engage your civic spirit."

Ralph Nader

"*Like many of the people* who attended the World Trade Organization teach-ins in Seattle, I was motivated to be there because of David Korten's work. *When Corporations Rule the World* continues to be at the very center of this expanding global dialogue. This revised and updated edition is even more powerful than the original in its articulation of the issues, its stories of the struggle, and its compelling call to each and every one of us to become participants in what I believe to be a sacred trust . . . creating a world that works for all."

Danny Glover
Activist and Actor

"*Periodically,* there comes along a book which really must be read by everybody associated with business and/or politics. I think this is one such book."

Social & Environmental Accounting

"*Should be high on the list* of 'must-read' books for even the busiest corporate executive."

The Financial Times (*London*)

"*Korten's book is creating* an intellectual framework for dealing with the issues of the entry of humankind into the 21st century."

Klaus Schwab
President, World Economic Forum

"*If you work in business,* or know someone who does, this book is required reading. Korten defines the business agenda for the next 20 years."

Peter Block
Author of *Stewardship and Flawless Consulting*

"*An incomparable presentation* of those forces and institutions that are ruling the nations and ruining the Earth. One of the most important books of this century."

Thomas Berry
Theologian and Author of *The Dream of the Earth*

"*A clear-eyed, rational critique.* . . . Korten's book deserves a large readership."

Academy of Management Review

"*This book should be read* by every thinking person in the developing world."

Rashmi Mayur
International Environmental Scientist
Director, International Institute for a Sustainable Future, Bombay

"*Regular readers of* publications such as *The Economist* or *Business Week* might well think they are having a bad dream when they open David Korten's latest book. The realities that Korten describes in the corporate-led trend toward economic globalization are far different from the glowing reports of growth opportunities and strategic positioning depicted in the mainline business press. . . . This book is riveting reading, relevant to the everyday experiences of life, and rich in current detail."

The Marketplace

"*A profoundly important book.* Required reading for the modern day revolutionary struggling against corporate globalization. When Korten spoke at our Action Camp before the Seattle WTO demonstrations I'd swear that he was channeling Thomas Payne."

John Sellers
Director, The Ruckus Society

"*This book has been a 'must read'* route map for many of us who found ourselves on the wrong (right!) side of the police lines at the Seattle protests. Now this essential update finds hope in the burgeoning counterbalance that citizen groups are bringing to bear on big business—tempering its vast power with a conscience, and, God forbid, maybe even a heart!"

Anita Roddick
Founder and Co-Chair, The Body Shop

"*I recommend this book* to any business executive as a 'must read.' It deals with one of the most important questions we can ask these days: What is the future role of business on the planet? The book is tough-minded, hard-hitting, and right on the money. It might at first glance strike some readers as anti-business, but it is not. It is just pro-people and pro-planet."

Willis Harman
President, Institute of Noetic Sciences

"*A wise, learned,* and inspiring book about the challenge of the new world economy. Korten's impressive analysis of global corporations is essential reading for anyone who places a higher value on the welfare of human beings than on money. The book is indispensable help in the search for a more hopeful path into the twenty-first century."

Richard J. Barnet
Co-author of *Global Dreams: Imperial Corporations and the New World Order*

"*A revealing portrait* of the effects of corporations on the global scene along with proposals for a transformation that will bring the massive global economy into tune with human values. Highly recommended."

In Context *magazine*

"*Never in history* has there occurred the economic gamble that is taking place today in the form of economic globalization. David Korten's important work begins the critical process of economic reformation that will surely follow this universal loss of sovereignty, self, and community."

Paul Hawken
Author of *The Ecology of Commerce*

"*Korten is an honest witness* to the disastrous betrayal of common people and future generations that is being carried out by corporations, governments, and multilateral banks. He cuts through the loud rhetoric of economic growth and global economic integration to the facts of increasing poverty, inequality, and dependence. I hope that this book is widely read."

Herman E. Daly
Senior Research Scholar, University of Maryland

"*David Korten is an eloquent critic* of globalization that is untempered by either compassion or vision. He will move you to profoundly rethink out collective direction, and to take steps towards redirecting your own life."

Joe Dominguez and Vicki Robin
Co-authors of *Your Money or Your Life*

"Taking us beyond the myths and illusions of the global economy, Korten's proposals for change bear careful consideration by all who care about the future we leave to our children."

Doug Tompkins
Cofounder and ex-CEO, Esprit

"The world system is not working for most people. In this courageous volume David Korten confronts the illusions of unlimited growth and domination of global corporations. He describes an alternative to a global system rooted in participatory communities, spiritual values, and mutual respect. A compelling vision."

John Al Lapp
Executive Secretary, Mennonite Central Committee

"The transnational corporations that control the global economy are working hard to assure that nothing interferes with their short-term interests. In this masterful book, David Korten spells out the dramatic implications and shows why our greatest priority today must be to bring economic activities once more under democratic control."

Teddy Goldsmith
Founding Editor of *The Ecologist*
Recipient of The Right Livelihood Award,
commonly known as the Alternative Nobel Prize

"Hard-nosed and idealistic, Korten challenges corporate and financial leaders as intensively as grassroots community organizers. Korten's wide-ranging and controversial views enrich the dialogue among those who must address the widening gap between the rich and the poor and the future of the planet—that is the dialogue among all of us."

Claire L. Gaudiani
President, Connecticut College

"When Corporations Rule the World spells out the reality and consequences of a corporate-dominated globalization process and how it is undermining democracy. It sets forth an agenda for regaining citizen sovereignty that is an important starting point on the long road back to democracy."

Maude Barlow
National Chairperson, Council of Canadians

When
Corporations
Rule
the World

When
Corporations
Rule
the World

David C. Korten

A Copublication of
Kumarian Press, Inc.
and Berrett-Koehler Publishers, Inc.

BK

BERRETT-KOEHLER PUBLISHERS, INC.
San Francisco

KUMARIAN
PRESS

When Corporations Rule the World, Second Edition

Published 2001 in the United States of America by Kumarian Press, Inc.,
and Berrett-Koehler Publishers, Inc.

Kumarian Press, Inc.
1294 Blue Hills Avenue
Bloomfield, Connecticut 06002 USA
(860) 243-2098

Berrett-Koehler Publishers, Inc.
450 Sansome Street, Suite 1200
San Francisco, California 94111-3320
(415) 288-0260

*Design by Nicholas A. Kosar. Copyedited by Beth Richards.
Proofread by Jody El-Assadi. Indexed by Barbara DeGennaro.
The text of this book is set in Adobe Minion 11/14.*

Printed in Canada on acid-free paper by
Transcontinental Printing and Graphics, Inc.
Text printed with vegetable oil-based ink.

∞ The paper used in this publication meets the minimum requirements
of the American National Standard for Information Sciences—Permanence of
Paper for Printed Library Materials, ANSI Z39.48–1984.

Library of Congress Cataloging-in-Publication Data
Korten, David C.
    When corporations rule the world / David C. Korten — 2nd ed.
        p.   cm.
    Includes index.
    ISBN 1–887208–04–6 (alk. paper).
    1. Corporations—Political aspects. 2. Industries—Environmental aspects
  3. Industrialization—Social aspects. 4. Big business. 5. Power (Social sciences).
  6. Business and politics. 7. International business enterprises.
  8. International economic relations. 9. Sustainable development. I. Title.
  HD2326 .K647 2001
  322'.3—dc21   00–054452

    10 09 08 07 06 05 04 03 02   10 9 8 7 6 5 4

First Printing 2001

To the courageous youth who put their lives on the line
in Seattle, Washington on November 30, 1999
in defense of life and democracy
and gave the world hope.

And

To my life partner, Dr. Frances F. Korten,
who shares the incredible journey
on a road less traveled.

CONTENTS

FOREWORD

by Danny Glover

HOW DO WE CREATE A MORE SUSTAINABLE, and at the same time a more economically and socially just world? Sustainable in the sense that we steward responsibly, and for the benefit of all this magnificently beautiful, small blue planet that we are blessed to call home. It is the major challenge of our time. In this revised edition of *When Corporations Rule the World*, David Korten presents us with a brilliant and incisive analysis of the problem, the challenge, and the opportunity.

An important first step toward addressing the challenge is to grasp the magnitude of the problem. For the past several years, as a Goodwill Ambassador for the United Nations Development Program (UNDP), I have been focusing on the issues of HIV/AIDS and poverty, particularly in Africa. In that capacity, I have had an opportunity to grapple deeply with some of the underlying issues related to poverty and development. This has also presented me with an opportunity to witness first hand, the ravaging effects of the widening economic gap between rich and poor. I see that growing gap everywhere, within and between families, neighborhoods, and nations.

Much of the prevailing public dialogue treats such problems as though they were merely personal issues to be worked out by individuals who have failed to get their own lives in order—without reference to the larger struggle to create a just world. It leads us to a dead end of cynicism and despair.

Meeting David Korten and reading the earlier edition of *When Corporations Rule the World* have had a profound impact on my own thinking and sense of my life mission. It has helped me see the larger context of the inequities people everywhere are experiencing and understand their root causes. Only as we begin to see ourselves in an ever enlarging, interconnected context can we fully appreciate the extent to which the problems we face as individuals, and the solutions to those problems, are global.

From here it is a short step to the obvious, but neglected, truth that to redeem ourselves we must also redeem our institutions. We must all lend our passion and creative energy to the collective work of institutional transformation to create a world of justice for all.

Like many of the people who in November 1999 attended the WTO teach-ins in Seattle, I was motivated to be there because of David's work and the profound opportunity that the occasion presented to deepen our collective understanding. I was deeply moved by the stories; stories of courage, resistance and compassion shared by people from every corner of the globe.

When Corporations Rule the World continues to be at the very center of this expanding global dialogue. This revised and updated edition is even more powerful than the original in its articulation of the issues, its stories of the struggle, and its compelling call to each and every one of us to become participants in what I believe to be a sacred trust. That trust involves creating a world that works for all; a world that we, through our consciousness and our collective actions have a responsibility to help bring into existence for ourselves, for our children, and for the yet unborn. Accepting this profound responsibility takes us to a whole new place as human beings.

Such is the power of this dialogue toward the articulation and realization of a vision of the human possibility. I'm humbled to be a part of it.

ACKNOWLEDGMENTS

From its inception this book has been the product of an international collaboration involving many wonderful colleagues. I am especially indebted to Tony Quizon, Sunimal Fernando, Bishan Singh, Chandra de Fonseca, Felix Sugitharaj, and Sixto Roxas, with whom I shared a ten-day retreat in Baguio, Philippines, in November 1992. The basic argument of *When Corporations Rule the World* was originally framed by the collective report we produced from that retreat.

Krishna Sondhi and Ian Mayo-Smith of Kumarian Press, which published many of my previous books, unrelentingly prodded me to undertake this project and gave me extraordinary support to make it happen. They commissioned Henry Berry as editorial and marketing consultant to help me make the transition from writing for a specialized development audience to writing for a broader trade audience. They also developed a unique copublication partnership with Berrett-Koehler Publishers that brought to this project the creative talents of Steve Piersanti, Pat Anderson, and their colleagues.

Frances Korten helped shape the book's core arguments through many hours of dinner table conversation, and with great love, devotion, and an unrelentingly critical eye read and edited every chapter—several times. An editorial advisory board of Anwar Fazal, Robert Gilman, Willis Harman, Stanley Katz, and Donella Meadows provided ideas, inspiration, and advice throughout. Michelle Beesten and Claudia Radel provided voluntary research and editorial assistance.

In addition, extensive critical input and feedback was provided by Nancy Alexander, Robin Broad, John Cavanagh, Walter Coddington, Sandy Cohen, Herman Daly, Richard Douthwaite, Neva Goodwin, Jonathan Greenberg, Ross Jackson, Elizabeth Kramer, Mark Leach, Jerry Mander, and Marilyn Mehlmann. Other colleagues who made special contributions to the underlying ideas and analysis include Fatma Alloo, Gar Alperovitz, Roy Anderson, Winifred Armstrong, Patricia Bauman, Walden Bello, David Bonbright, Jeremy Brecher, Ruth Caplan, Robert Cassani, Mary Clark, Clifford Cobb, Harriet Crosby, Joëlle Danant, Joe Dominguez, Duane Elgin, Bill Ellis, Linda Elswick, Gustavo Esteva, Joyce Gillilan-Goldberg, Edward Goldsmith, Alisa Gravitz, Nathan Gray, Leanne Grossman, Richard Grossman, Ted Halstead, Wendy Harcourt, Paul Hawken, Judy Henderson, Noeleen Heyzer, Janet Hunt, Tom Keehn, Danny Kennedy, Martin Khor, Andy Kimbrell, Alicia Korten, Smitu Kothari, Sigmund Kvaloy, Kathy Lawrence, Michael Lerner, Tina Liamzon, Jerry Mander, Peter Mann, Atherton Martin, Michael McCoy, Luis Lopezllera Méndez, Victor Menotti, John Mohawk, Ward Morehouse, David Morris, Shierry Nicholsen, Helena Norberg-Hodge, Michael Northop, Sharlye Patton, David Perrin, George Porter, William Rees, David Richards, Mark Ritchie, Neil Ritchie, James Robertson, Vicki Robin, Atila Roque, Nola Kate Seymoar, Isagani Serrano, Vandana Shiva, Michael Shuman, Greg Thompson, Sally Timpson, Edgardo Valenzuela, Steve Viederman, Paul Wachtel, Lori Wallach, and Paul Wangoola. The extraordinary musical creations of Jeff Clarkson—friend and colleague, New Zealand composer, synthesizer artist, and environmental activist—created a relaxed and reflective mood during the long periods of writing.

Many of those mentioned above remain close colleagues. Joe Dominguez, Joyce Gillilan-Goldberg, Willis Harman, Michael McCoy, Donella Meadows, and George Porter have since passed on. Especially important contributions to the development of my thinking since writing the original edition of *When Corporations Rule the World* have come from Mae-Wan Ho, Nicanor Perlas, and Elisabet Sahtouris. Others who have made important contributions to my thinking and understanding since the publication of the original edition include Sherry Anderson, Mark Anielski, Rod Arakaki, Jean-Bertrand Aristide, Maude Barlow, Janine Benyus, Jeff Barber, David Balduc, Elise Boulding, Tony Clarke, John B. Cobb, Jr., Richard Conlin, Susan Davis, Kevin Danaher, Charles Derber, Ronnie Duggar, Riane Eisler, Carol Estes, Ralph Estes, Keven Fong, Barbara Gaughen, Susan George, Danny Glover, William Greider, Colin Hines, Marjorie Kelly, Satish Kumar, Sara Larrain, Chee Yoke Ling, Joanna Macy, Rashmi Mayur, Victor Menotti, Robert Monks, Jane Anne Morris, Bill Moyer, Robert Muller, Gifford Pinchott, Libba Pinchott, Paul Ray, Anita Roddick, Gordon Roddick, Belvie Rooks, Johnathan Rowe, Klaus Schwab, John Sellers, Claude Smadja, David Solnit, Ali Starr, John Stauber, Victoria Tauli-Corpuz, Lynn Twist, Jakob von Uexkull, Steve Usher, Sarah van Gelder, and Verlene Wilder.

Both editions have been prepared as a project of the People-Centered Development Forum (PCDForum). Specific financial support for the original edition was provided to the Forum by the Jenifer Altman Foundation.

The PCDForum is a purely voluntary organization that pays no salaries. I have received no personal compensation from any source for the preparation of either the original or the new edition of this book, and all royalties go to the PCDForum. Further information on the PCDForum can be found on the web at www.pcdf.org.

The views expressed in this book are mine and do not necessarily represent those of the PCDForum or its contributors. I extend my deepest appreciation to all who helped make this book possible.

INTRODUCTION: DEEPENING CRISIS— CAUSE FOR HOPE

Perhaps the greatest threat to freedom and democracy in the world today comes from the formation of unholy alliances between government and business. This is not a new phenomenon. It used to be called fascism.... The outward appearances of the democratic process are observed, but the powers of the state are diverted to the benefit of private interests.
— George Soros, *international financier*[1]

It would be a grave mistake to dismiss the uproar witnessed in the past few years in Seattle, Washington, D.C., and Prague. Many of the radicals leading the protests may be on the political fringe. But they have helped to kick-start a profound rethinking about globalization among governments, mainstream economists, and corporations that, until recently, was carried on mostly in obscure think tanks.
— Business Week, *November 6, 2000*[2]

THE ORIGINAL EDITION OF *When Corporations Rule the World* grew out of my deep concern for the human future. As a young man, I wanted to help eliminate world poverty and to that end spent thirty years of my life as a development worker in Africa, Latin America, and Asia. I saw extraordinary changes in the world—especially in Asia, where I lived for fifteen years. By the early 1990s many of the cities I had experienced as dingy and remote sported luxurious modern airports, super highways crowded with late model cars, five-star hotels, gated residential communities, and air-conditioned mega-shopping malls stocked with state-of-the-art electronics and elegant designer clothing from all over the world.

At the dawning of the Third Millennium, such signs of progress in Southern countries are even more pervasive. To those who look no further, it seems that development has been a stunning success. Yet look a little deeper, and it is like visiting an elaborate movie set and finding there is nothing behind the carefully constructed facade. Yes, tens of thousands of people are living extremely well, and hundreds of thousands are enjoying far higher levels of consumption than ever before. But behind the facade billions face an ever more desperate struggle for survival. By the hundreds of millions they are being displaced from the lands on which they once made a modest living, to make way for dams, agricultural estates, forestry plantations, resorts, golf courses, and myriad other development projects. Follow the money and you will find that many of these projects are financed by the World Bank and other public development agencies. Invariably they benefit those already better off than those displaced. Often the most evident beneficiary is a global corporation.

The displaced, lacking other options, move onto marginal, environmentally unstable lands to eke out a living as best they can—often at great human and environmental cost. Others move into squalid urban squatter settlements, pushing wages down and rents up. Once-lush hillsides are stripped bare of trees. Coral reefs once vibrant with life become underwater wastelands. The air is thick with pollutants. Cultures grounded in strong spiritual, family, and community values give way to materialism and violence.

BREAKING THE SILENCE, TAKING TO THE STREETS

In the late 1980s my mind began to open to the full dimensions of the unfolding human tragedy. Earlier I had assumed that I was seeing only a local phenomenon confined to the Asian countries in which I was most involved. Then I began to look more seriously at data from the rest of the world. The full horror struck when I realized that similar trends toward social and environmental disintegration were playing out nearly everywhere in the world—including in the United States, Europe, and Japan—the supposed pinnacles of development achievement. Eventually I arrived at the inescapable truth. In the name of creating new wealth, humanity is in fact impoverishing itself, placing its very survival at risk. Once the magnitude of the problem became clear, I turned to the obvious question: Why?

When Corporations Rule the World presents the results of my inquiry. Through deregulation and the removal of national economic borders we have created a global economy more powerful than any national government—and it is flying on autopilot right into the face of a great mountain. Yet in 1992, the year I moved from Manila, Philippines, to New York City and began writing *When Corporations Rule the World*, few seemed to notice. The number of people in the United States actively concerned about the issues of corporate globalization could have met around a very small conference table. Gradually the excesses of CEO compensation, the unceremonious firing of tens of thousands of employees by companies reporting record profits, the wholesale movement of previously well-paid jobs to countries where workers are paid pennies an hour, and the wave of buyouts by corporate raiders began to attract public attention. More and more lives were being disrupted or ruined in the pursuit of quick profits.

The timing of *When Corporations Rule the World*'s release in October 1995 was remarkable. In hindsight it is clear that the tension people were feeling had reached a critical level. The indigenous people of Chiapas had already let the world know their views by initiating an armed rebellion on January 1, 1994, the inaugural day of NAFTA. Elsewhere, however, the tension many were feeling had remained largely invisible, as there was no outlet for its expression. Politicians addicted to corporate campaign contributions and the corporate-owned media still had only praise for free trade and the efforts of U.S. corporations to make themselves more globally competitive through mergers, downsizing, and the export of jobs. Individuals were reluctant to express their concerns for fear of being dismissed as backward-looking malcontents.

Then in November 1995 the International Forum on Globalization (IFG), a newly formed global alliance of activists engaged in opposition to NAFTA, GATT, and other free-trade agreements, held its first public teach-in on corporate globalization in New York City. It featured many of the movement's most informed and eloquent speakers, including Vandana Shiva, Martin Khor, Sara Larrain, Maude Barlow, Helena Norberg-Hodge, Jerry Mander, Lori Wallach, Jeremy Rifkin, and many others. It was hoped the event might attract as many as 400 people. The response to the event so exceeded those hopes that the venue was moved from a lecture hall at Columbia University to the much larger Riverside Church. The Church accommodated fifteen hundred people from all across the United States, Canada, and other countries. Hundreds more were turned away at the door. I was, and am, a charter member of the Forum and had the privilege of being among the speakers at this now-historic event. This was the moment when many of us first became aware of the depth of public concern.

There followed countless teach-ins, conferences, and seminars on the issues of corporate globalization organized by civil society groups around the world. Dozens of popular books, articles, newsletters, and e-mail listserves told the story the corporate media and corporate political parties avoided or dismissed.

Four years after the first IFG teach-in, on November 30, 1999, some 50,000 union members, people of faith, environmentalists, youth, indigenous peoples, peace and human rights activists, feminists, small farmers, and others took to the streets in Seattle, Washington to express their opposition to the World Trade Organization (WTO) and its role in sacrificing democracy to global corporate rule. On that historic Tuesday thousands of protestors committed to nonviolent resistance courageously stood their ground in the face of the rubber bullets, tear gas, and pepper spray of violent police battalions. Ultimately they played a major role in bringing the WTO negotiations to a standstill. The week of teach-ins, marches, debates, and seminars involved as many as 60,000 to 70,000 people.[3]

Because Seattle was the epicenter of what happened on that day, some called it "The Battle of Seattle" or "The Protest of the Century." Some simply called it "Seattle '99." Seattle, however, was only the tip of a very large iceberg. Simultaneous protests around the world brought hundreds of thousands of people to the streets. Millions have participated in related protests—both before and since—in India, France, Thailand, England, Bolivia, Switzerland, Brazil, and many other countries.

DEFINING THE ISSUES

The debates, dialogues, and street protests have brought into sharp focus a deepening struggle grounded in two sharply divergent worldviews. On one side are the forces of corporate globalization advanced by an alliance between the world's largest corporations and most powerful governments. This alliance is backed by the power of money, and its defining project is to integrate the world's national economies into a single, borderless global economy in which the world's mega-corporations are free to move goods and money anywhere in the world that affords an opportunity for profit, without governmental interference. In the name of increased efficiency the alliance seeks to privatize public services and assets and strengthen safeguards for investors and private property. In the eyes of its proponents, corporate globalization is the result of inevitable and irreversible historical forces driving a powerful

THE MOVEMENT WITH NO NAME

The movement has been referred to by many labels, including the Fair Trade Movement, the Anti-Globalization Movement, the Pro-Democracy Movement, and the Living Democracy Movement. Given that the movement's clearest underlying themes are life and democracy, I've chosen for purposes of this book to use the name "global movement for a living democracy" or "living democracy movement," which is the name of India's million-member Living Democracy Movement. It remains to be seen what the global movement will choose to call itself, which is why I express the name in lower case letters rather than capitalizing it in the normal convention for proper names.

engine of technological innovation and economic growth that is strengthening human freedom, spreading democracy, and creating the wealth needed to end poverty and save the environment.

On the other side are the forces of a newly emerging global movement advanced by a planetary citizen alliance of civil society organizations. This alliance is bringing together the most important social movements of our time in common cause, is self-organizing, depends largely on voluntary social energy, and is driven by a deep value commitment to democracy, community, equity, and the web of planetary life. It is a movement of a million leaders, each contributing ideas and initiatives toward shaping the whole. In the eyes of its members, corporate globalization is neither inevitable nor beneficial, but rather the product of intentional decisions and policies promoted by the World Trade Organization, the World Bank, the IMF, global corporations, and politicians who depend on corporate money. They believe corporate globalization is enriching the few at the expense of the many, replacing democracy with rule by corporations and financial elites, destroying the real wealth of the planet and society to make money for the already wealthy, and eroding the relationships of trust and caring that are the essential foundation of a civilized society.

Whether out of ignorance or intent to discredit, pundits of the corporate press portrayed the Seattle demonstrators as selfish, ill-informed, and disheveled malcontents who sought to close national borders, end trade, and consign the poor to perpetual misery. In other words the pundits completely missed the real story, a troubling reminder of the sorry state of the corporate news media in the United States.

The Seattle demonstrations announced the birth of perhaps the most truly international movement in human history—a movement with a well developed analysis, a deep commitment to economic justice, and an informed and articulate membership for whom concern for issues relating to trade is incidental to their concerns for human and planetary life and their commitment to the democratic ideal that every person has the right to a voice in the decisions that affect their lives.

In public, members of the establishment echoed the press in dismissing the demonstrations as the work of hooligans. In private they expressed shock at the protestors' ability to stall the plans of the world's most powerful nations and corporations. They soon mobilized to suppress, contain, or co-opt the dissenters through a combination of police repression and invitations to multistakeholder dialogues and partnerships. The tide of public opinion seems increasingly to align with the protestors and even a few establishment voices are beginning to call for more substantive reform.

In its September 11, 2000 cover story, "Too Much Corporate Power?" *Business Week* released survey results that found 72 percent of Americans believe corporations have too much power over too many aspects of American life. Seventy-three percent feel the top executives of U.S. companies are overpaid. Only 4 percent believe that America is best served when corporations pursue only one purpose—making the most profit for their shareholders. Ninety-five percent believe corporations should sacrifice some profit for the sake of making things better for their workers and communities. Respondents made a clear distinction between corporations and small business. While 74 percent said big companies have too much influence over government policy and politicians, eighty-two percent said small business has too little.

Business Week observed that although corporations are providing profits and material goods in large quantities, most people believe there should be more to life, and corporations seem either unable or unwilling to provide it. The article further noted that people are experiencing a sharp disconnect between the warm and caring images that corporations attempt to cultivate for themselves and what people actually experience when corporations invade their privacy, provide poor service, pay less than living wages for jobs that exhaust them and leave no time for loved ones, show disregard for their health and safety, and corrupt democracy with huge campaign contributions. A related editorial made four recommendations to *Business Week*'s corporate readers that could have been copied right off protestor banners, "First, get out of politics . . . then take responsibility for overseas factories," spread the wealth, and pay attention to social issues.[4]

The issues will not be swept away by police oppression, public relations spin, or empty promises. They are structural and persistent and can be corrected only through deep change. The resistance grows out of an awakening of the human consciousness to humanity's deeply destructive path, the shallowness of lives devoted to mindless material consumption, and the possibility of creating a world that values life more than money. An awakened consciousness will not be denied.

CONTINUING THE PERSONAL JOURNEY

As steadfastly as the corporate media ignored *When Corporations Rule the World*, the independent media embraced it—as did tens of thousands of enthusiastic readers. I was initially startled by the number of readers who reported that despite the book's troubling message, it left them feeling both hopeful and empowered. Reader after reader told me it affirmed their sanity by assuring them that what they felt and thought had a firm basis in reality. Furthermore, they said that once they understood the nature of the problem, they knew it was not inevitable—it resulted from human decisions that can be changed. That knowledge gave them hope.

Selling more than 90,000 copies in thirteen languages in the five years following its original release, *When Corporations Rule the World* has become something of a classic. The title alone helped to name what millions of people now embrace as a defining issue of our time. Some refer to it as a bible of the living democracy movement.

Since 1995 there has been a growing realization within the movement that while resistance is essential to slow the damage, resistance alone is a losing strategy. To win it is necessary to seize the initiative by articulating an effective and attractive counter to the corporate libertarian's disempowering mantra: "There Is No Alternative."[5] Consequently, my attention has turned increasingly toward a deeper exploration of the alternatives to corporate globalization.

My first major step in this direction came in 1996, when I joined with Sarah van Gelder to cofound the Positive Futures Network, located on

Bainbridge Island, Washington, publisher of *YES! A Journal of Positive Futures*. I have since chaired the board. *YES!* magazine is grounded in a critique much like that presented in *When Corporations Rule the World*. Its focus, however, is on bringing greater visibility to the people and positive initiatives that are laying the foundation for transformative change. Look for the subscription card at the back of this book. Also find *YES!* on the web at www.yesmagazine.org or call 1-800-937-4451.

In 1998 Fran, my life partner, accepted an invitation to become executive director of The Positive Futures Network. We moved from New York City—the belly of the corporate beast—to Bainbridge Island, a suburb of Seattle in the Pacific Northwest—the land of Ecotopia—just a year and a half before the demonstration that shook the world.

It was on Bainbridge Island that I finished writing *The Post-Corporate World: Life After Capitalism*, a sequel to *When Corporations Rule the World*, which explores the alternatives to the global corporate economy based on the application of principles derived from the study of healthy living systems.

The recommendations for change put forth in *When Corporations Rule the World* seek to restrain corporate power. *The Post-Corporate World* concludes that the publicly traded, limited liability corporation is a pathological organizational form that must join monarchy as an extinct institutional species. *The Post-Corporate World* delves further into the distinction between capitalism and a true market economy and the practical implications of the difference.

Although *When Corporations Rule the World* is a book about the structure and dynamics of capitalism, I rarely used the term in the original edition. We were still too close to the day when it was assumed that those who spoke of capitalism were socialists, which I am not. I believe that in complex modern societies properly regulated markets are the most efficient way to allocate resources and that direct participation by all people in the ownership of the productive assets on which their livelihood depends is an essential foundation of political democracy. This is not socialism, which centralizes the ownership and management of productive assets in distant governmental bureaucracies. Neither is it capitalism, which centralizes the ownership and management of productive assets in distant corporations with internal economies even larger than those of most nation-states. Socialism and capitalists are both destructive of life, democracy, and ethical values, which are essential foundations of a civil or civilized society.

Capitalism's proponents now speak freely of capitalism to celebrate its global triumph, so now I too use the term to raise awareness of its actual meaning. Proponents usually equate capitalism with private property, without noting that capitalism is an extremist ideology that advances the concentration and rights of ownership without limit, to the exclusion of the needs and rights of the many who own virtually nothing. It is both possible and necessary to eliminate capitalism's excesses of unaccountable concentration, without eliminating individual participation in ownership—a distinction critical to any search for alternatives to the extremist economic ideologies that dominated much of the political and economic discourse of the twentieth century.

A NEW EDITION

In early 2000, Steve Piersanti of Berrett-Koehler Publishers urged me to prepare a new edition of *When Corporations Rule the World*. Subsequent events had further confirmed its basic analysis regarding the inherent instability of the global financial casino, the tightening grip of corporate political and economic domination, and the increasingly devastating social and environmental consequences. At the same time, the rapidly growing resistance movement had added a new dimension to the equation and opened new possibilities for constructive action.

Soon after Piersanti made his appeal, Krishna Sondhi of Kumarian Press asked me to write a new introduction for a proposed low cost edition of *When Corporations Rule the World*. It seemed a doable task, but if there was to be a new edition, a more thorough revision and update seemed in order. We also decided that the new edition should be presented and priced to reach the widest possible audience.

This second edition of *When Corporations Rule the World* is the result. In addition to this introduction, this edition features three new chapters and a new epilogue. Chapter 21 "Making Money, Growing Poorer" updates the deepening human crisis of an economy that is making money for the rich at the expense of the life of society and the planet. Chapter 22 "The Living Democracy Movement" documents and examines the nature and implications of the growing citizen movement that has emerged in response to the issues spelled out in this volume. Chapter 23 "A Civil Society" provides a framework for describing the critical role of spirit and culture in distinguishing between a civil society and a capitalist society. It also addresses the centrality of culture to the political and institutional changes ahead. The new epilogue "A Story for Our Time" places the current struggle between the forces of democracy and corporate tyranny in its larger evolutionary context to provide insight into its deeper purpose and meaning.

Other changes have been made throughout the book to clean up awkward wording, clarify arguments, and eliminate unnecessary technical material—to simplify the reader's task while making room for the new chapters. Chapter 20 "Agenda for Change" has been updated to include new proposals put forward by the International Forum on Globalization and other civil society groups for the restructuring of global economic governance. Elsewhere, unless otherwise specifically noted, the time frame of the prologue through Chapter 20 remains consistent with the period 1994–1995 when the original edition was completed.

PROLOGUE:
A PERSONAL JOURNEY

I think there are good reasons for suggesting that the modern age has ended. Today, many things indicate that we are going through a transitional period, when it seems that something is on the way out, and something else is painfully being born. It is as if something were crumbling, decaying and exhausting itself, while something else, still indistinct, were arising from the rubble.

—Václav Havel, president of the Czech Republic[1]

MY PERSONAL JOURNEY OF THE PAST several years has brought me into contact with people of widely diverse backgrounds in countries as different as the Philippines, Hungary, New Zealand, Bangladesh, Brazil, South Africa, Thailand, and the United States. Everywhere I travel, I find an almost universal sense among ordinary people that the institutions on which they depend are failing them. Many are increasingly fearful of a future that seems to offer declining prospects for themselves and their children. In the United States and elsewhere, this fear is creating a growing sense of political frustration and alienation that is finding current expression in falling voter turnouts, a taxpayer revolt, and the rejection of political incumbents. Yet the real issues go far deeper than a simple rejection of big government.

Although politicians and the press play to the public's frustration over governmental failure, they display little understanding of the root causes of rising poverty and unemployment, inequality, violent crime, failing families, and environmental deterioration that lead so many people to foresee a dark future. Our leaders seem to be unable to move beyond blaming their political opponents and promoting the same old ineffectual solutions—accelerating economic growth through deregulation, cutting taxes, removing trade barriers, giving industry more incentives and subsidies, forcing welfare recipients to work, hiring more police, and building more jails.

Often, the people who live ordinary lives far removed from the corridors of power have the clearest perception of what is really happening. Yet they are often reluctant to speak openly about what they believe in their hearts to be true, because it is too frightening and differs too dramatically from what those with more impressive credentials and access to the media are saying. These suppressed insights leave people feeling isolated and helpless. The questions nag: Are things really as bad as they seem to me? Why don't others see it? Am I stupid? Am I being intentionally misinformed? What can I do? What can anyone do?

I have been struggling for a number of years with the same questions, at first with a similar sense of isolation, but increasingly with an awareness that millions of others are asking these same questions. Even so, each time I prepare to speak to a new group I am invariably nervous that what I have to say will be rejected out of hand in a world committed to growth, big business, and deficit financing. Yet the usual response is an outpouring of affirmation from people who express their relief and pleasure at the experience of having their own perspectives affirmed in a public forum. Getting the difficult and unpleasant truth on the table for discussion is a necessary first step toward action. Fear of the unknown may immobilize us, but the truth empowers us to act.

ROOTS OF THE INQUIRY

For me, each book I write is a new step in a continuing intellectual journey. It may be helpful for you to know something about the experiences that led me to the views I now hold and that I share in the following pages. The history of these experiences also provides an overview of the central arguments of *When Corporations Rule the World*.

I was born in 1937 into a conservative, white, upper-middle-class family and grew up in Longview, Washington, a small timber-industry town of some 25,000 people. Assuming that one day I would manage the family's retail music and appliance business, I had no particular interest in venturing beyond the borders of the United States. As a psychology major at Stanford University, I focused on musical aptitude testing and the uses of psychology to influence buying behavior. Then in 1959, during my senior year, a curious thing happened.

At that time a very conservative Young Republican, I was deeply fearful of the spread of Communism and the threat it posed to the American way of life I held so dear. This fear drew me to take a course on modern revolutions taught by Robert North, a professor of political science. There I learned that poverty was fueling revolutions the world over. In one of those rare, deeply life-changing moments, I made a decision. I would devote my life to countering this threat by bringing the knowledge of modern business management and entrepreneurship to those who had not yet benefited from it.

I prepared myself with an MBA in international business and a PhD in organizational theory from the Stanford Business School. Three years in Ethiopia setting up a business school with the help of my newlywed life partner Frances Korten provided my apprenticeship. I did my obligatory military service during the Vietnam War as a captain in the U.S. Air Force, fulfilling staff assignments at the Special Air Warfare School, the Office of the Secretary of the Air Force, and the Office of the Secretary of Defense. I then signed up for what turned out to be a five-and-a-half-year tour on the faculty of the Harvard University Graduate School of Business.

For three of my Harvard Business School years I served as the Harvard advisor to the Nicaragua-based Central American Management Institute (INCAE), a graduate business school catering to the elite business families of the Central American and Andean countries. After returning to Boston, I taught for two more years at the Business School and then moved to the Harvard Institute for International Development and the Harvard School of Public Health. At the beginning of 1978, Fran and I joined the Ford Foundation staff in the Philippines and remained in Southeast Asia for the next fourteen years. While Fran stayed with Ford, I moved on to spend eight years as a senior advisor on development management at the U.S. Agency for International Development (USAID), the official U.S. foreign aid program.

I share this detail to establish the depth of my conservative roots. The more interesting part of my story, however, has to do with my gradual awakening to the conclusion that the conventional development practice espoused by most conservatives and even many liberals is a leading cause of—not the solution to—a rapidly accelerating and potentially fatal human crisis of global proportions.

The first step toward my awakening came with the course on modern revolutions. Then in 1961, a summer in Indonesia immersed me in the realities of underdevelopment and brought me into contact with the heroic struggles, spiritual grounding, and generosity of people who live in desperate poverty. It was an aspect of the human experience I had not previously encountered. While at INCAE in the early 1970s, I wrote a number of Harvard Business School–style management cases for a course I was teaching on the management of change. They were based on Latin American experiences, and many involved efforts by government, business, and voluntary agencies to improve the conditions of the urban and rural poor. Many of these cases carried a disturbing message: externally imposed "development" was seriously disrupting human relationships and community life and causing significant hardship for the very people it claimed to benefit. By contrast, when people found the freedom and self-confidence to develop themselves, they demonstrated enormous potential to create a better world. I became fascinated with the challenge of transforming development programs to support these kinds of self-led, grassroots processes.

During our INCAE and Harvard years, Fran and I also became involved in efforts to improve the management of family-planning programs. This brought us into contact with many local initiatives, including those of poor people who were trying to gain control of their lives on a declining resource base.

When Fran and I left Harvard to join the Ford Foundation staff in Manila, Fran inherited a portfolio of grants that included a small grant to the Philippine National Irrigation Administration (NIA). It was intended to strengthen the NIA's ability to assist small farmer-owned-and-operated irrigation systems. This led to a long-term cooperation between the NIA and the Ford Foundation that ultimately transformed the NIA from an engineering-and-construction-centered organization that dictated to farmers to one that worked in partnership with farmer organizations and encouraged a substantial degree of local self-governance.

We were able to see the powerful energies that people and communities can mobilize on their own behalf when development initiatives are actually centered in people. We saw firsthand how foreign-funded development projects commonly overwhelm such efforts—even many projects that seek to embrace them. We also learned how careful strategic grant making can be used to debureaucratize large centralized public agencies and strengthen control of local resources by local people. USAID invited me to help it apply the lessons of this experience to its programming in Asia. I focused on this task for eight years, only to conclude that USAID was too big and bureaucratic to be effective as a catalyst in helping other development agencies become less bureaucratic.

These experiences left me with a deep conviction that real development cannot be purchased with foreign aid monies. Development depends on people's ability to gain control of and effectively use the real resources of their

localities—land, water, labor, technology, and human ingenuity and motivation—to meet their own needs. Yet most development interventions transfer
control of local resources to ever larger and more centralized institutions that
are unaccountable to local people and unresponsive to their needs. The greater
the amount of money that flows through these central institutions, the more
dependent people become, the less control they have over their own lives and
resources, and the more rapidly the gap grows between those who hold central power and those who seek to make a living for themselves within local
communities.

I came to see the difference between those things that increase economic
growth and those that result in better lives for people. This difference raised a
basic question: What would development look like if instead of being growth
and money centered it were truly people centered—with people being both
its purpose and its primary instrument? In 1984, I edited the anthology, *People-
Centered Development*, published by Kumarian Press. In 1986, I edited another Kumarian anthology, *Community Management*, which focused on the
importance of getting resource control in the hands of people.

The more I saw development's presumed beneficiaries struggling to maintain their dignity and the quality of their lives in the face of the systemic attack
by the development agencies and projects that were colonizing their resources,
the more alienated I became from mainstream development thinking. In 1988,
I left USAID but remained in Southeast Asia.

Having become disillusioned with official development agencies, I immersed myself in the world of nongovernmental organizations (NGOs) and
soon found myself among NGO colleagues who were raising similar questions about the nature and process of development. I became a synthesizer
and scribe of the collective insights emerging from an increasingly dynamic
dialogue within the NGO community. It was a period of intense personal learning that led to my next book, *Getting to the 21st Century: Voluntary Action and
the Global Agenda*, published by Kumarian Press in 1990. That book focused
on the threefold human crisis of deepening poverty, environmental destruction, and social disintegration, and it traced the roots of the crisis to models
that made growth the goal of development and treated people as mere means.
It concluded that since the dominant institutions of modern society are creations of a growth-centered development vision, the leadership for change
must necessarily come from voluntary citizen action.

Embracing this argument to recast my own commitments, I joined a number of colleagues to found the People-Centered Development Forum
(PCDForum), a global citizen network engaged in articulating and advancing

a people-centered vision of the future and redefining development practice in line with that vision. The PCDForum has particularly examined the role of national and global structures and institutions in depriving people and place-based communities of the power to meet their own needs in responsible, sustainable ways. This explains what some people may see as a paradox: although I talk of the need for local empowerment, much of my attention is focused on the transformation of global institutions. I am among those who seek to transform the global to empower the local.

In November 1992, I went to Baguio, a Philippine mountain resort town, to meet with the leaders of several Asian NGOs. We engaged in a ten-day reflection on Asian development experience and its implications for NGO strategies. We were concerned that Asia's economic success is dangerously superficial. Beneath the surface of dynamic competitive economies lies a deeper reality of impoverishment and spreading disruption of the region's social and ecological foundations. Our discussions turned to the need for a theory that would explain and provide guidance in addressing the deeper causes of the crisis. Without a theory, we were like a pilot without a compass. Late one night in a small Chinese restaurant, our discussions began to converge on two fundamental insights. First, we did not need an alternative theory of development as our guide. Rather, we needed a theory of sustainable societies that would apply to Northern and Southern countries alike. Second, the theory must go beyond the sterile formulations of economics to explain why human societies have become so alienated from natural processes.

As we continued our discussion over the next few days, the pieces began to fall into place. The Western scientific vision of a mechanical universe has created a philosophical or conceptual alienation from our own inherent spiritual nature. This has been reinforced in our daily lives by the increasing alignment of our institutions with the monetary values of the marketplace. The more dominant money has become in our lives, the less place there has been for any sense of the spiritual bond that is the foundation of community and a balanced relationship with nature. The pursuit of spiritual fulfillment has been increasingly displaced by an all-consuming and increasingly self-destructive obsession with the pursuit of money—a useful but wholly substanceless and intrinsically valueless human artifact.

It seemed evident from our analysis that to reestablish a sustainable relationship to the living earth, we must break free of the illusions of the world of money, rediscover spiritual meaning in our lives, and root our economic institutions in place and community so that they are integrally connected to people and life. Consequently, we concluded that the task of people-centered development in its fullest sense must be the creation of life-centered societies in which the economy is but one of the instruments of good living—not the purpose of human existence. Because our leaders are trapped in the myths and the reward systems of the institutions they head, the leadership in this creative process of institutional and values re-creation must come from within civil society.

It was in so many ways an unremarkable insight. We had accomplished little more than to rediscover the ancient wisdom that a deep tension exists between our spiritual nature and our economic lives, and that healthy social and spiritual function depends on keeping the two in proper balance and perspective. Nor was there anything new in recognizing the importance of civil society, which has always been the foundation of democratic governance. Yet we felt that we had deepened our own insights into the practical relevance of these ideas for the crisis that imperils contemporary societies. *When Corporations Rule the World* builds from these insights and flows from my commitment to my Asian NGO friends and colleagues to help communicate their concerns and the lessons of their experience to a Northern audience.

RETURNING HOME

In the summer of 1992, shortly before the Baguio retreat, Fran and I left Southeast Asia to return to the United States. We had announced our decision to friends and colleagues in our Christmas letter with the following explanation:

> We were drawn to these far-away regions in the early 1960s by a belief that they were the locus of the development problems to which we had decided as young university students to dedicate our careers. We began these careers challenged by a mission—to help share the lessons of America's success with the world—so that "they" could become more like "us."
>
> Development as we understood it thirty years ago, and as it is to this day vigorously promoted by the World Bank, the IMF [International Monetary Fund], the Bush administration, and most of the world's powerful economic institutions, isn't working for the majority of humanity. And the roots of the problem are not found among the poor of the "underdeveloped" world. They are found in the countries that set global standards for wasteful extravagance and dominate

the global policies that are leading our world to social and ecological self-destruction.

Now thirty years older and hopefully a good deal wiser, Fran and I have come to realize the extent to which America's "success" is one of the world's key problems. Indeed, the ultimate demonstration of this assertion is found in America itself.

From our vantage point in Asia we have watched in horror as the same policies the United States has been advocating for the world have created a Third World within its own borders as revealed in its growing gap between rich and poor, dependence on foreign debt, deteriorating educational systems, rising infant mortality, economic dependence on the export of primary commodities—including the last remaining primary forests—indiscriminate dumping of toxic wastes, and the breakdown of families and communities.

While we have been away from home, the powerful have consolidated the nation's wealth in their own hands and absolved themselves of responsibility for their less fortunate neighbors. Labor unions have withered as American workers desperate to keep their jobs have been forced to compete with the even more desperate unemployed of Mexico, Bangladesh, and other Third World countries by negotiating for wage cuts with corporations that may still bear American names but honor no national allegiance.

We feel that our own education has been the primary product of our years abroad and that it is now time to return home to face up to our responsibilities to confront the problem at its geographical source. New York, a major center of economic power manifesting all the qualities of a contemporary Third World city—including wandering armies of the homeless juxtaposed with the extravagant lifestyles of the rich and famous, incapacitated government, and indiscriminate violence—seemed an appropriate choice. So we are moving to the belly of the beast, bringing the perspectives gained from our thirty years of learning about the causes of these conditions.

We had set out to solve for others the problems we perceived to reside in them by making them more like us. We now came back home to help our own compatriots better understand the ways in which the United States has contributed to placing the world, ourselves included, on a self-destructive course. Only when we are prepared to assume responsibility for changing ourselves will others be able to fully reclaim the social and environmental spaces we have appropriated from them and recover their ability to meet their own needs within a just, democratic, and sustainable world of cooperative partnerships.

DISCLOSURE STATEMENT

As the issues discussed in these pages are inseparable from basic questions of values, I believe it is appropriate to disclose the underlying political and spiritual values I bring to the exchange. With regard to political values, I remain a traditional conservative in the sense that I retain a deep distrust of large institutions and their concentrations of unaccountable power. I also continue to believe in the importance of the market and private ownership. However, unlike many contemporary conservatives, I have no more love for big business than I have for big government. Nor do I believe that possession of wealth should convey special political privilege.

I share the liberal's compassion for the disenfranchised, commitment to equity, and concern for the environment and believe that there are essential roles for government and limits to the rights of private property. I believe, however, that big government can be as unaccountable and destructive of societal values as can big business. Indeed, I distrust any organization that accumulates and concentrates massive power beyond the bounds of accountability. And I believe that every individual shares a responsibility to and for the whole of life. In short, I align with those who are defining a new path that is more pragmatic than ideological and who cannot be easily pigeonholed within the conventional conservative-liberal spectrum of political choice.

I first encountered economics in college when I chose it as my undergraduate major. I soon found it mechanistic, boring, and detached from reality, so I switched to the study of human behavior and organization. I've since come to realize that economic systems are the dominant systems for organizing behavior in modern societies and are most appropriately studied as behavioral systems.

Although this book takes a harshly critical look at the institution of the corporation and the system within which business functions, I have never been, and am not now, anti-business. An efficient system of industry and commerce is essential to human well-being. As an MBA student, I believed that global corporations might offer an answer to the problems of poverty and human conflict. I have since concluded, however, that the systemic forces nurturing the growth and dominance of global corporations are at the heart of the current dilemma. I now believe that to avoid collective catastrophe we must radically transform the underlying system of business to restore power to the small and local.

With regard to spiritual values, I was raised in the Protestant Christian faith but find wisdom in the teachings of all the great religions. I believe that each person has access to an inner spiritual wisdom and that our collective salvation as a species depends, in part, on tapping into this wisdom from which the institutions of modern science, the market, and even religion have deeply alienated us. Through this rediscovery we may achieve the creative balance between market and community, science and religion, and money and spirit that is essential to the creation and maintenance of healthy human societies.

I hope that this introduction will help you approach this book as you would an active conversation with a valued friend. In reading this book, you are in fact engaging in an exchange with many friends who have had important roles in shaping the analysis and the vision it presents. If you are not already involved in the larger conversation on these issues, I hope that this book will encourage you to become so engaged with your friends and colleagues. I ask, however, that readers not attempt to contact me directly for personal guidance or to discuss issues raised in my writing as I simply do not have the time and resources to respond individually—as much as I wish I did.

If you are among those who work in a large corporation, I urge you to step out of your corporate role while reading *When Corporations Rule the World*. Read it from the perspective of your role as a citizen and a parent concerned for the future of your children. This may make it easier and less painful to hear and assess the book's underlying message objectively and to consider its invitation to join the movement to transform the system.

Please read what follows actively and critically. Bring your own perspectives and insights to bear. Question. Challenge. Consider the implications for the way you want to live your life. Discuss it with friends. Tell them where you agree, where you disagree, what new insights you gained, where you find it incomplete. Get their thoughts. Explore new avenues together. Take the conversation to a new level. And act.

Although the general direction we must travel becomes clearer with each passing day, no one has yet been where we must go. If we seek a well-marked road, we will look in vain. To borrow from the title of a book of conversations between Myles Horton and Paulo Freire, two of the great social activists of our time, we set our sights on a destination beyond the distant horizon and then "We make the road by walking."

THE ARGUMENT

Part of our inability to come to terms with institutional systems failure stems from the fact that television reduces political discourse to sound bites and academia organizes intellectual inquiry into narrowly specialized disciplines. Consequently, we become accustomed to dealing with complex issues in fragmented bits and pieces. Yet we live in a complex world in which nearly every aspect of our lives is connected in some way with every other aspect. When we limit ourselves to fragmented approaches to dealing with systemic problems, it is not surprising that our solutions prove inadequate. If our species is to survive the predicaments we have created for ourselves, we must develop a capacity for whole-systems thought and action.

Whole-systems thinking calls for skepticism about simplistic solutions, willingness to seek connections between problems and events that conventional discourse ignores, and the courage to delve into subject matter that may lie outside our direct experience and expertise. In taking a whole-systems perspective, this book covers a broad territory with many elements. To help you keep in mind how the individual arguments that are developed and documented throughout the book link into a larger whole, the overall argument is summarized here. I don't ask you to accept these many arguments at face value, only to keep an open mind until you have had the opportunity to examine the reasoning and documentation underlying each of them. At that point, I trust that you will exercise your own independent critical judgement and eventually build your own syntheses that may or may not correspond with mine. Always bear in mind that we are all participants in an act of creation, and none of us can claim a monopoly on truth in our individual and collective search for understanding of these complex issues.

The point of departure of *When Corporations Rule the World* is the evidence that we are experiencing accelerating social and environmental disintegration in nearly every country of the world—as revealed by a rise in poverty, unemployment, inequality, violent crime, failing families, and environmental deterioration. These problems stem in part from a fivefold increase in economic output since 1950 that has pushed human demands on the ecosystem beyond what the planet is capable of sustaining. The continued quest for economic growth as the organizing principle of public policy is accelerating the breakdown of the ecosystem's regenerative capacities and the social fabric that sustains human community; at the same time, it is intensifying the competition for resources between rich and poor—a competition that the poor invariably lose.

Governments seem wholly incapable of responding, and public frustration is turning to rage. This situation is more than a failure of government bureaucracies, however. It is a crisis of governance born of a convergence of ideological, political, and technological forces behind a process of economic globalization that is shifting power away from governments responsible for the public good and toward a handful of corporations and financial institutions driven by a single imperative, the quest for short-term financial gain. This has concentrated massive economic and political power in the hands of an elite few whose absolute share of the products of a declining pool of natural wealth continues to increase at a substantial rate—thus reassuring them that the system is working perfectly well.

Those who bear the costs of the system's dysfunctions have been stripped of decision-making power and remain confused about the cause of their distress because the corporate-dominated media incessantly bombards them with interpretations of the resulting crisis based on the perceptions of the power holders. An active propaganda machine controlled by the world's largest corporations constantly reassures us that consumerism is the path to happiness, governmental restraint of the market is the cause of our distress, and corporate globalization is both a historical inevitability and a boon to the human species. In fact, these are all myths propagated to justify profligate greed and mask the extent to which the global transformation of human institutions is a consequence of the sophisticated, well-funded, and intentional interventions of a small elite whose money enables them to live in a world of illusions apart from the rest of humanity.

These forces have transformed once-beneficial corporations and financial institutions into instruments of a market tyranny that reaches across the planet like a cancer, colonizing ever more of the planet's living spaces, destroying livelihoods, displacing people, rendering democratic institutions impotent, and feeding on life in an insatiable quest for money. As our economic system has detached from place and gained greater dominance over our democratic institutions, even the world's most powerful corporations have become captives of a globalized financial system that has delinked the creation of money from the creation of real wealth and rewards extractive over productive investment. The big winners are the corporate raiders who strip sound companies of their assets for short-term gain and the speculators who capitalize on market volatility to extract a private tax from those who are engaged in productive work and investment.

Faced with pressures to produce greater short-term returns, the world's largest corporations are downsizing to shed people and functions. They are not, however, becoming less powerful. While tightening their control over markets and technology through mergers, acquisitions, and strategic alliances, they are forcing both subcontractors and local communities into a standards-lowering competition with one another to obtain the jobs that global corporations control. The related market forces are deepening our dependence on socially and environmentally destructive technologies that sacrifice our physical, social, environmental, and mental health to corporate profits.

The problem is not business or the market per se but a badly corrupted global economic system that is gyrating far beyond human control. The dynamics of this system have become so powerful and perverse that it is becoming increasingly difficult for corporate managers to manage in the public interest, no matter how strong their moral values and commitment.

Driven by the imperative to replicate money, the system treats people as a source of inefficiency and is rapidly shedding them at all system levels. As the first industrial revolution reduced dependence on human muscle, the information revolution reduced dependence on our eyes, ears, and brains. The first industrial revolution dealt with the resulting unemployment by colonizing weaker peoples and sending the surplus populations off as migrants to less populated lands. People in colonized countries fell back on traditional social structures to sustain themselves. With the world's physical frontiers largely exhausted and social economies greatly weakened by marked intrusion, few such safety valves remain. Consequently, the redundant now end up as victims of starvation and violence, homeless beggars, welfare recipients, or residents of refugee camps. Continuing on our present course will almost certainly lead to accelerating social and environmental disintegration.

It is within our means, however, to reclaim the power that we have yielded to the institutions of money and re-create societies that nurture cultural and biological diversity—thus opening vast new opportunities for social, intellectual, and spiritual advancement beyond our present imagination. Millions of people throughout the world are already acting to reclaim this power and to rebuild their communities and heal the earth. These initiatives are being melded into global alliances that form the foundation of a powerful political movement grounded in a global consciousness of the unity of life.

When Corporations Rule the World outlines a citizens' agenda to enhance these efforts by getting corporations out of politics and creating localized economies that empower communities within a system of global cooperation. Having reached the limits of the materialistic vision of the scientific and industrial era ushered in by the Copernican Revolution, we are now on the threshold of an ecological era called into being by an Ecological Revolution grounded in a more holistic view of the spiritual and material aspects of our nature. This revolution now calls to each of us to reclaim our political power and rediscover our spirituality to create societies that nurture our ability and desire to embrace the joyful experience of living to its fullest.

Part I

COWBOYS IN A SPACESHIP

1

FROM HOPE TO CRISIS

People who celebrate technology say it has brought us an improved standard of living, which means greater speed, greater choice, greater leisure, and greater luxury. None of these benefits informs us about human satisfaction, happiness, security, or the ability to sustain life on earth.
—*Jerry Mander*[1]

THE LAST HALF OF THE TWENTIETH CENTURY has been perhaps the most remarkable period in human history. Scientifically we have unlocked countless secrets of matter, space, and biology. We have virtually dominated the planet with our numbers, technology, and sophisticated organization. We have traveled beyond our world to the moon and reached out to the stars. A mere fifty years ago, within the lifetime of my generation, many of the things we take for granted today as essential to a good and prosperous life were unavailable, nonexistent, or even unimagined. These include the jet airplane and global commercial air travel, computers, microwave ovens, electric typewriters, photocopying machines, television, clothes dryers, air-conditioning, freeways, shopping malls, fax machines, birth-control pills, artificial organs, suburbs, and chemical pesticides—to name only a few.

This same period saw the creation of the first consequential institutions of global governance: the United Nations, the International Monetary Fund, the World Bank, and the General Agreement on Tariffs and Trade (GATT). Western Europe was transformed from a continent of warring states into a peaceful and prosperous political and economic union. The superpower conflict between East and West, and its dark specter of nuclear Armageddon, already seems a distant historical memory, eclipsed by a rush of business deals, financial assistance, and scientific and cultural exchanges. There has been a dramatic spread of democracy to nations formerly ruled by authoritarian governments. We have conquered many once-devastating illnesses such as smallpox and polio, increased life expectancy in developing countries by more than a third in the past thirty years, and cut their infant and under-five mortality rates by more than half.[2]

One of the most significant human commitments of the last half of the twentieth century has been to economic growth and trade expansion, and we have been spectacularly successful in accomplishing both. Global economic output expanded from $6.4 trillion in 1950 to $35.5 trillion in 1995 (constant 1997 dollars), a 5.5-fold increase. This means that, on average, we have added more to total global output *in each of the past four decades* than was added from the moment the first cave dweller carved out a stone axe up to the middle of the present century. During this same period, world trade soared from total exports of $0.4 trillion to $5 trillion (1997 dollars)—an 11.5-fold increase, and well over twice the rate of increase in total economic output.[3] More than a billion people now enjoy the abundance of affluence.

These are only a few of the extraordinary accomplishments of the last half-century. We have arrived at a time in history when we truly seem to have the knowledge, technology, and organizational capacity to accomplish bold goals, including the elimination of poverty, war, and disease. This should be a time filled with hope for a new millennium in which societies will be freed forever from concerns of basic survival and security to pursue new frontiers of social, intellectual, and spiritual advancement.

A THREEFOLD HUMAN CRISIS

The leaders and institutions that promised a golden age are not delivering. They assail us with wondrous new technological gadgets, such as airplane seats with individual television monitors, and an information highway that makes it possible to connect to the Internet while sunning ourselves on the beach. Yet the things that most of us really want—a secure means of livelihood, a decent place to live, healthy and uncontaminated food to eat, good education and health care for our children, a clean and vital natural environment—seem to slip further from the grasp of most of the world's people with each passing day.

Fewer and fewer people believe that they have a secure economic future. Family and community units and the security they once provided are disintegrating. The natural environment on which we depend for our material needs is under deepening stress. Confidence in our major institutions is evaporating, and we find a profound and growing suspicion among thoughtful people the world over that something has gone very wrong. These conditions are becoming pervasive in almost every locality of the world and point to global-scale failure of our institutions.

Even in the world's most affluent countries, high levels of unemployment, corporate downsizing, falling real wages, greater dependence on part-time and temporary jobs without benefits, and the weakening of unions are creating a growing sense of economic insecurity and shrinking the middle class. The employed find themselves working longer hours, holding multiple part-time jobs, and having less real income. Many among the young—especially of minority races—have little hope of ever finding jobs adequate to provide them with basic necessities, let alone financial security. The advanced degrees and technical skills of many of those who have seen their jobs disappear and their incomes and security plummet mock the idea that simply improving education and job training will eliminate unemployment.

In rich and poor countries, as competition for land and natural resources grows, those people who have supported themselves with small-scale farming, fishing, and other resource-based livelihoods find their resources are being expropriated to serve the few while they are left to fend for themselves. The economically weak find their neighborhoods becoming the favored sites for waste dumps or polluting smokestacks.

Small-scale producers—farmers and artisans—who once were the backbone of poor but stable communities are being uprooted and transformed into landless migrant laborers, separated from family and place. Hundreds of thousands of young children, many without families, make lives for themselves begging, stealing, scavenging, selling sex, and doing odd jobs on the streets of cities in Asia, Africa, and Latin America. There are an estimated 500,000 child prostitutes in Thailand, Sri Lanka, and the Philippines alone.[4] Millions migrate from their homes and families in search of opportunity and a means of survival. In addition to the 25 to 30 million people working outside their own countries as legal migrants, an estimated 20 to 40 million are undocumented migrant workers, economic refugees without legal rights and with little access to basic services. Some, especially women, are confined and subjected to outrageous forms of sexual, physical, and psychological abuse.[5]

The world is increasingly divided between those who enjoy opulent affluence and those who live in dehumanizing poverty, servitude, and economic insecurity. While top corporate managers, investment bankers, financial speculators, athletes, and celebrities bring down multimillion-dollar annual incomes, approximately 1.2 billion of the world's people struggle desperately to live on less than $1 a day. One need not go to some remote corner of Africa to experience the disparities. I could see it daily within a block of my apartment in the heart of New York City. Shiny chauffeured stretch limousines with built-in bars and televisions discharged their elegantly coifed occupants at trendy, expensive restaurants while homeless beggars huddled on the sidewalk wrapped in thin blankets to ward off the cold.

Evidence of the resulting social stress is everywhere: in rising rates of crime, drug abuse, divorce, teenage suicide, and domestic violence; growing numbers of political, economic, and environmental refugees; and even the changing nature of organized armed conflict. Violent crime is increasing at alarming rates all around the world.[6]

The seemingly impossible dream of millions of young people in the United States—especially those of color—is simply to have a stable family and survive to adulthood. More than half of all children in the United States are being raised in single parent families.[7] On an average day in the United States, 100,000 children carry guns with them to school, and forty of them are wounded or killed. Rare is the city, or even small town, in which people feel truly secure in their property and persons. Private security guards and systems have become a major growth industry around the world.

In developing countries, an estimated one-third of wives are physically battered. Of every 2,000 women in the world, one is a reported rape victim. There may be as many as 9,000 dowry-related deaths of women in India each year.[8]

In the era of "peace" that began in 1945 with the end of World War II, more than 20 million people have died in armed conflicts. Only three of the eighty-two armed conflicts between 1989 and 1992 were between states. The remainder were wars in which the combatants were killing those of their own nationality. Ninety percent of war casualties at the beginning of the twentieth century were military combatants. As the century ended, 90 percent were civilians.[9]

The increase in the number of internal wars is a primary cause of an alarming increase in the number of refugees in the world. In 1960, the United Nations listed 1.4 million international refugees. By 1992, the number had grown to 18.2 million. And it was estimated that an additional 24 million people were displaced within the borders of their own countries.[10]

Environmentally, although there have been important gains in selected localities in reducing air pollution and cleaning up polluted rivers, the deeper reality is one of a growing ecological crisis. The ever-present threat of nuclear holocaust has been replaced by the threat of increasing exposure to potentially deadly ultraviolet rays as the protective ozone layer thins. The younger generation worries whether they may be turned into environmental refugees by climate changes that threaten to melt the polar ice caps, flood vast coastal areas, and turn fertile agricultural areas into deserts.

Even at present population levels, nearly a billion people go to bed hungry each night. Yet the soils on which we depend for food are being depleted faster than nature can regenerate them, and one by one the world's productive fisheries are collapsing from overuse. Water shortages have become pervasive, not simply from temporary droughts but also from depleted water tables and rivers taxed beyond their ability to regenerate. We hear of communities devastated by the exhaustion of their forests and fisheries and of people much like ourselves discovering that they and their children are being poisoned by chemical and radioactive contamination in the food they eat, the water they drink, and the earth on which they live and play.

As we wait for a technological miracle to resolve these apparent limits on continued economic expansion, as of 1999 some 77 million people were being added every year to the world's population. Each new member of the human family aspires to a secure and prosperous share of the planet's dwindling bounty. In 1950, the year I entered high school, the world population was 2.5 billion people. On October 12, 1999, world population officially reached 6 billion. The United Nations estimates that it will reach nearly 9 billion by 2050.[11] Bear in mind that demographers make their projections using mathematical models based only on assumptions about fertility rates. These models take no account of what the planet can sustain. Given the environmental and social stresses created by current population levels, it is likely that if we do not voluntarily limit our numbers, famine, disease, and social breakdown will do it for us.

Taken together, these manifestations of institutional systems failure constitute a threefold global crisis of deepening poverty, social disintegration, and environmental destruction. Most elements of the crisis share an important characteristic: solutions require local action—household by household and community by community. This action can be taken only when local resources are in local hands. The most pressing unmet needs of the world's people are for food security, adequate shelter, clothing, health care, and education—the lack of which defines true deprivation. With rare exception, the basic resources and capacity to meet these needs are already found in nearly every country. The natural inclination of local people is usually to give these needs priority. If, however, control lies elsewhere, different priorities usually come into play.

Unfortunately, in our modern world, control seldom rests with local people. More often it resides either with central governmental bureaucracies or with distant corporations that lack both the capacity and the incentive to deal with local needs. The result is a crisis of confidence in our major institutions.

LOSS OF INSTITUTIONAL LEGITIMACY

Public-opinion polls reveal a growing sense of personal insecurity and loss of faith in major institutions all around the world. Particularly telling is the public attitude in the United States, the country that defines for many of the world's people their vision of prosperity, democracy and high-tech consumerism. Here the polls tell us that the real dream of the vast majority of Americans is not for fast sports cars, fancy clothes, caviar, giant TV screens, and country estates, as the popular media might lead one to believe. Rather, it is for a decent and secure life[12]—which American institutions are failing to provide. The single greatest fear of Americans in 1994 was job loss.[13] Only 51 percent of nonmanagement employees in the United States felt that their jobs were secure—down from 75 percent ten years earlier. A similar drop occurred in the sense of job security among management employees.[14] Fifty-five percent of adult Americans no longer believed that one could build a better life for oneself and one's family by working hard and playing by the rules.[15] The U.S. job market has subsequently improved, but the long-term trend is toward growing instability and insecurity.

The Louis Harris polling organization's annual index of confidence in the leaders of twelve major U.S. institutions fell from a base level of 100 in 1966 to 39 in 1994. At the bottom of the list were the U.S. Congress (8 percent of respondents expressed great confidence), the executive branch of government (12 percent), the press (13 percent), and major companies (19 percent). Meanwhile, the Louis Harris "alienation index," which taps feelings of economic inequity, disdain about people with power, and powerlessness, rose from a low of 29 in 1969 to 65 in 1993. A Kettering Foundation report captured the mood of the American electorate: "Americans . . . describe the present political system as impervious to public direction, a system run by a professional political class and controlled by money, not votes."[16] International polls generally support similar results for other industrial countries.[17]

Confidence in our major institutions and their leaders has fallen so low as to put their legitimacy at risk—and for good reason. On the threshold of the golden age, these institutions are working for only a fortunate few. For the many, they are failing disastrously to fulfill the promise that once seemed within our reach.

2

END OF THE OPEN FRONTIER

If current predictions of population growth prove accurate and patterns of human activity on the planet remain unchanged, science and technology may not be able to prevent either irreversible degradation of the environment or continued poverty for much of the world.
    —*Royal Society of London and U.S. National Academy of Sciences*[1]

[I]t is impossible for the world economy to grow its way out of poverty and environmental degradation . . . As the economic subsystem grows it incorporates an even greater proportion of the total ecosystem into itself and must reach a limit at 100 percent, if not before.
    —*Herman Daly*[2]

WHAT HAS GONE WRONG? Why is the dream that should be in our grasp turning to a nightmare? The fundamental nature of our problem was dramatically articulated in 1968 by Kenneth Boulding in his classic essay "The Economics of the Coming Spaceship Earth."[3] Boulding suggested that our problem results from acting like cowboys on a limitless open frontier when in truth we inhabit a living spaceship with a finely balanced life-support system.

COWBOYS AND ASTRONAUTS

How different are the lives of the cowboy and the astronaut. The cowboys of earlier frontier societies, such as the great American West, lived in a world of sparsely populated expanses blessed with seemingly inexhaustible material resources. Except for the presence of indigenous peoples who felt that they had rights to the lands on which they and their ancestors had lived for centuries, everything was free for the taking, to be used and discarded at will for the earth to absorb and the restless winds to scatter. The opportunities for those willing to work seemed limitless, and anyone who presumed that the gain of one must be the loss of another was dismissed as shortsighted and lacking vision. Each person was expected to compete in search of his or her fortune with the assumption that the gains of the individual would in the end be a gain for the community as well.

Astronauts live on spaceships hurtling through space with a human crew and a precious and limited supply of resources. Everything must be maintained in balance, recycled; nothing can be wasted. The measure of well-being is not how fast the crew is able to consume its limited stores but rather how effective the crew members are in maintaining their physical and mental health, their shared resource stocks, and the life-support system on which they all depend. What is thrown away is forever inaccessible. What is accumulated without recycling fouls the living space. Crew members function as a team in the interests of the whole. No one would think of engaging in nonessential consumption unless the basic needs of all were met and there was ample provision for the future.

Boulding's analogy conveys a basic truth. Modern societies are practicing *cowboy economics* in what has become a *spaceship world*. We still treat nature's bounty and waste-disposal services as free for the taking; we honor the strong and equate progress with never-ending increases in the rates of our consumption. As we surmise that ancient Egyptians measured themselves by the size of their pyramids, a future civilization may look back on our era and conclude that we measured our progress by the size of our garbage dumps. Living like cowboys in a spaceship world has tragic consequences:

- It overburdens the life-support system, resulting in its breakdown and a decrease in the level of human activity it can ultimately sustain.
- It creates intense competition between the more powerful and weaker members of the crew for a shrinking pool of life-support services. Some crew members consume wastefully, others are deprived of basic sustenance, social tensions mount, and the legitimacy of governance structures erodes—creating significant potential for social breakdown and violence.

To address the crisis, we must come to terms with a basic reality: we have passed over the historic threshold from an open frontier to a spaceship world. *Our lives depend on the life-support systems of the natural world, and that world is now full.* We must adjust ourselves to the principles of a life-centered space-ship economics.[4] On our current course, we are at once plundering our planet and tearing apart the fabric of nonmarket social relationships that are the foundation of human civilization, a direct consequence of our misperception of the human relationship to natural systems.

FROM OPEN FRONTIERS TO FULL WORLD

Throughout most of human history, the aggregate demand placed on the planetary ecosystem by human economic activities has been inconsequential compared with the enormous regenerative capacity of those systems, and we have not been forced to take the issue of resource limits seriously. When industrialization caused countries to exceed their national resource limits, they simply reached out to obtain what was needed from beyond their own borders, generally by colonizing the resources of nonindustrial people. Although the consequences were sometimes devastating for the colonized people, the added impact on the planetary ecosystem was scarcely noticed by the colonizers.

Thus, Europe's industrialization was built on the backs of its colonies in Africa, Asia, and Latin America. For the United States, this same need was met largely by colonizing its western frontiers at the expense of the Native Americans who inhabited them and by expanding its economic domain to embrace Latin America and the Philippines. Japan, a more recent colonizer, used a sophisticated combination of aid, foreign investment, and trade to colonize the resources of its neighbors in East and Southeast Asia. Asia's newly industrializing countries, South Korea and Taiwan, are now reaching out in a similar manner, as are Thailand and Malaysia.

When only a small portion of the world was industrialized, environmental frontiers were available for exploitation through settlement, trade, and traditional colonization. Similarly, frontier territories served as a social safety valve to absorb surplus population from industrial societies. Between 1850 and 1914, difficult economic conditions in Britain (average population of 32 million) prompted an outward migration of more than 9 million people mainly to the United States.[5]

The era of colonizing open frontiers is now in its final stage. The most readily available frontiers have been exploited, and the competition for the few that remain in such remote locations as Iran Jaya, Indochina, Papua New Guinea, Siberia, and the Brazilian Amazon is intensifying.

It is relevant to our current inquiry to note that the out-migration from Britain in the late nineteenth and early twentieth centuries suggests that the commonly held idea—that colonialism benefited the people of the colonizing countries—is largely myth. The situation was more ambiguous and has much in common with the new corporate colonialism of economic globalization. For the most part, its benefits went to the monied classes, not to the average citizen. A recent study of the British colonial experience by two American historians found that although wealthy investors profited from investments in the colonies, the middle class received only the tax bills that supported the vast military establishment required to maintain the empire. The study concluded, "Imperialism can best be viewed as a mechanism for transferring income from the middle to the upper classes."[6] Economic globalization is a modern form of the same imperial phenomenon, and it carries the same consequence.

The bottom line for our species is that because of population growth and the more than fivefold economic expansion since 1950, the environmental demands of our economic system now fill the available environmental space of the planet. This has brought us to a historic transition point in the evolutionary development of our species from living in a world of open frontiers to living in a full world in a mere historical instant (see Figure 2.1). We now have the option of adjusting ourselves to this new reality or destroying our ecological niche and suffering the consequences.

The first environmental limits that we have confronted, and possibly exceeded, are not the limits of renewable resources and the environment's ability to absorb our wastes—referred to by ecologists as "sink functions." Evidence of our encounter with these limits is everywhere. Acid rain has damaged 31 million hectares of forest in Europe alone. At the global level, each year deserts encroach on another 6 million hectares of once productive land. The area covered by tropical forest is reduced by 11 million hectares, there is net loss of 26 billion tons of soil from oxidation and erosion, and 1.5 million hectares of prime agricultural land are abandoned due to salinization from irrigation projects. Per capita grain production has been falling since 1984. Five percent of the ozone layer over North America, and probably globally, was lost between 1980 and 1990. There has been a 2 percent increase in atmospheric carbon dioxide in the past 100 years.[7]

There is now a vast literature and much debate assessing the data about whether a particular limit has been exceeded or will be passed within the next few years. Such exactness is far less important than coming to terms with the basic truth that we have no real option other than to re-create our economic institutions in line with the reality of a full world.

Figure 2.1: Transition to a Full World

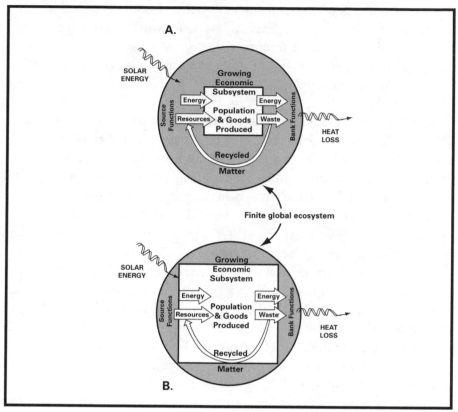

Source: Robert Goodland, Herman E. Daly, and Salah El Serafy, *Population, Technology and Lifestyle: The Transition to Sustainability* (Washington, D.C.: Island Press, 1992), p. 5.

The countries that are consuming beyond their own environmental means control the rule-making process of the international economy. They adjust the rules to ensure their own ability to make up their national environmental deficits through imports—often without being mindful of the implications for the exporting countries.

El Salvador and Costa Rica . . . grow export crops such as bananas, coffee, and sugar on more than one fifth of their cropland. Export cattle ranches in Latin America and southern Africa have replaced rain forest and wildlife range. At the consumer end of the production line, Japan imports 70 percent of its corn, wheat, and barley, 95 percent of its soybeans, and more than 50 percent of its wood, much of it

from the rapidly vanishing rain forests of Borneo ... [In the Nether-
lands] millions of pigs and cows are fattened on palm-kernel cake
from deforested lands in Malaysia, cassava from deforested regions of
Thailand, and soybeans from pesticide-dosed expanses in the south
of Brazil in order to provide European consumers with their high-fat
diet of meat and milk.[8]

The lands used by Southern countries to produce food for export are unavailable to the poor of those countries to grow the staples they require to meet
their own basic needs. The people who are displaced to make way for export-
oriented agriculture add to urban overcrowding or move to more fragile and
less productive lands that quickly become overstressed. The grains that many
Southern countries import from the North in exchange for their own food
exports are often used primarily as feedstocks to produce meat for upper-
income urban consumers. The poor are the double losers.

These dynamics are invisible to Northern consumers, who, if they do raise
questions, are assured that this arrangement provides needed jobs and income for the poor of the south, allowing them to meet their food needs more
cheaply than if they grew the basic grains themselves. It seems like a plausible
theory, but in practice the only certain beneficiaries of this shift from food
economy to trade dependence have been the transnational agribusiness corporations that control global commodities trade.

Just as wealthy countries import resources when their demands exceed
their own limits, they also export their surplus wastes when the volume exceeds their absorptive capacity. Indeed, waste-disposal practices reveal with
particular clarity the relationship between power and the allocation of environmental costs. Polluting factories and waste-disposal sites are so consistently
located in poor and minority neighborhoods or communities that we might
use them as proxy indicators of the geographical distribution of political power.

Adding insult to injury, the rich commonly point to the miserable environmental conditions in which the poor are often forced to live as proof that
the poor are less environmentally responsible than the wealthy. Such claims
divert attention from two important realities. First, most environmental stress
is a direct function of human consumption, and rich people unquestionably
consume far more than do poor people. Second, poor people are far more
likely to live next to waste dumps, polluting factories, and clear cut forests
than are wealthy people, but this doesn't mean that poor people's wastes are
filling those dumps or that they are major consumers of the products produced in those factories or from those forests. Nor does it mean that they

wouldn't prefer to live in more environmentally pristine settings. It simply means that wealthy people have the economic and political power to make sure that pollutants and wastes are dumped somewhere other than in their neighborhoods and to ensure that their neighborhoods remain pleasantly green and that polluting factories are located elsewhere. Poor people do not have this power. What we are seeing is a consequence of income inequality, not a difference in environmental awareness and concern. It can be corrected only by equalizing power.

Economic globalization has greatly expanded opportunities for the rich to pass their environmental burdens to the poor by exporting both wastes and polluting factories. This has been a particularly common practice among Japanese companies, with nearby Southeast Asia being a major recipient. The figures are striking. Japan has reduced its domestic aluminum smelting capacity from 1.2 million tons to 140,000 tons and now imports 90 percent of its aluminum.[9]

What this involves in human terms is suggested by a case study of the Philippine Associated Smelting and Refining Corporation (PASAR). PASAR operates a Japanese-financed and constructed copper smelting plant in the Philippine province of Leyte to produce high-grade copper cathodes for shipment to Japan. The plant occupies 400 acres of land expropriated by the Philippine government from local residents at giveaway prices. Gas and wastewater emissions from the plant contain high concentrations of boron, arsenic, heavy metal, and sulfur compounds that have contaminated local water supplies, reduced fishing and rice yields, damaged the forests, and increased the occurrence of upper-respiratory diseases among local residents. Local people whose homes, livelihoods, and health have been sacrificed to PASAR now largely depend on the occasional part-time or contractual employment they are offered to do the plant's most dangerous and dirtiest jobs.

The company has prospered. The local economy has grown. The Japanese people have a supply of copper at no environmental cost to themselves. The local poor—the project's professed beneficiaries—have lost their means of livelihood and suffer impaired health. The Philippine government is repaying the foreign aid loan from Japan that financed the construction of supporting infrastructure for the plant. And Japanese are congratulating themselves for the cleanliness of their domestic environment and their generous assistance to the poor of the Phillippines.[10]

There is nothing particularly special about this case, other than the fact that it has been documented. Thousands of similar stories illustrate the realities of corporate globalization. *The Economist*, an ardent globalization proponent, has argued that those who criticize such toxic dumping practices would deprive the poor of needed economic opportunities.[11]

Although an open trading system is sometimes advocated as necessary to make up for the environmental deficits of those who have too little, it more often works in exactly the opposite way—increasing the environmental deficits of those who have too little to provide additional environmental resources for those who already have more than their need. Furthermore, an open trading system makes it easier for the rich to keep the consequences of this transfer out of their own sight. The further out of sight those consequences are, the easier it is for those who hold power to ignore or rationalize them.

CONSUMPTION, POPULATION, AND EQUITY

We have endured far too many debates in which the representatives of rich countries condemn the population growth of the poor and refuse to discuss overconsumption and inequality, and the representatives of poor countries refuse to discuss population growth. In a full world, consumption, population, and equity are inseparably linked and must be dealt with holistically. Three studies illustrate these links.

The first is a study by William Rees, an urban planner at the University of British Columbia. Rees estimates that four to six hectares of land are required to maintain the consumption of the average person living in a high-income country, including the land that would be required to maintain current levels of energy consumption using renewable sources. In 1990, the total available ecologically productive land area (land capable of generating consequential biomass) in the world was estimated to be only 1.7 hectares per capita.[12] Rees estimates that the population of the Netherlands, for example, consumes an output equivalent of some 14 times as much productive land as is contained within its borders.[13] The deficits of the Netherlands and other industrial countries is covered up in part by drawing down their own natural resource stocks and in part through international trade that allows them to expropriate the resources of lower-income countries.

Among the industrial countries, per capita resource consumption is generally highest in the United States and Canada. However, since Europe and Japan have higher population densities, the case can be made that they are living even further beyond their own ecological means.

A study by Friends of the Earth Netherlands took such an analysis a step further, asking: What would be the allowable annual levels of consumption of environmental resources and waste-absorption services for the average Dutch person in the year 2010 if (a) resource consumption levels are equal among all people living on the earth at that time and (b) the global level of resource consumption is sustainable? The results are sobering. The researchers found that in almost every area of consumption, the average person in the Netherlands is consuming far beyond his or her means and is thereby depriving people in poorer countries of the ability to meet their basic needs.[14]

Friends of the Earth USA applied the Dutch estimates to the United States and reached a similar conclusion.[15] For example, current annual per capita carbon dioxide emissions are 19.5 tons in the United States and 12 tons in the Netherlands. To meet suggested targets for the reduction of global warming, world per capita carbon dioxide emission levels from fossil fuel use must be brought down to 4 tons by 2010. If the burden of achieving this target were shared equitably, each person would be reduced in 2010 to consuming no more than one liter of carbon-based fuel per day. "A Dutch person will be given the choice of traveling 24 km (15.5 mi.) by car, 50 km (31 mi.) by bus, 65 km (40 mi.) by train or 10 km (6.2 mi.) by plane per day. A flight from Amsterdam to Rio de Janeiro can probably be undertaken only once every twenty years!"[16]

For those whose only transportation option is walking, such standards may seem luxurious. They are sobering indeed, however, for those of us accustomed to spending much of our lives in cars, planes, buses, and trains. It is even more sobering to note that our allowance of one liter of fossil fuel a day is our allowance not only for direct personal travel but for the fuels used to produce, transport, and market the items we consume as well—burdens we place on the environment but never see and tend to neglect.

A third study, presented at the annual meeting of the American Association for the Advancement of Science by Cornell University professor David Pimentel and his colleagues, asked similar questions but also looked at interactions among sectors and took population as a variable. For example, the study took into account that although we might cultivate more land, doing so would require more water. We could get more of our energy from the sun, but only by using more land. Each hectare of agricultural land could produce higher yields, but only by using more energy inputs.

The Cornell researchers also took into account that although we continue to bring new land under cultivation, 10 million hectares of productive arable land are already being abandoned each year due to severe degradation. These abandoned lands must be replaced simply to maintain existing food consumption levels. An additional 5 million hectares of new land must be put into production to feed the annual net addition to the world population, before making any dent in reducing existing malnutrition. Most of this new agricultural land comes from clearing forests.[17]

The Cornell research team concluded that the earth can sustain a population of one to two billion people consuming at a level roughly equivalent to the current per capita standard of Europe. To highlight the trade-off involved, they posed a fundamental question: "Does human society want 10 to 15 billion humans living in poverty and malnourishment or one to two billion living with abundant resources and a quality environment?"[18]

The calculations presented by all three studies are at best preliminary approximations based on controversial assumptions and the use of fragmented and often unreliable data. They are, however, important to any realistic discussion of sustainability as they bring into focus the inescapable relationship in a full world between consumption, population, and equity and point to three important realities. First, if the earth's sustainable natural output were shared equally among the earth's present population, the needs of all could be met. Second, it is a physical impossibility, even with the most optimistic assumptions about the potential of new technologies, for all the world's people to consume at levels even approximating those in North America, Europe, and Japan. Third, each doubling of world population reduces each individual's share of the earth's regenerative output by half.

If we are to have a world that works for all, we must free ourselves of the myth that economic growth is the foundation of human progress and direct our attention to ending overconsumption, deprivation, population growth, and inequality—all of which are inextricably linked.

3

THE GROWTH ILLUSION

To address poverty, economic growth is not an option: it is an imperative.
—Mahbub ul Haq, former World Bank vice president[1]

Economic growth provides the conditions in which protection of the environment can be best achieved.
—International Chamber of Commerce[2]

PERHAPS NO SINGLE IDEA IS MORE deeply embedded in modern political culture than the belief that economic growth is the key to meeting most important human needs, including alleviating poverty and protecting the environment. Anyone who dares to speak of environmental limits to growth risks being dismissed out of hand as an antipoor doomsayer. Thus most environmentalists call simply for "a different kind of growth," although it is seldom evident what kind it would be.

Nobel laureate economist Jan Tinbergen and his distinguished colleague Roefie Hueting point out that there are two ways for an economy to grow, according to our current mode of reckoning. One is to increase the number of people employed. The other is to increase the labor productivity—the value of output per worker—of those already employed. Historically, increases in labor productivity have been the most important source of growth. About 70 percent of this productivity growth has been in the 30 percent of economic activity accounted for by the petroleum, petrochemical, and metal industries; chemical-intensive agriculture; public utilities; road building and transportation; and mining—specifically the industries that are most rapidly drawing down natural capital, generating the bulk of our most toxic wastes, and consuming a substantial portion of our nonrenewable energy reserves.[3]

Furthermore, the more environmentally burdensome ways of meeting a given need are generally those that contribute most to the gross domestic product (GDP).[4] For example, driving a mile in a car contributes more to GDP than riding a mile on a bicycle. Turning on an air conditioner adds more than opening a window. Relying on processed packaged food adds more than using natural foods purchased in bulk in reusable containers. We might say that GDP, technically a measure of the rate at which money is flowing through the economy, might also be described as a measure of the rate at which we are turning resources into garbage.

We could expend a lot of effort on the probably unrealistic goal of making GDP go up indefinitely without creating more garbage. But why not instead concentrate on ending poverty, improving our quality of life, and achieving a balance with the earth. These are achievable goals—if we can free ourselves from the illusion that growth is *the* path to better living.

A DISILLUSIONED ECONOMIST

In 1954, R. A. Butler, the British chancellor of the Exchequer, spoke to a Conservative Party conference in which he pointed out that a 3 percent annual growth rate would double the national income per capita by 1980 and make every man and woman twice as rich as his or her father had been at the same age. The speech proved to be a turning point in British life. Previously, national goals had been set in terms of specific targets, such as building 300,000 houses a year or establishing a national health service. Henceforth, the primary goal would be economic growth. The ideological debate between the Left and the Right as to how a fixed pie would be distributed was largely defused. Attention centered on how to increase the size of the pie.

In 1989, Irish economist Richard Douthwaite set out to document the benefits of the subsequent doubling of Britain's per capita income. In his own words:

> Problems only arose when I attempted to identify what they (the benefits) were, especially as it quickly became apparent that almost every social indicator had worsened over the third of a century the experiment had taken. Chronic disease had increased, crime had gone up eight fold, unemployment had soared and many more marriages were ending in divorce. Almost frantically I looked for gains to set against these losses which, in most cases I felt, had to be blamed on growth.
> . . . [E]ventually . . . I gave up. The weight of evidence was over-

whelming: the unquestioning quest for growth had been an unmitigated social and environmental disaster. Almost all of the extra resources the process had created had been used to keep the system functioning in an increasingly inefficient way. The new wealth had been squandered on producing pallets and corrugated cardboard, non-returnable bottles and ring-pull drink cans. It had built airports, supertankers and heavy goods lorries, motorways, flyovers and car parks with many floors. It had enabled the banking, insurance, stock brokering, tax collecting and accountancy sector to expand from 493,000 to 2,475,000 employees during the thirty-three years. It had financed the recruitment of over three million people to the "reserve army of the unemployed." Very little was left for more positive achievements when all these had taken their share.[5]

We might apply a similar test to the more than fivefold increase in global output since 1950. The advocates of growth persistently maintain that economic growth is the key to ending poverty, stabilizing population, protecting the environment, and achieving social harmony. Yet during this same period, the number of people living in absolute poverty has kept pace with population growth: both have doubled. The ratio of the share of the world's income going to the richest 20 percent to that going to the bottom 20 percent poor has doubled. And indicators of social and environmental disintegration have risen sharply nearly everywhere. Although economic growth did not necessarily create these problems, it certainly has not solved them.

THE LIMITS OF GROWTH

Few would dispute that there has been real and consequential human progress over the past several centuries and that advances in technology and the consequent productivity increases have resulted in real gains in human well-being. At the same time, as this chapter elaborates, there is little basis for assuming that economic growth, as we currently define and measure it, results in automatic increases in human welfare. As British economist Paul Ekins points out, it is possible to conclude that a particular instance of growth has been a good thing only by:

- Showing that the growth has taken place through the production of goods and services that are inherently valuable and beneficial;

- Demonstrating that these goods and services have been distributed widely throughout the society; and
- Proving that these benefits outweigh many detrimental effects of the growth process on other parts of society.[6]

Our measures of GDP make no such distinctions. Indeed, a major portion of what shows up as growth in GDP is a result of:

- Shifting activities from the non-money social economy of household and community to the money economy, with the consequent erosion of social capital;
- Depleting natural resource stocks such as forests, fisheries, and oil and mineral reserves at far above their recovery rates; and
- Counting as income the costs of defending ourselves against the consequences of growth, such as disposing of waste, cleaning up toxic dumps and oil spills, providing health care for victims of environmentally-caused illnesses, rebuilding after floods resulting from human activities such as deforestation, and financing pollution-control devices.

Standard financial accounting deducts from income an allowance for the depreciation of capital assets. The economic accounting systems by which economic growth is measured make no comparable adjustment for the depletion of social and natural capital. Indeed, economic accounting counts many costs of economic growth as economic gains, even though they clearly reduce rather than increase our well-being. The results are sometimes ludicrous. For example, the costs of cleaning up the *Exxon Valdez* oil spill on the Alaska coast and the costs of repairing damage from the terrorist bombing of the World Trade Center in New York both counted as net contributions to economic output. According to this distorted logic, disasters that are tragic for the people and the environment are beneficial to society.

In their book *For the Common Good*, Herman Daly and John Cobb Jr. reconstruct the national income accounts for the United States from 1960 to 1986, counting only those increases in output that relate to improvements in well-being and adjusting downward for the depletion of human and environmental resources. The result is an index of real economic welfare rather than simply aggregate output. Their index reveals that, on average, individual welfare in the United States peaked in 1969, then remained on a plateau and fell during the early and mid-1980s. Yet from 1969 to 1986, GNP per person went up by 35 percent, and fossil fuel consumption increased by around 17 percent.

The main consequence of this growth has been that most of us are now working harder to maintain a declining quality of life.[7]

Often, how the economic pie is allocated is more important to our well-being than its absolute size. United Nations Development Programme (UNDP) studies show that it is *not* necessary to have particularly high economic output for a country to meet the basic needs of its people. In fact, some countries with relatively modest economic output do better in this regard than other countries with much higher GDP. Saudi Arabia's literacy rate is lower than Sri Lanka's despite the fact that its per capita income is fifteen times higher. Brazil's child mortality rate is four times that of Jamaica, even though its per capita income is twice as high.[8]

Obviously, some minimum level of economic output is essential to meet basic needs, and this required level is probably a good deal higher than the current output of the world's poorest countries. However, for most of the world's people, the question of whether their basic needs are met depends less on the absolute level of per capita income than on how productive output is allocated. If the priority is to provide people with a good diet, shelter, clothing, clean water, health care, basic transport, education, and other essentials of good living, then it is within the means of most countries to do so and thus alleviate human deprivation within existing levels of productive output. In many instances it would require little more than reallocating the resources now devoted to military purposes.

Clean water and proper sanitation are perhaps the most important contributors to good health and long life. Experience in places such as the state of Kerala in India prove that such necessities can be provided at quite modest income levels. By contrast, countries with high income levels are experiencing increases in rates of cancer, respiratory illnesses, stress and cardiovascular disorders, and birth defects, as well as falling sperm counts. A growing body of evidence links all these phenomena to the by-products of economic growth—air and water pollution, chemical additives and pesticide residues in food, high noise levels, and increased exposure to electromagnetic radiation.[9]

Suburbanization, greater dependence on the automobile for mobility, and increased use of television for entertainment are associated with economic growth. Each has reduced the normal human contacts and interactions that used to be a regular part of village and urban life as people met on paths and sidewalks, created family and community entertainment, and congregated in local shops and coffee stalls.

Rapid economic growth in low-income countries brings modern airports,

television, express highways, and air-conditioned shopping malls with sophisticated consumer electronics and fashion labels for the fortunate few. It rarely
improves living conditions for the many. This kind of growth requires gearing
the economy toward exports to earn foreign exchange to buy the things that
wealthy people desire. Thus the lands of the poor are appropriated for export
crops. The former tillers of these lands then find themselves subsisting in urban slums on starvation wages paid by sweatshops producing items for export. Families are broken up, the social fabric is strained to the breaking point,
and violence becomes endemic. Those whom growth has favored then need
still more foreign exchange to import arms to protect themselves from the
rage of the excluded.

GROWTH AND THE POOR

Any mention of the need to end growth elicits protests that doing so would
condemn the poor to perpetual deprivation. Ironically, the argument that the
well-being of the poor depends on economic growth comes mainly from professional development workers, economists, financiers, corporation heads, and
others who have no problem putting food on their tables. When the poor
speak for themselves, they more often talk of secure rights to the land and
waters on which they live and from which they obtain their livelihoods. They
seek decent jobs that pay a living wage. They want health care and education
for their children. In a world in which all things come to those with money,
they may also say, "We need money." Rarely, if ever, do they say, "We must have
economic growth." Growth is a rich man's game.

It is all too common for poor people's deprivation to increase during periods of rapid economic expansion and decrease during periods of economic
contraction. The reason is simple: the policies that favor economic expansion
commonly shift income and assets to those who own property at the expense of
those who labor for their livelihood. Although growth does not necessarily cause
poverty, the policies advanced in its name often do.[10] Consider, for example, the
following policy outcomes typically associated with economic growth:

- Depleting natural resources often provides financial gains for the economically powerful at the expense of people whose livelihood base is
  disrupted.
- Shifting activities from the social (nonmoney) economy to the money
  economy increases the dependence of the working classes on money

and thereby on those who own assets, provide professional services, and control access to jobs.

- Shifting control of agricultural lands, forests, and fisheries from those engaged in creating subsistence livelihood to property owners engaged in investing for profit adds to measured economic output, redistributes the ownership of these assets to the capital-owning classes, expands the pool of low-cost wage labor, and pushes wages downward.

For centuries, the indigenous Igorot ("people of the mountains") of Benguet province, Philippines, have engaged in small-scale "pocket mining" of the rich gold veins found on their ancestral lands. The men dug small, round caves into the mountain. Women and children hammered the gold-bearing rocks into nuggets the size of corn kernels.[11] The lands of the Igorot are now dominated by huge open-pit mines operated by the Benguet Corporation—owned in approximately equal shares by wealthy Filipinos, the Philippine government, and U.S. investors—to produce gold for export. Dozens of bulldozers, cranes, and trucks cut deep gashes into the mountain, stripping away the trees and topsoil and dumping enormous piles of rocky waste into the riverbeds. The local people tell visitors how, with their water sources destroyed, they can no longer grow rice and bananas and must go to the other side of the mountain for water to drink and bathe. Even their mining grounds are threatened, and their rights ignored.[12]

Instead of using water to separate the gold from the rock, as the Igorot do, the mining company uses toxic chemicals, including cyanide compounds, and flushes them down the river, poisoning the water and killing the cattle that drink it. Downstream, rice farmers in the affected area of Panasinan province are losing an estimated 250 million pesos a year as the mine tailings cover their irrigated fields and cause sharp declines in yields, resulting in a net population exodus. Further down the river, fisherfolk in the gulf report substantial reductions in their catch as tailings smother the coral reefs. It's good for growth. Benguet and the other major mining companies involved earn combined net profits of 1.1 billion pesos a year—a massive resource transfer from the poor to the rich.[13] Countless such stories are told wherever mining companies operate.

The poor suffer similar consequences when timber companies move in to strip their forests bare, usually without regard for the rights of local people. As a young peasant woman in a remote community of San Fernando in the southern Philippine province of Bukidnon explained to visitors, "Without trees there is no food and without food, no life." An old man explained that before the logging trucks came to his village, "There was plenty of fish, plenty of corn, and plenty of rice." People went on to describe how their rivers have changed shape, turned muddier, shallower. During the monsoons, the river now overflows its banks and swallows adjacent fertile fields in formerly flood-free areas. Creeks that once nourished the fields during the dry season have disappeared; landslides have become common during the rainy season. The rat population, which previously found food in the forests and was kept in check by forest predators, now ravages farmers' fields at night. In a once prosperous community, more than four out of five children suffer some degree of malnutrition.[14]

In the name of promoting economic growth, such devastation is often heavily supported by public subsidies. For each ton of mine tailings they produce, the typical Philippine mining company earns 96.73 pesos and pays 0.5 pesos of taxes.[15] In the Unites States, the government gives away mining rights to federal lands for $12 a hectare or less. Adding insult to injury, miners are able to take a tax deduction of 5 to 22 percent of their gross income as a "depletion allowance" to compensate them for the depletion of these federal lands. In Japan, the government offers loans, subsidies, and tax incentives for domestic mineral exploration and development.[16] Infrastructure costs associated with mining and timber extraction by Japanese companies in Southern countries are commonly funded by loans disbursed under the Japanese foreign aid program to be repaid by the host country with public funds.

As opportunities for industrial employment have declined in high-income countries, economists have looked to the service economy to pick up the slack. Little note is taken of the fact that much of the service economy expansion results from colonizing the social economies of households and communities. These social economies once productively engaged more than half the working hours of the adult population, mostly women, in meeting many of the basic needs of families and carrying out the countless neighborly functions essential to the maintenance of healthy, caring communities. Indeed, there was a time when social economies engaged both women and men in carrying out most of the productive and reproductive activities through which people met their basic needs for food, shelter, clothing, child care, health care, care of the elderly, housekeeping, education, physical security, and entertainment. Social economies are by nature local, nonwaged, nonmonetized, and nonmarket. They are energized more by love than by money.

As productive and reproductive functions such as child care, health care, food preparation, entertainment, and physical security are transferred from the social economy to the market economy, they show up as additions to economic output and thus contributors to economic growth—though this transfer does little or nothing to improve the quality of the services we receive. This shift also increases the demand for economic overhead functions, which are counted as additions to economic output although they are actually an enormous source of economic inefficiency. Consider that when family and community members worked directly with and for one another, there were no tax collectors, managers, government regulators, accountants, lawyers, stockbrokers, bankers, middlemen, advertising account executives, marketing specialists, investment brokers, or freight haulers collecting their share of the output of those who did the actual productive work. The full value of the goods and services produced was shared and exchanged within the family and the community, among those who actually created the value.[17] The result was an extraordinarily efficient use of resources to meet real needs.

Many people find that the market economy's overhead costs have become so high that, even with two wage earners and longer work hours, they cannot adequately meet needs that they once met quite satisfactorily on their own. Parents—or more often a single, impoverished female parent—are left with little time, energy, or encouragement to do more than function as income earners and night guardians. The modern urban home has become little more than a place to sleep and watch television. Few people find time to participate in the vast array of community activities and services that once made neighborhoods more than a physical address. The dense fabric of relationships based on long-term sharing and cooperation that social economies once maintained comes unraveled. High rates of deprivation, depression, divorce, teenage pregnancy, violence, alcoholism, drug abuse, crime, and suicide are among the more evident consequences in both high and low-income countries.[18]

Because such shifts have given women new opportunities, they are often hailed as a victory for women's equality. Yet rather than promoting new partnerships that involve men more fully in family and community as women expand their participation in the workplace, the change has more often simply increased the burden on women. This has placed heavy stresses on family relationships and left communities dependent on paid professional staff to perform functions that neighbors once provided for one another. Many children grow up in commercial day-care centers or are left at home or in the streets without any adult supervision. Many women who started working to expand their options now find themselves tied to poorly compensated and unfulfilling jobs on which their families have become dependent.

Economists applaud the economic growth that results from creating new highly paid professional classes and new opportunities for the health care, social services, and security services industries to deal with the resulting family and community breakdown. The net costs to societies—and especially to the poor, for whom the money economy provides inadequate opportunities—are ignored.

The displacement of the poor from the lands on which they live and obtain their livelihoods has been a long historical process. Time after time the consequence has been economic growth for the strong and deprivation for the weak. Economists estimate that between 1750 and 1950, Britain's per capita income roughly doubled, but the quality of life for the majority of people steadily declined. Before 1750, travelers to the British countryside reported little evidence of deprivation. For the most part, people had adequate food, shelter, and clothing, and the countryside had a prosperous appearance. Most farming was done on open fields, with families holding the rights to farm small, scattered strips of land. Even those without such rights were able to provide for themselves from the common lands, which provided grazing for their animals, rabbits to eat, and wood for their fires. A few industrious souls managed to consolidate larger properties through exchange, rental, and purchase and to hedge or wall them off from the rest—a process commonly referred to as enclosure, but this was a slow and cumbersome process.[19]

Then landed interests chose to speed up the process through the introduction of legislation that made enclosure a requirement. As enclosure progressed, the poor were increasingly deprived of access to the lands from which they once derived their living. With no other source of livelihood, they were forced to work as laborers for the larger farmers. The resulting surge in the labor pool depressed wages and increased the profits of the larger landowners. The introduction of land taxes forced many smaller farmers to sell the bits of land they held. The result was a major consolidation of landholdings and a continuing flow of labor from the countryside to the city to supply the factories of the industrial revolution with workers—many of them women and young children—who were willing to accept employment in factories that "were viler than prisons . . . So appalling were these conditions that British factory employees in the early nineteenth century were probably worse off than the slaves on American plantations."[20]

In contrast to their experience during this early period of "economic expansion," conditions for ordinary people in Britain improved from 1914, the year World War I began, through the end of World War II, including the years between the wars, when there was no overall growth in Britain's national income. As explained by Douthwaite, the wars made it politically necessary to control the forces of capitalism. The government introduced heavy taxes on top incomes and controlled wages. Although it held wage increases below the level of inflation, more people were employed, and their work was steady. As a consequence, the real purchasing power of most wage-earner households improved. Furthermore, when the government sanctioned wage increases, it frequently authorized the same absolute increase for everyone. Thus the raises for unskilled workers were proportionally higher than for skilled workers. The overall result was a massive shift toward equity.[21]

Following World War I, a reduction of the workweek from fifty-four hours to forty-six or forty-eight hours to absorb the influx of returning military personnel kept unemployment low and wages high. Those without jobs were protected by the national employment insurance scheme introduced in 1911. Paid for by the substantial taxes on high incomes, it systematically transferred income from wealthier taxpayers to those most in need.

World War II resulted in much the same consequence for the poor. The benefit came not from the growth in output that accompanied the war effort but from a combination of high demand for labor, the erosion of wage differentials, government control of profits, and the implementation of a highly progressive tax structure. Income equality increased dramatically, and the enforced saving that resulted from rationing left an enormous pent-up demand following the war, easing the transition to a peacetime economy.

Similar patterns were experienced in the United States. The imperatives of the depression of the 1930s and World War II galvanized political action behind measures that resulted in a significant redistribution of income and built the strong middle class that came to be seen as the hallmark of America's economic strength and prosperity.

The resulting structure of relative equity and shared economic prosperity remained more or less intact until the 1970s, when a combination of economic competition from East Asia, labor unrest, inflation, and a rebellious youth culture mobilized conservative forces to reassert themselves. An all-out political attack on labor unions, social safety nets, market regulation, and trade barriers realigned the institutional forces of American society behind big-money interests. In the 1970s and 1980s, the percentage of working Americans whose wages placed them below the poverty line increased sharply, and the society become increasingly polarized between haves and have-nots with respect to employment opportunities and earnings.[22]

Those who call for expanding the economic pie as the answer to poverty overlook an important reality. Whether or not a person has access to the resources required for survival depends less on absolute income than on relative income. In a free-market economy, each individual is in competition for access to the limited environmental space, and the person with the most money invariably wins.

As we have seen above, economic growth often raises the incomes of the wealthy faster than those of the poor. Even if all incomes were to increase at the same rate, the consequence would be much the same—the absolute gap between rich and poor would increase. It is simple arithmetic. Take the uniform annual 3 percent global increase in per capita income that the Brundtland Commission on the Environment and Development proposed as the answer to global poverty and environmental problems. That would translate into a first-year annual per capita increase (in U.S. dollars) "of $633 for the United States; $3.60 for Ethiopia; $5.40 for Bangladesh; $7.50 for Nigeria; $10.80 for China and $10.50 for India. By the end of ten years, such growth will have raised Ethiopia's per capita income by $41—hardly sufficient to dent poverty there—while that of the United States will have risen by $7,257."[23] The per capita *increase* in purchasing power for the United States would thus be 177 times that of Ethiopia.

Without concurrent redistribution, an expanding pie brings far greater benefit to the already wealthy than to the poor, increases the absolute gap between rich and poor, and further increases the power advantage of the former over the latter. This advantage becomes a life-and-death issue in a resource-scarce world in which the rich and poor are locked in mortal competition for a depleting resource base.

If the prophets of illusion who promote growth as the answer to poverty are really concerned with the plight of the poor, let them advocate measures that directly increase the ability of the poor to meet their basic needs—not tax breaks for the rich.

GROWTH IN THE NAME OF DEVELOPMENT

Many development economists believe that moving a country on the path to industrialization requires that labor be forced off the farm and into the cities so that agriculture can be modernized and an urban industrial labor pool can be created. The parallels to the enclosure process in Britain are striking. Costa Rica provides a particularly egregious contemporary example of how it works.

Before the International Monetary Fund (IMF) and the World Bank restructured Costa Rica's economic policies in the name of easing its foreign debt problems, Costa Rica was widely known as one of the most stable, peaceful, prosperous, and equitable of Southern countries. It had a strong base of small farmers and few of the large landholdings characteristic of other Latin American societies. The policies imposed by the IMF and the World Bank shifted the economic incentives away from small farms producing foods that Costa Ricans eat toward large estates producing for export. As a consequence, thousands of small farmers have been displaced, their lands have been consolidated into large ranches and agricultural estates producing for export, and Costa Rica's income gap is becoming more like that of the other Latin American countries. An increase in crime and violence has required sharp increases in public expenditures on police and public security. The country now depends on imports to meet basic food requirements, and the foreign debt that structural adjustment was supposed to reduce has doubled. As outrageous as the consequences of their policies have been, the IMF and the World Bank point to Costa Rica as a structural adjustment *success* story because economic growth has increased and the country is now able to meet its growing debt service payments.[24]

In Brazil, the conversion of agriculture from smallholders producing food for domestic consumption to capital-intensive production for export displaced 28.4 million people between 1960 and 1980—a number greater than the entire population of Argentina.[25] In India, large-scale development projects have displaced 20 million people over a forty-year period.[26] In 1989, ongoing World Bank projects were displacing 1.5 million people, and projects in preparation threatened another 1.5 million. Bank staffers were unable to point to a single bank-funded project in which the displaced people had been relocated and rehabilitated to a standard of living comparable to what they enjoyed before displacement.[27] A conference on Asian development sponsored by Asian nongovernmental organizations working at the grassroots on environmental and poverty issues revealed an aspect of Asia's development experience that the gushing reports in World Bank documents and business periodicals never mention:

In Thailand, ten million rural people face eviction from the land they live on to make way for commercial tree farms. Ground water is depleted and mangroves are continually destroyed by export-oriented shrimp farms. Tribal people struggle for recognition of ancestral land rights in the forests of Eastern Malaysia and Indonesia. In the Philippines, the government's land reform program is systematically eroded by the conversion of prime agricultural lands into industrial estates and other non-agricultural uses–even as the country needs to spend its scarce foreign exchange on rice imports. Agricultural chemicals and toxic industrial wastes, including those brought to the region by foreign corporations and agencies under the guise of international assistance, continue to poison us. Dams and geothermal projects displace people and destroy agricultural and forest lands to meet the energy demands of export-oriented industries. Slum dwellers are evicted to make way for industries and shopping centers that benefit others. Destructive fishing practices, commonly supported by corporate interests serving foreign markets, deprive our fisherfolk of their livelihoods and threaten the regenerative capacities of our oceans.[28]

Urban development plans in Bangkok, Thailand, call for the eviction of 300,000 people for highways and other urban development projects. Low-income families that resist find their water and electricity cut off. Further resistance is likely to result in the arson or bulldozing of their homes.[29] A million Mexican families were displaced from their farms as a consequence of the North American Free Trade Agreement. The engine of economic growth has proved far more effective in creating development refugees than in fulfilling its promise to end human deprivation in the world's low-income countries.

If our concern is with sustainable human well-being for all people, then we must penetrate the economic myths embedded in our culture by the prophets of illusion, free ourselves of our obsession with growth, and dramatically restructure economic relationships to focus on two priorities:

1. Bring human uses of the environment into balance with the regenerative capacities of the ecosystem; and
2. Give priority in the allocation of available natural capital to ensuring that all people have the opportunity to fulfill their physical needs adequately and to pursue their full social, cultural, intellectual, and spiritual development.

Among the barriers to accomplishing this transformation is the powerful coalition of political interests aligned behind an institutional agenda that is taking us in a quite different direction. These are the corporate interests that benefit when societies make the pursuit of economic growth the organizing principle of public policy.

Part II

CONTEST FOR SOVEREIGNTY

4

RISE OF CORPORATE POWER IN AMERICA

Chartered privileges are a burden, under which the people of Britain, and other European nations, groan in misery.
—*Thomas Earle, pamphleteer, 1823*

Today's business corporation is an artificial creation, shielding owners and managers while preserving corporate privilege and existence. Artificial or not, corporations have won more rights under law than people have—rights which government has protected with armed force.
—*Richard L. Grossman and Frank T. Adams[1]*

THE FACT THAT THE INTERESTS OF CORPORATIONS and people of wealth are closely intertwined tends to obscure the significance of the corporation as an institution in its own right. On the more positive side, the corporate charter is a social invention created originally to aggregate financial resources in the service of a public purpose. On the negative side, it allows one or more individuals to leverage massive economic and political resources behind narrowly focused private agendas while protecting themselves from legal liability for the public consequences.

Less widely recognized is the tendency of individual corporations, as they grow in size and power, to develop their own institutional agendas aligned with imperatives inherent in their nature and structure that are not wholly under the control even of the people who own and manage them. These agendas center on increasing their own profits and protecting themselves from the uncertainty of the market. They arise from a combination of market competition, the demands of financial markets, and efforts by individuals within them to advance their careers and increase their personal income.

Large corporations commonly join forces to advance shared political and economic agendas. In the United States, they have been engaged for more than 150 years in restructuring the rules and institutions of governance to suit their interests. Some readers may feel uneasy with my anthropomorphizing the corporation, but I do so advisedly, because once created corporations tend to take on a life of their own beyond the intentions of their human participants.

Corporations have emerged as the dominant governance institutions on the planet, with the largest among them reaching into virtually every country of the world and exceeding most governments in size and power. Increasingly, it is the corporate interest rather than the human interest that defines the policy agendas of states and international bodies.

INSTRUMENTS OF COLONIAL EXTRACTION

It is instructive to recall that the modern corporation is a direct descendant of the great merchant companies of fifteenth- and sixteenth-century England and Holland. These were limited liability, joint stock companies to which the crown granted charters that conferred on them the power to act as virtual states in dealing with vast foreign territories.

For example, in 1602 the Dutch Crown chartered the United East India Company, giving it a monopoly over Dutch trade in the lands and waters between the Cape of Good Hope at the Southern tip of Africa and the Straits of Magellan at the tip of South America. Its charter vested it with sovereign powers to conclude treaties and alliances, maintain armed forces, conquer territory, and build forts. It subsequently defeated the British fleet and established sovereignty over the East Indies (now Indonesia) after displacing the Portuguese.[2] Early on it acquired large tracts of land in Eastern Indonesia through a system of loans to cultivators that led to their eventual dispossession. It prohibited the growing of cloves on lands not in Dutch hands. Unable to produce sufficient food to sustain themselves on the remaining infertile land of their islands, the local people were obliged to buy rice from the company at inflated prices, eventually ruining the local economy and reducing the population to poverty.[3]

The British East India Company was the primary instrument of Britain's colonization of India, a country it ruled until 1784 much as if it were a private estate. The company continued to administer India under British supervision until 1858 when the British government assumed direct control.[4]

In the early 1800s, the British East India Company established a thriving business exporting tea from China and paying for its purchases with illegal opium. China responded to the resulting social and economic disruption by confiscating the opium warehoused in Canton by the British merchants. This precipitated the Opium War of 1839 to 1842—which Britain won. As tribute, the British pressed a settlement on China that included the payment of a large indemnity to Britain, granted Britain free access to five Chinese ports for trade, and secured the right of British citizens accused of crimes in China to be tried by British courts.[5] This settlement was a precursor to modern "free trade" agreements imposed by powerful Northern nations on weaker Southern nations.

British crown corporations also played an important role in the colonization of North America. The London Company founded the Virginia colony and for a time ruled it as company property. The Massachusetts Bay Company held rights to trade and colonization in the New England region. The Hudson's Bay Company, which was founded to establish British control over the fur trade in the Hudson's Bay watershed area of North America, was an important player in the British colonization of what is now Canada.

The corporate charter represented a grant from the crown that limited an investor's liability for losses of the corporation to the amount of his or her investment in it—a right not extended to individual citizens. Each charter set forth the specific rights and obligations of a particular corporation, including the share of profits that would go to the crown in return for the special privileges extended. Such charters were bestowed at the pleasure of the crown and could be withdrawn at any time. Not surprisingly, the history of corporate-government relations since that day has been one of continuing pressure by corporate interests to expand corporate rights and to limit corporate obligations.

HOLDING CORPORATIONS AT BAY

Much of America's history has been shaped by a long and continuing struggle for sovereignty between people and corporations. Although there have been similar struggles in other Western democracies, the U.S. experience assumes special importance because of the dominant role the United States has had in shaping the institutions of the world economy since the end of World War I. This global role became increasingly self-conscious and assertive when the United States emerged from World War II as the world's most powerful nation.

Even as its economic power declined compared with that of Japan and Europe, the United States remained the dominant player in shaping international institutions such as the United Nations, the International Monetary Fund, the World Bank, and the World Trade Organization. As we shall see in following chapters, corporate interests have figured prominently in how the United States has defined its national interest in relation to these and other global institutions. Thus the history of corporate power in the United States is more than purely national significance. America was born of a revolution against the abusive power of the British kings and the chartered corporations used by the crown to maintain control over colonial economies.[6]

The English Parliament, which during the seventeenth and eighteenth centuries was made up of wealthy landowners, merchants, and manufacturers, passed many laws intended to protect and extend their private monopoly interests. One set of laws, for example, required that all goods imported to the colonies from Europe or Asia first pass through England. Similarly, specified products exported from the colonies also had to be sent first to England. The Navigation Acts required that all goods shipped to or from the colonies be carried on English or colonial ships manned by English or colonial crews. Furthermore, although they had the necessary raw materials, the colonists were forbidden to produce their own caps, hats, and woolen and iron goods. Raw materials were shipped from the colonies to England for manufacture, and the finished products were returned to the colonies.[7]

These practices were strongly condemned by Adam Smith in *The Wealth of Nations*. Smith saw corporations, much as he saw governments, as instruments for suppressing the beneficial competitive forces of the market. His condemnation of corporations was uncompromising. He specifically mentioned them twelve times in his classic thesis, and not once did he attribute any favorable quality to them. Typical is his observation that: "It is to prevent this reduction of price, and consequently of wages and profit, by restraining that free competition which would most certainly occasion it, that all corporations, and the greater part of corporation law, have been established."[8]

It is noteworthy that the publication of *The Wealth of Nations* and the signing of the U.S. Declaration of Independence both occurred in 1776. Each was, in its way, a revolutionary manifesto challenging the abusive control of markets to capture unearned profits and inhibit local enterprise. Smith and the American colonists shared a deep suspicion of both state and corporate power. The U.S. Constitution instituted the separation of governmental powers to create a system of checks and balances that was carefully crafted to limit opportunities for the abuse of state power. It makes no mention of corporations, which suggests that those who framed it did not foresee or intend that corporations would have a consequential role in the affairs of the new nation.

In the young American republic, there was little sense that corporations were either inevitable or necessary. Family farms and businesses were the mainstay of the economy, much in the spirit of Adam Smith's ideal, although neighborhood shops, cooperatives, and worker-owned enterprises were also common. This was consistent with a prevailing belief in the importance of keeping investment and production decisions local and democratic.[9]

The corporations that were chartered were kept under watchful citizen and governmental control. The power to issue corporate charters was retained by the individual states rather than being given to the federal government so that it would remain as close as possible to citizen control. Many provisions were included in corporate charters and related laws that limited use of the corporate vehicle to amass excessive personal power.[10] The early charters were limited to a fixed number of years and required that the corporation be dissolved if the charter were not renewed. Generally, the corporate charter set limits on the corporation's borrowing, ownership of land, and sometimes even its profits. Members of the corporation were liable in their personal capacities for all debts incurred by the corporation during their period of membership. Large and small investors had equal voting rights, and interlocking directorates were outlawed. Furthermore, a corporation was limited to conducting only those business activities specifically authorized in its charter. Charters often included revocation clauses. State legislators maintained the sovereign right to withdraw the charter of any corporation that in their judgment failed to serve the public interest, and they kept close watch on corporate affairs. By 1800, only some 200 corporate charters had been granted by the states.[11]

In the nineteenth century an active legal struggle emerged between corporations and civil society regarding the right of the people, through their state governments, to revoke or amend corporate charters. Action by state legislators to amend, revoke, or simply fail to renew corporate charters was fairly common throughout the first half of the century. However, this right came under attack in 1819 when New Hampshire attempted to revoke the charter issued to Dartmouth College by King George III before U.S. independence. The Supreme Court overruled the revocation on the ground that the charter contained no reservation or revocation clause.

Outraged citizens, who saw this decision as an attack on state sovereignty, insisted that a distinction be made between a corporation and the property rights of an individual. They argued that corporations were created not by birth but by the pleasure of state legislatures to serve a public good. Corporations were therefore public, not private, bodies, and elected state legislators thereby had an absolute legal right to amend or repeal their charters at will. The public outcry led to a significant strengthening of the legal powers of the states to oversee corporate affairs.[12]

As late as 1855, in *Dodge v. Woolsey*, the Supreme Court affirmed that the Constitution confers no inalienable rights on a corporation, ruling that the people of the states have not

> released their power over the artificial bodies which originate under the legislation of their representatives . . . . Combinations of classes in society . . . united by the bond of a corporate spirit . . . unquestionably desire limitations upon the sovereignty of the people . . . But the framers of the Constitution were imbued with no desire to call into existence such combinations.[13]

SPOILS OF THE CIVIL WAR

The U.S. Civil War (1861–65) marked a turning point for corporate rights. Violent antidraft riots rocked the cities and left the political system in disarray. The huge profits pouring in from military procurement contracts allowed industrial interests to take advantage of the disorder and rampant political corruption to virtually buy legislation that gave them massive grants of money and land to expand the Western railway system. The greater its profits, the tighter the emergent industrial class was able to solidify its hold on government to obtain further benefits.[14] Seeing what was unfolding, President Abraham Lincoln observed just before his death:

> Corporations have been enthroned . . . An era of corruption in high places will follow and the money power will endeavor to prolong its reign by working on the prejudices of the people . . . until wealth is aggregated in a few hands . . . and the Republic is destroyed.[15]

The nation was divided against itself by the war; the government was weakened by the assassination of Lincoln and the subsequent election of alcoholic war hero Ulysses S. Grant as president. The nation was in disarray. Millions of Americans were rendered jobless in the subsequent depression, and a tainted presidential election in 1876 was settled through secret negotiations.[16]

Corruption and insider deal-making ran rampant. President Rutherford B. Hayes, the eventual winner of those corporate-dominated negotiations, subsequently complained, "This is a government of the people, by the people, and for the people no longer. It is a government of corporations, by corporations, and for corporations."[17] In his classic *The Robber Barons*, Matthew Josephson wrote that during the 1880s and 1890s, "The halls of legislation were transformed into a mart where the price of votes was haggled over, and laws, made to order, were bought and sold."[18]

These were the days of men such as John D. Rockefeller, J. Pierpont Morgan, Andrew Carnegie, James Mellon, Cornelius Vanderbilt, Philip Armour, and Jay Gould. Wealth begot wealth as corporations took advantage of the disarray to buy tariff, banking, railroad, labor, and public lands legislation that would further enrich them.[19] Citizen groups committed to maintaining corporate accountability continued to battle corporate abuse at state levels, and corporate charters continued to be revoked both by courts and state legislatures.[20]

Gradually, however, corporations gained sufficient control over key state legislative bodies to virtually rewrite the laws governing their own creation. Legislators in New Jersey and Delaware took the lead in watering down citizens' rights to intervene in corporate affairs. They limited the liability of corporate owners and managers and issued charters in perpetuity. Corporations soon had the right to operate in any fashion not explicitly prohibited by law.[21]

A conservative court system that was consistently responsive to the appeals and arguments of corporate lawyers steadily chipped away at the restraints a wary citizenry had carefully placed on corporate powers. Step by step, the court system set new precedents that made the protection of corporations and corporate property a centerpiece of constitutional law. These precedents eliminated the use of juries to decide fault and assess damages in cases involving corporate-caused harm and took away the right of states to oversee corporate rates of return and prices. Judges sympathetic to corporate interests ruled that workers were responsible for causing their own injuries on the job, limited the liability of corporations for damages they might cause, and declared wage and hours laws unconstitutional. They interpreted the common good to mean maximum production, no matter what was produced or who it harmed.[22] These were important concerns to an industrial sector in which, from 1888 to 1908, industrial accidents killed 700,000 American workers—roughly 100 a day.[23]

In 1886, in a stunning victory for the proponents of corporate sovereignty, the chief justice of the Supreme Court declared in *Santa Clara County v. Southern Pacific Railroad* that a private corporation is a natural person under the U.S. Constitution—although, as noted above, the Constitution makes no mention of corporations. Subsequent court decisions interpreted this to mean that corporations are entitled to the full protections of the Bill of Rights, including the right to free speech and other constitutional protections extended to individuals.[24]

Thus corporations came to claim the full rights enjoyed by individual citizens while being exempted from many of the responsibilities and liabilities of citizenship. In being guaranteed the same right to free speech as individual citizens, they achieved, in the words of Paul Hawken, "precisely what the Bill of Rights was intended to prevent: domination of public thought and discourse."[25] The subsequent claim by corporations that they have the same right as any individual to influence the government in their own interest pits the individual citizen against the vast financial and communications resources of the corporation and mocks the constitutional intent that all citizens have an equal voice in the political debates surrounding important issues.

These were days of violence and social instability brought on by the excesses of capitalism that Karl Marx described to powerful political effect. Working conditions were appalling, and wages scarcely covered subsistence. Child labor was widespread. By one estimate, 11 million of the 12.5 million families in America in 1890 subsisted on an average of $380 a year and had to take in boarders to survive.[26] Both organized and wildcat strikes were common, as was industrial sabotage. Employers used every means at their disposal to break strikes, including private security forces and federal and state military troops. Violence evoked violence, and many died in the industrial wars of this era.

These conditions gave impetus to a growing labor movement. Between 1897 and 1904, union membership rose from 447,000 to 2,073,000.[27] Unions provided fertile ground for the thriving socialist movement that was taking root in America and called for the socialization and democratic control of the means of production, natural resources, and patents. These were times of open class warfare, with zealous new recruits joining the army of the dispossessed in growing numbers, ready to fight and sacrifice for the cause. Socialists who sought to organize labor along class lines vied for primacy with more conventional unionists who preferred to organize along craft or industrial lines.[28]

These movements united ethnic groups. An emergence of black pride and culture began to unify blacks. The women's movement took hold, with women forming their own labor unions, leading strikes, and assuming active roles in populist and socialist movements.[29] In 1920, female suffrage (the right to vote) was guaranteed by a constitutional amendment.

In the end, the conditions of chaos and violence that characterized the period of explosive free-market industrial expansion were not conducive to the interests of either industrialists or labor. Competitive battles between the most powerful industrialists were cutting into profits. There was considerable fear among industrialists of the growing political power of socialist and other popular movements, which threatened to bring fundamental change that might eliminate their privileged position.

This set the stage for consolidation and compromise, which transformed social and institutional relationships among the corporate barons. Industrialists merged their individual empires to consolidate their power and limit competition among them. Formerly bitter rivals, J. P. Morgan and John D. Rockefeller joined forces in 1901 to amalgamate 112 corporate directorates, combining $22.2 billion in assets under the Northern Securities Corporation of New Jersey. This massive sum was equivalent to twice the total assessed value of all property in thirteen states in the southern United States. The result was:

> The heart of the American economy had been put under one roof, from banking and steel to railroads, urban transit, communications, the merchant marine, insurance, electric utilities, rubber, paper, sugar refining, and assorted other mainstays of the industrial infrastructure.[30]

Eventually, major industrialists came to realize that by providing better wages, benefits, and working conditions, they could undercut the appeal of socialism and at the same time win greater worker loyalty and motivation. There was a parallel interest in regularizing loosely organized, craft-based production processes to take greater advantage of the methods of industrial engineering and mass production. This meant organizing around more highly structured, rule-driven production processes that demanded worker stability and discipline.

Big business came to see advantages in working with large moderate (non-socialist) labor unions that negotiated uniform wages and standards throughout an industry and enforced worker discipline according to agreed-upon rules. These arrangements increased stability and predictability within the system without ultimately challenging the power of the industrialists or the market system.[31]

These reforms took place against a backdrop of continuing struggle. A pro-business judicial system that consistently ruled against labor interests prompted the labor movement to become increasingly political, resulting in labor's development of a legislative agenda and an alliance with the Democratic Party. Reform legislation at local, state, and national levels began to set new social standards and reshape the context of labor relations. Particularly important to labor was the Clayton Anti-Trust Act, which banned court injunctions against striking workers.[32]

Even so, during the Roaring Twenties, corporate monopolies were allowed to flourish within a loosely regulated national economy. A stock market fueled by borrowed money seemed to be a limitless engine of wealth creation. With faith in the free market and the power of big business at its peak, an ebullient President Herbert Hoover proclaimed, "We shall soon with the help of God be within sight of the day when poverty will be banished from the nation." Irving Fisher, perhaps the leading U.S. economist of the day, announced that the problem of the business cycle had been solved and that the country had settled on a high plateau of endless prosperity.[33]

It was evident that the average American family was better fed, better dressed, and blessed with more of life's amenities than any average family in history.[34] This reality masked the enormous underlying inequality of an America in which just one percent of families controlled 59 percent of the wealth.[35] In October 1929, only a few months after Fisher announced the end of business cycles, the highly leveraged financial system came crashing down. Financial fortunes evaporated almost overnight. It took World War II to provide the impetus for a new social contract between government, business, and labor based on Keynesian economic principles that set the global economic system back on the track of prosperity.

ASCENDANCE AND REVERSAL OF PLURALISM

By the time Franklin D. Roosevelt became president in 1933, business excesses of the 1920s, the depression, and the resulting plight of farmers, laborers, the elderly, blacks, women, and others had produced a wave of political and cultural radicalism throughout the United States. Roosevelt feared that without dramatic action, this radicalism might overwhelm the entire structure of government. He set about to save the system by pushing through an epic agenda of social and regulatory reforms. Congress's passage of his National Industrial Recovery Act (NIRA) was key, as it gave government a mandate to play a more active role in achieving an economic recovery that market forces alone seemed unable to manage.

On May 27, 1935, the Supreme Court voided the NIRA and ruled that states could not set minimum wage standards. This decision continued a century-old pattern of Supreme Court defense of business and corporate rights over civil or human rights. The Supreme Court's action on NIRA and the minimum wage radicalized a furious Roosevelt, motivating his commitment to a sweeping reform of American institutions. He set about to break up the business trusts, strengthen the regulation of business and financial markets, and push through legislation providing stronger guarantees for worker rights. Programs of public employment were started, and a social safety net was put into place.

Roosevelt attacked the Supreme Court with a vengeance and tried to expand its membership with new appointments of his choice. His attempt to "pack" the Court failed, but his charges had a distinct impact on the justices themselves, and the majority became more supportive of progressive initiatives. In the end, Roosevelt's long period in office allowed him to appoint justices to fill seven of the Court's nine seats, setting the Court on a liberal course that lasted until the 1970s, when Republican President Richard Nixon began to re-create the Court in its earlier pro-business image.[36]

World War II brought the government into an even more central and politically accepted role in managing economic affairs. The government placed controls on consumption, coordinated industrial output, and decided how national resources would be allocated in support of the war effort. A combination of a highly progressive tax system put in place to finance the war effort, full employment at good wages, and a strong social safety net brought about a massive shift in wealth distribution in the direction of greater equity. In 1929, there were 20,000 millionaires in the United States and two billionaires. By 1944 there were only 13,000 millionaires and no billionaires. The share of total wealth held by the top 0.5 percent of U.S. households fell from a high of 32.4 percent in 1929 to 19.3 in 1949.[37] It was a great victory for the expanding middle class and for those among the working classes who rose to join its ranks.

Pluralism flourished into the 1960s, a period of cultural rebellion in the United States. A new generation, the flower children, vocally challenged basic assumptions about lifestyles, the military-industrial complex, foreign military intervention, the exploitation of the environment, the rights and roles of women, civil rights, equity, and poverty. The U.S. corporate establishment was badly shaken by the apparent threat to its values and interests. Perhaps most threatening of all was that the young were dropping out of the consumer culture. This generation was rebelling not so much against poverty and the deprivations of exploitation as against the excesses of affluence. This rejection of materialism by a new generation of Americans in some ways presented a more fundamental threat to the system than had earlier generations of angry workers seeking a living wage and safe working conditions.

The names of consumer activist Ralph Nader and environmentalist Rachel Carson became household words. Liberal Democrats had firm control of Congress and were passing important legislation that extended the scope of governmental regulation to strengthen environmental protection and product and worker safety. The government was aggressively pursuing antitrust cases to break up monopolies and keep markets competitive.

Abroad, U.S. corporations were under attack on two fronts. Japan and Asia's newly industrializing countries (NICs)—Taiwan, South Korea, Singapore, and Hong Kong—had become enormously successful in penetrating U.S. markets. At the same time, U.S. corporations were being prevented from fully penetrating Southern economies, including those of the NICs, by aggressive government support of domestic industries, protectionism, and foreign investment restrictions. U.S. corporations felt these Southern government policies put them at an unfair disadvantage. With high taxes on corporations and investor incomes and rigorous enforcement of environmental and labor standards at home, U.S. corporations felt doubly handicapped in global competition. U.S. corporations cried foul and demanded the creation of "a level playing field."[38]

It was a critical historical moment, and the corporate establishment rallied to protect its interests, as will be examined in more detail in Part III. The election of Ronald Reagan as president in 1980 ushered in a concerted and highly successful effort to roll back the clock on the social and economic reforms that had created the broad-based prosperity that made America the envy of the world and to create a global economy that was more responsive to U.S. corporate interests.

In his insightful book *Dark Victory*, Philippine economist Walden Bello provides a Southern perspective on the Reagan agenda:

[A] highly ideological Republican regime in Washington . . . abandoned the grand strategy of "containment liberalism" abroad and the New Deal modus vivendi at home. Aside from defeating communism, Reaganism in practice was guided by three other strategic concerns. The first was the re-subordination of the South within a U.S.-dominated global economy. The second was the rolling back of the challenge to U.S. economic interests from the NICs, or "newly industrializing countries," and from Japan. The third was the dismantling of the New Deal's "social contract" between big capital, big labor and big government which both Washington and Wall Street saw as the key constraints on corporate America's ability to compete against both the NICs and Japan.[39]

The debt crisis of 1982 provided the opportunity to address the threat of prospective new NICs. The U.S.-dominated World Bank and International Monetary Fund moved to restructure the economies of debt-burdened Southern countries to open them to penetration by foreign corporations. The structural adjustment policies imposed by these institutions rolled back government involvement in economic life in support of domestic entrepreneurs, eliminated barriers to imports from the North, lifted restrictions on foreign investment, and integrated Southern economies more tightly into the Northern-dominated world economy. Trade policy was the weapon of choice for imposing similar reforms on the NICs.[40]

The full political resources of corporate America were mobilized to regain corporate control of the political agenda and the court system. High on the political agenda were domestic reforms intended to improve the global competitiveness of the United States by getting government "off the back" of business. Taxes on the rich were radically reduced and restraints on corporate mergers and acquisitions removed. Enforcement of environmental and labor standards was weakened. The government sided with aggressive U.S. corporations seeking to make themselves more globally competitive by breaking the power of unions, reducing wages and benefits, downsizing corporate workforces, and shifting manufacturing operations abroad to benefit from cheap labor and lax regulation.[41]

As these measures took hold in the United States, unemployment became a chronic problem, and labor unions lost members and political clout. Wages began to decline, as did the incomes of the poorest households. A fortunate few profited handsomely. The earnings of big investors, top managers, entertainers, star athletes, and investment brokers skyrocketed. The number of billionaires in the United States increased from one in 1978 to 120 in 1994.[42] Lending abuses by a deregulated savings and loan industry left U.S. taxpayers with a bill for $500 billion to clean up the mess. These were hard times for ordinary citizens. Greed had a field day.

As the Reagan initiatives took hold abroad, backed by similar conservative revivals in other Western nations, the same patterns emerged in most of the other Western countries as well as the indebted countries of the South. Inequality increased within and between countries. Unemployment rose to alarming levels, and many social indicators that had shown steady improvement over the previous three decades stagnated or in some instances began to decline. Many of the indebted Southern countries fell even further into international debt. The number of billionaires in the world increased from 145 in 1987 to 358 in 1994.[43]

The Reagan Administration had pledged to arrest U.S. decline. However, it made a number of strategic policy blunders that strengthened U.S. military might and economic growth in the short term, but seriously weakened the U.S. position in the global economy over the longer term. First, massive deficit spending on the military contributed to making the United States the world's leading international debtor country. The main holder of that debt was Japan, the major competitor of the United States. Second, by denying any government role in economic planning and priority setting, the Reagan administration left the economic future of the United States entirely in the hands of corporations that were being pressed by the capital markets to focus only on short-term profits. Third, by allowing corporations to pursue their anti-labor strategy, the United States squandered its key resource in the competitive global marketplace—its human capital.[44] Overall, however, the strategy has worked brilliantly for the largest corporations, their top managers, and their wealthiest shareholders—at the expense of the planet and most of the world's people.

This was not the result of a formal conspiracy. Major shifts in national policy do not come about as a consequence of corporate and political elites gathering in a conference room to define a grand strategy to consolidate their personal power. They are far too independent minded and represent too broad a range of conflicting interests. As Bello observes:

> What usually occurs is a much more complex social process in which *ideology* mediates between interests and policy. An ideology is a belief-system—a set of theories, beliefs and myths with some internal coherence—that seeks to universalize the interests of one social sector to the whole community. In market ideology, for instance, freeing market forces from state restraints is said to work to the good not only of business, but also to that of the whole community.
>
> Transmitted through social institutions such as universities, corporations, churches or parties, an ideology is internalized by large numbers of people, but especially by members of the social groups whose interests it principally expresses. An ideology thus informs the actions of many individuals and groups, but it becomes a significant force only when certain conditions coincide . . . Market ideology became a dominant force only when a political elite which espoused it

ascended to state power on the back of an increasingly conservative middle-class social base, at the same time that the corporate establishment was deserting the liberal Keynesian consensus in its favor, because of the changed circumstances of international economic competition.[45]

A QUESTION OF GOVERNANCE

Interwoven into the political discourse about free markets and free trade is a persistent message: the advance of free markets is the advance of democracy. Advocates of the free market would have us believe that an unregulated market is a more efficient and responsive mechanism for political expression than the ballot, because business is more efficient and more responsive to people's preferences than are uncaring politicians and inefficient bureaucrats. The logic is simple: In the marketplace, people express their priorities directly and precisely by how they spend their consumer dollars. A vote for one among the available political candidates is by comparison a blunt instrument for expressing choice. Therefore the market is the most effective and democratic way to define the public interest.

Given the growing distrust of government, it is a compelling message, and it embodies an important truth: markets and politics are both about governance, power, and the allocation of society's resources. It is also a misleading message that masks an important political reality. In a political democracy, each person gets one vote. In the market, one dollar is one vote, and you get as many votes as you have dollars. No dollar, no vote. Markets are inherently biased in favor of people of wealth.

Equally important, markets have a strong bias in favor of very large corporations, which command more massive financial resources than even the wealthiest individuals. As markets become freer and more global, the power to govern increasingly passes from national governments to global corporations, and the interests of those corporations diverge ever farther from the broader human interest—assertions documented in detail in Parts III and IV.

People, even the greediest and most ruthless, are living beings with needs and values beyond money. We need air to breathe, water to drink, and food to eat. Most of us have families. Nearly all of us find inspiration in things of beauty, such as a natural landscape or a newborn baby. Our bodies are flesh, and real blood runs through our veins.

Behind its carefully crafted public relations image and the many fine, ethical people it may employ, the body of a corporation is its corporate charter, a legal document, and money is its blood. At its core it is an alien entity with one goal: to reproduce money to nourish and replicate itself. Individuals are dispensable. The corporation owes only one true allegiance: to the financial markets, which are more totally creatures of money than even the corporation itself.

The problem is deeply embedded in the structure and rules by which corporations are compelled to operate. The marvel of the corporation as a social innovation is that it can bring together hundreds of thousands of people within a single structure and compel them to act in accordance with a corporate purpose that is not necessarily their own. Those who revolt or fail to comply are expelled and replaced by others who are more compliant.[46]

As Washington journalist William Greider writes in *Who Will Tell the People?*:

> [The corporations'] . . . tremendous financial resources, the diversity of their interests, the squads of talented professionals—all these assets and some others are now relentlessly focused on the politics of governing. This new institutional reality is the centerpiece in the breakdown of contemporary democracy. Corporations exist to pursue their own profit maximization, not the collective aspirations of the society. They are commanded by a hierarchy of managers, not the collective aspirations of the society.[47]

Human societies have long faced the question whether the power to rule will reside only with the rich or be shared by all. We now face a different and even more ominous question, which—to the extent that its implications are fully understood—should unite rich and poor alike in a common cause. Will the power to rule reside with people, no matter their financial circumstance, or will it reside with the artificial persona of the corporation?

During this critical historical moment, in which our species faces the fundamental challenge of rediscovering the purpose and unity of life, we must decide whether the power to govern will be in the hands of living people or will reside with corporate entities driven by a different agenda. To regain control of our future and bring human societies into balance with the planet, we must reclaim the power we have yielded to these artificial entities. One important step will be to free ourselves from the ideological illusions and policies that free corporations from human accountability.

5

ASSAULT OF THE CORPORATE LIBERTARIANS

If there were an Economist's Creed, it would surely contain the affirmation, "I believe in the Principle of Comparative Advantage." And "I believe in free trade."

—*Paul Krugman, MIT economist[1]*

The difference between a system dominated by General Motors and Exxon and one based upon the individual landholding farmer and small business person of an earlier day in American history may very well be greater—in the real life experience of the average person—than the difference between a system based upon large private bureaucracies in the United States and public bureaucracies in socialist nations.

—*Gar Alperovitz[2]*

IN THE QUEST FOR ECONOMIC GROWTH, free-market ideology has been embraced around the world with a near-religious fervor. Money is its sole measure of value, and its practice advances policies that are deepening social and environmental disintegration everywhere. The economics profession serves as its priesthood. It champions values that demean the human spirit. It assumes an imaginary world divorced from reality. And it restructures our institutions of governance in ways that make our most urgent problems more difficult to resolve. Yet to question its doctrine has become heresy, invoking risk of professional censure and damage to one's career in most institutions of business, government, and academia. In the words of Australian sociologist Michael Pusey, it has reduced economics to "an ideological shield against intelligent introspection and civic responsibility,"[3] and infused the study of economics in most universities with a strong element of ideological indoctrination.

THE SANCTIFICATION OF GREED

The beliefs espoused by free-market ideologues are familiar to anyone conversant with the language of contemporary economic discourse:

- Sustained economic growth, as measured by gross national product, is the path to human progress.
- Free markets, unrestrained by governments, generally result in the most efficient and socially optimal allocation of resources.
- Economic globalization, achieved by removing barriers to the free flow of goods and money anywhere in the world, spurs competition, increases economic efficiency, creates jobs, lowers consumer prices, increases consumer choice, increases economic growth, and is generally beneficial to almost everyone.
- Privatization, which moves functions and assets from governments to the private sector, improves efficiency, lowers prices, and increases responsiveness to consumer preferences.
- The primary responsibility of government is to provide the infrastructure necessary to advance commerce, maintain public order, protect property rights, and enforce contracts.

These beliefs are based on a number of explicit, underlying assumptions embedded in the theories of neoclassical economics:

- Humans are motivated by self-interest, which is expressed primarily through the quest for financial gain.
- The action that yields the greatest financial return to the individual or firm also yields the most benefit to society.
- Competitive behavior is more rational for the individual than cooperative behavior and ultimately more beneficial for society.
- Human progress and improvements in well-being are best measured by increases in the aggregate market value of economic output.

To put it in harsher language, these ideological doctrines assume that:

- People are by nature motivated only by greed.
- The drive to acquire is the highest expression of what it means to be human.
- The relentless pursuit of greed and acquisition leads to socially optimal outcomes.
- The interests of human societies are best served by encouraging, honoring, and rewarding the above values.

A number of valid ideas and insights about markets have become twisted into an extremist ideology that raises the baser aspects of human nature to a self-justifying ideal. Although this ideology denigrates the most basic human values and ideals, it has become so deeply embedded within our values, institutions, and popular culture that we accept it almost without question. This pervasive ideology plays a critical role in shaping nearly every aspect of public policy. It plays to the declining economic fortunes of the majority and to well-founded public distrust of big government to build a populist political constituency for agendas with decidedly nonpopulist consequences.

Reminiscent of twentieth-century Marxist ideologues, advocates of this extremist ideology seek to cut off debate by proclaiming the inevitability of the historical forces advancing their cause. They tell us that a globalized free market that leaves resource allocation decisions in the hands of giant corporations is inevitable, and we had best concentrate on learning how to adapt to the new rules of the game. They warn that those who hold back and fail to get on board will be swept aside; the rewards will go only to those who acquiesce.

The extremist quality of their position is revealed in the stark choices they pose between a "free" market unencumbered by any form of governmental restraint or a Soviet-style, centrally planned, state-controlled economy in which government makes all economic decisions. They countenance no middle ground, such as a market that functions within a framework of democratically determined rules.

Similarly, they divide the world into two groups: "free" traders who would remove all economic borders to allow goods and money to flow unimpeded by public oversight; and protectionists who would build impenetrable walls around countries, cutting off all trade and exchange with others. Again, in defiance of history and logic they recognize no middle ground, such as the possibility that governments might establish appropriate rules to assure that cross border exchanges are fair and balanced to the mutual benefit of people on both sides.

In its various guises, this ideology is known by different names—neoclassical, neoliberal, or libertarian economics; neoliberalism, market capitalism, or market liberalism. In Australia and New Zealand, Michael Pusey's book *Economic Rationalism in Canberra* has popularized the term economic rationalism and injected it into the public debate.[4] Latin Americans commonly use the term neoliberalism. However, in most countries, including the United States, it goes without a generally recognized name. Unnamed, it goes undebated, and its underlying assumptions remain unexamined.

The more descriptive label for those of this ideological persuasion, however, is *corporate libertarian*, because whatever they call themselves, the "free" market, "free" trade policies they advocate do *not* free trade, markets, or people. Rather they free global corporations to plan and organize the world's economic affairs to the benefit of their bottom line, without regard to public consequences.

THE CORPORATE LIBERTARIAN ALLIANCE

Three major constituencies have joined in a powerful political alliance to advance the ideological agenda of corporate libertarianism with a dogmatic fervor normally associated with religious crusades.

Neoclassical Economists Most mainstream economists align with the neoclassical school of economic rationalism. Rationalism is defined as "the doctrine that knowledge comes wholly from pure reason, without aid from the senses."[5] This is the underlying doctrine of contemporary mainstream economics, which builds its economic models deductively from first principles, without reference to the real world. This commitment to rationalism has given economics its standing as the only truly objective, value-free social science—and led it to conclusions that often defy both common sense and observable reality. Most of the profession embraces two first principles as fundamental articles of faith. One is that individuals are motivated solely by self-interest. The other is that individual choice based on the unrestrained pursuit of self-interest leads to socially optimal outcomes. It is immediately evident to most anyone without advanced training in economics that both principles are demonstrably false.

Mainstream economists also treat corporations the same as individual people and presume that maximizing the freedom of corporations is the same as maximizing the freedom of real people—ignoring the reality that the corporate charter is a vehicle for creating massive concentrations of authoritarian power, and that more freedom for corporations inevitably means less freedom for most people. Through this distorting bit of intellectual sleight of hand, neoclassical economists provide corporate libertarianism with a patina of *intellectual* legitimacy. In return, corporate interests provide neoclassical economists with generous funding and a powerful political constituency.

Property Rights Advocates   Ardent property rights advocates, sometimes called "market liberals," commonly present themselves as libertarians dedicated to the defense of individual rights and freedom. While true libertarians seek to defend individual freedom against intrusion from coercive institutions of any kind, market liberals are mostly concerned with protecting the rights of property from public accountability. This highly elitist ideology in effect apportions rights to people in proportion to the property they own. According to Roger Pilon of the Cato Institute, a libertarian think tank in Washington, D.C., market liberals believe that "rights and property are inextricably connected . . . Broadly understood . . . property is the foundation of all our natural rights. Exercising those rights, consistent with the rights of others, we may pursue happiness in any way we wish." In the exercise of these rights individuals form voluntary associations with others through the mechanism of the contract.[6] In the eyes of a market liberal, the only responsibility attached to the rights of property are to respect the same rights of others, obey the law, and honor contractual agreements. Those without property have no rights that the market liberal is bound to respect.

Like the neoclassical economists, market liberals make little distinction between individuals and corporations. Corporations are presumed to have the same right as an individual to use their property in any way that suits their self-interest. Market liberals give corporate libertarianism its cast of *moral* legitimacy. In return, corporate interests give leading proponents of market liberalism, such as the Cato Institute, the same financial support and political leverage they give to the neoclassical economists.

Corporations and Members of the Corporate Class   Corporations and members of the corporate class—such as corporate managers, lawyers, consultants, public-relations specialists, financial brokers, and wealthy investors—comprise the third pillar of the corporate libertarian alliance. Some are drawn to corporate libertarianism purely by financial self-interest or because they are paid to do so, others by moral conviction. Although few members of the corporate class have a serious interest in the fine points of academic theories or moral philosophy, they find a natural common cause with those who provide an intellectual and ethical case for freeing corporations from the restraining hand of government and absolving them of moral responsibility for the social and environmental consequences of their actions. Furthermore, they have the financial resources at their disposal to handsomely reward those who legitimate their power.

This combination of economic theory, moral philosophy, and elite political interest makes for a powerful alliance. Yet in many ways it has served even its own members poorly, as its corrupting influence has not been limited to the broader society. It has led neoliberal economists to seriously debase the integrity and social utility of economics by reducing it to a system of ideological indoctrination that violates its own theoretical foundations and is deeply at odds with reality. It has similarly engaged libertarians in a cause that violates their own commitment to individual freedom, as corporations infringe on the property rights of real people and use their growing power to suppress the individual freedoms of all but society's wealthiest members. The enormous political success of the alliance in shielding corporations from public accountability has created a monster that even the members of the corporate class no longer control and is creating a world that they would scarcely wish to bequeath to their children.

The contemporary corporation increasingly exists as an entity apart— even from the people who work for it. Every member of the corporate class, no matter how powerful his or her position within the corporation, has become expendable, as many top executives have learned. As corporations gain in autonomous institutional power and become more detached from people and place, the human interest and the corporate interest increasingly diverge. It is like being invaded by alien beings intent on colonizing our planet, reducing us to serfs, and then eliminating those of us they don't need.

THE BETRAYAL OF ADAM SMITH AND DAVID RICARDO

It is ironic that corporate libertarians regularly pay homage to Adam Smith as their intellectual patron saint, since it is obvious to even the most casual reader of his epic work *The Wealth of Nations* that Smith would have vigorously opposed most of their claims and policy positions. For example, corporate libertarians fervently oppose any restraint on corporate size or power. Smith, on the other hand, opposed any form of economic concentration on the ground that it distorts the market's natural ability to establish a price that provides a fair return on land, labor, and capital; to produce a satisfactory outcome for both buyers and sellers; and to optimally allocate society's resources.

Through trade agreements, corporate libertarians press governments to provide absolute protection for the intellectual property rights of corporations. Smith was strongly opposed to trade secrets as contrary to market principles[7] and would have vigorously opposed governments enforcing a person or corporation's claim to the right to monopolize a lifesaving drug or device and to charge whatever the market would bear.

Corporate libertarians maintain that the market turns unrestrained greed into socially optimal outcomes. Smith would be outraged by those who attribute this idea to him. He was talking about small farmers and artisans trying to get the best price for their products to provide for themselves and their families. That is self-interest, not greed. Greed is a high-paid corporate executive firing 10,000 employees and then rewarding himself with a multimillion-dollar bonus for having saved the company so much money. Greed is what the economic system being constructed by the corporate libertarians encourages and rewards.

Smith strongly disliked both governments and corporations. He viewed government primarily as an instrument for extracting taxes to subsidize elites and intervening in the market to protect corporate monopolies. In his words, "Civil government, so far as it is instituted for the security of property, is in reality instituted for the defense of the rich against the poor, or of those who have some property against those who have none at all."[8] Smith never suggested that government should not intervene to set and enforce minimum social, health, worker safety, and environmental standards in the common interest or to protect the poor and nature from the rich. Given that most governments of his day were monarchies, the possibility probably never occurred to him.

The theory of market economics, in contrast to free-market ideology, specifies a number of basic conditions needed for a market to set prices efficiently in the public interest. The greater the deviation from these conditions, the less socially efficient the market system becomes. Most basic is the condition that markets must be competitive. I recall the professor in my elementary economics course using the example of small wheat farmers selling to small grain millers to illustrate the idea of perfect market competition. Today, four companies—Conagra, ADM Milling, Cargill, and Pillsbury—mill nearly

60 percent of all flour produced in the United States, and two of them—Conagra and Cargill—control 50 percent of grain exports.[9]

In the real world of unregulated markets, successful players get larger and, in many instances, use the resulting economic power to drive or buy out weaker players to gain control of even larger shares of the market. In other instances, "competitors" collude through cartels or strategic alliances to increase profits by setting market prices above the level of optimal efficiency. The larger and more collusive individual market players become, the more difficult it is for newcomers and small independent firms to survive, the more monopolisitic and less competitive the market becomes, and the more political power the biggest firms can wield to demand concessions from governments that allow them to externalize even more of their costs to the community.

Given this reality, one might expect the neoliberal economists who claim Smith's tradition as their own to be outspoken in arguing for the need to re-strict mergers and acquisitions and break up monopolistic firms to restore market competition. More often, they argue exactly the opposite position—that to "compete" in today's global markets, firms must merge into larger com-binations. In other words, they use a theory that assumes small firms to advo-cate policies that favor large firms.

Market theory also specifies that for a market to allocate efficiently, the full costs of each product must be born by the producer and be included in the selling price. Economists call it cost internalization. Externalizing some part of a product's cost to others not a party to the transaction is a form of subsidy that encourages excessive production and use of the product at the expense of others. When, for example, a forest products corporation is al-lowed to clear-cut government lands at giveaway prices, it lowers the cost of timber products, thus encouraging their wasteful use and discouraging their recycling. While profitable for the company and a bargain for consumers, the public is forced, without its consent, to bear a host of costs relating to water shed destruction, loss of natural habitat and recreational areas, global warm-ing, and diminished future timber production.

The consequences are similar when a chemical corporation dumps wastes without adequate treatment, thus passing the resulting costs of air, water, and soil pollution to the community in the form of health costs, genetic deformi-ties, discomfort, lost working days, a need to buy bottled water, and the cost of cleaning up contamination. If the users of the resulting chemical products were required to pay the full cost of their production and use, there would be a lot less chemical contamination in our environment, our food and water would be cleaner, there would be fewer cancers and genetic deformities, and we would have more frogs and songbirds. If the full cost of producing and driving cars were passed on to the consumer we would all benefit from a dramatic reduction in urban sprawl, traffic congestion, the paving over of productive lands, pollution, global warming, and depletion of finite petroleum reserves.

There is good reason why cost internalization is one of the most basic principles of market theory. Yet in the name of the market, corporate libertarians actively advocate eliminating government regulation and point to the private cost savings for consumers while ignoring the social and environmental consequences for the broader society. Indeed, in the name of being internationally competitive, corporate libertarians urge nations and communities to increase market distorting subsidies—including resource giveaways, low wage labor, lax environmental regulation, and tax breaks—to attract the jobs of footloose corporations. An unregulated market invariably encourages the externalization of costs because the resulting public costs become private gains. In the end it seems that corporate libertarians are more interested in increasing corporate profits than in defending market principles.

The larger the corporation and the "freer" the market, the greater the corporation's ability to force others to bear its costs and thereby subsidize its profits. Some call this theft. Economists call it "economies of scale."

Neva Goodwin, ecological economist, head of the Global Development and Environment Institute at Tufts University, and an advocate of cost internalization, puts it bluntly. "Power is largely what externalities are about. What's the point of having power, if you can't use it to externalize your costs—to make them fall on someone else?"[10]

Corporate libertarians tirelessly inform us of the benefits of trade based on the theories of Adam Smith and David Ricardo. What they don't mention is that the benefits the trade theories predict assume the local or national ownership of capital by persons directly engaged in its management. Indeed, these same conditions are fundamental to Adam Smith's famous assertion in *The Wealth of Nations* that the invisible hand of the market translates the pursuit of self-interest into a public benefit. Note that the following is the only mention of the famous invisible hand in the entire 1,000 pages of *The Wealth of Nations*.

> By preferring the support of domestic to that of foreign industry, he [the entrepreneur] intends only his own security, and by directing that industry in such a manner as its produce may be of the greatest value, he intends only his own gain, and his is in this, as in many other

cases, led by an invisible hand to promote an end which was no part
of his intention. [11]

Smith assumed a natural preference on the part of the entrepreneur to invest
at home where he could keep a close eye on his holdings. Of course, this was
long before jet travel, telephones, fax machines, and the Internet. Because local investment provides local employment and produces local goods for local
consumption using local resources, the entrepreneur's natural inclination contributes to the vitality of the local economy. And because the owner and the
enterprise are both local they are more readily held to local standards. Even on
pure business logic, Smith firmly opposed the absentee ownership of companies.

> The directors of such companies, however, being the managers rather
> of other people's money than of their own, it cannot well be expected,
> that they should watch over it with the same anxious vigilance with
> which the partners in a private copartnery frequently watch over their
> own. . . . Negligence and profusion, therefore, must always prevail,
> more or less in the management of the affairs of such a company.[12]

Smith believed the efficient market is composed of small, owner-managed
enterprises located in the communities where the owners reside. Such owners
normally share in the community's values and have a personal stake in the
future of both the community and the enterprise. In the global corporate
economy, footloose money moves across national borders at the speed of light,
society's assets are entrusted to massive corporations lacking any local or national allegiance, and management is removed from real owners by layers of
investment institutions and holding companies.

We find similar contradictions when we look at David Ricardo's theory of
comparative advantage, which corporate libertarians regularly invoke as proof
of their argument that unrestrained free trade advances the public good. This
theory, originally articulated by Ricardo in 1817, provides an elegant demonstration that, *under certain conditions*, trade between two countries works to
the benefit of the people of both. Three conditions, among others, are fundamental to this outcome: capital must not be allowed to cross national borders
from a high-wage to a low-wage country, trade between the participating countries must be balanced, and each country must have full employment.

When these conditions are met, investment in each country will tend to
flow toward those activities in which each has a comparative advantage based

on differences in their natural endowments. To use Ricardo's example, because of difference in climate it may be relatively more efficient to produce wine in Portugal and woolen goods in England. In the event of open trade between the two, the hapless vintner in England who finds himself unable to compete with imported Portugese wines will covert his wine fields to pasture lands for sheep and his winery to a woolens mill employing the same people.

In Ricardo's time, most trade involved the exchange of finished national goods produced by national enterprises. Today, products are commonly assembled using components and services produced in many different countries. Global corporations, rather than national economies, are likely to be the coordinating units, with the result that roughly a third of the $3.3 trillion in goods and services traded internationally in 1990 consisted of transactions within a single firm.[13] A growing portion of international trade is intraindustry, meaning that countries are exchanging the same product—as when the United States and Japan sell automobiles to each other—making it difficult to argue that natural comparative advantage is involved and rendering trade theory irrelevant in assessing the consequent costs and benefits.

In the pursuit of free trade, corporate libertarians actively promote the removal of restrictions on the transfer of factories across borders and the free international movement of money, belittle trade balances as irrelevant, and look to unemployment as a beneficial brake on inflation—in each instance disregarding essential conditions of the trade theory they invoke to support their cause. In truth, the "trade agreements" advocated by corporate libertarians are not about trade; they are about economic integration. Although the theory of comparative advantage applies to balanced trade between otherwise independent national economies, a very different theory—the theory of downward leveling—applies when national economies are integrated.

When capital is confined within the national borders of trading partners, it must flow to those industries in which its home country has a comparative advantage. When the economies are merged, capital flows to whatever locality offers the maximum opportunity to externalize costs through cash subsidies, tax breaks, substandard pay and working conditions, and lax environmental standards. Income is thus shifted from workers to investors, and costs are shifted from investors to the community.[14] It seems a common practice for corporate libertarians to justify their actions based on theories that apply only in the world that by their actions they seek to dismantle.

Economist Neva Goodwin suggests that neoclassical economists have invited this distortion and misuse of economic theory by drawing narrow boundaries around their field that exclude most political and institutional reality.

She characterizes the neoclassical school of economics as the political economy of Adam Smith minus the political and institutional analysis of Karl Marx:

> The classical political economy of Adam Smith was a much broader, more humane subject than the economics that is taught in universities today. . . . For at least a century it has been virtually taboo to talk about economic power in the capitalist context; that was a communist (Marxist) idea. The concept of class was similarly banned from discussion. [15]

Adam Smith was as acutely aware of issues of power and class as he was of the dynamics of competitive markets. However, the neoclassical economists and the neo-Marxist economists bifurcated his holistic perspective on the political economy, one taking those portions of the analysis that favored the owners of property, and the other taking those that favored the sellers of labor. Thus, the neoclassical economists left out Smith's considerations of the destructive role of power and class, and the neo-Marxists left out the beneficial functions of the market. Both advanced extremist social experiments on a massive scale that embodied a partial vision of society, with disastrous consequences.

ECONOMIC DEMAGOGUERY

On the evening of December 1, 1994, a lame-duck session of the U.S. Senate approved by a margin of seventy-six to twenty-four the Uruguay round agreement of the General Agreement on Tariffs and Trade (GATT) that created the World Trade Organization. Responding to their corporate financial sponsors, a broad coalition of Republican and Democratic senators supported the measure in defiance of widespread and growing opposition among those Americans familiar with the agreement and its threat to jobs, the environment, and democracy. The strong and unequivocal backing of the agreement by President Bill Clinton and Vice President Al Gore deepened the chasm between them and their core labor and environmental constituencies.

C-SPAN, a cable television news channel, held a telephone call-in session following the vote. Doug Harbrecht, the trade editor of *Business Week*, was the guest resource person. As caller after caller phoned in to express outrage at the politicians who voted for the agreement in support of big-money interests and total disregard of the popular will, Harbrecht commented that the pro-GATT position represented impeccable economics but bad politics. As did many of his colleagues, Harbrecht mistook free-market ideology for good economics. The global economic integration advanced through GATT and the World Trade Organization is at odds with the most basic principles of market economics and puts in place an economic system designed to self-destruct at an enormous cost to human societies. This can scarcely be considered the practice of "impeccable" economics.

How can neoclassical economists advocate economic integration if it advances conditions that are at odds with those required for efficient market function? An important part of the answer is found in their legendary ability to assume away reality. This ability has been immortalized in an apocryphal story about three scientists—a physicist, a chemist, and an economist—marooned on a desert island. They've salvaged a can of beans from the wreck of their ship, but unfortunately, they have no evident means of opening it. They agree that with so much scientific brainpower among them, they can surely complete this simple task. The physicist points to a nearby palm tree and suggests that she will climb the tree and drop the can on a rock below at the proper angle to pop it open. The chemist points out that the beans will be spilled on the ground and suggests that they might use salt water to create a chemical reaction that will rust away the top. Then the economist says, "You are both making this simple task too complicated. First, we will assume a can opener." Like this economist, when the real world diverges from the conditions necessary to support their preferred policy options, economic rationalists are prone to solve the conflict by assuming the conditions that support their recommendations.

Take the case of the obvious reality that the human economy is embedded in and dependent on the natural environment. As far back as 1798, Thomas Robert Malthus suggested that environmental limits might make population growth a problem for the future of humanity. Neoclassical economists have dealt with this inconvenience by adopting an analytical model that assumes economies consist of isolated, wholly self-contained, circular flows of exchange values (labor, capital, and goods) between firms and households without reference to the environment. In other words, they avoid the problem of environmental limits by creating a model that assumes the environment doesn't exist. They then conclude from this model that the economy does not depend on the environment and dismiss those who challenge the possibility of infinite growth on a finite planet with the stinging epithet "Neo-Malthusianism!"

A belief in the possibility of unlimited growth is the very foundation of the ideological doctrine of corporate libertarianism, because to accept the reality of physical limits is to accept the need to limit greed and acquisition in favor of economic justice and sufficiency. This would require a fundamental reorientation of economic priorities to focus on equity rather than growth.

The propensity of the neoclassical economists to choose their assumptions to fit their conclusions is revealed with particular clarity in the computer simulations they use to demonstrate the economic benefits of lowering trade barriers. During the public debates on the North American Free Trade Agreement (NAFTA), proponents of the agreement aggressively brandished the results of computer simulations, known as general equilibrium models, as proof that NAFTA would create large numbers of new jobs for each of the participating NAFTA countries: Canada, Mexico, and the United States.[16]

Economist James Stanford examined the models used to generate these projections and found that each one incorporated assumptions from classical trade theory sharply at odds with economic reality. To illustrate the contradictions, he related the following hypothetical discussion between an auto worker in the midwestern United States and one of the pro-NAFTA economic modelers. The worker related to the modeler her fears that:

> If NAFTA is approved, Ford will surely move its Taurus plant to Mexico where it can hire workers for a tenth of my pay with no independent union and export cars back to the United States. With the labor market already depressed in this part of the country I don't see any prospect of finding a job at comparable pay.

The economic modeler, looking surprised, assures her that he is an expert on the subject of trade and that her fears are entirely unfounded:

> Don't worry. I've constructed a computer simulation that shows you will actually benefit from the trade agreement because of the new jobs NAFTA will create in America. Here's how it works. In my model I assume *capital is immobile*. Therefore, Ford cannot move its plant to Mexico. Nor would it want to, because I assume *unit labor* costs are the same in both countries and in my model *Americans have a clear preference for U.S.-made products, even if they are more expensive*.
>
> My model also assumes *full employment* and specifies that *anything imported to the U.S. from Mexico must be balanced by American exports*, so new export industries will necessarily spring up here to replace any industries that might be displaced by Mexican imports. Since you earn above-average wages at Ford, you obviously possess valuable skills. With full employment you will certainly find another

job very shortly in one of these new export industries, probably with higher pay than your current job. So NAFTA will be great for you.

A worker confronted with such an explanation might conclude that the economic modeler had just arrived from an alien planet with little knowledge of affairs on Earth. Although the discussion is hypothetical, the assumptions articulated by the economist (italicized for ease of identification) are not. Each of them is built into one or more of the economic models that trade experts used to prove that the United States would realize employment gains from NAFTA. In comparing the models and their results, Stanford found a direct relationship between unrealistic assumptions and favorable job projections— the less realistic the assumptions, the more optimistic the projections. The more realistic models predicted either negative or negligible economic consequences for at least one of the partners.[17]

Those who use these models to press their case make no mention of the underlying assumptions. The misrepresentations are so flagrant and persistent that one sometimes suspects an intent to misinform the public. For example, during the NAFTA debates, the unabashedly pro-free trade *New York Times* took the unusual step of presenting a trade economics primer on its front page. The primer provided a textbook explanation of the theory of comparative advantage to bolster its editorial position in support of the NAFTA legislation. No mention was made, however, of the underlying assumptions of the theory, let alone of how those assumptions diverge from reality. Letters submitted by me and others to the editor of the *New York Times* pointing out the omission were not published.

Those who engage in such distortion lend legitimacy to flawed economic policies that advantage the greediest among us to the disadvantage of the rest.

THE MORAL JUSTIFICATION OF INJUSTICE

The moral philosophers of market liberalism perpetrate similar distortions by neglecting the distinction between the rights of property and the rights of people. Indeed, they equate the freedom and rights of individuals with market freedom and property rights. The freedom of the market is the freedom of those with money. When rights are a function of property rather than personhood, only those with property have rights.

It is a basic premise of democracy that each individual has equal rights before the law and an equal voice in political affairs—one person, one vote.

We can rightfully look to the market as a democratic arbiter of rights and preferences only to the extent that money and property are equitably distributed. Although a market can allocate efficiently with less than complete equality, when 358 billionaires enjoy a combined net worth of $760 billion—equal to the net worth of the poorest 2.5 billion of the world's people—the market is neither just nor efficient and it loses all legitimacy as a democratic institution.[18]

Publications such as *Fortune, Business Week, Forbes, The Wall Street Journal,* and *The Economist*—all ardent advocates of corporate libertarianism—rarely if ever praise an economy for its progress toward eliminating poverty or achieving greater equity. Rather, they regularly evaluate the performance of economies by the number of millionaires and billionaires they produce, the competence of managers by the cool dispassion with which they fire thousands of employees, the success of individuals by how many millions of dollars they acquire in a year, and the success of companies by the global reach of their power and their ability to dominate global markets.

Take for example, the cover story of the July 5, 1993, issue of *Forbes,* trumpeting the extraordinary accomplishments of the free market under the banner "Meet the World's Newest Billionaires":

> As disillusion with socialism and other forms of statist economics spreads, private, personal initiative is being released to seek its destiny. Wealth, naturally, follows. The two big openings for free enterprise in this decade have come in Latin America and the Far East. Not surprisingly, the biggest clusters of new billionaires on our list have risen from the ferment of these two regions. Eleven new Mexican billionaires in two years, seven more ethnic Chinese.[19]

Taking a slightly more populist view, *Business Week* presented a special report titled "A Millionaire a Minute" in its November 29, 1993, issue. It included this breathless account of what the free market has accomplished in Asia:

> Wealth. To most Asians just one generation ago, it meant moving to the U.S.—or selling natural resources to Japan. But now, East Asia is generating its own wealth on a speed and scale that probably is without historical precedent. The number of non-Japanese Asian multimillionaires is expected to double to 800,000 by 1996. . . . East Asia will surpass Japan in purchasing power within a decade. And with savings increasing $550 billion annually it is becoming the world's

biggest source of liquid capital. "In Asia," says Olarn Chaipravat, chief
executive of Siam Commercial Bank, "money is everywhere." . . . There
are new markets for everything from Mercedes Benz cars to Motorola
mobile phones to Fidelity mutual funds. . . . To find the nearest prece-
dent, you need to rewind U.S. history 100 years to the days before
strong unions, securities watchdogs and antitrust laws.[20]

Such stories do not simply glorify the pursuit of greed, they perversely elevate
it to the level of a religious mission. Never mind that although a few Asians
have made vast fortunes and a tiny minority of Asians have risen to the
overconsumer class, the suffering of the 675 million Asians who live in absolute poverty continues unabated. In a special 1994 issue, "21st Century Capitalism," *Business Week* confirmed that market economics is a class issue and
that the corporate libertarians are clear as to whose class interests they are
advancing:

> The death throes of communism clearly gave birth to the new era,
> leaving most nations with only one choice—to join . . . the market
> economy. . . . Almost 150 years following the publication of the Com-
> munist Manifesto, and more than half a century after the rise of to-
> talitarianism, the bourgeoisie has won.[21]

It seems the corporate libertarians are a good deal more concerned with making money for the rich than with meeting human needs. Even the oft-cited
claim of neoclassical economics to "value-free objectivity" supports this bias
as it rests on the questionable premise that a decision is objective and value
free if it is based solely on financial return. Never mind that such calculations
almost always work to the advantage of those who have the money to which
the returns are being calculated at the expense of those without money. Seldom has this been more starkly revealed than in a widely publicized staff memo
written by Lawrence Summers [U.S. Secretary of the Treasury in the final years
of the Clinton administration] in his capacity as chief economist of the World
Bank. Summers argued that it is economically most efficient for the rich countries to dispose of their toxic wastes in poor countries, because poor people
have both shorter life spans and less earning potential than wealthy people.[22]
In a subsequent commentary on the Summers memo, *The Economist* argued
that it is a moral duty of the rich countries to export their pollution to poor
countries because this provides poor people with economic opportunities of
which they would otherwise be deprived.[23]

In a further twist of moral logic, corporate libertarians also argue that it is the moral duty of the rich to help the poor by consuming more. In international affairs this translates into an appeal for rich countries to increase their consumption of exports from poor countries—a convenient rationalization for colonizing more of the world's resources to support more consumption by those least in need.[24] The possibility that the productive resources of low income countries might better be used by their own people to produce the things they need to improve their own lives is never considered.

If corporate libertarians had a serious allegiance to market principles and human rights, they would be calling for policies aimed at achieving the conditions under which markets function in a democratic fashion in the public interest. They would be calling for an end to corporate welfare, the breakup of corporate monopolies, the equitable distribution of property ownership, the internalization of social and environmental costs, local ownership, a living wage for working people, rooted capital, and a progressive tax system. Corporate libertarianism is not about creating the conditions that market theory argues will optimize the public interest, because its real concern is with private, not public, interests.

Millions of thoughtful, intelligent people who are properly suspicious of big government, believe in honest and hard work, have deep religious values, and are committed to family and community are being deceived by the false information and distorted intellectual and moral logic repeated constantly in the corporate media. They are being won over to a political agenda that runs counter to both their values and their interests. Those who work within our major corporate, academic, political, governmental, and other institutions find the culture and reward systems so strongly aligned with the corporate libertarian ideology that they dare not speak out in opposition for fear of jeopardizing their jobs and their careers. We must break through the veil of illusion and misrepresentation that is holding us in a self-destructive cultural trance and get on with the work of re-creating our economic systems in service to people and the living earth.

6

DECLINE OF DEMOCRATIC PLURALISM

What an astounding thing it is to watch a civilization destroy itself be-
cause it is unable to re-examine the validity under totally new circum-
stances of an economic ideology.

—*Sir James Goldsmith*[1]

From the results, one can easily see that the whole point of privatization
is neither economic efficiency nor improved services to the consumer but
simply to transfer wealth from the public purse—which could redistrib-
ute it to even out social inequalities—to private hands.

—*Susan George*[2]

THE CHAMPIONS OF CORPORATE libertarianism gleefully greeted the disintegration of the Soviet empire in 1989 as a victory of the free market and a
mandate to press forward their cause. Francis Fukuyama proclaimed that the
long path of human evolution was reaching its ultimate conclusion, a universal, global consumer society. He called it the end of history.[3]

The governments and corporations of the West quickly reached out to
urge Eastern Europe and the countries of the former Soviet Union to embrace
the lessons of Western success by opening their borders and greening their
economies. Armies of Western experts were fielded to help these and other
"transition states" write laws that would prepare the way for Western corporations to penetrate their economies.

Simultaneously, the industrial West intensified its effort to create a unified global economy through the General Agreement on Tariffs and Trade
(GATT), establish a powerful World Trade Organization (WTO), and create

regional markets through such initiatives as the North American Free Trade Agreement (NAFTA), Maastricht (the European common market), and the Asia-Pacific Economic Community (APEC). Anxious to please powerful corporate interests and lacking other viable ideas, U.S. President Bill Clinton embraced economic globalization as both his jobs program and his foreign policy.

Marxist socialism died an ignoble death. However, it is no more accurate to attribute the West's economic and political triumph to the unfettered marketplace than it is to blame the U.S.S.R.'s failure on an activist state. Contrary to the boastful claims of corporate libertarians, the West did not prosper in the post–World War II period by rejecting the state in favor of the market. Rather, it prospered by rejecting extremist ideologies of both Right and Left in favor of democratic pluralism: a system of governance based on a pragmatic, institutional balance among the forces of government, market, and civil society.

Driven by the imperatives of depression and war, America emerged from World War II with government, market, and civil society working together in a healthier, more dynamic, and more creative balance than at any time since the pre–Civil War years. A relatively egalitarian income distribution created an enormous mass market, which in turn drove aggressive industrial expansion. America certainly was far from socialist, but neither was it truly capitalist. We might more accurately call it pluralist. This is the America that readily withstood the challenges posed by the Soviet empire to emerge as the Cold War victor. The America of democratic pluralism and equality defeated communism, not "free" market America.

Although the specifics differed, similar patterns of democratic pluralism prevailed in most of the Western industrial democracies. Some moved more toward public ownership and management of nationalized industries than others but within a pluralistic framework in which both market and government were strong players.

In contrast, the Soviet system embraced an ideological extremism so strongly statist that the market and the private ownership of property were virtually eliminated. The same ideology resulted in eliminating the civic sector's essential public oversight role. This left only a hegemonic and unaccountable state. Lacking the pluralistic balance and civic accountability afforded by the civic and market sectors, the Soviet economy was both unresponsive to popular needs and inefficient in the use of resources. The consequent suffering of the Soviet people was not a consequence of an activist state. It was the consequence of an extremist ideology that excluded everything except the state.

The West is now on a similar extremist ideological path; the difference is that we are captive to detached and unaccountable corporations rather than to a detached and unaccountable state. It is ironic that the closer the corporate libertarians move us toward their ideological ideal of *laissez faire* capitalism, the less responsive the economy becomes to the real needs of people and planet. Ironically, the reasons for the failure are virtually identical to the reasons the Marxist economies failed:

- Both lead to the concentration of economic power in unaccountable centralized institutions—the state in the case of Marxism, and the transnational corporation in the case of capitalism.
- Both create economic systems that destroy the living systems of the earth in the name of economic progress.
- Both produce a disempowering dependence on mega-institutions that erodes the social capital on which the efficient function of markets, governments, and society depends.
- Both take a narrow economistic view of human needs that undermines the sense of spiritual connection to the earth and to the community of life essential to maintaining the moral fabric of society.

An economic system can remain viable only as long as society has mechanisms to counter the concentration and abuse of both state and market power and the erosion of the natural, social, and moral capital that such abuses commonly exacerbate. Democratic pluralism isn't a perfect answer to the governance problem, but it seems to be the best we have discovered in our imperfect world.

MAINTAINING COMPETITIVE MARKETS

Although business often complains that government interferes unduly with its affairs, most calls for freeing the market ignore a basic reality: the efficient function of a market economy depends on a strong government. This need is well established in contemporary market economic theory and has been demonstrated in practice. In their exhaustive critique of corporate libertarianism *For the Common Good*, Herman E. Daly and John Cobb Jr. list the conditions on which the market depends for its efficient function yet cannot provide for itself.[4]

Fair Competition By its nature, competition creates winners and losers. Winners become more powerful as they grow. Losers disappear. The bigger the winners, the more difficult it is for new entrants to gain a foothold and the more monopolistic the market becomes. Even children who play the family board game Monopoly know how it works. As the game progresses, Monopoly players acquire property on which they charge one another rent. Those who get property early in the game eventually drive the less fortunate bankrupt. The game officially ends when all players have gone bankrupt save one. Astute players know that anyone who arrives late and joins the game after others have acquired initial properties doesn't stand a chance. Most players drop out after one player gains substantial advantage as there is no prospect of a clever or lucky player coming from behind to win a surprise victory. Interest is restored only when assets are redistributed and a new game is started.

Real-world monopoly is much the same, except that the larger players have the additional advantage of being able to use their financial power to influence legislators to rewrite the rules of the game to give themselves even more advantage. The result is an inexorable tendency toward monopoly that can be restrained only by government action, backed by a politically aware citizenry, to regularly break up concentrations of economic power.

Moral Capital Although market theory assumes self-interested individuals and real-world markets often reward greedy, dishonest, and immoral behavior, the day-to-day interactions of an efficient market depend on trust. A market in which participants are driven purely by greed and desire to obtain momentary competitive advantage by any means—a market without trust, cooperation, compassion, and individual integrity—is not just an unpleasant place to do business. It is also highly inefficient, incurring inordinate costs for lawyers, security guards, and other defensive measures. Neither a society nor a market economy can function efficiently without a moral foundation.

Public Goods Many investments and services that are essential to the public good—such as investments in basic scientific research, public security and justice, public education, roads, and national defense—are not supplied by the market because once they have been produced, they are freely available for anyone to use. Even most corporate libertarians recognize a role for government in providing such public goods, at least those essential for the profitable function of private business. The actual work may be done by private contractors, but the bills must be paid by governments out of tax revenues.

Full-Cost Pricing   The market produces an optimal allocation of resources only when sellers and buyers bear the full cost of the products they produce, purchase, and consume. Rarely, if ever, will full costs be internalized in an unregulated market, because competitive pressures make it necessary to externalize costs whenever possible. A producer that successfully externalizes social and environmental costs will gain a higher profit and attract more investors and thus can offer a lower price and capture a greater market share. It is wonderful when a company discovers inherent economic advantages in reducing its waste and paying its workers a fair wage, but experience shows that there is nothing inherent in the workings of the market to ensure that social and environmental costs will be internalized without active governmental intervention.

Just Distribution   In a market system there is a strong tendency, especially during periods of economic expansion, for the owners of capital to increase their wealth and incomes while the incomes of those who sell their labor lag or decline. A market in which economic power is unjustly distributed will allocate resources to producing luxuries for those with money while depriving those with no money of even the most basic necessities of life, which is neither just nor socially efficient. Market efficiency and institutional legitimacy depend on governmental intervention to constantly restore the equity that market forces inexorably erode.

Ecological Sustainability   As the human economy grows to fill its ecological space, limiting the scale of the economic subsystem to maintain an optimal balance with nature becomes necessary for species survival. Carbon dioxide emissions must be maintained below absorption levels. Fisheries harvests must be held to sustainable levels. Unfortunately, the unregulated market is blind to countless such constraints. Government must set the limits and ensure that appropriate signals are sent to the market. Even proposed "market solutions" to environmental problems, such as tradable pollution permits, depend on government intervention to set the limits, issue permits, and monitor compliance.

The market produces socially optimal outcomes *only* when government and civil society are empowered to act to maintain these six conditions of market efficiency. A market freed from governmental restraint is inherently unsustainable because it erodes its own institutional, social, and environmental foundations.

THE CORROSIVE EFFECTS OF GLOBALIZATION

Market mechanisms are essential to modern societies. However, for the market to serve the public good, business must recognize and accept the essential roles of government and civil society in maintaining the conditions on which the economic and social efficiency of markets depends, even though this may reduce corporate profits, limit the freedom of corporate action, and increase the prices of some consumer goods. The payoffs for society include good jobs that pay a living wage and protect the health and safety of workers and the community, a clean environment, economic stability, job security, and strong and secure families and communities.

There will also be cases of government inefficiency, just as there are cases of corporate inefficiency. It is appropriate to reduce the costs of such inefficiency both to taxpayers and to business. It is also appropriate to ensure that increases in consumer prices do not make it more difficult for people of modest incomes to meet their basic needs. However, we should *not* be concerned when governmental intervention in the public interest makes it more costly to consume things that we may not really need, reduces excessive corporate profits, and gives corporations fewer freedoms than people.

To play its essential role in relation to the market, a government must have jurisdiction over the economy within the borders of its territory. It must be able to set the rules for the domestic economy without having to prove to foreign governments and corporations that such rules are not barriers to international trade and investment. A government must be able to assess taxes and regulate the affairs of corporations that conduct business within its jurisdiction without being subject to corporate threats to sue for lost profits, withhold critical technologies, or transfer jobs to foreign facilities. For such jurisdiction to be maintained, economic boundaries must coincide with political boundaries. If not, government becomes impotent, and democracy becomes a hollow facade. When the economy is global and governments are national, global corporations and financial institutions function largely beyond the reach of public accountability, governments become more vulnerable to inappropriate corporate influence, and citizenship is reduced to making consumer choices among the products that corporations find it most profitable to offer.

Domestic economies that favor locally owned businesses—serving community interests in ways that foreign producers and footloose investors cannot—need not exclude imported goods and outside investors. Where a community finds benefits in foreign trade and investment, it should surely welcome them. But people have both the right and the need to be in control of their own economic lives through their own enterprises and the rules they set for themselves through their own democratically elected governments. If they wish to place economic speed bumps on their borders to create an advantage for local investment, they have every moral right to do so. Such a strategy worked for the Western nations during the post–World War II economic boom and resulted in the broad domestic sharing of economic benefits.

Sweden offers an instructive case study of what democratic pluralism was able to accomplish during the mid-twentieth century and of the dynamics that ultimately led to its breakdown in favor of rule by a small corporate and financial elite.

THE CASE OF SWEDEN

Sweden is known among the Western industrial countries for its success in achieving prosperity and equity through mixing elements of both capitalist and socialist models within a strong framework of democratic pluralism. Sweden's experience offers instructive insights into the dynamics of pluralism and the consequences of globalization.

Few realize that industrialization came a hundred years later to Sweden than to England. Until the years following World War II, Sweden remained an extremely poor country. In the countryside, many people lived on small farms that, given the poor soil and climate, barely provided them a living. Some died in famines or emigrated. Many others, even well into this century, lived in serf-like conditions on large estates. Illiteracy was widespread. In the late 1940s, it was still common for a family to live in an apartment consisting of one room plus a kitchen (toilet facilities were shared with other families). Even the Swedish royal house was relatively poor by the standards of most of its European cousins.[5]

Sweden's modern success was a creation of the Swedish Social Democratic Party, which melded and sustained a national consensus that kept it in power for forty-four years, from 1932 to 1976.[6] The Social Democrats built Sweden's elaborate social welfare system. Their wage policies brought working people into the middle class and created a substantial degree of wage equity—including greater equity between the wages of women and men—than in any other Western country.[7] The Social Democrats place a high priority on maintaining full employment. To encourage Swedish transnational firms such as Volvo, Electrolux, Saab, and Ericsson to concentrate their operations in Sweden, the

applicable effective tax rate was much lower for profits generated in Sweden
than for those generated abroad. [8]

An alliance between the major Swedish industrial corporations and organized labor served as the party's political base and supported the centralized
and peaceful negotiation of wages and working conditions by national union
and employers' organizations. This alignment produced significant benefits
for both big labor and big capital.

The arrangement had important structural flaws, however, that eventually destabilized it. One was a tax system that subsidized larger firms that were
expanding and investing at the expense of small-scale and family firms. This
led to increasing concentration and monopolization of ownership of the Swedish economy. Although wage policies stressed equality within the working class,
the gap between the working class and those who controlled capital grew substantially. At the time, this gap was considered the price of maintaining the
industrialists' commitment to the coalition. In the end, it brought about the
coalition's destruction. [9]

When the first shock of rising oil prices hit in 1973–74, the resulting economic slowdown brought a fiscal crisis and triggered popular resistance to
higher taxes. During this same period, Sweden was opening its economic borders and becoming a more active player in the international economy. This
loosened the bonds that tied capital to local labor and weakened national labor movements.

In the early stages of globalization, the outward expansion of Swedish
firms generated new employment at home, and the objectives of the two sides
of the alliance did not significantly conflict. But once Sweden's transnationals
began to define their own interests as global rather than national, the alliance
between blue-collar workers and the owners of capital began to disintegrate.
By this time, Sweden's highly educated white-collar workers outnumbered blue-
collar workers, and the younger generation was taking the welfare state for
granted, further weakening the political base of Sweden's Social Democrats. [10]

The growing contradiction between government support for the global
expansion of Swedish transnationals and the need to create employment and
rising real wages at home could no longer be sustained. In 1976, the Social
Democrats lost the election to a three-party, center-right coalition government.

When the Social Democrats returned to power in 1982, they were a chas-
tened party intent on promoting policies that would allow Sweden's industrialists sufficient profit margins on domestic investment to keep them "believ-
ing in Sweden," a phrase coined by P. G. Gyllenhammar, the chairman of Volvo.
Maintaining a belief in Sweden meant increasing the share of the national

product going to profits compared with wages so that Sweden's industrialists would find it worthwhile to invest at home. This was accepted as the price of maintaining full employment at a time when unemployment elsewhere in Europe was running at 8 to 9 percent or higher.[11]

The resulting policies pushed corporate profits to previously unimaginable levels. With so much more money in their pockets than could be absorbed by productive investments, Swedish investors turned to speculation, driving up the prices of real estate, art, stamps, and other speculative goods. To stop the upward spiral, the government loosened monetary controls so that the excess funds could spill over into Europe. Money flowed out at such a rate that it helped push real estate prices in London and Brussels to record highs. As the speculative bubble fed on itself, the quick profits offered by speculation drained funds away from productive investments within Sweden. When the bubble in Swedish real estate finally burst, the Swedish banking system lost $18 billion in uncollectible loans. The bill was picked up by the state and passed on to the Swedish taxpayers.[12]

During this period, Sweden's major industrialists played an active role in dismantling the "Swedish model" constructed by the Social Democratic alliance. The Swedish Employers' Federation rejected centralized wage bargaining, which had been one of the model's cornerstones, and allied itself with the Conservative Party. It also bankrolled think tanks espousing a corporate libertarian economic ideology and conducted a major public-relations effort praising individualism and the free market while denouncing the Social Democratic state as oppressive and inept.[13] This weakened the political apparatus of the state and its ability to define long-term policies.

In 1983, Volvo chairman P.G. Gyllenhammar stepped in to fill the void by forming the Roundtable of European Industrialists, made up of the heads of the leading European transnationals, including Fiat, Nestle, Philips, Olivetti, Renault, and Siemens. The purpose was to define long-term policies for the state and to serve as an international lobby to press for their implementation.[14]

By the end of 1992, the richest 2 percent of Swedish households owned 62 percent of the value of the shares traded on the Stockholm stock exchange and 23 percent of all wealth in the country. While the average Swedish household grew poorer from 1978 to 1988, the richest 450 households doubled their assets.[15] Unemployment had been below 3 percent when the Social Democrats were first voted out of office.[16] It rose to 5 percent in 1992 and was projected to reach 7 percent, even though another 7 percent of the workforce was already engaged in countercyclical retraining programs and public employment projects.

From the beginning, the Swedish model contained the seeds of its own destruction. It built a powerful financial elite whose interests were far removed from those of the majority middle class. It bred a sense of welfare complacency among the Swedish people and failed to instill in the younger generation an awareness of democracy's need to be continually re-created through constant citizen vigilance and political activism. And its prosperity had been built on the unsustainable exploitation of Sweden's natural resources of timber, iron ore, and hydroelectric power.

As the elites gained more financial power, they were able to pyramid their claims on the resources of society without making a corresponding productive contribution. As the economic borders were opened, the jobs of those who depended on earning wages for doing productive work became hostage to those who controlled capital. The more the government, in its desperation to keep jobs at home, gave in to the demands of the financial elite, the greater the amount of money that passed into their hands, the greater their power to dictate public policy in their own interest, and the greater the stresses on the social fabric. The parallels to the U.S. experience examined in Part III are striking.

The Swedish experience reveals a lesson of fundamental importance: democratic pluralism cannot long survive extreme inequality.

THE NEED FOR CREATIVE BALANCE

Communism established the hegemony of the state. Capitalism establishes the hegemony of financial markets and the corporation. A healthy society is built on the balanced interaction of three distinct yet interlinked sectors of activity: civic, governmental, and economic. All are human creations and a given individual may participate in all three, yet the integrity of the whole depends on clearly distinguishing their roles and their legitimate sources of power.

Civic[17]   Less formally institutionalized than the other three sectors, the civic sector affords the greatest creative freedom to the individual to act from a sense of inner spiritual connection to life and community. The distinctive role of the civic sector is to generate, maintain, and renew the sense of meaning and the symbols of cultural identity that are the foundation of the coherence and integrity of a healthy society. An active civic sector is the conscience of the society, the source of its cultural vitality and renewal, and a counter to the abuse of power by governmental and economic institutions.

Governmental   Government is the sector to which the civic sector freely, but reluctantly, gives the authority to use coercive power in the public interest, including the power to confiscate property and to deprive a person of physical liberty and even life. By the exercise of this authority government carries out such essential functions as maintaining public order and national security, collecting taxes, and reallocating society's resources to maintain equity and meet other public needs. Government's distinctive competence is in reallocating wealth, not in creating it. Its power must be continually checked by an active civil society.

Economic   The economic sector specializes in producing goods and services. Market economies respond to consumer demand. Markets are, however, ill-equipped to set society's larger priorities. Markets have no mechanism for preventing the unscrupulous from selling guns, drugs, and tobacco products to children, creating environmental damage, endangering workers, or for insuring the accuracy of product labels. They cannot maintain public streets, run schools for poor children, or mandate recycling. Nor do they distinguish between profits earned from the efficient production of goods and unearned profits gained by exercising monopoly power, externalizing costs, expropriating common property resources, or creating artificial demand for unnecessary and even harmful products. In each instance there is a need for democratically elected governments to establish the boundaries of behavior acceptable to the society.

Democratic pluralism melds the forces of the market, government, and civil society to maintain a dynamic balance among the often competing societal needs for essential order and equity, the efficient production of goods and services, the accountability of power, the protection of human freedom, and continuing institutional innovation. This balance finds expression in the *regulated* market, not the *free* market, and in trade policies that link national economies to one another within a framework of rules that maintains domestic competition and favors domestic enterprises that employ local workers, meet local standards, pay local taxes, and function within a robust system of democratic governance.

In a healthy society the civic sector is appropriately considered to be the first sector as it is the arena of citizenship, individual expression, and democratic participation. At the same time, the health of the society depends on the vitality of all three sectors. Without the institutions of government and the economy the society will be lawless and impoverished. Since government is the body through which citizens establish and maintain the rules for all sectors, it is appropriately considered the second sector. The role of the economic sector is to serve society's needs as defined by people through their purchases, their choice of work, and the rules and priorities determined democratically through their participation in government. It is therefore properly subordinate to both the civic and governmental sectors and is appropriately designated the third sector.

PLAYING BY DIFFERENT RULES

Contrary to popular myth, capitalist economies and market economies operate by different rules to different ends. The institutions of a capitalist economy are designed to concentrate control of the means of production in the hands of the few to the exclusion of the many. A capitalist economy is characterized by concentrations of monopoly power, financial speculation, absentee ownership, deregulation, public subsidies, the externalization of costs, and central economic planning by mega-corporations.

By contrast the institutions of a market economy, as envisioned by Adam Smith and described by market theory, are intended to facilitate the self-organizing processes by which people engage in the production and exchange of goods and services to create adequate and satisfying livelihoods for themselves and their families. A true market economy features human-scale enterprises, honest money, rooted local ownership, and a framework of democratically chosen rules intended to maintain the conditions of efficient market function—including equity and cost internalization. It is a natural companion to democracy and a pluralistic society.

The publicly traded, limited liability corporation is capitalism's institutional form of choice because it allows the virtually unlimited concentration of power with minimal public accountability or legal liability. Actual shareholders, the real owners, rarely have any role in corporate affairs and bear no personal liability beyond the value of their investments. Directors and officers are protected from financial liability for acts of negligence or commission by the corporation's massive legal resources and company paid insurance policies. The same criminal act that would result in a stiff prison sentence, or even execution, if committed by an individual, brings a corporation only a fine—usually inconsequential in relation to corporate assets and likely less than what it gained by committing the infraction.[18] The prosecution of corporate executives for illegal corporate acts is extremely rare. It is with good reason that William M. Dugger characterizes the corporation as "organized irresponsibility."[19]

Unlike real people, who are eventually rendered equal by the grave, corporations are able to grow and reproduce themselves without limit, "living" and amassing power indefinitely. Eventually, that power evolves beyond the ability of any mere human to control, and the corporation becomes an autonomous entity unto itself, using its power to "create its own culture, using the lens of career to focus corporate culture on profit, size, and power."[20] Those who serve the corporate interest are well rewarded and derive substantial personal power from their positions. But in the end, they are only employees who serve the institution at its pleasure.

Few real persons can begin to match the political resources that a large corporation is able to amass in its behalf. Corporations may lack the right to vote, but that is a minor inconvenience, given their ability to mobilize hundreds of thousands of votes from among their workers, suppliers, dealers, customers, and the public, and to package millions of dollars in political contributions.

Left to their devices, corporations colonize markets and defeat the very mechanisms that theory tells us make the market work in the public interest. The limited liability, publicly traded corporation may be the favored institution of capitalism, but it is not a market institution. To the contrary, it is aggressively *anti*market, because it works tirelessly to erode the essential conditions of the market's social efficiency.

It is fully appropriate, therefore, that citizens view corporations with the same skepticism as did the early American settlers, granting corporate charters judiciously only to serve well-defined public purposes, setting clear rules for corporate function, holding corporations fully accountable for their actions, and barring them from political participation of any kind.

The owners and managers of corporations have the full rights of any citizen—in their capacity as citizens—to participate in defining public goals and policies. However, corporations are not people. They are alien to the ways of life, blind to the complex nonmaterial needs of human societies, and have no proper role in the political processes by which real people define the public interest and set standards for corporate conduct.

A corporate charter represents a privilege—not a right—that is granted by a government subject to the will of its people in return for the acceptance of corresponding obligations. It is up to the people who comprise the electorate—not the fictitious persona of the corporation—to define these privileges and obligations. We are learning through harsh experience that the survival of democracy depends on holding firmly to this principle.

Democratic pluralism faces a paradox. During times of change, societies need to mobilize the full creative potential of their citizens in a way that can be achieved only under democratic pluralism. Yet it is in such stressful times that democratic pluralism seems least adequate and most susceptible to the certainty offered by the simplistic appeals of ideological demagogues. Instead of offering direction, democratic pluralism calls on people to find their own direction with a view to the good of the whole. Instead of certainty, it nurtures variety to the point of apparent chaos. These are its weakness, but also its genius. Democratic pluralism provides a framework within which each citizen contributes what he or she can toward addressing—in the context of family, community, and nation—the countless changing needs faced by complex, dynamic human societies. Gradually, through a diffuse and chaotic social learning process, the lessons from countless innovations are distilled into changes in local, national, and ultimately global institutions and policies.

Democratic pluralism provides the institutional framework within which people can bring to bear their full creative powers toward finding innovative solutions to shared problems and, in the process, create societies that are responsive to the challenges of the unfolding Ecological Revolution. We need that creative power now as never before.

7

ILLUSIONS OF THE CLOUD MINDERS

This troubled planet is a place of the most violent contrasts. Those that receive the rewards are totally separated from those who shoulder the burdens. It is not a wise leadership.

—Spock, "The Cloud Minders," Star Trek[1]

With the information technologies already available, I can sit on the beach of my Florida home with a laptop computer and a cellular telephone and monitor the video cameras installed throughout my manufacturing company in Ohio to insure that my people are on the job and doing their work properly.

—Interview with company owner on U.S. National Public Radio, August 31, 1994

"THE CLOUD MINDERS," EPISODE 74 of the popular science fiction television series *Star Trek*, took place on the planet Ardana. First aired on February 28, 1969, it depicted a planet whose rulers devoted their lives to the arts in a beautiful and peaceful city, Stratos, suspended high above the planet's desolate surface. Down below, the inhabitants of the planet's surface, the Troglytes, worked in misery and violence in the planet's mines to earn the interplanetary exchange credits used to import from other planets the luxuries the rulers enjoyed on Stratos. In this modern allegory, an entire planet had been colonized by rulers who successfully detached and isolated themselves from the people and the localities of the planet's surface on whose toil their luxuries depended.

The imagery of this *Star Trek* episode has stuck vividly in my mind. How like our own world it is, where the truly rich and powerful work in beautifully appointed executive suites in tall office towers; travel to meetings by limousine and helicopter; jet between continents high above the clouds, pampered with the finest wines by an attentive crew; and live in protected estates, affluent suburbs, and penthouse suites amid art, beauty, and a protected environment. They are as insulated from the lives of the ordinary people of our planet as those who lived on Stratos were insulated from the lives of the Troglytes. They too are living in a world of illusion, draining the world of its resources and so isolated from reality that they know not what they do, nor how else to live.

THE MAGIC MARKET

The isolation of the rich and powerful is exemplified by the annual gathering of the directors of the World Bank and the International Monetary Fund (IMF). The following is an account by journalist Graham Hancock from one such meeting:

> I had come [to Washington, D.C.] simply to attend the joint annual meeting of the Boards of Governors of the World Bank and the International Monetary Fund, two institutions that play a central role in mobilizing and disbursing funds for impoverished developing countries .... The total cost of the 700 social events laid on for delegates during that single week was estimated at $10 million .... A single formal dinner catered by Ridgewells cost $200 per person. Guests began with crab cakes, caviar and *creme fraîche*, smoked salmon and mini Beef Wellingtons. The fish course was lobster with corn rounds followed by citrus sorbet. The *entrée* was duck with lime sauce, served with artichoke bottoms filled with baby carrots. A hearts of palm salad was also offered accompanied by sage cheese soufflés with a port wine dressing. Dessert was a German chocolate turnip sauced with raspberry coulis, ice-cream bonbons and flaming coffee royale.... Washington limousine companies were doing a roaring trade. [2]

At the same meeting that favored its delegates with $10 million worth of lavish meals and social events, Barber Conable, the former U.S. congressman and then recently appointed president of the World Bank, presented the following charge to the 10,000 men and women present:

> Our institution is mighty in resources and in experience but its labours will count for nothing if it cannot look at our world through the eyes

of the most underprivileged, if we cannot share their hopes and their fears. We are here to serve their needs, to help them realise their strength, their potential, their aspirations .... Collective action against global poverty is the common purpose that brings us together today. Let us therefore rededicate ourselves to the pursuit of that great good.[3]

If the delegates had indeed made an effort to look at their world through the eyes of the most underprivileged, they might well have lost their appetites. Take, for example, this simple interview with a sharecropper's child in nearby Selma, Alabama, by Raymond Wheeler of CBS TV:

"Do you eat breakfast before school?"
"Sometimes, sir. Sometimes I have peas."
"And when you get to school, do you eat?"
"No, sir."
"Isn't there any food there?"
"Yes, sir."
"Why don't you have it?"
"I don't have the 35 cents."
"What do you do while the other children eat lunch?"
"I just sits there on the side" (his voice breaking).
"How do you feel when you see the other children eating?"
"I feel ashamed" (crying).[4]

Far from encouraging delegates to see the world through the eyes of the poor, the organizers of World Bank–IMF meetings take great care to shield them from the specter of poverty.

The World Bank and IMF are leading proponents of economic rationalism and free-market, export-led growth strategies. They have for years been lauding South Korea, Taiwan, Singapore, and Hong Kong as examples of success. Thus when the directors met in Bangkok, Thailand, in October 1991, it was natural that the meeting served as a celebration of the recent "success" story of free-market, export-led growth in Thailand.

No expense or inconvenience was spared by Thailand's government to impress the delegates that Thailand had arrived as a full member of the elite club of newly industrialized nations (NICs). To ensure the desired impression, a shiny new convention complex was rushed to completion in downtown Bangkok to host the conference. Two hundred families were evicted from their homes to widen roads to and from the site.[5] A nearby squatter settlement was leveled so that the delegates would not be troubled by unpleasant views of Bangkok's poverty. Schools and government offices were closed to limit traffic congestion and help clear the air of emissions so that the delegates might rush with the least inconvenience, free of respiratory distress in their air-conditioned cars, between elegant cocktail parties and official dinners along routes chosen—and walled off, where necessary—to avoid disconcerting views of Bangkok's slums. English-speaking engineers, doctors, and lawyers were pressed into service as drivers of the delegates; nurses and teachers waited tables in the conference restaurants to ensure that instructions were understood and that no need of a visiting dignitary would go unmet.

Such cosmetic measures could only partially hide the reality that Bangkok, a once beautiful city, has been ravaged by the consequences of its development "success." Amid shining shopping malls, high-rise office buildings, and luxury hotels, filth and squalor abound. Three hundred thousand new vehicles are added to Bangkok's monumental traffic jams each year, slowing traffic to an average of less than ten kilometers (about six miles) per hour. On more than 200 days a year, air pollution in Bangkok exceeds maximum World Health Organization safety limits, and emissions are increasing by 14 percent a year.[6]

The World Bank–IMF meeting in Thailand was a fitting metaphor for the illusion within which the world's power holders live. The illusion is maintained in part through the construction of a life of luxury set apart in enclaves, and in part by self-justifying belief systems, such as corporate libertarianism, and by the adulation of wealth and the wealthy by the business press and a plethora of economic researchers and consultants. Most of all, it is maintained by the dysfunctions of an economic system that lavishes rich rewards on power holders for decisions that place terrible burdens on the rest of humanity.

THE GREAT DIVIDE

The gap that separates the world's rich and poor, both within and between countries, is unconscionable and growing. In 1992, the United Nations Development Programme (UNDP) dramatized the inequity by representing the world's income distribution with a graph in the shape of a champagne glass.[7]

As shown in Figure 7.1, the 20 percent of the world's people who live in the world's wealthiest countries receive 82.7 percent of the world's income; only 1.4 percent of the world's income goes to the 20 percent who live in the world's poorest countries. In 1950, about the time the commitment was made to globalize the development process, the average income of the 20 percent of

Figure 7.1: Transition to a Full World

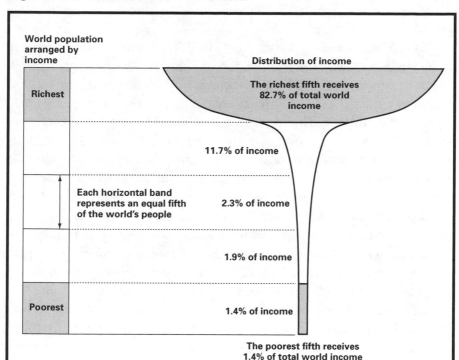

World population arranged by income

Distribution of income

Richest

The richest fifth receives 82.7% of total world income

11.7% of income

Each horizontal band represents an equal fifth of the world's people

2.3% of income

1.9% of income

Poorest

1.4% of income

The poorest fifth receives 1.4% of total world income

Source: UNDP, *Human Development Report 1992* (New York: Oxford University Press, 1992).

people living in the wealthiest countries was about thirty times that of the 20 percent living in the poorest countries. By 1989, this ratio had doubled to sixty times.

Based on national averages, these figures represent disparities among countries and substantially understate the disparity among people. For example, all Americans are placed in the world's top income category, including the homeless, the rural poor, and the urban slum dwellers. When the UNDP estimated the global distribution based on individual incomes rather than on national averages, the average income of the top 20 percent was 150 times that of the lowest 20 percent.

Even this figure masks the extreme inequity revealed when the incomes of the top 20 percent are desegregated. Although global data are not available, data from the United States illustrate the point. In 1989, the top 20 percent of American households had an average income of $109,424 a year. [8] However, those households in the eightieth to ninetieth percentiles received, on average, a relatively modest $65,900. Those in the top 1 percent averaged $559,795— receiving as a group more total income than the bottom 40 percent of all Americans.[9]

Yet even this is mere pocket change to Wall Street investment brokers such as the infamous Michael Milken, who in one year took home a cool half-billion dollars for his labors selling junk bonds on Wall Street, and to the chief executives officers (CEOs) of America's major corporations and the top-earning celebrities. In 1992, Thomas F. Frist Jr., CEO of Hospital Corporation of America, led the pack of overpaid American executives with $127 million, nearly 780,000 times the average $163 per capita income of the poorest 20 percent of the world's people! The 1992 average take of the CEOs of the 1,000 largest corporations surveyed by *Business Week* was $3.8 million—up 42 percent from the previous year. Furthermore, the gap between the pay of top executives and the pay of those who work for them is growing rapidly.[10] In 1960, the average CEO of a major company received forty times the compensation of the average worker. In 1992, he (there were only two women among *Business Week*'s top 1,000 CEOs) received 157 times as much.[11]

These well-paid executives are, however, only pretenders to wealth compared with the wealth of those who live by the earnings of their investment portfolios. *Forbes*'s "four hundred richest people in America" enjoyed an increase in their combined net worth of $92 billion between 1982 and 1993, bringing them to a total of $328 billion[12]—more than the combined 1991 gross national products (GNPs) shared by a billion people living in India, Bangladesh, Sri Lanka, and Nepal.[13]

Eager to assure its wealthy readers that their good fortune was not at the expense of others, *Forbes* prefaced its inventory of the wealthiest Americans with the following caveat:

> Aha! Then the redistributionists are right. The rich have gotten richer. Yes and no. The truly rich may have gotten richer, but there's no evidence that their proportionate share of the nation's wealth has grown. The price of admission to the Forbes Four Hundred has increased approximately as much as the stock market, as measured by the Dow Jones index. The tremendous increase in the stock market—which has rubbed off nicely on the super rich—rubs off on every pension holder and shareholder in America as well . . . .
>
> Weep not for the rich. But don't get the dumb idea that they have gotten rich off the rest of us.[14]

Surely there were some widows and pensioners of modest means among the beneficiaries of the stock market gains. However, the protestation of *Forbes* (a publication of and for the Stratos dwellers) that equity has been maintained is but one manifestation of the isolation of the Stratos dwellers and their belief that their world is the world. The 400 richest Americans may not have increased their share of total stock wealth, but apart from stocks owned by pension funds, 83.1 percent of the stock market wealth owned by American households is owned by the wealthiest 10 percent. Moreover, 37.4 percent of stock wealth is owned by the richest 0.5 percent. [15]

From 1977 to 1989, the average real income of the top 1 percent of U.S. families increased by 78 percent, whereas that of the bottom 20 percent *decreased* by 10.4 percent. [16] Thus the poorest among us became not only relatively poorer but also absolutely poorer. What these figures don't tell us is that these absolute decreases occurred in spite of the fact that those who were employed in 1989 were working longer hours than they had in 1977, and far more families had two people working full time as more women entered the workforce. For many U.S. families among the bottom 60 percent, even longer hours and an extra breadwinner were not enough to make up for the decline in wages.

The simple truth that the *Forbes* editors and other Stratos dwellers are prone to ignore is that each time a major corporation announces a cut back of thousands of jobs, the stratos families get richer and the incomes of the thousands of workers whose jobs have been eliminated decline. It is part of an ongoing process of shifting wealth and economic power from those who are engaged in the production of real value to those who already have large amounts of money and believe it is their right to see those amounts grow without limit, regardless of their own needs or productive contributions.

Is it possible for those who sip from the lip of the champagne glass to truly appreciate the lot of the vast mass of humanity that shares only the meager dregs that settle into the stem? If they were to acknowledge that their own abundance is the cause of the plight of those so deprived, could any person bear the terrible moral burden? There is substantial incentive to avoid facing such moral contradictions by maintaining the reassuring cultural illusions of Stratos.

A DIFFERENT WORLD

Forbes prefaced its 1993 listing of the 400 richest people in America with an article on the struggle of the very rich to make ends meet in today's economy. In one year's time, the price of a one-kilo tin of beluga malossol caviar had

increased by 28 percent to $1,408. A Sikorsky S-780 helicopter with full execu-
tive options had increased 8 percent to $7 million. And a suitable night's hotel
lodging in New York was up 15 percent to $750. [17] Theirs is a different world.

When Henry Kissinger, long one of the most influential players in U.S.
foreign policy circles, takes his dog, Amelia, with him on his morning constitutional, a bodyguard follows behind to handle the scooper duties. When Henry
goes on vacation, Amelia rides by limousine to Mrs. Peepers' kennel in rural
Maryland, where she stays as a houseguest in a private room. [18] Many Americans were amused when the press caught George Bush gazing in wonder at a
grocery checkout scanner and realized that he was one of the last people in the
United States to encounter this addition to the checkout routine.

When Alexander Trotman assumed the post of chairman, president, and
CEO of Ford Motor Company in 1993, he was responsible for making more
than 3 million vehicles a year. Yet he did not own a car of his own and had
never bought one from a dealer. Ford, as is common practice in the auto industry, provides all its top executives with new cars—ensuring that they always have cars that are in perfect working order without ever having the experience of negotiating with a dealer and hassling with registration, insurance,
repairs, and maintenance. [19]

In 1989, Lone Star Industries took a $271 million loss. Its CEO, James E.
Stewart, ordered layoffs, sold off $400 million of corporate assets, eliminated
the dividend to stockholders, and told his managers to fly coach. Yet he maintained a $2.9 million expense account for himself and continued to commute
in the corporate jet between his home in Florida and the company headquarters in Stamford, Connecticut. As CEO of RJR Nabisco, F. Ross Johnson built
a palatial hangar in Atlanta to house the corporation's ten planes and twenty-
six corporate pilots. Next door he built a three-story VIP lounge complete
with inlaid mahogany walls, Italian marble floors, and an atrium with a Japanese garden. [20] Ivan Boesky, the global financier, was known to order eight en-
trees from the menu at the exclusive Cafe des Artistes, sample each, and then
decide which he would eat. [21]

In June of 1991, I attended the annual conference of the American Forum for
Global Education in Hartford, Connecticut. Ed Pratt, the chairman and CEO
of Pfizer, Inc., a drug and medical products producer with annual worldwide
sales of $7 billion, was an opening speaker. He received an award for his con-
tributions to global education and shared his insights on educational needs
with several hundred American educators, telling them that the education of
young Americans must focus on giving them the greatest competitive edge in

the new global economy. In his view, there was no time for unnecessary frills —such as studying foreign languages. He reported that in his travels around Pfizer's world operations, he found that everyone with whom there was any need to talk already spoke English. So he advised that the classroom hours that children in other countries spend learning English be devoted to teaching American students science and economics.

Nike, a major footwear company, refers to itself as a "network firm." This means that it employs 8,000 people in management, design, sales, and promotion and leaves production in the hands of some 75,000 workers hired by independent contractors. Most of the outsourced production takes place in Indonesia, where a pair of Nikes that sells in the United States or Europe for $73 to $135 is produced for about $5.60 by girls and young women paid as little as fifteen cents an hour. The workers are housed in company barracks, there are no unions, overtime is often mandatory, and if there is a strike, the military may be called to break it up. The $20 million that basketball star Michael Jordan reportedly received in 1992 for promoting Nike Shoes exceeded the entire annual payroll of the Indonesian factories that made them.[22]

When asked about the conditions at plants where Nikes are produced, John Woodman, Nike's general manager in Indonesia, gave a classic Stratos-dweller response. Although he knew that there had been labor problems in the six Indonesian factories making Nike shoes, he had no idea what they had been about. Furthermore he said, "I don't know that I need to know. It's not within our scope to investigate." [23]

The Nike case is a striking example of the distortions of an economic system that shifts rewards away from those who produce real value to those whose primary function is to create marketing illusions to convince consumers to buy products they do not need at inflated prices. It is little wonder that many managers, like the Nike manager who avoided contact with Indonesian workers, prefer to avoid talking to too many people outside the elite circles.

It seems fitting that in 1993 the winner in the annual executive compensation package sweepstakes was master illusionist Michael Eisner, chairman of the Walt Disney Company, a corporation dedicated to the creation of fantasy worlds. Eisner's compensation package of $203.1 million equaled 68 percent of the company's total profits of $299.8 million for that year—surely ample to create a few personal illusions of his own.[24]

This is the cloud world in which the architects of the global economic order live. For themselves and their corporations, local markets become too confining. No amount of wealth and power is enough. They must constantly push new frontiers, build new empires, and colonize new markets. There is good reason to conclude that people who are so isolated from the daily reality of those they rule are ill prepared to define the public interest.

REDEFINING NORTH—SOUTH

Great wealth and the embrace of a world of illusion are not found only in "wealthy" countries. The *Forbes* 1993 directory of the world's wealthiest people listed eighty-eight billionaires from low- and middle-income countries, up from sixty-two only a year earlier. Mexico headed the list with twenty-four billionaires in 1993, up from thirteen in 1992.[25]

Consider the Philippines, a poor economic performer by the standards of East and Southeast Asia. Its per capita GNP is $730, and an estimated 60 percent of its people lack adequate incomes to provide even a minimum healthy diet for themselves and their families. *Forbes* listed two Philippine billionaires in 1992 and five in 1993.

From 1988 to 1992, I worked from an office located on the eleventh floor of a high-rise building in Makati, the commercial and financial center of Manila, the capital city of the Philippines. From my window I looked out on three of Manila's five-star hotels and a number of high-rise bank buildings. Almost any time of the day I could see one or more private helicopters ferrying Manila's business elites to and from the tops of these high-rise buildings far above the cars stalled in Manila's legendary traffic jams and the lines of carless commuters waiting amid thick diesel fumes for public transportation. On the other side of Manila, thousands of less fortunate Filipinos had built their shacks of scavenged materials on top of Smokey Mountain, a steaming garbage dump, and made their livings picking through the stinking mountain of garbage for bottles, bits of plastic, and other salable items.

Hundreds of thousands of Filipinos go abroad each year in a desperate search for work to sustain themselves and their families. Many of the women arrive in Japan to work as "entertainers" or take jobs as household servants in the Middle East. They commonly find themselves working under conditions of virtual slavery and the objects of sexual exploitation. The Philippine government considers its overseas workers to be an essential source of foreign exchange earnings to pay for, among other things, imports to stock the country's luxurious, air-conditioned mega-malls with advanced consumer electronics and designer fashions and to service the country's $32 billion foreign debt.

In an earlier day, when economies were defined by national borders and even by individual localities, rich and poor alike who lived within the borders of a nation or a town generally shared a sense of national and community interest. No matter how great the conflict among them might be, their destinies intertwined. Industrialists had a stake in the educational system that produced their workers and in the physical infrastructure of transportation and other public facilities on which their productive enterprises depended. No matter how begrudgingly, they accepted the obligation to pay taxes to help support essential social and physical infrastructures.

In recent years, one of the demographic realities of the United States has been an increasing geographical segregation by income. Those in the upper income brackets have been clustering in affluent suburban communities organized as independent political jurisdictions, where they share facilities only with members of their own affluent class. Thus, they are able to finance good schools and other public services without the need to pay additional taxes to contribute toward providing similar facilities for lower-income families. Low-income families thus become similarly clustered in low-income jurisdictions that have a far greater need for social services than the wealthier clusters but lack the tax base to finance them.[26]

The consequences of this separation by political jurisdiction were exacerbated in the United States during the 1980s when the federal government began shifting greater responsibility to local jurisdictions for funding social services. In 1978, when federal transfers to local government peaked, almost 27 percent of state and local funding came from federal grants. By 1988, federal funding had fallen to 17 percent. This was all part of a larger effort by the Reagan administration to dismantle the income-redistribution mechanisms that earlier administrations had put into place during America's era of democratic pluralism. Robert Reich refers to it as the secession by the privileged few from the rest of America. The result has been a growing gap in the quality of education and other public services enjoyed by rich and poor; a deepening of the class divide, commonly exacerbated by racial lines; and an increasing isolation of the wealthy in their worlds of illusion.[27]

Of the many countries I have visited, Pakistan most starkly exemplifies the experience of elites living in enclaves detached from local roots. The country's three modern cities—Karachi, Lahore, and Islamabad—feature enclaves of five-star hotels, modern shopping malls, and posh residential areas within a poor and feudalistic countryside governed by local lords who support private armies with profits from a thriving drug and arms trade and who are inclined to kill any central government official who dares to enter. Health and education indicators for Pakistan's rural areas are comparable to those for the most deprived African nations.

On two of my visits to Pakistan, I was the guest of some of the country's most successful businessmen. Widely traveled and graduates of the best British and American universities, they spoke and moved with the confidence, gracious demeanor, and sense of hospitality typical of cosmopolitan aristocrats who are fully at ease with their money and position. My hosts regularly traveled the world to supervise their widespread business interests, moving easily among the global business elites and feeling as much at home in New York or London as in Karachi, Lahore, or Islamabad.

Particularly striking, however, was the extent to which—in contrast to their knowledge of and interest in the rest of the world—they had little knowledge of or interest in what was happening in their own country beyond the borders of their enclave cities. It was as though the rest of Pakistan were an inconsequential foreign country not worthy of notice or mention. They were almost completely detached from any sense of national interest. What I failed to realize at the time was that this phenomenon was not an aberration of underdevelopment so much as the cutting edge of a global social and political trend—a melding of the world's financial elites into a stateless community in the clouds, detached from the world in which the vast majority of ordinary mortals live.

We have long thought of the world as divided into rich and poor countries. As economic globalization progresses, we find growing islands of great wealth in poor countries and growing seas of poverty in rich countries. The North and South distinction is now most meaningfully used to acknowledge the reality of a world divided by class lines more than by geography.

A SELF-DESTRUCTING SYSTEM

The global economic system is rewarding corporations and their executives with generous profits and benefits packages for contracting out their production to sweatshops paying substandard wages, for clear-cutting primal forests, for introducing labor-saving technologies that displace tens of thousands of employees, for dumping toxic wastes, and for shaping political agendas to advance corporate interests over human interests. The system shields those who take such actions from the costs of their decisions, which are borne by the system's weaker members—the displaced workers who no longer have jobs, the replacement workers who are paid too little to feed their families, the forest dwellers whose homes have been destroyed, the poor who live next to the toxic dumps, and the unorganized taxpayers who pick up the bills. The consequence of delinking benefits from their costs is that the system is telling the world's most powerful decision makers that their decisions are creating new benefits, when in fact they are simply shifting more of the earth's available wealth to themselves at the expense of people and the planet.

Systems theorists, who concern themselves with understanding the dynamics of complex, self-regulating systems, would say that the economic system is providing these decision makers with positive feedback, rewarding them for decisions that upset the system's dynamic equilibrium and cause the system to oscillate out of control, risking eventual collapse. Stable systems depend on negative feedback signals that provide incentives to correct errant behavior and move the system back toward equilibrium.

The genius of Adam Smith's concept of a market economy is that although he never used the cybernetic terminology of the systems theorists, he was one of the first to recognize the basic principles of a complex, self-regulating human system. Implicitly, he applied those principles to create an idealized model of a self-regulating economic system that would efficiently allocate society's resources to produce those things that people most want without the intervention of a powerful central ruler. It was a brilliant intellectual achievement and had enormous appeal to intellectuals who were attracted to elegant theories, to populists who had a deep distrust of powerful rulers—and to propertied elites who found in it a moral justification for greed.

Unfortunately, the economic rationalists who are Smith's intellectual descendants took a narrower and more mechanistic view of economic systems and embraced market freedom as an ideology, without Smith's focus on the conditions required to maintain the market's self-regulating balance. Ideologues make poor system designers because they are oriented to simplistic prescriptions rather than to the creation of balanced, self-regulating systems.

As resulting social tensions mount and the system's failures become more evident, established political alignments are becoming increasingly strained. Capitalizing on a growing sense of public uncertainty and fear, political demagogues and opportunists are now having a field day. In the United States, they are attacking big government and environmentalists while calling for tax cuts, government downsizing, the restoration of family values and individual responsibility, the elimination of restrictions on natural resource exploitation, increased defense expenditures, a tougher stand on crime, market deregulation, and free trade. Posing as conservatives committed to protecting ordinary people from the abuses of big government, they play simultaneously to the self-reliant, who distrust government; to the economically burdened, who seek tax relief; to workers in resource-based industries, who fear environmental restrictions; and to corporate interests, which are eager for greater freedom to increase profits by externalizing costs. The proposals offered to attract these varied constituencies are rife with contradictions. Few of the proposals will contribute to restoring the values of family, community, and self-reliance. To the contrary, they allow the world's largest corporations the freedom to colonize still more of the world's markets and resources to the benefit of the already rich, further shift tax burdens from those best able to pay to those least able to pay, and enlarge the police powers of the state to stem the resulting social unrest.

The opportunists and demagogues of corporate libertarianism have linked corporate money and power with populist interests to advance an agenda that results in placing corporate interests above human interests. This contradiction remains unexposed as long as the corporate libertarians are allowed to define the issues as a struggle between tax-and-spend, big-government liberals and family-values conservatives fighting for individual freedom and responsibility. In this guise, they have enjoyed great success in attacking social programs for the poor, providing tax breaks for the rich, and giving greater freedom to corporations. The consequence, however, is to shift still more power and wealth to the big and central—the corporate world of the cloud minders— at the expense of the small and local. Ironically, the cause that many conservative voters believe themselves to be serving is that of reclaiming power for the small and local.

The terms of the political debate must be redefined to focus clearly on the real issue: the contest for power between the big and central and the small and local—between corporations and ordinary people. The time is ripe for a realignment of political alliances, which is likely to come into full flower only when the true populists realize that their enemy is not only big government but also the giant corporations that owe no allegiance to place, people, or human interest.

Economic globalization is the foundation on which the empires of the new corporate colonialism are being built. The corporate libertarians tell us that the process of economic globalization is advancing in response to immutable historical forces and that we have no choice but to adapt and learn to compete with our neighbors. It is a disingenuous claim that belies the well-organized, generously funded, and purposeful efforts by the cloud minders to dismantle national economies and build the institutions of a global market. In Part III we examine their vision and how they have gone about realizing it.

Part III

CORPORATE COLONIALISM

8

DREAMING OF GLOBAL EMPIRES

The world economy has become more integrated. But to travel is not the same as to arrive. Full integration will be reached only when there is free movement of goods, services, capital and labour and when governments treat firms equally, regardless of their nationality.

—The Economist[1]

The men who run the global corporations are the first in history with the organization, technology, money, and ideology to make a credible try at managing the world as an integrated economic unit . . . . What they are demanding in essence is the right to transcend the nation-state, and in the process, transform it.

—*Richard J. Barnet and Ronald E. Muller*[2]

THE PAST TWO DECADES HAVE SEEN the most rapid and sweeping institutional transformation in human history. It is a conscious and intentional transformation in search of a new world economic order in which business has no nationality and knows no borders. It is driven by global dreams of vast corporate empires, compliant governments, a globalized consumer monoculture, and a universal ideological commitment to corporate libertarianism. To counter the economic, social, and environmental devastation being wrought nearly everywhere by the realization of this corporate colonial vision, we must learn to recognize its message and the methods of its propagation.

THE VISION

One of the most respected and articulate visionaries of the new economic order is Akio Morita, the founder and chairman of Sony Corporation. The June 1993 *Atlantic Monthly* carried an open letter from Morita to the heads of state who were then preparing for the 1993 G-7 Summit in Tokyo. He called on them to find:

> the means of lowering *all* economic barriers between North America, Europe, and Japan—trade, investment, legal, and so forth—in order to begin creating the nucleus of a new world economic order that would include a harmonized world business system with agreed rules and procedures that transcend national boundaries. [3]

Morita went on to make clear that, in his view, it is time for all local interests, including local cultures and other symbols of local identity, to give way to the larger good that the free-market system makes possible. In his ideal world:

> Japanese rice farmers would not be able to keep their market closed, nor would Japanese *keiretsu* be allowed to exclude foreign suppliers from their production systems or imported goods from retail shelves. But neither would Americans be able to deal with perceived unfairness through methods such as unilateral tariffs. And Europeans would not be able to sit in unilateral judgment on what is or isn't a "European" car.
>
> Over time we should seek to create an environment in which the movement of goods, services, capital, technology, and people throughout North America, Europe, and Japan is truly free and unfettered. [4]

Within such a world order, complaints about restrictions on foreign access to markets would be quickly investigated and resolved by a supranational arbitration panel that would "propose specific remedies to facilitate foreign entry in areas found to be unfair or insufficiently open." [5] Governmental efforts to maintain competition through antitrust regulations would be tempered by acceptance of the needs of companies that are "sharing research and development, carrying out joint manufacturing, or forming various kinds of beneficial partnerships and alliances." Governments would coordinate exchange rates to reduce arbitrary risks from currency fluctuations incurred by global corporations as they move goods and capital freely around the world to wherever offers the greatest return. [6]

The underlying message is clear. Local people, acting through their governments, should no longer have the right to govern their own economies in the local interest. Government should respond instead to the needs of the global corporation. Morita's words echo those of George Ball, America's undersecretary of state for economic affairs, who in 1967 said to the British National Committee of the International Chamber of Commerce:

> [T]he political boundaries of nation-states are too narrow and constricted to define the scope and activities of modern business . . . . By and large, those companies that have achieved a global vision of their operations tend to opt for a world in which not only goods but all the factors of production can shift with maximum freedom.[7]

In the July 15, 1991, issue of its official newsletter, the International Monetary Fund drew on a study by DeAnne Julius, the chief economist of Shell International Petroleum Company, to stress the importance of trade agreements that would assure capital the same freedom of movement as goods. It proposed three principles:

- Foreign companies should have complete freedom of choice as to whether they participate in a local market by importing goods or by establishing a local production facility.
- Foreign firms should be governed by the same laws and be accorded the same rights in a country as domestic firms.
- Foreign firms should be allowed to undertake any activity in a country that is legally permissible for domestic firms to undertake.

Carla Hills, U.S. trade representative under the Bush administration, expressed her commitment to this goal: "We want corporations to be able to make investments overseas without being required to take a local partner, or export a given percentage of their output, to use local parts, or to meet any of a dozen other restrictions."[8] It is a view widely shared in corporate circles. An international survey of business executives conducted by the *Harvard Business Review* in 1990 found that some 12,000 respondents from twenty-five countries agreed by a substantial margin that there should be free trade between nations and the least possible protection for domestic enterprise. By a similar margin, they rejected the idea that businesses should be committed to their home country or face barriers to moving facilities to another part of the world.[9]

The corporate empire builders are rapidly making their dream a reality. From 1965 to 1992, the percentage of world economic output traded between countries rose from just under 9 percent to just under 19 percent.[10] Overall, trade has been expanding at roughly twice the rate of growth in economic output. From 1983 to 1990, worldwide foreign investment grew four times faster than world output and three times faster than world trade, leading *The Economist* to conclude that foreign investment is the area "where the most rapid progress has been made since 1980."[11] Given that as much as 70 percent of world trade is controlled by just 500 corporations,[12] and a mere 1 percent of all multinationals own half the total stock of foreign direct investment,[13] it seems that *The Economist* measures progress by the rate at which a few transnational corporations are consolidating their hold on the global economy.

CORPORATIONS BEYOND NATIONAL INTERESTS

It has become a matter of pride and principle for corporate executives to proclaim that their firms have grown beyond any national interest. Typical is the statement of Charles Exley, CEO of National Cash Register, who proudly told the *New York Times*, "National Cash Register is not a U.S. corporation. It is a world corporation that happens to be headquartered in the United States."[14] According to C. Michael Armstrong, senior vice president in charge at IBM World Trade Corporation, "IBM, to some degree, has successfully lost its American identity."[15]

Such statements are not mere posturing. IBM Japan employs 18,000 Japanese workers and is one of Japan's major computer exporters, including to the United States.[16] In 1993, General Motors Corporation of the United States announced an agreement with Toyota Motor Corporation of Japan under which General Motors would produce up to 20,000 cars a year in the United States for sale in Japan under the Toyota brand name.[17]

In truth, the question of national origin of the content of a product has become so complex that it is nearly impossible to determine with certainty. It is not evident that even the companies in question know, or particularly care, the percentage distribution of the national origin of their products' content. In a 1990 cover story, *Business Week* noted:

> Though few companies are totally untethered from their home countries, the trend toward a form of "stateless" corporation is unmistakable. The European, American, and Japanese giants heading in this direction are learning how to juggle multiple identities and multiple loyalties . . . . These world corporations are developing chameleon-like abilities to resemble insiders no matter where they operate. At the

same time, they move factories and labs "around the world without particular reference to national borders," says Unisys Corp. Chairman W. Michael Blumenthal.[18]

In other words, in their day-to-day operations, the allegiance of the world's largest corporations is purely to their own bottom lines—without regard to any national or local interest.

During the transition phase from national to transnational, many corporations styled themselves as "multinational," which meant they took on many national identities, maintaining relatively autonomous production and sales facilities in individual countries, establishing local roots and presenting themselves in each locality as a good local citizen. Globalized operations might be linked to one another, but they were as well deeply integrated into the individual local economies in which they operated. During this phase, many did function to some extent as local citizens.

As structural adjustment programs and free trade agreements rendered national economic borders increasingly irrelevant, most corporations that operate internationally became self-consciously transnational. This commonly involved building their operations around globally integrated supplier networks. For example, when Otis Elevator set about to create an advanced elevator system, it contracted out the design of the motor drives to Japan, the door system to France, the electronics to Germany, and small geared components to Spain. System integration was handled from the United States.[19] The goal is to eliminate considerations of nationality in an effort to maximize the economies of centralized global procurement.[20]

Although a transnational corporation may choose to claim local citizenship when that posture suits its purpose, local commitments are temporary. Only when asking its "home government" for special tax breaks, subsidies, or governmental representation in negotiations that bear on its global marketing and investment interests is a transnational corporation likely to wrap itself in a national flag and profess its deep commitment to strengthening "national" competitiveness.

The Economist has suggested that the appropriate strategy for those who own the rights to products or processes in a fully globalized economy is not to produce anything. Instead, they should simply license rights to these products and processes for an amount sufficient to yield the same profits they would have made if they had produced the products locally or for export.[21] In other worlds, those who hold monopoly control of patented technologies should not be expected to produce anything—they should simply collect the profits.

This is a far cry from Adam Smith's ideal of a competitive market economy in which the returns go to small producers.

The more protected individual markets are, the more a global firm is forced to function in a multinational mode, producing locally in each setting to achieve access to that market and integrating itself into the local economy. As local settings are opened to the global economy, it becomes possible, and highly profitable, for a firm to take advantage of the differences between localities with regard to wages, market potential, employment standards, taxes, environmental regulations, local facilities, and human resources. This means arranging its global operations to produce products where costs are lowest, sell them in more affluent markets, and shift the resulting profits to where tax rates are least burdensome. The ability to shift production from one country to another weakens the bargaining power of any given locality and shifts the balance of power from the local human interest to the global corporate interest.

The more readily a firm is able to move capital, goods, technology, and personnel freely among localities in search of such advantage, the greater the competitive pressure on localities to subsidize investors by absorbing their social, environmental, and other production costs. The larger and more open the markets, the greater the profit opportunity for firms that are sufficiently large and nimble to capitalize on the differences—and the greater the larger firms' competitive advantage over smaller local firms that remain rooted in a particular community and play by its rules.

A recent study of multinational enterprises (MNEs) by the Office of Technology Assessment of the U.S. Congress observed:

> [B]ecause they span national borders, many MNEs are less concerned with advancing national goals than with pursuing objectives internal to the firm—principally growth, profits, proprietary technology, strategic alliances, return on investment, and market power .... The U.S. economy (or any other, for that matter) cannot remain competitive unless MNEs that sell and conduct business in America also contribute to its research and technology base, employment, manufacturing capabilities, and capital resources ....
>
> The interests of all nations ought to be fairly straightforward—quality jobs, a rising standard of living, technological and industrial development, ensured rights of workers and consumers, and a high-quality environment at home and globally .... As compared to nations, the interests of MNEs are far more situation-oriented and linked to opportunity.[22]

In general, Japanese firms have been more oriented toward a Japanese national interest than have American firms, which have taken the lead in rejecting national interests in favor of a more narrowly defined corporate interest. European firms tend to fall somewhere in between. The clear trend, however, is toward corporate transnationalism.

GOVERNMENTS IN THE SERVICE OF CONSUMERISM

Kenichi Ohmae, managing director of McKinsey & Company Japan, is another respected guru of the new economic order. In his widely read book *The Borderless World*, Ohmae tells national governments that clinging to their traditional roles as managers of national economies is futile, because national economies no longer exist. For example, when governments attempt to use traditional interest rate and money supply instruments to stimulate a nonexistent national economy, the jobs that result may well be created in other countries that experience a resulting increase in demand for their exports. If a government raises interest rates to control inflation, foreign funds will gush in from abroad and render the policy meaningless.[23]

Globalization has rendered many of the political roles of government obsolete as well. Companies with globalized operations routinely and effortlessly sidestep governmental restrictions based on old assumptions about national economies and foreign policy. For example, Honda circumvents restrictions on importing Japanese cars into Taiwan, South Korea, and Israel by shipping Honda vehicles to these countries from its U.S. plant in Ohio. When Japan opened bidding on new telecommunications facilities to U.S. manufacturers, Canada's Northern Telecom Ltd. moved many of its production facilities to the United States so that it could win Japanese contracts as a U.S. company. When U.S. President Ronald Reagan ordered economic sanctions against Libya in January 1986, Brown & Root, Inc., a Houston engineering concern, simply shifted a $100 million contract for work on Libya's Great Man-Made River Project to its British subsidiary.[24]

The appropriate response for the bureaucrats, in Ohmae's view, is to yield to the inevitable—accept the reality that government is obsolete, get out of the way, and let goods and money flow freely in response to market forces:

> [M]ultinational companies are truly the servants of demanding consumers around the world . . . . When governments are slow to grasp the fact that their role has changed from protecting their people and

their natural resource base from outside economic threats to ensuring that their people have the widest range of choice among the best and the cheapest goods and services from around the world—when, that is, governments still think and act like the saber-rattling mercantilist ruling powers of centuries past—they discourage investment and impoverish their people. Worse, they commit their people to isolation from an emerging world economy, which, in turn effectively dooms them to a downward spiral of frustrated hopes and industrial stagnation. . . . [As] recent events in Eastern Europe have shown, the people—as consumers and as citizens—will no longer tolerate this antiquated role of government.[25]

Ohmae counsels governments to actively join global corporations in assuring consumers that they should not be concerned about where a product is produced. He supports his argument by pointing out that production costs are typically only about 25 percent of the end-user price; the major contribution to a product's price comes increasingly from marketing and support functions. "Such functions as distribution, warehousing, financing, retail marketing, systems integration, and services are all legitimate parts of the business system and can create as many, and often more jobs than simply manufacturing operations."[26] In effect, Ohmae is arguing that a country can meet its employment needs by concentrating on marketing and consuming goods that are produced elsewhere.

The United States has already largely embraced Ohmae's vision as the organizing principle of its economy. Foreign producers now supply 30 percent of the goods, other than oil, sold in the U.S. domestic market—up from 15 percent at the beginning of the 1980s.[27] Meanwhile, the United States became the world's leading international debtor nation, while suffering rising unemployment and falling wages.

If people were indeed only consumers, there might be merit to Ohmae's argument. But people have other roles and values that lead to real and legitimate concerns about such matters as where a good is produced and what rules will govern local economic affairs. The human interest and the corporate interest differ.

COMMUNITY VERSUS CORPORATE INTERESTS

The global economy has created a dynamic in which competition among localities has become as real as competition among firms. Moore Country, South

Carolina, won a competitiveness bid in the 1960s and 1970s when it lured a number of large manufacturers from the unionized industrial regions of the northeastern United States with promises of tax breaks, lax environmental regulations, and compliant labor. Proctor Silex was one of the companies attracted. Later, when Proctor Silex expanded its local plant, Moore County floated a $5.5 million municipal bond to finance necessary sewer and water hookups—even though nearby residents were living without running water and other basic public services. Then in 1990, the company decided that Mexico offered more competitive terms and moved again. It left behind 800 unemployed Moore County workers, drums of buried toxic waste, and the public debts the county had incurred to finance public facilities in the company's behalf.[28]

Americans need go no farther than the Mexican border to get an idea of what it now takes to be globally competitive. The *maquiladoras* are assembly plants in the free-trade zone on the Mexican side of the border with the United States. The zone has become a powerful magnet, attracting many U.S. companies, including General Electric, Ford, General Motors, GTE Sylvania, RCA, Westinghouse, and Honeywell, that are seeking low-cost locations in which to produce for the U.S. market.[29] Growth has been explosive, from 620 *maquiladora* plants employing 119,550 workers in 1980 to 2,200 factories employing more than 500,000 Mexican workers in 1992. Many feature the most modern high-productivity equipment and technology. Although the productivity of Mexican workers who work in modern plants is comparable to that of U.S. workers, average hourly wages in *maquiladora* factories are just $1.64, compared with an average manufacturing wage of $16.17 in the United States.

To maintain the kind of conditions transnational corporations prefer, the Mexican government has denied workers the right to form independent labor unions and has held wage increases far below productivity increases. In the summer of 1992, more than 14,000 Mexican workers at a Volkswagen plant turned down a contract negotiated by their government-dominated labor union. The company fired them all, and a Mexican court upheld the company's action. In 1987, in the midst of a bitter two-month strike in Mexico, Ford Motor Company tore up its union contract, fired 3,400 workers, and cut wages by 45 percent. When the workers rallied around dissident labor leaders, gunmen hired by the official government-dominated union shot workers at random in the factory.

Loose enforcement of environmental regulations is another attraction. An investigative team from the U.S. General Accounting Office reported to

Congress that all six newly opened U.S. plants it inspected in Mexico were operating without the required environmental licenses. Other studies have found evidence of massive toxic dumping in the *maquiladora* zones, polluting rivers, groundwater, and soils, and causing severe health problems among workers and deformities among babies born to young women working in the zone.

Since investors are exempted from property taxes on their factories, public infrastructure—roads, water, housing, and sewage lines—is grossly inadequate. The workers live in shantytowns that stretch for miles. The dwellings are constructed of scrap materials and have no sewer systems; most have no running water. Worker families commonly store water in discarded barrels—the markings show that they once contained toxic chemicals.

According to Professor Valdes-Villalva of the Colegio de la Frontera Norte in Juarez:

> We have begun to see more fourteen-year-olds in the plants. Because of the intensive work it entails, there is a constant burnout. If they've been here three or four years, workers lose efficiency. They begin to have problems with eyesight. They begin to have allergies and kidney problems. They are less productive.[30]

Mexican workers, including children, are heroes of the new economic order in the eyes of corporate libertarians—sacrificing their health, lives, and futures on the altar of global competition.

Not all global corporations locate in Mexico. In 1993, South Carolina was again being praised by business publications for its aggressive efforts to win the favor of international investors. Its major coup was a successful bid for a new BMW auto plant. BMW had spent three years assessing offers from 250 localities in ten countries before deciding to place its $400 million facility in South Carolina. According to *Business Week*, company officials were attracted by the temperate climate, year-round golf, and the availability of a number of mansions at affordable prices. They also liked the region's cheap labor, low taxes, and limited union activity. When BMW indicated that it favored a 1,000-acre tract on which a large number of middle-class homes were already located, the state spent $36.6 million to buy the 140 properties and leased the site back to the company at $1 a year. The state also picked up the costs of recruiting, screening, and training workers for the new plant and raised an additional $2.8 million from private sources to send newly hired engineers for training in Germany. The total cost to the South Carolina taxpayers for these and other subsidies to attract BMW will be $130 million over thirty years.[31]

This is an all-too-typical example of how taxpayers are subsidizing the production costs of major global companies. In 1957, corporations in the United States provided 45 percent of local property tax revenues. By 1987, their share had dropped to about 16 percent.[32] A 1994 study by the Progressive Policy Institute of the Democratic Leadership Conference identified what it considered to be unjustified subsidies and tax benefits extended to corporations in the United States amounting to $111 billion over five years.[33] The trend is clear. The largest corporations are paying less taxes and receiving more subsidies.

This is the globally competitive market at work, forcing localities to absorb private costs to increase private profits. The game of global competition is rigged. It pits companies against people in a contest that the people almost always lose.

A serious reading of the financial press and the treatises of the architects of globalization suggests that the ideal world of the global dreamers can be characterized as one in which:

- The world's money, technology, and markets are controlled and managed by gigantic global corporations;
- A common consumer culture unifies all people in a shared quest for material gratification;
- There is perfect global competition among workers and localities to offer their services to investors at the most advantageous terms;
- Corporations are free to act solely on the basis of profitability without regard to national or local consequences;
- Relationships, both individual and corporate, are defined entirely by the market; and
- There are no loyalties to place and community.

Embellished by promises of limitless and effortless affluence, the vision of a global economy has an entrancing appeal. Beneath its beguiling surface, however, we find a modern form of enchantment, a siren song created by the skilled image makers of Madison Avenue, enticing societies to weaken community to free the market, eliminate livelihoods to create wealth, and destroy life to increase unneeded and often unsatisfying consumption. Contrary to what the corporate libertarians would have us believe, the seductive melodies that beckon us are not produced by inexorable historical forces beyond human influence. They come from the well-rehearsed human voices of Stratos dwellers calling out to us from their city in the clouds across a great gap that most of humanity can never cross.

9

BUILDING ELITE CONSENSUS

We must find new lands from which we can easily obtain raw materials and at the same time exploit the cheap slave labour that is available from the natives of the colonies. The colonies would also provide a dumping grounds for the surplus goods produced in our factories.
—Cecil Rhodes, "founder" of Rhodesia[1]

Strong growth in the poorer parts of the world will be needed to sustain enough growth in the West to maintain adequate levels of employment and to enable Western governments to deal with their pressing social problems.
—Felix Rohatyn[2]

IT IS HELPFUL TO UNDERSTAND how the corporate globalization agenda has been crafted and carried forward largely outside the public discourse. It is not a matter of a small elite group meeting in secret to craft a master plan for taking over the world. It works much more like any networking or shared culture-building process out of which alliances among individuals and groups emerge and evolve. There is no conspiracy, though in practical terms, the consequences are much as if there were.

In this chapter, we take a brief look at each of three major forums that have served the consensus-building process in support of economic globalization: the Council on Foreign Relations, the Bilderberg, and the Trilateral Commission. They are not the only organizations important to this process. But they are distinctive in their effectiveness in bringing together key individuals from government, business, the media, and academia to create a consensus that aligns our most powerful institutions with the economic globalization agenda.

VISIONS OF AMERICAN HEGEMONY

The roots of the current drive toward economic globalization go back to the trauma of the depression that preceded World War II. America's policy elites were deeply concerned about ensuring that nothing similar would ever recur. There were two prevailing ideas as to how this might be accomplished. One would have required major reforms of the U.S. economy, including strong governmental intervention in the market. The other depended on ensuring the domestic American economy sufficient access to foreign markets and raw materials to sustain the continuous expansion required to maintain full employment without market reforms. The latter was by far the more popular alternative among those in power, including a small elite group of foreign policy planners associated with the Council on Foreign Relations.

A meeting ground for powerful members of the U.S. corporate and foreign policy establishments, the Council on Foreign Relations styles itself as a forum for the airing of opposing views—an incubator of leaders and ideas. Its activities are organized around dinner meetings and study programs for its members—often involving influential world figures or foreign policy thinkers—in settings that are conducive to candid, off-the-record discussion. It similarly styles its influential *Foreign Affairs* journal as a forum for the open debate of significant foreign policy issues.[3]

The portion of the Council's history that is of particular interest to our present inquiry began on September 12, 1939, less than two weeks after the outbreak of World War II. On that day, Walter Mallory, executive director of the Council, and Hamilton Armstrong, the editor of *Foreign Affairs*, met in Washington with George Messersmith, assistant secretary of state and a member of the Council. They outlined a long-range planning project to be carried out by the Council in close collaboration with the State Department on long-term problems of the war and plans for peace. Several war and peace studies groups composed of foreign policy experts would produce confidential expert recommendations for President Franklin D. Roosevelt,[4] who, during his tenure as governor of New York, had lived in a town house next door to the Council's headquarters. Relations between Roosevelt and the Council continued to be close. At that point in history, the State Department lacked the funds and personnel to undertake such studies, so its leadership accepted the Council's proposal. By the end of the war, the partnership had produced 682 confidential memoranda for the government, with funding provided in part from the Rockefeller Foundation.[5]

The planners anticipated that the defeat of Germany and Japan and the wartime devastation of Europe would leave the United States in an undisputed position to dominate the postwar economy. They believed the more open that economy was to trade and foreign investment, the more readily the United States would be able to dominate it. Working from that logic, the plans produced by the State Department-Council planning groups placed a substantial emphasis on creating an institutional framework for an open global economy.[6]

In April 1941, a confidential memo from the Council's Economic and Financial Group provided the government with the following suggestion on how to frame the public presentation of U.S. objectives for propaganda purposes during the war:

> If war aims are stated which seem to be concerned solely with Anglo-American imperialism, they will offer little to people in the rest of the world, and will be vulnerable to Nazi counter promises. Such aims would also strengthen the most reactionary elements in the United States and the British Empire. The interests of other peoples should be stressed, not only those of Europe, but also of Asia, Africa, and Latin America. This would have a better propaganda effect.[7]

Memorandum E-B34, issued by the Council to the president and the State Department on July 24, 1941, outlined the concept of a "Grand Area." This was the area of the world that the United States would need to dominate economically and militarily to ensure materials for its industries with the "fewest possible stresses."[8] The minimum necessary Grand Area would consist of most of the non-German world. Its preferred scope would consist of the Western Hemisphere, the United Kingdom, the remainder of the British Commonwealth and Empire, the Dutch East Indies, China, and Japan. The concept outlined in the memo involved working for economic integration within the largest available core area and then expanding outward to weave other areas into the core, as circumstances allowed.

This same memorandum called for the creation of worldwide financial institutions for stabilizing currencies and facilitating programs of capital investment in the development of backward and underdeveloped regions.[9] This recommendation aligned with similar proposals being put forward by Harry White at the U.S. Department of Treasury that led to establishment of the International Monetary Fund (IMF), to be responsible for keeping currencies stable and liquid to facilitate trade, and the International Bank for Reconstruction and Development (IBRD), commonly known as the World Bank, to facilitate capital investments in "backward and underdeveloped" regions and open them for development.[10]

The subsequent U.S. initiative on behalf of economic globalization worked from two basic premises. First, in order to maintain the existing capitalist economic system, the United States must have access to the resources and markets of much of the world so that it could create a sufficient export surplus to maintain full employment at home. Second, by spreading the U.S. economic model throughout the world within a globalized economy, the world would become united in peace and prosperity. Apparently, little note was taken of the evident contradiction that if maintaining the prosperity of a U.S.-style economy required gaining control of most of the world's resources and markets, it would be impossible for other countries to replicate the U.S. experience. Nor is it evident that much thought was given to the contradiction of financing industrial exports to low-income countries with international development loans that could be repaid by these countries only if they developed export surpluses with the countries that had initially extended the loans.

If such questions were raised, they were quickly pushed into the background by the urgency of the war effort and the powerful interests the vision served. Furthermore, much as the U.S. foreign policy planners anticipated, the United States was in the driver's seat immediately following World War II. America's foreign policy elites were gripped by a sense of America's newfound power and responsibility in the world. A bit of hubris was perhaps inevitable.

THE NORTH ATLANTIC ALLIANCE

Europe's emergence from the ashes of war, the decision to form a European political and economic union, and the West's confrontation with the communist empire of the Soviet Union created an imperative to expand the earlier hegemonic U.S. vision to embrace the idea of a North Atlantic community that would provide the leadership in a Western-dominated global system. This created an obvious need for mechanisms through which the policies of the North Atlantic countries might be coordinated. The formal mechanisms, such as the North Atlantic Treaty Organization (NATO) formed in 1949 and the Organization for Economic Cooperation and Development (OECD) established in 1961 are well known to the public.

Less known is a powerful but unofficial group with no acknowledged membership known simply as the Bilderberg, named for the Hotel de Bilderberg of Oosterbeek, Holland, at which a group of North American and

European leaders first met in May 1954. Subsequent Bilderberg meetings and the relationships they nurtured played a significant role in advancing the European union and shaping a consensus among leaders of the Atlantic nations.[11] Participants include heads of state, other leading politicians, key industrialists and financiers, and an assortment of intellectuals, trade unionists, diplomats, and influential representatives of the press with demonstrated sympathy for establishment views. One Bilderberg insider observed that "today there are very few figures among governments on both sides of the Atlantic who have not attended at least one of these meetings.[12]

U.S. President Eisenhower regularly sent Gabriel Hauge, his White House domestic policy chief and former director and treasurer of the Council on Foreign Relations, as his personal representative to Bilderberg meetings. President Kennedy appointed Bilderberg alumni to virtually every senior position in his State Department—Secretary of State Dean Rusk, Undersecretary of State George W. Ball, George McGhee, Walter Rostow, McGeorge Bundy, and Arthur Dean.[13]

Joseph Retinger, a founder and permanent secretary of Bilderberg until his death in 1960 and a leading proponent of European unification, explained that the Bilderberg meetings provided a freedom in discussing difficult issues that more official forums could not provide:

> Even if a participant is a member of a government, a leader of a political party, an official of an international organization or of a commercial concern, he does not commit his government, his party or his organization by anything he may say. . . . Bilderberg does not make policy. Its aim is to reduce differences of opinion and resolve conflicting trends and to further understanding, if not agreement, by hearing and considering various points of view and trying to find a common approach to major problems. Direct action has therefore never been contemplated, the object being to draw the attention of people in responsible positions to Bilderberg's findings.[14]

TRILATERALISM

The subsequent emergence of Japan as a third economic force within the orbit of the West led to the idea of a trilateral alliance that would merge the economic interests of three regional partners: North America (the United States and Canada), Western Europe, and Japan. This idea became a frequent topic of discussion at Bilderberg meetings. It was decided to create a new forum that included the Japanese and had a more formal structure than Bilderberg.

In 1973, the Trilateral Commission was formed by David Rockefeller, chairman of Chase Manhattan Bank, and Zbigniew Brzezinski, who served as the Commission's director and coordinator until 1977, when he became national security advisor to U.S. President Jimmy Carter.[15] The Trilateral Commission describes itself as follows:

> The Commission's members are about 325 distinguished citizens, with a variety of leadership responsibilities from these three regions. When the first triennium of the Trilateral Commission was launched in 1973, the most immediate purpose was to draw together—at a time of considerable friction among governments—the highest level unofficial group possible to look together at the common problems facing our three areas. At a deeper level, there was a sense that the United States was no longer in such a singular leadership position as it had been in earlier post-World War II years, and that a more shared form of leadership—including Europe and Japan in particular—would be needed for the international system to navigate successfully the major challenges of the coming years. These purposes continue to inform the Commission's work.[16]

In contrast to Bilderberg, which is known for its secrecy, the Trilateral Commission is a more transparent organization that readily distributes its membership and publication lists to anyone who calls its publicly listed phone number, and its publications are available for sale to the public. Whereas Bilderberg includes many heads of state, other top government officials, and royalty, members of the Trilateral Commission who assume high level administrative positions in government resign from the Commission for the period of their tenure.[17]

The collective power of the Commission's members is impressive. They include the heads of four of the world's five largest nonbanking transnational corporations (ITOCHU, Sumitomo, Mitsubishi, and Mitsui & Co.); top officials of five of the world's six largest international banks (Sumitomo Bank, Fuji Bank, Sakura Bank, Sanwa Bank, and Mitsubishi Bank); and heads of major media organizations (Japan Times, Ltd.; Le Poit; Times Mirror Co.; the Washington Post Co.; Cable News Network [CNN]; and Time Warner).

U.S. Presidents Jimmy Carter, George Bush, and Bill Clinton were all members of the Trilateral Commission, as was Thomas Foley, former Speaker of the U.S. House of Representatives. Many key members of the Carter administration were both Bilderbergers and Trilateral Commission members, including Vice President Mondale, Secretary of State Vance, National Security Advisor Brzezinski, and Treasury Secretary Blumenthal.[18] Former members of the Trilateral Commission who went on to hold key positions under the Clinton administration include Warren Christopher, secretary of state; Bruce Babbitt, secretary of the interior; Henry Cisneros, secretary of housing and urban development; Alan Greenspan, chairman of the U.S. Federal Reserve System; Joseph Nye Jr., chairman of the National Intelligence Council, Central Intelligence Agency; Donna E. Shalala, secretary of health and human services; Clifton Wharton Jr., deputy secretary of state; and Peter Tarnoff, undersecretary of state for political affairs.[19]

Although the Commission publishes its own position papers, its views are conveyed through many outlets not necessarily associated with it. The trilateralist vision of Sony chairman Akio Morita that was published in *Atlantic Monthly* and discussed in the previous chapter is an example. At the time he published the article, Morita was the Japanese chairman of the Trilateral Commission.

It is important to note that the Council on Foreign Relations, the Bilderberg, and the Trilateral Commission bring together heads of competing corporations and leaders of competing national political parties for closed-door discussions and consensus-building processes that the public never sees. Although the participants may believe that they represent a broad spectrum of intersectoral and even international perspectives, in truth it is a closed and exclusive process limited to elite Stratos dwellers. Participants are predominantly male, wealthy, from Northern industrial countries, and, except for the Japanese on the Trilateral Commission, Caucasian. Other voices are excluded.

The resulting narrowness of perspective is evident in the publications of the Trilateral Commission. They are written by seasoned and thoughtful professionals, and a diversity of views is presented. Yet they all accept without question the ideological premises of corporate libertarianism. The benefits of economic integration and a harmonization of the tax, regulatory, and other policies of the trilateral countries—and ultimately of all countries—are assumed as an article of faith. The debate centers on how, not whether.

No note is taken of the fact that harmonizing standards—which necessarily means setting standards—can be accomplished only through international negotiations, which by their nature must be carried out in secret by the administrative branches of governments. Thus, in the absence of an elected international parliament, a call to harmonize standards is a call to take decisions regarding the standards by which businesses will operate out of the hands of democratically elected national legislative bodies and pass them to the unelected bureaucrats who represent governments in international negotiations. Such a situation lends itself especially well to cozy insider deal making, especially when these bureaucrats come from the same elite circles as members of the Trilateral Commission. For example, Carla Hills, who as U.S. trade representative under President George Bush played a key role in negotiating the General Agreement on Tariffs and Trade (GATT) that established the new World Trade Organization, was a member of the Trilateral Commission.

The fact that George Bush and Bill Clinton were both members of the Trilateral Commission makes it easy to understand why there was such a seamless transition from the Republican Bush administration to the Democratic Clinton administration with regard to the U.S. commitment to pass the North American Free Trade Agreement (NAFTA) and GATT. Clinton's leadership in advancing what many progressives thought to be a Bush agenda on these agreements won him high marks from his colleagues on the Trilateral Commission but seriously alienated major elements of his core constituency, who had looked to him to provide a less corporatist view of the trade agenda. On this most fundamental of issues, the electoral system gave the voters only the illusion of choice.

The policy actions being advanced by the elite consensus constitute an increasingly effective attack on the institutions of democracy, the very purpose of which is to prevent a small inside elite from capturing control of the instruments of governance. Their dominance of the policy debate largely precludes any discussion of alternatives to prevailing assumptions.

Corporate globalization is neither in the human interest nor inevitable. It is axiomatic that political power aligns with economic power. The larger the economic unit, the larger its dominant players, and the more political power becomes concentrated in the largest corporations. The greater the political power of corporations and those aligned with them, the less the political power of the people, and the less meaningful democracy becomes. There is an alternative: to localize economies, disperse economic power, and bring democracy closer to the people. However, networks and alliances made up exclusively of Stratos dwellers are unlikely to articulate and pursue such an alternative. To the contrary, as we shall see in the next chapter, the Stratos dwellers are mobilizing the full resources of the world's largest corporations behind an effort to consolidate global corporate rule.

10

BUYING OUT DEMOCRACY

Funds generated by business (by which I mean profits, funds in business foundations and contributions from individual businessmen) must rush by multimillions to the aid of liberty . . . to funnel desperately needed funds to scholars, social scientists, writers, and journalists who understand the relationship between political and economic liberty.
—William Simon, former secretary of the U.S. Treasury Department[1]

Before NAFTA we thought corporations could only buy Southern governments. Now we see they also buy Northern governments.
—Ignacio Peon Escalante, Mexican Action Network on Free Trade

U.S. CORPORATIONS ENTERED THE 1970S besieged by a rebellious anticonsumerist youth culture, a mushrooming environmental and product safety movement, and a serious economic challenge from Asia. Not only was their dream of global hegemony in tatters, they even risked losing control of their own home turf. In response, they mobilized their collective political resources to regain control of the political and cultural agenda. Their methods included a combination of sophisticated marketing techniques, old-fashioned vote buying, funding for ideologically aligned intellectuals, legal action, and many of the same grassroots mobilization techniques that environmental and consumer activists had used against the corporations during the 1960s and 1970s. Their campaigns were well funded, involved sophisticated strategies, and were professionally organized. The major goals were deregulation, economic globalization, and the limitation of corporate liability—in short, to enlarge corporate rights and reduce corporate responsibilities. And their campaign continues in full force.

MOBILIZING CORPORATE POLITICAL RESOURCES

In 1971, the U.S. Chamber of Commerce sought the advice of Virginia attorney and future Supreme Court Justice Lewis Powell about the problems facing the business community. Powell produced a memorandum, "Attack on American Free Enterprise System," that warned of an assault by environmentalists, consumer activists, and others who "propagandize against the system, seeking insidiously and constantly to sabotage it." He argued that it was time "for the wisdom, ingenuity, and resources of American business to be marshaled against those who would destroy it."[2] This set the stage for an organized effort by a powerful coalition for business groups and ideologically compatible foundations to align the U.S. political and legal system with their ideological vision.

Among Powell's recommendations was a proposal that the business community create a business-organized and -funded legal center to promote the general interests of business in the nation's courts. This led to the formation of the Pacific Legal Foundation (PLF) in 1973. Housed in the Sacramento Chamber of Commerce building, it was the first of a number of corporate-sponsored "public-interest" law firms dedicated to promoting the interests of their sponsoring corporations.[3] The PLF specialized in defending business interests against "clean air and water legislation, the closing of federal wilderness areas to oil and gas exploration, workers' rights, and corporate taxation." Some 80 percent of its income was from corporations or corporate foundations.[4]

In a 1980 speech, PLF's managing attorney Raymond Momboisse turned reality on its head by attacking environmentalists for their "selfish, self-centered motivation . . .; their ability to conceal their true aims in lofty sounding motives of public interest; their indifference to the injury they inflict on the masses of mankind; their ability to manipulate the law and the media; and, most of all, their power to inflict monumental harm on society."[5]

Business interests funded the establishment of law and economics programs in leading law schools to support scholarly research advancing the premise that the unregulated marketplace produces the most efficient—and thereby the most just—society. Business funded all-expense-paid seminars at prestigious universities such as George Mason and Yale to introduce sitting judges to these economic principles and their application to jurisprudence.[6]

Before the 1970s, business interests were represented by old-fashioned corporate lobbying organizations with straightforward names: Beer Institute,

National Coal Association, Chamber of Commerce, or American Petroleum Institute. As aggressive public-interest groups succeeded in mobilizing broad-based citizen pressures on Congress, business decided that another approach was needed.

Corporations began to create their own "citizen" organizations with names and images that were carefully constructed to mask their corporate and sponsorship and their true purpose. The National Wetlands Coalition, which features a logo of a duck flying blissfully over a swamp, was sponsored by oil and gas companies and real estate developers to fight for the easing of restrictions on the conversion of wetlands into drilling sites and shopping malls. Corporate-sponsored Consumer Alert fights government regulations of product safety. Keep America Beautiful attempts to give its sponsors, the bottling industry, a green image by funding anti-litter campaigns, while those same sponsors actively fight mandatory recycling legislation. The strategy is to convince the public that litter is the responsibility of consumers—not the packaging industry.[7]

The views of these and similar industry-sponsored groups—thirty-six of them are documented in *Masks of Deception: Corporate Front Groups in America*—are regularly reported in the press as the views of citizen advocates. The sole reason for their existence is to convince the public that the corporate interest *is* the public interest and that labor, health, and the environment are "special" interests. The top funders of such groups include Dow Chemical, Exxon, Chevron USA, Mobil, DuPont, Ford, Phillip Morris, Pfizer, Anheuser-Busch, Monsanto, Procter & Gamble, Phillips Petroleum, AT&T, and Arco.[8]

Business interests funded the formation of new conservative policy think tanks such as The Heritage Foundation and revived lethargic pro-establishment think tanks such as the American Enterprise Institute, which experienced a tenfold increase in its budget.[9] In 1978, the Institute for Educational Affairs was formed to match corporate funders with sympathetic scholars producing research studies supporting corporate views on economic freedom.[10]

In 1970, only a handful of the Fortune 500 companies had public affairs offices in Washington; by 1980, more than 80 percent did. In 1974, labor unions accounted for half of all political action committee (PAC) money. By 1980, the unions accounted for less than a fourth of this funding.[11] With the inauguration of U.S. President Ronald Reagan in 1981, the ideological alliance of corporate libertarians consolidated its control over the instruments of power.

Although many of those involved in these campaigns truly believe that they are acting in the public interest, what we are seeing is a frontal assault on democratic pluralism to advance the ideological agenda of corporate libertarianism. Though advanced in the name of freedom and democracy, this massive abuse of corporate power mocks them both.

BUILDING BUSINESS LOBBIES

Business roundtables are national associations of the chief executive officers (CEOs) of the largest transnational corporations. Whereas more inclusive business organizations such as national chambers of commerce and national associations of manufacturers include both large and small firms representing many different interests and perspectives, the members of business roundtables are all large transnational corporations firmly aligned with the economic globalization agenda.

The first Business Roundtable was formed in the United States in 1972. Its 200 members include the heads of forty-two of the fifty largest Fortune 500 U.S. industrial corporations, seven of the eight largest U.S. commercial banks, seven of the ten largest U.S. insurance companies, five of the seven largest U.S. retailers, seven of the eight largest U.S. transportation companies, and nine of the eleven largest U.S. utilities. In this forum, the CEO of DuPont chemical company sits with the CEOs of his three major rivals: Dow, Occidental Petroleum, and Monsanto. The head of General Motors sits with the heads of Ford and Chrysler—and so on with each major industry. In this forum, the heads of the world's largest U.S.-based corporations put aside their competitive differences to reach a consensus on issues of social and economic policy in America. The U.S. Business Roundtable describes itself as:

> an association of chief executive officers who examine public issues that affect the economy and develop positions which seek to reflect sound economic and social principles. Established in 1972, the Roundtable was founded in the belief that business executives should take an increased role in the continuing debates about public policy.
>
> The Roundtable believes that the basic interests of business closely parallel the interests of the American people, who are directly involved as consumers, employees, investors and suppliers .... Member selection reflects the goal of having representation varied by category of business and by geographic location. Thus, the members, some 200 chief executive officers of companies in all fields, can present a cross section of thinking on national issues.[12]

The Roundtable, surely one of America's most exclusive and least diverse membership organizations, has an unusually narrow notion of what constitutes a "cross section" of thinking on national issues. With few, if any, exceptions, its membership is limited to white males over fifty years of age whose annual compensation averages more than 170 times the U.S. per capita gross national product.[13] Its members head corporations that disavow a commitment to national interests and stand to gain substantially from economic globalization. Once positions are defined, the Roundtable organizes aggressive campaigns to gain their political acceptance, including personal visits by its member CEOs to individual senators and representatives.

The Roundtable took an especially active role in campaigning for the North American Free Trade Agreement (NAFTA). Recognizing that the public might see free trade as a special-interest issue if touted by an exclusive club of the country's 200 largest transnationals, the Roundtable created a front organization, USA*NAFTA, that enrolled some 2,300 U.S. corporations and associations as members. Although USA*NAFTA claimed to represent a broad constituency, every one of its state captains was a corporate member of the Business Roundtable. All but four Roundtable members enjoyed privileged access to the NAFTA negotiation process through representation on advisory committees to the U.S. trade representative. Roundtable members bombarded Americans with assurances through editorials, op-ed pieces, news releases, and radio and television commentaries that NAFTA would provide them with high-paying jobs, stop immigration from Mexico, and raise environmental standards.

Nine of the USA*NAFTA state captains (Allied Signal, AT&T, General Electric, General Motors, Phelps Dodge, United Technologies, IBM, ITT, and TRW) were among the U.S. corporations that, according to the Interhemispheric Resource Center, had already shipped up to 180,000 jobs to Mexico during the twelve years prior to the passage of NAFTA. Some among the NAFTA captains were corporations that had been cited for violating worker rights in Mexico and for failing to comply with worker safety standards. Many were leading polluters in the United States and had exported to or produced in Mexico products that were banned in the United States.[14]

DEMOCRACY FOR HIRE

Washington D.C.'s major growth industry consists of for-profit public-relations firms and business-sponsored policy institutes engaged in producing facts, opinion pieces, expert analyses, opinion polls, and direct-mail and tele-phone solicitation to create "citizen" advocacy and public-image-building cam-paigns on demand for corporate clients. William Greider calls it "democracy for hire."[15] Burson Marsteller—the world's largest public-relations firm, with net 1992 billings of $204 million—worked for Exxon during the *Exxon Valdez* oil spill and for Union Carbide during the Bhopal disaster. The top fifty pub-lic-relations firms billed over $1.7 billion in 1991.[16]

In the United States, the 170,000 public-relations employees engaged in manipulating news, public opinion, and public policy to serve the interests of paying clients now outnumber actual news reporters by about 40,000—and the gap is growing. These firms will organize citizen letter-writing campaigns, provide paid operatives posing as "housewives" to present corporate views in public meetings, and place favorable news items and op-ed pieces in the press. A 1990 study found that almost 40 percent of the news content in a typical U.S. newspaper originates from public-relations press releases, story memos, and suggestions. According to the *Columbia Journalism Review*, more than half of *The Wall Street Journal*'s news stories are based solely on press releases.[17] The distinction between advertising space and news space grows less distinct with each passing day.

While the Republicans have long been known as the party of money, the Demo-cratic Party was historically the party of the people, with strong representa-tion of working-class and minority interests. The Democrats once depended heavily on their strong grassroots political organization—on people more than money—to deliver the votes on election day. These structures in turn forced politicians to maintain some contact with the grassroots and ensured a degree of local accountability. Ties to the party were strong. With the growing role of television in American life and the decline in the U.S. labor movement, costly television-based media campaigns have become increasingly central in decid-ing election outcomes. As a consequence, the grassroots organization that was once the foundation of the Democratic Party structure has disintegrated, caus-ing it to lose its populist moorings and leaving those who once constituted its political base feeling unrepresented.

With the breakdown of this structure, those who run for office under the Democratic Party banner have become increasingly dependent on developing their own fund-raising organizations. This has left them more vulnerable to the influence of monied interests and greatly strengthened the hand of big business in setting policy agendas of both parties. William Greider maintains that the policy direction of the Democratic Party is now set largely by six Washington law firms that specialize in selling political influence to monied clients and in raising money for Democratic politicians. Working closely with Republicans as well, these firms are in the business of brokering power to whomever will pay their fees.[18] This is the sorry state of American democracy.

The Republican Party has responded most handily to the new circumstances, expertly adapting sophisticated techniques of mass marketing to the task of winning elections. With these techniques, it has accomplished the improbable task of exploiting the alienation of powerless citizens to build a populist political base in support of an elitist agenda.

> As men of commerce, Republicans naturally understood marketing better than Democrats, and they applied what they knew about selling products to politics with none of the awkward hesitation that inhibited old-style politicians. As a result, voters are now viewed as a passive assembly of "consumers," a mass audience of potential buyers. Research discovers through scientific sampling what it is these consumers know or think and, more important, what they feel, even when they do not know their own "feelings." A campaign strategy is then designed to connect the candidate with these consumer attitudes. Advertising images are created that will elicit positive responses and make the sale.[19]

American democracy isn't for sale only to America's transnational corporations. The Mexican government spent upwards of $25 million and hired many of the leading Washington lobbyists to support its campaign for NAFTA. In the late 1980s, Japanese corporations were spending an estimated $100 million a year on political lobbying in the United States and another $300 million building a nationwide grassroots political network to influence public opinion. Together, the Japanese government and Japanese companies employed ninety-two Washington law, public-relations, and lobbying firms on their behalf. This compared with fifty-five for Canada, forty-two for Britain, and seven for the Netherlands. The purpose is to rewrite U.S. laws in favor of foreign corporations—and it often works.[20]

Corporate libertarianism—an ideology whose claims and promises are as false and self-serving as the claims of cigarette companies that nicotine is nonaddictive and cigarette smoke poses no health hazard—has become the dominant philosophy of our political culture and of our most powerful institutions. This is the accomplishment of a persistent campaign that uses the most sophisticated techniques yet developed by the masters of mass marketing and media manipulation. It is one element of a larger campaign to globalize markets and to embed corporate libertarianism and consumerism as defining values of a homogenized global culture.

11

MARKETING THE WORLD

Whoever has the power to project a vision of the good life and make it prevail has the most decisive power of all. . . . American business, after 1890, acquired such power and . . . in league with key institutions, began the transformation of American society into a society preoccupied with consumption, with comfort and bodily well-being, with luxury, spending, and acquisition, with more goods this year than last, more next year than this.

—William Leach[1]

Corporate executives dream of a global market made up of people with homogenized tastes and needs. . . . Logos on bottles, boxes, and labels are global banners, instantly recognizable by millions who could not tell you the color of the U.N. flag.

—Richard J. Barnet and John Cavanagh[2]

IN MODERN SOCIETIES, TELEVISION HAS arguably become our most important institution of cultural reproduction. Our schools are probably the second most important. Television has already been wholly colonized by corporate interests, which are now laying claim to our schools. The goal is not simply to sell products and strengthen the consumer culture. It is also to create a political culture that equates the corporate interest with the human interest in the public mind. In the words of Paul Hawken, "Our minds are being addressed by addictive media serving corporate sponsors whose purpose is to rearrange reality so that viewers forget the world around them."[3]

The rearrangement of reality begins with the claim that in a market economy, the consumer decides and the market responds. In a world of small buyers and sellers, this may have been true. No individual seller could expect to create a new culture conducive to buying his or her product. This is not our current reality. Present-day corporations have no reservations about reshaping the values of whole societies to create a homogenized culture of indulgence. As corporate demand has grown for supporting services in advertising, graphics, media, creative production, consumer research, marketing education, and countless others, whole industries have emerged to help corporations create insatiable desires for the things they sell and cultivate political values aligned with the corporate interest.

FIRST AMERICA, THEN THE WORLD

There was a day when the prevailing American culture was the mass marketer's worst nightmare. Frugality and thrift were central to the famed "Puritan ethic" that the early Puritan settlers brought with them to America. The Puritans believed in hard work, participation in community, temperate living, and devotion to a spiritual life. Their basic rule of living was that one should not desire more material things than could be used effectively. They taught their children, "Use it up, wear it out, make do, or do without."[4]

The Quakers also had a strong influence on early America and, although more tolerant and egalitarian, shared with the Puritans the values of hard work and frugality as important to one's spiritual development. Ralph Waldo Emerson and Henry David Thoreau, both important early American writers, viewed simplicity as a path to experiencing the divine.[5]

The consumer culture emerged largely as a consequence of concerted efforts by the retailing giants of the late nineteenth and early twentieth centuries to create an ever-growing demand for the goods they offered for sale. American historian William Leach has documented in *Land of Desire: Merchants, Power, and the Rise of a New American Culture* how they successfully turned a spiritually oriented culture of frugality and thrift into a material culture of self-indulgence. Leach finds the claim that the market simply responds to consumer desires to be nothing more than a self-serving fabrication of those who make their living manipulating reality to convince consumers to buy what corporations find it profitable to sell:

> Indeed, the culture of consumer capitalism may have been among the most nonconsensual public cultures ever created, and it was nonconsensual for two reasons. First, it was not produced by "the people" but by commercial groups in cooperation with other elites

comfortable with and committed to making profits and to accumulating capital on an ever-ascending scale. Second, it was nonconsensual because, in its mere day-to-day conduct (but not in any conspiratorial way), it raised to the fore only one vision of the good life and pushed out all others. In this way, it diminished American public life, denying the American people access to insight into other ways of organizing and conceiving life, insight that might have endowed their consent to the dominant culture (if such consent were to be given at all) with real democracy.[6]

The populist cultures that grew out of the hearts and aspirations of ordinary people in America stressed the democratization of property and the virtues of a republic based on independent families owning their own land and tools, producing for themselves much of what they consumed, and participating in communities of sharing. Theirs was the model of a strong social economy, supplemented by involvement in the money economy at the margin of their lives.

The shift from a social economy of household and community production to a primarily monetized economy took place in America in the mid-1800s, during the period in which the large corporations came into ascendance. As late as 1870, however, the average number of workers in a given firm was still fewer than ten. Markets remained predominantly local or regional, and most businesses were individually owned and managed—a world still close to the ideal of Adam Smith.

Large corporations became increasingly skillful in creating desire for their products. Eventually, marketing was born as a management specialty, and the early business schools began offering courses to meet the demand. As more people became dependent on wage employment in the factories, governments gained a stake in promoting consumerism as a way of maintaining employment.

Business became skilled in using colors, glass, and light to create exciting images of a this-world paradise conveyed by elegant models and fashion shows. Museums offered displays depicting the excitement of the new culture. Gradually, the individual was surrounded by messages reinforcing the culture of desire. Advertisements, department store show windows, electric signs, fashion shows, the sumptuous environments of the leading hotels, and billboards all conveyed artfully crafted images of the good life. Credit programs made it seem effortless to buy that life. According to Leach:

The United States was the first country in the world to have an economy devoted to mass production and it was the first to create the mass consumer institutions and the mass consumer enticements that rose up in tandem to market and sell the mass-produced goods. More effectively and pervasively than any other nation, America . . . forged a unique bond among different institutions that served to realize business aims.[7]

Today, television is the primary medium through which corporations shape the culture and behavior of Americans. The statistics are chilling.[8] The average American child between the ages of two and five watches three and a half hours of television a day; the average adult, nearly five hours. Only work and sleep occupy more of the average adult's life, with television effectively replacing community and family life, cultural pursuits, and reading. At this rate, the average American adult is seeing approximately 21,000 commercials a year, most of which carry an identical message: "Buy something—do it now!" The 100 largest corporations in America pay for roughly 75 percent of commercial television time and 50 percent of public television time. With a half minute of prime-time network advertising selling for between $200,000 and $300,000, only the largest corporations can afford it. Although there may be no overt control over program content, television producers are hired to produce television programming that advertisers will buy and necessarily have these corporations and their views of proper programming content constantly in mind.

Jerry Mander explains why television is a nearly ideal communications medium for serving the corporate purpose:

By its ability to implant identical images into the minds of millions of people, TV can homogenize perspectives, knowledge, tastes, and desires, to make them resemble the tastes and interests of the people who transmit the imagery. In our world, the transmitters of the images are corporations whose ideal of life is technologically oriented, commodity oriented, materialistic, and hostile to nature. And satellite communications is the mechanism by which television is delivered into parts of the planet that have, until recently, been spared this assault.[9]

As global corporations reach out to the four corners of the earth, they bring with them not only established products and brand names but also their fa-

vored media and the sophisticated marketing methods by which they colonize every culture they touch.

The Economist reported that in 1989, global corporate spending for advertising totaled more than $240 billion. Another $380 billion was spent on
packaging, design, and other point-of-sale promotions. Together, these expenditures amounted to $120 for every single person in the world.[10] Although
the bulk of this corporate expenditure is directed toward creating demand for
specific products, it also contributes to creating a generalized global consumer
culture and to making a connection in the public mind between corporate
interests—in particular the interests of large corporations—and the public
interest.

Overall, corporations are spending well over half as much per capita to
create corporation-friendly consumers as the $207 per capita ($33 for Southern countries) the world spends on public education.[11] Furthermore, growth
in advertising expenditures far outpaces increases in education spending. Advertising expenditures have multiplied nearly sevenfold since 1950—one-third
faster than the world economy.[12]

THE ONE WORLD OF MTV KNOWS—"COKE IS BEST"

In his Atlantic Monthly article in praise of economic integration, Akio Morita
identified distinctive local cultures as a trade barrier.[13] The need to respect
local tastes and cultural differences as a condition of gaining consumer acceptance greatly complicates global marketing campaigns. The dream of corporate marketers is a globalized consumer culture united around brand-name
loyalties that will allow a company to sell its products with the same advertising copy in Bangkok as in Paris or New York. It is happening. In the words of
Robert C. Goizueta, chairman of Coca-Cola Company, "people around the
world are today connected by brand-name consumer products as much as by
anything else."[14] Coca-Cola's success in making itself a global symbol has served
as an inspiration for corporate executives everywhere.

Few media provide greater potential for realizing this advertisers' dream
than MTV, the rock music television channel. Its near-universal appeal to teen-
agers and preteens around the world makes it an ideal instrument for the globalization of the consumer culture. By 1993, MTV's popular rock-and-roll
programming, with its kaleidoscope of brief, disconnected images, was available on a daily basis to 210 million households in seventy-one countries. According to Richard J. Barnet and John Cavanagh, the MTV entertainment net-

work, which specializes in pop videos and serves as a continuous commercial for a wide array of commercial products, "may be the most influential educator of young people on five continents." They continue:

> The performances and the ads merge to create a mood of longing—for someone to love, for something to happen, for an end to loneliness, and for things to buy—a record, a ticket to a rock concert, a T-shirt, a Thunderbird. The advertising is all the more effective because it is not acknowledged as such. . . . All across the planet, people are using the same electronic devices to watch or to listen to the same commercially produced songs and stories.[15]

Sarah Ferguson believes that the commercialization of youth culture, especially the music that was once a primary instrument of expressive rebellion for adolescents, keeps youth from owning even their own rebellion and actively inhibits the development of a counterculture. She writes, "The loop taken by a new musical style from the underground to the mainstream is now so compressed that there's no moment of freedom and chaos when a counterculture can take root."[16]

Among the most aggressive efforts to universalize the consumer culture is that of the Avon beauty products company. On August 2, 1994, the show *TV Nation* documented the campaign by Avon to win new customers among dirt-poor campesinas in the Amazon basin of Brazil, where 70,000 Avon saleswomen take the Avon message to every rural doorstep. Ademar Serodio, president of Avon Brazil, explained, "Instead of asking people to buy more from us, we start discovering people who never bought from us before." As revealed in footage of Avon saleswomen making door-to-door house calls in the remote village of Santarem, many of these new customers are thin, aging, wrinkled women living with their barefoot children in shacks with dirt floors. Most people in Santarem don't read or write, and the average household income is $3 per day.

Hundreds of Avon saleswomen were fielded in Santarem to follow up on TV advertising showing romantic scenes of sensuous, young, light-skinned women with dashingly handsome young men. They tell the aged women, broken by years of childbearing and toil in the sun, that they can be beautiful if they use Avon products. A major promotion centers on a skin-renewal product called Renew—costing $40 a jar—which works by burning off the top layer of the user's skin. A TV ad uses special effects to create the image of a woman peeling away years of aging from her face to appear magically younger. According to Rosa Alegria, communications director for Avon Brazil, "Women do everything to buy it. They stop buying other things like clothes, like shoes. If they feel good with their skin they prefer to stop buying clothes and buy something that is on the television. People think it is a real miracle."[17]

CORPORATIONS IN THE CLASSROOM

Corporations are now moving aggressively to colonize the second major institution of cultural reproduction, the schools. According to Consumers Union, 20 million U.S. schoolchildren used some form of corporate-sponsored teaching materials in their classrooms in 1990. Some of these are straightforward promotions of junk food, clothing, and personal-care items. For example, the National Potato Board joined forces with Lifetime Learning Systems to present "Count Your Chips," a math-oriented program celebrating the potato chip for National Potato Lovers' Month. NutraSweet, a sugar substitute, sponsored a "total health" program.[18]

Corporations have also been aggressive in getting their junk foods into school vending machines and school lunch programs. Trade shows and journals aimed at school food-service workers are full of appeals such as: "Bring Taco Bell products to your school!" "Pizza Hut makes school lunch fun." Coca-Cola launched a lobbying attack on proposed legislation to ban the sale of soft drinks and other items of "minimal nutritional value" in public schools. Randal W. Donaldson, a spokesman for Coca-Cola in Atlanta, said: "Our strategy is ubiquity. We want to put soft drinks within arms' reach of desire. We strive to make soft drinks widely available, and schools are one channel we want to make them available in."[19]

Other messages seek to indoctrinate young minds in the beliefs and values of corporate libertarianism. Thus Mobil Corporation, which is well known for buying op-ed space in the *New York Times* to promote its view of the public interest, offered a curriculum module produced by the Learning Enrichment Corporation for classroom use that claimed to help students evaluate the North American Free Trade Agreement (NAFTA), mainly by touting its benefits.

Faced with the inevitability of an environmentally aware public, corporations have responded by painting themselves green and seeking to define the problem and its solutions in ways that support corporate objectives. Another Mobil contribution to public education is a video prepared for classroom use that touts plastic as the best waste to put in landfills. An Exxon module titled "Energy Cube" omits discussion of fuel efficiency, alternatives to fossil fuels, and global warming. Indeed, it attempts to equate gasoline with solar energy in students' minds by explaining that its "energy value comes from solar energy stored in its organic chemical bonds."

Mobil and other corporations actively support the National Council on Economic Education, whose mission is to promote the teaching of economics in elementary and high schools. A paid Mobil op-ed piece in the *New York Times* lamented the fact that high school seniors were able to give correct answers to only 35 percent of questions on a national economic literacy survey. Obviously, Mobil has its own idea of what a correct answer is. The op-ed piece noted:

> When it comes to domestic issues, it helps to understand the impact that raising or cutting taxes will have on job security and your standard of living. And when it comes to environmental policy and regulations, it's necessary to comprehend basic economic principles such as supply and demand, cost versus benefit and a company's need for profits.[20]

General Motors mailed a video "I Need the Earth and the Earth Needs Me" to every public, private, and parochial elementary school in the country. Against a backdrop of happy children swimming in sparkling waters and running in picturesque landscapes, the GM video promotes such activities as planting trees and recycling. There is no mention of mass transit or the need to redesign cities to reduce transportation needs. GM recommends forming car pools and recycling used motor oil. All the statements made in the video and the accompanying teacher's guide are accurate. Yet the overall picture is misleading because it omits critical facts and ideas.

Channel One, an advertiser-sponsored school television program, beams its news and ads for candy bars, fast food, and sneakers directly into the classroom for twelve minutes a day in more than 12,000 schools. In exchange for a satellite dish and video equipment for each classroom, the school must agree that Channel One will be shown on at least 90 percent of school days to 90 percent of the children. *Teachers are not allowed to interrupt the show or turn it off.* A survey found that most students thought that since Channel One was shown in school, the products advertised on it must be good for them.[21]

Mark Evans, a senior vice president of Scholastic, Inc., presented the following challenge to business in an essay in *Advertising Age:*

More and more companies see educational marketing as the most com-pelling, memorable and cost-effective way to build share of mind and market into the 21st century.... [A Gillette program introducing teen-agers to its safety razors is] ... building brand and product loyalties through classroom-centered, peer-powered lifestyle patterning.... Can you devise promotions that take students from the aisles in school rooms to the aisles in supermarkets?[22]

If not, presumably Scholastic, Inc., one of the leading U.S. producers of school curriculum materials, stands ready to help.

Other corporations are proposing to operate public schools on a for-profit basis. The possibilities for profiting by turning classrooms into new mass media outlets for corporate marketing, image building, and ideological molding pitched to young and malleable minds are staggering—and frightening.

THE WORLD OF 1984

Corporations spend money on advertising, lobbying, advocacy, and public relations, whether in schools or the mass media, to encourage individual and public actions that support and advance corporate interests using whatever methods will elicit the desired consumer response. Paul Hawken describes their methods:

Soft-focus shots of deer in virgin forests are used as totemic proof of a paper company's commitment to the future even as they continue to clear-cut and fight congressional renewal of the Endangered Spe-cies Act. Native Americans look approvingly over a littered wildflower meadow being cleaned up by children using plastic bags advertised as biodegradable which in fact are not. (Mobil Oil was sued and chas-tised by attorney generals in several states for this ad.) Simpson Paper introduces a line of "recycled" paper with fractional amounts of post-consumer waste under the names of Thoreau, Whitman, and Leopold. British nuclear power companies announce that nuclear energy is green energy since it does not pollute the air.[23]

Tobacco companies spend millions to convince the public that there is no scientific basis for claims that smoking is harmful to their health; auto manu-facturers fight emissions standards; gun manufacturers fight gun controls;

chemical companies illegally dump their toxic wastes; and drug companies engage in monopoly pricing. It happens every day. For all the corporate claims to the contrary, *Business Week* itself said it well: "Modern multinationals are not social institutions. They will play governments off one another, shift pricing to minimize taxes, seek to sway opinion, export jobs, or withhold technology to maintain a competitive edge."[24]

Corporate efforts to shape our culture and our politics through control of television bring to mind George Orwell's *1984* and his images of an authoritarian society ruled by ever-present television monitors that manipulate citizens' perceptions of the world. Our reality is more subtle and the techniques more sophisticated than Orwell anticipated. And the strings are pulled by corporations rather than governments. We are ruled by an oppressive market, not an oppressive state.

The techniques have an elegant simplicity. They center on manipulating the cultural symbols in which our individual identities and values are anchored. Before mass media, these symbols were collective creations of people relating to one another and expressing their inner feelings through artistic media. They represented our collective sense of who we are. The more time we spend immersed in the corporate-controlled and packaged world of television, the less time we have for the direct human exchanges through which cultural identity and values were traditionally expressed, reinforced, and updated. Increasingly, those who control mass media control the core culture.

The architects of the corporate global vision seek a world in which universalized symbols created and owned by the world's most powerful corporations replace the distinctive cultural symbols that link people to particular places, values, and human communities. Our cultural symbols provide an important source of identity and meaning; they affirm our worth, our place in society. They arouse our loyalty to and sense of responsibility for the health and well-being of our community and its distinctive ecosystem. When the control of our cultural symbols passes to corporations, we are essentially yielding to them the power to define who we are. Instead of being Americans, Norwegians, Egyptians, Filipinos, or Mexicans, we become simply members of the "Pepsi generation," detached from place and any meaning other than those a corporation finds it profitable to confer on us. Market tyranny may be more subtle than state tyranny, but it is no less effective in enslaving the many to the interests of the few.

12

ELIMINATING THE PUBLIC INTEREST

They no longer use bullets and ropes. They use the World Bank and the IMF.

—Jesse Jackson[1]

To attract companies like yours . . . we have felled mountains, razed jungles, filled swamps, moved rivers, relocated towns . . . all to make it easier for you and your business to do business here.

—Philippine government ad in Fortune[2]

IN THE FLURRY OF GLOBAL INSTITUTION BUILDING that followed World War II, the spotlight of public attention was focused on the United Nations (UN), which was to include all countries, each with an equal voice—at least in its General Assembly. Delegates to the UN are public figures, and debates are open to public view and often heated. Yet the General Assembly has little real power. The real ability to act is vested in the Security Council, in which each of the major powers maintains the right of veto. Judging from its governance structures, it must be concluded that the UN was created primarily to function as a forum for debate.

In contrast, three other multilateral institutions were created with relatively little fanfare to operate outside the public eye—the International Bank for Reconstruction and Development (commonly known as the World Bank), the International Monetary Fund (IMF), and the General Agreement on Tariffs and Trade (GATT)—now the World Trade Organization (WTO). These three agencies are commonly referred to as the Bretton Woods institutions, in tribute to a meeting of representatives of forty-four nations who gathered in

Bretton Woods, New Hampshire, July 1–22, 1944, to reach agreement on an institutional framework for the post–World War II global economy. The public purpose of what became known as the Bretton Woods system was to unite the world in a web of economic prosperity and interdependence that would preclude nations' taking up arms. Another purpose in the eyes of its architects was to create an open world economy unified under U.S. leadership that would ensure unchallenged U.S. access to the world's markets and raw materials.[3] Two of the Bretton Woods institutions—the IMF and the World Bank—were actually created at the Bretton Woods meeting. The GATT was created at a subsequent international meeting.

Although formally designated as "special agencies" of the UN, the Bretton Woods institutions function autonomously from it. Their governance and administrative processes are secret, carefully shielded from public scrutiny and democratic debate. Indeed, the internal operating processes of the World Bank are so secretive that access to many of its most important documents relating to country plans, strategies, and priorities is denied to even its own governing executive directors. In the World Bank and the IMF, the big national powers have both veto power over certain decisions and voting shares in proportion to their shares of the subscribed capital—ensuring their ability to set and control the agenda.[4]

In this chapter, we examine how, in playing out their roles, the World Bank and the IMF have worked in concert to deepen the dependence of low-income countries on the global system and then to open their economies to corporate colonization. In the following chapter, we look at how the GATT and its successor, the World Trade Organization (WTO), are being used by the world's largest corporations to consolidate their power and place themselves beyond public accountability.

CREATING A DEMAND FOR DEBT

The primary original purpose of the World Bank was to finance European reconstruction. However, there was very little demand from the European countries for World Bank loans. What Europe needed was rapidly dispersing grants or concessional loans for balance-of-payment support and imports to temporarily meet basic needs while its own economies were being rebuilt. The U.S. Marshall Plan provided this type of assistance; the World Bank did not. By 1953—nine years after its establishment—total Bank lending was only $1.75 billion, of which only $497 million was for European reconstruction.

That amount paled in comparison to the $41.3 billion transferred to Europe under the Marshall Plan.[5]

The Bank's annual report for 1947–48 acknowledged that lack of demand for its loans was not limited to Europe. As the Bank began to look to the low-income countries for customers, it ran into a similar problem. Countries were not presenting the Bank with acceptable projects.

The Bank's claim that it simply responds to the needs and requests of borrowing countries is as false as the claim by corporate libertarians that the market simply responds to consumer demand. The Bank did what the big retail outlets did in the late 1800s when faced with a frugal culture that failed to produce sufficient customers. It set about to reshape values and institutions in ways that would create customers for its product. And much like the corporations that chose this course, the Bank gave scant attention to the larger consequences of actions taken primarily to meet its own needs.

WHEN THE BILL COLLECTOR CALLS

Lending from the World Bank and its sister regional banks was a fairly orderly process until the late 1970s, when the rise in oil prices effected by the OPEC countries caused the foreign debts of Southern countries to skyrocket. From 1970 to 1980, the long-term external debt of low-income countries increased from $21 billion to $110 billion.[6] As real interest rates soared, it became evident that the borrowing countries were so seriously overextended that default was imminent, leading potentially to a collapse of the whole system. The World Bank and the IMF, acting as overseers of the global financial system, stepped in—much as court-appointed receivers in bankruptcy cases—to set the terms of financial settlements between virtually bankrupt countries and the international lenders.

In their capacity as international receivers, the World Bank and the IMF imposed packages of policy prescriptions on indebted nations under the rubric of *structural adjustment*. Each structural adjustment package called for sweeping economic policy reforms intended to channel more of the adjusted country's resources and productive activity toward debt repayment, privatize public assets and services, and further open national economies to the global economy. Restrictions and tariffs on both imports and exports were reduced, and subsidies were offered to attract foreign investors.

Some of the reforms, such as a reduction of subsidies to the rich, were long overdue. However, others provided new subsidies for exporters and foreign investors. Government spending on social services for the poor was reduced to free more funds for loan repayment. In adjusted countries in Africa and Latin America aggregate governmental spending per person declined between 1980 and 1987, while the share of the total budget devoted to interest payments increased. The share of all other budget categories—including defense—decreased. In Latin America, the portion of government budgets allocated to interest payments increased from 9 percent to 19.3 percent. In Africa, it rose from 7.7 percent to 12.5 percent.[7]

The World Bank and the IMF proclaimed their structural adjustment programs to be a resounding success and declared the debt crisis resolved. They pointed to the fact that many of the adjusted countries subsequently experienced higher growth rates, expanded their export sectors, increased the total value of their exports, attracted new foreign investment, and became current on their debt repayments. Yet international debts and trade deficits increased and social conditions deteriorated.

To attract foreign investors, adjusted governments suppress union organizing to hold down wages, benefits, and labor standards. They give special tax breaks and subsidies to foreign corporations and cut corners on environmental regulations. The fact that dozens of countries seek to increase foreign exchange earnings by increasing the export of natural resources and agricultural commodities drives down the prices of their export goods in international markets, creating pressures to extract and export even more to maintain foreign exchange earnings. Falling prices for export commodities, profit repatriation by foreign investors, and increased demand for manufactured imports stimulated by the reduction of tariff barriers result in continuing trade deficits for most countries. From 1980 (the beginning of the World Bank-IMF decade of structural adjustment) to 1992, the aggregate trade deficit of low-income countries increased from $6.5 billion to $34.7 billion.

The Bank and the IMF responded with more loans to cover the growing trade deficits as a reward for carrying out structural adjustment. As a result, the international indebtedness of low-income countries increased from $134 billion in 1980 to $473 billion in 1992. Annual interest payments on this debt increased from $6.4 billion to $18.3 billion.[8] Rather than increasing their self-reliance, the world's low-income countries, under the guidance of the World Bank and the IMF, mortgage yet more of their futures to the international system each year.

We may infer from the programs and policies of the World Bank and the IMF that they favor a world in which all goods for domestic consumption are imported from abroad and paid for with money borrowed from foreign banks.

All domestic productive assets and natural resources are owned by foreign corporations and devoted to export production to repay the foreign loans. And all public services are operated by foreign corporations on a for-profit basis. It makes no sense if the goal is help the poor. It makes perfect sense if the goal is to increase the power and profits of global corporations.

IF THE POOR MATTERED

Properly understood, development is a process by which people increase their human, institutional, and technical capacities to produce the goods and services needed to achieve sustainable improvements in their quality of life using the resources available to them. Many of us call such a process people-centered development, not only because it benefits people but also because it is centered *in* people. It is especially important to involve the poor and excluded, thus allowing them to meet their own needs through their own productive efforts.[9] A small amount of help from abroad can be very useful in a people-centered development process, but too much foreign funding can prevent real development and even break down the existing capabilities of a people to sustain themselves.

Let's reduce the problem to its basics. Poverty—generally defined as a lack of adequate money—is not the issue. Deprivation associated with a lack of money is the problem—the lack of access to adequate food, clothing, shelter, and other essentials of a decent life. This simple fact suggests a people-centered alternative to both the import-substitution and export-led development models that were considered to be the only available choices in early development debates: pursuing policies that create opportunities for people who are experiencing deprivation to produce the things that they need to have a better life.

This is, in many respects, what Japan, Korea, and Taiwan did. Each made significant investments to achieve a high level of adult literacy and basic education, carried out radical land reform to create a thriving rural economy based on small farm production, and supported the development of rural industries that produced things needed by small farm families. These became the foundation of larger industries. The development of these countries was equity-led, not export-led—contrary to the historical revisionism of corporate libertarians. Only after these countries had developed broad-based domestic economies did they become major exporters in the international economy.

From the standpoint of transnational corporate capital and the World Bank, a people-centered development strategy presents a major problem. Since it creates very little demand for imports, it also creates little demand for foreign loans. Furthermore, it favors local ownership of assets and thus provides few investment opportunities for global corporations.

Foreign aid, even grant aid, becomes actively antidevelopmental when the proceeds are used to build dependence on imported technology and experts, encourage import-dependent consumer lifestyles, fund waste and corruption, displace domestically produced products with imports, and drive millions of people from the lands and waters on which they depend for their livelihoods—all of which are common outcomes of World Bank projects and structural adjustment programs.

In addition, there is evidence that most Bank projects are failures, even by the Bank's own narrowly defined economic criteria. In 1992, an internal Bank study team headed by Willi Wapenhans published a report, "Effective Implementation: Key to Development Impact," which concluded that 38 percent of Bank-funded projects completed in 1991 were failures at the time of completion.[10] Earlier, the Bank's Operations Evaluation Department had conducted four- to ten-year follow-up evaluations on projects that the Bank had rated as successful at the time of completion. The study found that twelve of twenty-five projects rated as successful when completed eventually turned out to be failures.[11] If only half of the 62 percent of projects rated successful at completion in 1991 eventually achieved their projected returns, then less than a third of all Bank projects will have provided sufficient economic return to justify the original investment. However, failures or not, the loan must be repaid in scarce foreign exchange. The Bank bears no liability for its own errors.

If measured by contributions to improving the lives of people or strengthening the institutions of democratic governance, the World Bank and the IMF have been disastrous failures, imposing an enormous burden on the world's poor and seriously impeding their development. In terms of fulfilling the mandates set for them by their original architects—advancing economic globalization under the domination of the economically powerful—they both have been resounding successes. Together, the Bank and the IMF have helped build powerful political constituencies aligned with corporate libertarianism, weakened the democratic accountability of Southern governments, usurped the functions of democratically elected officials, and removed most consequential legal and institutional barriers to the recolonization of Southern economies by transnational corporations.

THE WORLD'S HIGHEST JUDICIAL AND LEGISLATIVE BODY

The third institution called for by the Bretton Woods meeting—the International Trade Organization—was stillborn because of concerns in the U.S. Congress that its powers would infringe on U.S. sovereignty. The General Agreement on Tariffs and Trade (GATT) served in its stead, with a somewhat ambiguous status, as the body through which multilateral trade agreements were fashioned for nearly fifty years, until the Uruguay round of GATT negotiations quietly gave birth to the World Trade Organization (WTO) on January 1, 1995. It was a landmark triumph for corporate libertarianism. What the World Bank and the IMF had accomplished in institutionalizing the doctrines of corporate libertarianism in low-income countries, the WTO now had a mandate and enforcement powers to carry forward in both high- and low-income countries.

The key provision in the 2,000-page agreement creating the WTO is buried in paragraph 4 of Article XVI: "Each member shall ensure the conformity of its laws, regulations and administrative procedures with its obligations as provided in the annexed Agreements." The "annexed Agreements" include all the substantive multilateral agreements relating to trade in goods and services and intellectual property rights. This provision allows a WTO member country to challenge any law of another member country that it believes deprives it of benefits it expected to receive from the new trade rules. This includes virtually any law that requires imported goods to meet local or national health, safety, labor, or environmental standards that exceed WTO-accepted international standards. Unless the government against which the complaint is lodged can prove to the WTO panel that a number of restrictive provisions have been satisfied, it must bring its own laws into line with the lower international standard or be subject to perpetual fines or trade sanctions.

The WTO's goal is to "harmonize" international standards. Regulations requiring that imported products meet local standards on such matters as recycling, use of carcinogenic food additives, auto safety, toxic substances, labeling, and meat inspection are all subject to challenge. The offending country must prove that a purely scientific justification exists for its standards. The fact that its citizens simply do not want to be exposed to the higher level of risk associated with the lower WTO standards isn't acceptable.

Conservation measures that restrict the export of a country's own resources—such as forestry products, minerals, and fish products—can be ruled unfair trade practices, as can requirements that locally harvested timber or other resources be processed locally to provide local employment. Cases may also be brought against countries that attempt to give preferential treatment to local over foreign investors or that fail to protect the intellectual property rights (patents and copyrights) of foreign companies. Local interests are no longer a valid basis for local laws under the new WTO regime. The interests of international trade, which are primarily the interests of transnational corporations, take priority.

Challenges may also be brought against the laws of state and local governments located within the jurisdiction of a member country, even though these governments are not signatories to the new agreement. The national government under whose jurisdiction they fall becomes obligated to take all reasonable measures to ensure the compliance of these state or local administrations. Such "reasonable measures" include preemptive legislation, litigation, and withdrawal of financial support.

The fact that local laws are subject to challenge under the WTO does not necessarily mean that they will be. However, there are numerous cases in which these same types of laws were successfully challenged under the previous, less stringent, GATT rules. Even before the GATT-WTO was ratified, the United States, Canada, the European Community, and Japan had each compiled extensive lists of one another's laws that they intended to target for challenge once the agreement was in place.

Although the GATT-WTO is an agreement among countries, and challenges are brought by one country against another, the impetus for a challenge normally comes from a transnational corporation that believes itself to be disadvantaged by a particular law. For example, tobacco companies have repeatedly used trade agreements to fight health reforms intended to reduce harm from cigarette smoking.[12]

When a challenge to a national or local law is brought before the WTO, the contending parties present their case in a secret hearing before a panel of three trade experts, generally lawyers who have made careers of representing corporate clients on trade issues. There is no provision for the presentation of alternative perspectives, such as amicus briefs from nongovernmental organizations, unless a given panel chooses to solicit them. Documents presented to the panels are secret, except that a government may choose to release its own documents. The identification of the panelists who supported a position or conclusion is explicitly forbidden. The burden of proof is on the defendant to prove that the law in question is not a restriction of trade as defined by the WTO.

When a panel decides that a domestic law violates WTO rules, it may recommend that the offending country change its law. It becomes, in effect, the world's highest court. Countries that fail to make the recommended change within a prescribed period face financial penalties, trade sanctions, or both.

Under the proposed rules, the recommendations of the review panel are automatically adopted by the WTO sixty days after presentation unless there is a *unanimous* vote of WTO members to reject them. This means that over 100 countries, including the country that won the decision, must vote against a panel decision to overturn it—rendering the appeals process virtually meaningless.

The WTO has legislative as well as judicial powers. GATT allows the WTO to change certain trade rules by a two-thirds vote of WTO member representatives. The new rules become binding on all members. The WTO becomes, in effect, an unelected global parliament of trade lawyers with the power to amend its own charter without referral to national legislative bodies.

GOVERNANCE IN THE CORPORATE INTEREST

The world's major transnational corporations have had a highly influential insider role in GATT negotiations and are similarly active in the WTO. They are especially well represented in the U.S. delegation, which has had a pivotal role in shaping the GATT agreements. The key to this corporate access is the U.S. Trade Act of 1974, which provides for a system of trade advisory committees to bring a public perspective to U.S. trade negotiations.[13] The trade committees are supposed to conform to the Federal Advisory Committee Act of 1972, which sets guidelines for the membership of all such federal advisory committees. These include a requirement that public representation must be "fairly balanced in terms of points of view represented and the functions to be performed by the advisory committee." Advisory committee processes are also required to be open to public scrutiny.

The U.S. trade representative's office has chosen to define this requirement to mean only that the advisory committee membership must represent of the business community with regard to "balance among sectors, product lines, between small and large firms, among geographical areas, and among demographic groups."[14] A study by Public Citizen's Congress Watch released in December 1991 found that of 111 members of the three main trade advisory committees, only two represented labor unions. An approved seat for an environmental advocacy organization had not been filled, and there were no consumer representatives. The trade panels rarely announced their meetings to the public and never allowed the public to attend.

The corporate interest, however, was well represented. The study found that ninety-two members of the three committees represented individual companies, and sixteen represented trade industry associations, ten of them from the chemical industry. Members of the Advisory Committee for Trade Policy and Negotiations, the most important of the panels, included such corporate giants as IBM, AT&T, Bethlehem Steel, Time Warner, 3M, Corning, BankAmerica, American Express, Scott Paper, Dow Chemical, Boeing, Eastman Kodak, Mobil, Amoco, Pfizer, Hewlett Packard, Weyerhaeuser, and General Motors—all of which were also members of the U.S. Business Roundtable. Of the corporate members all but General Motors were represented either by the chairman of the board or the president, in most instances, whichever of these officers functioned as CEO. According to Public Citizen's Congress Watch:

> Advisory committees are so intertwined with governmental trade negotiators that panel members require security clearances. One of the perks of membership is a special reading room filled with classified documents available for perusal by nongovernmental advisors. To enable trade advisors' opinions regarding the current GATT talks to reach negotiators more quickly, a database has been established that instantly puts an advisory committee member's words at the negotiators' fingertips. Government sponsors of the trade advisory system take enormous trouble to keep trade advisors fully informed of every twist and turn in the negotiating process. Despite their enormous influence, the corporate trade counselors work in near total obscurity.[15]

A 1989 Department of Commerce document described the involvement of advisory committee members in the 1979 Tokyo round of GATT:

> The advisory members spent long hours in Washington consulting directly with negotiators on key issues and reviewing the actual texts of proposed agreements. For the most part, government negotiators followed the advice of the advisory committee. . . . Whenever advice was not followed, the government informed the committees of the reasons it was not possible to utilize their recommendations.[16]

Of the ninety-two corporations represented on the three trade advisory panels, twenty-seven companies or their affiliates had been assessed fines by the

U.S. Environmental Protection Agency (EPA) totaling more than $12.1 million between 1980 and 1990 for failure to comply with existing environmental regulations. Five—DuPont, Monsanto, 3M, General Motors, and Eastman Kodak—made the EPA's top ten list of hazardous waste dischargers. Twenty-nine of the member companies or their affiliates had collectively contributed more than $800,000 in a failed attempt to defeat California's Safe Drinking Water and Toxics Enforcement Act, a statewide initiative to require accurate labeling on potentially cancer-causing products and to limit toxic discharges into drinking water. Twenty-nine had put up over $2.1 million in a successful bid to defeat another California initiative called Big Green, which, among other provisions, would have set tighter standards for the discharge of toxic chemicals.[17]

Clayton Yeutter, in his capacity as U.S. secretary of agriculture under George Bush, stated publicly that one of his main goals was to use GATT to overturn strict local and state food safety regulations. He rationalized, "If the rest of the world can agree on what the standard ought to be on a given product, maybe the U.S. or EC will have to admit that they are wrong when their standards differ."[18]

The WTO uses the global health and safety standards for food set by the Codex Alimentarius Commission, or Codex. Codex is an intergovernmental body established in 1963 and run jointly by the UN Food and Agriculture Organization (FAO) and the World Health Organization (WHO) to establish international standards on pesticide residues, additives, veterinary drug residues, and labeling. Critics of Codex observe that it is heavily influenced by industry and has tended to harmonize standards downward. For example, a Greenpeace USA study found that Codex safety levels for at least eight widely used pesticides were lower than current U.S. standards by as much as a factor of twenty-five.[19] The Codex standards allow DDT residues up to fifty times those permitted under U.S. law.[20]

Governmental delegations to Codex routinely include nongovernmental representatives, but they are chosen almost exclusively from industry. One hundred forty of the world's largest multinational food and agrochemical companies participated in Codex meetings held between 1989 and 1991. Of a total of 2,587 individual participants, only twenty-six came from public-interest groups.[21] Nestle, the world's largest food company, had thirty-eight representatives. A Nestle spokesperson explained, "It seems to me that governments are more likely to find qualified people in companies than among the self-appointed ayatollahs of the food sector."[22]

PROTECTING INTELLECTUAL PROPERTY MONOPOLIES

Many of the WTO provisions have been put forward as necessary to ensure the efficient functioning of competitive markets. Yet the WTO does nothing to limit the ability of transnational corporations to use their economic power to drive competitors out of the market by unfair means; absorb competitors through mergers and acquisitions; or form strategic alliances with competitors to share technology, production facilities, and markets. Indeed, one of the few areas in which the WTO calls for strengthening government regulations and standards is in its agreement on intellectual property rights: patents, copyrights, and trademarks. Here the WTO calls for strong government intervention to protect corporate monopoly rights to information and technology.

Particularly ominous is the effort to use the WTO to privatize the rights to genetic materials, including seeds and natural medicinals, through patenting. U.S. companies have aggressively pursued patent protection for seeds and genetic materials in the United States, convincing the U.S. government to extend patent protection to all genetically engineered organisms, from microorganisms to plants and animals, excluding only genetically engineered humans. By patenting the processes by which genes are inserted into a species of seeds, a few companies have effectively obtained monopoly rights over genetic research on an entire species and on any useful products of that research. These companies have been pressing hard to turn such patents into worldwide monopolies under the WTO. In 1992, Agracetus, Inc., a subsidiary of W.R. Grace, was granted a U.S. patent on all genetically engineered or "transgenic" cotton varieties and had applications pending for similar patents in other countries accounting for 60 percent of the world's cotton crop, including India, China, Brazil, and the European Union. In March 1994, it received a European patent on all transgenic soybeans and had a similar patent pending in the United States.

Through the ages, farmers have saved seed from one harvest to plant their next crop. Under existing U.S. patent law, a farmer who saves and replants the offspring of a patented seed violates patent law.[23] The corporate move to create global monopolies over seeds and other life-forms through patents has been the subject of massive demonstrations by farmers in India, who realized that under the GATT-WTO agreements, they could be prohibited from growing their own seed stocks without paying a royalty to a transnational corporation.[24]

The industry view of what is right and proper with regard to people's rights to their means of subsistence has been clearly expressed by Hans

Leenders, secretary general of the industry association of corporate seed houses and breeders:

> Even though it has been a tradition in most countries that a farmer can save seed from his own crop, it is under the changing circumstances not equitable that a farmer can use this seed and grow a commercial crop out of it without payment of a royalty. . . . The seed industry will have to fight hard for a better kind of protection.[25]

Vandana Shiva, a leader of the Southern opposition to the patenting of life-forms, says, "This is just another way of stating that global monopoly over agriculture and food systems should be handed over as a right to multinational corporations."[26] What we are seeing is a blatant effort by a few corporations to establish monopoly control over the common biological heritage of the planet.[27]

A review of the accomplishments of the three Bretton Woods institutions brings their actual functions into sharp focus. The World Bank has served as an export-financing facility for large Northern-based corporations. The IMF has served as the debt collector for Northern-based financial institutions. The GATT has served to create and enforce a corporate bill of rights protecting the world's largest corporations against intrusion in their affairs by people, communities, and democratically elected governments.

The Bank and the IMF celebrated their fiftieth anniversary in 1994. Citizen organizations from around the world marked the event by organizing a global campaign around the theme "Fifty Years Is Enough." Fifty years of Bretton Woods has indeed been far more than enough. The world's people and environment can scarcely afford more.

World War II did not end the global domination of the weak by strong states. It simply cloaked colonialism in a less obvious, more beguiling form. The new corporate colonialism is no more a consequence of immutable historical forces than was the old state colonialism. It is a consequence of conscious choices based on the pursuit of elite interest. This elite interest has been closely aligned with the corporate interest in advancing deregulation and economic globalization. As a consequence, the largest transnational corporations and the global financial system have assumed increasing power over the conduct of human affairs in the pursuit of interests increasingly at odds with the human interest. It is not possible to have healthy, equitable, and democratic societies when political and economic power is concentrated in a few gigantic corporations able to dictate public priorities. We have created a system that is now beyond the control even of those who created it and whom it richly rewards for serving its ends. In Part IV, we examine the nature and dynamics of this system.

Part IV

A ROGUE FINANCIAL SYSTEM

13

THE MONEY GAME

In this new market . . . billions can flow in or out of an economy in seconds. So powerful has this force of money become that some observers now see the hot-money set becoming a sort of shadow world government—one that is irretrievably eroding the concept of the sovereign powers of a nation state.

—Business Week[1]

The modern banking system manufactures money out of nothing. The process is perhaps the most astounding piece of sleight of hand that was ever invented. . . . If you want to be slaves of the bankers, and pay the costs of your own slavery, then let the banks create money.
—Lord Josiah Stamp, former director, Bank of England (1937)

EACH DAY, HALF A MILLION to a million people arise as dawn reaches their part of the world, turn on their computers, and leave the real world of people, things, and nature to immerse themselves in playing the world's most lucrative computer game: the money game.[2] On-line, they enter a cyberspace fantasy world constructed of numbers that represent money and complex rules by which the money can be converted into a seemingly infinite variety of forms, each with its own distinctive risks and reproductive qualities. Through their interactions, the players engage in competitive transactions aimed at acquiring for their own accounts the money that other players hold. Players can also pyramid the amount of money in play by borrowing from one another and bidding up prices. They can also purchase a great variety of exotic financial instruments that allow them to leverage their own funds without actually borrowing. It is played like a game. But the consequences are real.

The story of economic globalization is only partly a tale of the fantasy world of Stratos dwellers and the dreams of global empire builders. Another story of impersonal forces is at play, deeply embedded in our institutional systems—a tale of money and how its evolution as an institution is transforming human societies in ways that no one intended toward ends that are inimical to the human interest. It is a tale of the pernicious side of the market's invisible hand, of the tendency of an unrestrained market to reorient itself away from the efficient *production* of wealth to the *extraction* and *concentration* of wealth. It is a tragic tale of how good and thoughtful people have become trapped in serving, even creating, a system devoted to the unrestrained pursuit of greed, producing outcomes they neither seek nor condone.

Although the consequences are global, our primary focus here, as in previous chapters, is predominantly on the United States because, since World War II, the United States has had the dominant role in shaping the global economy and its institutions. Thus, there has been a tendency for the strengths and dysfunctions of the global system to be revealed first in the United States and then spread throughout the world.

DELINKING MONEY FROM VALUE

To understand what has happened to the global financial system, we must begin with an understanding of the nature of money. Money is one of humanity's most important inventions, created to meet an important need.

The earliest market transactions were based on the direct exchange of things of equal value, which meant that a transaction could occur only when two individuals met who each possessed an item they were willing to trade for an item possessed by the other. The useful expansion of commerce was greatly constrained. This constraint was partially relieved when people began to use certain objects that had their own intrinsic value as a medium of exchange—decorative shells, blocks of salt, bits of precious metals, or precious stones. Eventually, metal coins provided standard units of exchange based on the amount of precious metal, generally silver or gold, they contained. Later the idea emerged that it was more convenient to keep the precious metal in a vault and issue paper money that could be exchanged for the metal on demand. In a sense, the paper bill was originally the equivalent of a receipt showing that the bearer owned an amount of precious metal, but the paper receipt was more convenient and transportable.

Each of these innovations was, however, a step toward delinking money from things of real value. An additional step was taken at the historic 1944 Bretton Woods conference that created the World Bank and the International

Monetary Fund. The countries represented at this meeting agreed to create a new global financial system in which each participating government guaranteed to exchange its own currency on demand for U.S. dollars at a fixed rate. The U.S. government, in turn, guaranteed to exchange dollars on demand for gold at a rate of $35 per ounce. This effectively placed all the world's currencies on the gold standard, backed by the U.S. gold stored at Fort Knox. Many governments thus came to accept U.S. dollars as gold deposit certificates and chose to hold their international foreign exchange reserves in dollars rather than gold.

This system worked reasonably well for more than twenty years, until it became widely evident that the United States was creating far more dollars to finance its massive military and commercial expansion around the world than it could back with its gold. If all the countries that were holding dollars decided to redeem them for gold, the available supply would be quickly exhausted, and those who had placed their faith in the integrity of the dollar would be left holding nothing but worthless pieces of paper.

To preclude this eventuality, on August 15, 1971, President Richard Nixon declared that the United States would no longer redeem dollars on demand for gold. The dollar was no longer anything other than a piece of high-grade paper with a number and some intricate artwork issued by the U.S. government. The world's currencies were no longer linked to anything of value except the shared expectation that others would accept them in exchange for real goods and services.

Once computers came into widespread use, the next step was relatively obvious—eliminate the paper and simply store the numbers in computers. Although coins and paper money continue to circulate, more and more of the world's monetary transactions involve direct electronic transfers between computers. Money has become almost a pure abstraction delinked from anything of real value.

Four developments are basic to this transformation of the financial system:

1. The United States financed its global expansion with dollars, many of which now show up on the balance sheets of foreign banks and foreign branches of U.S. banks. These dollars are not subject to the regulations and reserve requirements of the U.S. Federal Reserve system.
2. Computerization and globalization melded the world's financial markets into a single global system in which an individual at a computer terminal can maintain constant contact with price movements in all major markets and execute trades almost instantaneously in any or all

of them. A computer can be programmed to do the same without human intervention, automatically executing transactions involving billions of dollars in fractions of a second.

3. Investment decisions that were once made by many individuals are now concentrated in the hands of a relatively small number of professional investment managers. The pool of investment funds controlled by mutual funds doubled in three years to total $2 trillion at the end of June 1994, as individual investors placed their savings in professionally managed investment pools rather than buying and holding individual stocks.[3] Meanwhile, there has been a massive consolidation of the banking industry—more than 500 U.S. banks merged or closed between September 1992 and September 1993 alone[4]—concentrating control of huge pools of funds within the major international "money center" banks. Pension funds, now estimated to total $4 trillion in assets, are managed mostly by trust departments of these giant banks, adding enormously to their financial power. The pension funds alone account for the holdings of about a third of all corporate equities and about 40 percent of corporate bonds.[5]

4. Investment horizons have shortened dramatically. The managers of these investment pools compete for investors' funds based on the returns they are able to generate. Mutual fund results are published daily in the world's leading newspapers, and countless services compare fund performance monthly and yearly. Individual investors have the ability to switch money among mutual funds with the push of a button on a phone or their personal computer mouse, based on these results. For the mutual fund manager, the short term is a day or less and the long term is perhaps a month. Pension fund managers have a slightly longer evaluation cycle.

Individual savings have become consolidated in vast investment pools managed by professionals under enormous competitive pressures to yield nearly instant financial gains. The time frames involved are far too short for a productive investment to mature, the amount of money to be "invested" far exceeds the number of productive investment opportunities available, and the returns the market has come to expect exceed what most productive investments are able to yield even over a period of years. Consequently, the financial markets have largely abandoned productive investment in favor of extractive investment and are operating on autopilot without regard to human consequences.

The financial system increasingly functions as a world apart at a scale that dwarfs the productive sector of the global economy, which itself functions increasingly at the mercy of the massive waves of money that the money game players move around the world with split-second abandon.

Joel Kurtzman, formerly business editor of the *New York Times* and subsequently editor of the *Harvard Business Review*, estimated that for every $1 circulating in the productive world economy, $20 to $50 circulates in the economy of pure finance, although no one knows the ratios for sure. In the international currency markets alone, some $800 billion to $1 trillion changes hands each day,[6] far in excess of the $20 billion to $25 billion required to cover daily trade in goods and services. According to Kurtzman:

> Most of the $800 billion in currency that is traded . . . goes for very short-term speculative investments—from a few hours to a few days to a maximum of a few weeks. . . . That money is mostly involved in nothing more than making money. . . . It is money enough to purchase outright the nine biggest corporations in Japan—overvalued though they are—including Nippon Telegraph & Telephone, Japan's seven largest banks, and Toyota Motors. . . . It goes for options trading, stock speculation, and trade in interest rates. It also goes for short-term financial arbitrage transactions where an investor buys a product such as bonds or currencies on one exchange in the hopes of selling it at a profit on another exchange, sometimes simultaneously by using electronics.[7]

This money is not associated with any real value. Yet the money managers who carry out the millions of high-speed, short-term transactions stake their reputations and careers on making that money grow at a rate greater than the prevailing rate of interest. This growth depends on the system's ability to endlessly increase the market value of the financial assets being traded, irrespective of what happens to the output of real goods and services. As this growth occurs, the financial or buying power of those who control the inflated assets expands, compared with the buying power of other members of society who are actually creating value but whose real and relative compensation is declining.[8]

THE GREAT MONEY MACHINE

There are two common ways to create money without creating value. One is by creating debt. Another is by bidding up asset values. The global financial system is adept at using both of these devices to create money delinked from the creation of value.

Debt

The way in which the banking system creates money by pyramiding debt is familiar to anyone who has taken an elementary economics course. In the United States it begins when the Federal Reserve buys government bonds in the open market. Say the Fed buys a $1,000 bond from Person A, who deposits the check in his account with Bank M. The Federal Reserve then credits the reserve account of Bank M with $1,000 to cover the purchase. As Bank M is only required to maintain a reserve of, say, ten percent of deposits, it is thus able to loan $900 against this reserve to Person B, which Person B deposits in her account in Bank N. Now Person A has a cash asset of $1,000 in Bank M, and Person B has a cash asset of $900 in Bank N. Keeping a 10 percent reserve, Bank N is able to loan $810 to Person C, who deposits it in Bank O, which then loans $729 to Person D, and so on. The original purchase of $1,000 bond by the Fed ultimately allows the banking system to generate $9,000 in new deposits by issuing $9,000 in new loans—money created without a single thing of value having necessarily been produced.

The total of $1,000 in new money interjected into the banking system by the Federal Reserve is thus pyramided into $10,000 in new money, of which $9,000 is in loans on which the banks involved expect to receive the going rate of interest, let us say 8 percent. This means that the banking system expects to obtain a minimum annual interest return of $720 on $9,000 that has been created simply by entering an amount in the account of a borrower and crediting themselves with a corresponding asset in the amount of the outstanding loan. Now you know why banking is such a good business.

In this instance, we have used the classic textbook example of how banks create money, assuming an average 10 percent reserve requirement—the actual varies from zero to 14 percent depending on the size of the bank and the nature of the account—that must be retained on deposit with the U.S. Federal Reserve system.[9] Without such a reserve requirement, the banking system could, in theory, create money without limit.

As the United States has spent beyond its means abroad, a growing portion of the total supply of dollars circulating in the world has accumulated in the accounts of foreign banks or foreign branches of U.S. banks. Known as Eurodollars, they are not subject to the reserve requirement of the U.S. Federal Reserve. If banks hold accounts where governments do not impose a reserve requirement, these banks can loan out the full amount of these deposits, should they choose to do so, giving the global banking system the capacity to endlessly expand the supply of dollars.

Asset Values

The price of a stock or of a tangible asset such as land or a piece of art is determined by the market's demand for it. In an economy awash with money and investors looking for quick returns, that demand is substantially influenced by speculators' expectations that other speculators will continue to push up the price. Nicholas F. Brady, who served as U.S. treasury secretary under President George Bush, observed, "If the assets were gold or oil, this phenomenon would be called inflation. In stocks, it is called wealth creation."[10] The process tends to feed on itself. As the price of an asset rises, more spectators are drawn to the action and the price continues to increase, attracting still more speculators—until the bubble bursts as when the crash of the overinflated Mexican stock market caused the 1995 peso crisis.

Vast changes in the buying power of people who own such assets can occur within a very short time, with no change whatever in the underlying value of the asset or in society's ability to produce real goods and services. We are so conditioned to the idea that changes in buying power are related to changes in real wealth that it is easy to overlook the fact that this relationship is often simply an illusion. Consider the following excerpt from Joel Kurtzman's book *The Death of Money*, describing what happened on October 19, 1987, when the New York Stock Exchange's Dow Jones Industrial Average fell by 22.6 percent in one day:

> If measured from the height of the bull market in August 1987, investors lost a little over $1 trillion on the New York Stock Exchange in a little more than two months. That loss was equal to an eighth of the value of everything that is manmade in the United States, including all homes, factories, office buildings, roads, and improved real estate. It is a loss of such enormous magnitude that it boggles the mind. One trillion dollars could feed the entire world for two years, raise the Third World from abject poverty to the middle class. It could purchase one thousand nuclear aircraft carriers.[11]

Those who invested in the stock market did indeed lose individual buying power. Yet the homes, factories, office buildings, roads, and improved real estate to which Kurtzman refers did not change in any way. In fact, this $1 trillion could not have fed the world for even five minutes for the simple reason that people can't eat money. They eat food, and the collapse of stock market values did not itself increase or decrease the world's actual supply of food by so much as a single grain of rice. Only prices at which shares in particular companies could be bought and sold changed. There was no change in the productive capacity of any of those companies or even in the cash available in their own bank accounts.

Furthermore, although stock values represent potential purchasing power for individual investors, they do not accurately reflect the aggregate buying power of all investors in the market for the simple reason that you can't buy much with a stock certificate. You cannot, for example, give one to the checkout clerk at your local grocery store for your purchase. You first have to convert the stock to cash by selling it. Now, although any individual can sell a stock certificate at the prevailing price and spend the money to buy groceries, if everyone decided to convert their stocks into money to buy groceries at the same time, much the same thing would happen as did on October 19, 1987. The aggregate value of their stock holdings would deflate like a punctured balloon. The "money"—the buying power—would instantly evaporate. What we are dealing with is market speculation that creates an illusion of wealth. It conveys real powers on those who hold it, but only as long as the balloon remains inflated.

The whole nature of trading these vast sums in the world's financial markets is changing dramatically. The trend is toward replacing financial analysts and traders with theoretical mathematicians, "quants," who deal in sophisticated probability analysis and chaos theory to structure portfolios on the basis of mathematical equations. Since humans cannot make the calculations and decisions with the optimal speed required by the new portfolio management strategies, trading in the world's financial markets is being done directly by computers, based on abstractions that have nothing to do with the business itself. According to Kurtzman:

> These computer programs are not trading stocks, at least in the old sense, because they have no regard for the company that issues the equity.... The computers are simply ... trading mathematically precise descriptions of financial products (stocks, currencies, bonds, options, futures). Which exact product fits the descriptions hardly matters as long as all the parameters are in line with the description contained in the computer program. For stocks, any one will do if its volatility, price, exchange rules, yield, and beta [risk coefficient] fit the computer's description. The computer hardly cares if the stock is IBM or Disney or MCI. The computer does not care whether the company makes nuclear bombs, reactors, or medicine. It does not care whether it has plants in North Carolina or South Africa.[12]

The decisions of the financial system are increasingly being made by computers on the basis of esoteric mathematical formulas with the sole objective of replicating money as a pure abstraction. This is a long way from the invisible hand of the market Adam Smith had in mind when *The Wealth of Nations* was published in 1776, but is the reality of a world ruled by "free-market" forces in the 1990s. The global financial system has become a parasitic predator that lives off the flesh of its host—the productive economy.

14

PREDATORY FINANCE

You can't make any money like this. The dollar is moving sideways, the movement is too narrow.... Anyone speculating or trading in the dollar or any other currency can't make money or lose money. You can't do anything. It's been a horror.

—Carmine Rotondo, foreign exchange trader
at Security Pacific Bank[1]

ONE OF THE IDEOLOGICAL PREMISES of corporate libertarianism is that investment is by nature *productive* in the sense that it increases the size of the economic pie, adds to the net well-being of society, and therefore is of potential benefit to everyone. In a healthy economy, most investment is productive. The global economy is not, however, a healthy economy. In all too many instances, it rewards *extractive* investors who do not create wealth but simply extract and concentrate existing wealth. The extractive investor's gain is at the expense of other individuals or the society at large.

In the worst case, an extractive investment actually decreases the overall wealth of the society, even though it may yield a handsome return to an individual. This occurs when an investor acquires control of a productive asset or resource—such as land, timber, or even a corporation—from a group that is maintaining the asset's productive potential, then liquidates it for immediate profit. The investor is extracting value, not creating it. In some instances, such as an ancient forest, the asset may be irreplaceable. An investment that simply creates money or buying power, such as through the inflation of land or stock values, without creating anything of corresponding value, is also a form of extractive investment. The investor creates nothing, yet his or her share of a society's buying power is increased.

Speculation is another form of extractive investment. The financial speculator is engaged in little more than a sophisticated form of gambling—betting on the rise and fall of selected prices. When a speculator wins, he or she is simply capturing claims to wealth created by others. When a large speculator funded with borrowed money loses, the survival of major financial institutions may be placed at risk, resulting in demands for a public bailout to save the financial system from collapse. In either instance, the public loses. Rarely does a speculator's activity contribute to the wealth or well-being of society.

Although there may be some merit to speculators' claims that their activities increase market liquidity and stability, these claims have a hollow ring in increasingly volatile, globalized financial markets in which speculative financial movements are a major source of instability and economic disruption. Furthermore, whatever contribution speculators may make to increasing the financial markets' efficiency, it comes at a substantial cost in terms of the profits and fees they extract. The additional risks and economic distortions created by a sophisticated class of financial instruments known as derivatives are an especially important source of concern.

The derivatives contracts that are currently a hot topic in the financial press involve bets on movements of stock prices, currency prices, interest rates, and even entire stock market indices. Futures contracts on interest rates didn't exist until the late 1970s. Now outstanding contracts on interest rates total more than half the gross national product of the United States.[2] The total value of outstanding derivatives contracts was estimated to be about $12 trillion in mid-1994, with growth projected to $18 trillion by 1999.[3] In 1993, *The Economist* estimated the value of the world's total stock of productive fixed capital to be around $20 trillion.[4]

What makes derivatives particularly risky is that they are commonly purchased on margin, meaning that the buyer initially puts up only a small deposit against the potential financial exposure. The largest players may not be required to put up any money at all, even though their potential financial exposure may run into hundreds of millions of dollars.[5]

The more sophisticated derivatives are highly complex and are often not well understood, even by those who deal in them. In the words of *Fortune*:

When they are employed wisely, derivatives make the world simpler, because they give their buyers an ability to manage and transfer risk. But in the hands of speculators, bumblers, and unscrupulous peddlers, they are a powerful leveraged mechanism for *creating* risk.[6]

CREATING UNCERTAINTY AND RISK

For global corporations engaged in producing and trading real goods and services, the sometimes considerable swings in the exchange relationships among different currencies can be a serious problem, possibly playing a larger role in determining profit or loss than productive efficiency or market share. Speculators, by contrast, thrive on volatility, as it is their source of extractive gain through:

1. Arbitraging temporary price differences for the same or similar commodities or financial instruments in two markets. The arbitrager makes a simultaneous purchase in the market where the price is lower and a corresponding sale in the market where the price is higher. The margins are narrow, but the action is essentially riskless, and when large sums of money are involved, the strategy can be quite profitable. The key is to act before anyone else notices the same opportunity. Speed is so important that one firm spent $35 million to buy a super-computer simply to gain a two-second advantage in arbitraging stock futures in Tokyo.[7]

2. Speculating on price changes in commodities, currency exchange rates, interest rates, and financial instruments such as stocks, bonds, and various derivative products. Speculation involves betting on short-term price fluctuations. These bets can involve significant risks, especially if they are leveraged with borrowed money.

3. Insuring others against the risks of future price changes. Those who sell derivatives contracts promote them as a form of risk insurance, as when a farmer locks in a price for his or her crop through a futures contract. However, the more complex derivatives have more to do with gambling than with insuring against risk.

There would be little opportunity for speculative profit in a stable financial market. In most instances, the extractive investor is taking advantage of price fluctuations to claim a portion of the value created by productive investors and by people doing real work—a private tax levied on the productive output of others. It is difficult to see, for example, how arbitraging electronically linked markets to reduce two-second differentials in price adjustments serves any public purpose. The greater the volatility of financial markets, the greater the opportunity for these forms of extraction.

The riskier and more destabilizing forms of extractive investments have received a major boost from the formation of a new breed of mutual funds—called hedge funds—that specialize in high-risk, short-term speculation and require a minimum initial investment of $1 million. The biggest of these, Quantum Fund headed by George Soros, controls more than $11 billion of investor money. Since aggressive hedge funds may leverage investor money to borrow $25 or more for every investor dollar, this would give a fund with $10 billion in equity potential control over as much as $250 billion. Many of the largest hedge funds produced a return of more than 50 percent for their shareholders in 1993. The downside risks are also substantial, however. One small hedge fund lost $600 million in two months in the mortgage markets and went out of business.[8]

The fact that hedge funds are generally highly leveraged greatly increases both the potential gains and the risks. It also ties up banking system funds in activities that are of questionable benefit to society when the credit needs of home buyers, farmers, and productive businesses go unmet.

The claim that speculators increase price stability by moving markets more quickly toward their equilibrium was recently debunked by George Soros himself in testimony before the Banking Committee of the U.S. House of Representatives. Soros told the committee that when a speculator bets that a price will rise and it falls instead, he is forced to protect himself by selling, which accelerates the price drop and increases market volatility. Soros, however, told the committee that price volatility is not a problem unless everyone rushes to sell at the same time and a "discontinuity" is created, meaning there are no buyers. In that case, those with positions in the market are unable to bail out and may suffer "catastrophic losses."[9] His testimony clearly revealed the perspective of the professional speculator, for whom volatility is a source of profits. If he were involved in productive forms of investment, he would surely have had a different opinion about price volatility.

Soros speaks from experience when he claims that speculators can shape the directions of market prices and create instability. He has developed such a legendary reputation as a shaper of financial markets that a *New York Times* article, "When Soros Speaks, World Markets Listen" credited him with being able to increase the price of his investments simply by revealing that he has made them. After placing bets against the German mark, he published a letter in the *Times* (London) saying, "I expect the mark to fall against all major currencies." According to the *New York Times*, it immediately did just that "as traders in the United States and Europe agreed that it was a Soros market."[10] On November 5, 1993, the *New York Times* business pages included the story,

"Rumors of Buying by Soros Send Gold Prices Surging."

In September 1992, Soros sold $10 billion worth of British pounds in a bet against the success of British Prime Minister John Major's effort to maintain the pound's value.[11] In so doing, he was credited with a major role in forcing a devaluation of the pound that contributed to breaking up the system of fixed exchange rates that governments were trying to put into place in the European union. Fixed exchange rates are anathema for speculators because they eliminate the volatility on which speculators depend. For his role in protecting the opportunity for speculative profits, Soros extracted an estimated $1 billion from the financial system for his investment funds.[12] The resulting gyrations in the money markets caused the British pound to fall 41 percent against the Japanese yen over eleven months. These are the kinds of volatility that speculators considered a source of opportunity.[13]

There is a substantial and growing basis for the conclusion of Felix Rohatyn, a senior partner with Lazard Freres & Co, that:

> In many cases hedge funds, and speculative activity in general, may now be more responsible for foreign exchange and interest-rate movements than interventions by the central banks.
> ... Derivatives ... create a chain of risks linking financial institutions and corporations throughout the world; any weakness or break in that chain (such as the failure of a large institution heavily invested in derivatives) could create a problem of serious proportions for the international financial system.[14]

The fact that many major corporations, banks, and even local governments have become active players in the derivatives markets as a means of boosting their profits began to attract the attention of the business press in 1994. The risks can be substantial, yet the institutions that have been major players generally do not disclose their financial exposure in derivatives in their public financial statements, preferring to treat them as "off-balance-sheet" transactions. This makes it impossible for investors and the public to properly assess the real risks involved.

The truth becomes known only as major losses are reported, as when Procter & Gamble announced a $102 million derivatives loss after interest rates rose more sharply than anticipated,[15] or when bad real estate loans required a federal bailout of the Bank of New England. The bank's balance sheet showed about $33 billion in total assets. Regulators, however, found that it had off-balance-sheet commitments of $36 billion in various derivatives instruments.[16]

The Paine Webber Group announced in July 1994 that it would spend $268 million to bail out one of its money market funds, which had been marketed as a safe and secure investment, when it came up short on a derivatives speculation. In 1994, BankAmerica and PiperJaffray Companies took similar actions.[17]

The most publicized derivatives shock of 1994 came in December, when California's Orange County announced that its investment fund of $7.4 billion in public monies from 187 school districts, transportation authorities, and cities faced losses of $1.5 billion. It had borrowed $14 billion to invest in interest-sensitive derivatives and lost its bet when interest rates rose. As a result, Orange County faced a severe cutback in public services, including its schools, and the possibility of sharp tax increases.[18]

The news broke on February 25, 1995, that a twenty-eight-year-old trader in the Singapore office of Barings Bank had, over roughly four weeks, bet $29 billion of the firm's money on derivatives tied to Japanese Nikkei stock-index futures and Japanese interest rates—and ran up losses of $1.3 billion. The loss wiped out the venerable 233-year-old bank's $900 million in capital and forced it into bankruptcy.[19] In the first four hours of trading following the announcement, the Tokyo Nikkei index fell by 4.6 percent.[20] That the actions of a single trader of no particular personal wealth or reputation could produce such a consequence is indicative of the reckless instability of a globalized financial system in which hundreds of billions of dollars may move instantly in response to the latest news break.

PROFITING FROM VOLATILITY

The financial resources that private speculators bring into play in the world's money markets mock governmental efforts to manage interest and exchange rates to maintain economic stability and growth. Allen Metzler, one of the world's leading authorities on central banks and monetary policy, estimated that if the world's central bankers agreed among themselves on a coordinated commitment to protect a currency from a speculative attack, they might at best be able to muster $14 billion a day, a mere drop in the bucket compared with the more than $800 billion that currency speculators trade daily.[21]

The U.S. dollar fell by approximately 10 percent against both the Japanese yen and the German mark during the first half of 1994. On June 24, 1994, the U.S. Federal Reserve and sixteen other central banks mobilized a coordinated intervention and bought an estimated 3 to 5 billion U.S. dollars to slow the fall. The market scarcely noticed.

We have reached a point at which such interventions do little to decrease volatility. They simply transfer taxpayer dollars into the hands of speculators.

The onset of the Mexican peso crisis in December 1994 gave new insight into how costly the financial system dysfunctions have become. Although little discussed by the financial press, the backdrop to Mexico's financial crisis was very different from the picture of an economic miracle that had been presented to the public by big business and the Clinton administration during their campaign to sell the North American Free Trade Agreement (NAFTA).

For years, Mexico increased its foreign borrowing—and thereby its foreign debt—to cover consumer imports, capital flight, and debt-service payments. This borrowing took many forms, including selling high-risk, high-interest bonds to foreigners; selling public corporations to private foreign interests; and attracting foreign money with the speculative binge that sent Mexico's stock market skyrocketing. As little as 10 percent of the $70 billion in foreign "investment" funds that flowed into Mexico over the previous five years actually went to the creation of capital goods to expand productive capacity and thereby create a capacity for repayment. Prices of many of the assets transferred to foreign ownership were based on fictitiously inflated balance sheets. Projected debt service payments alone came to exceed the country's projected export revenues. Mexico's "economic miracle" was little more than a giant Ponzi scheme.[22]

Who benefited from these inflows? A few Mexicans built huge fortunes during this period. *Forbes* identified fourteen Mexican billionaires in its 1993 survey of the world's billionaires. It identified twenty-four in its 1994 survey.[23]

The bubble burst in December 1994. The Mexican stock market lost more than 30 percent of its money value in peso terms as speculators rushed to pull their money out. Downward pressure on the overvalued peso due to the flight of money out of Mexico pushed the Mexican government into a deep financial crisis and forced it to devalue a highly overvalued peso. This resulted in a dramatic shift in the terms of trade between the United States and Mexico and priced most U.S. imports out of reach of the Mexican market. When it appeared that the Mexican government might be forced to default on its foreign obligations, the Wall Street investors who held Mexican bonds ran to the U.S. government with cries that the sky would fall unless U.S. taxpayers financed a bailout. President Clinton responded by circumventing a reluctant Congress to put together a bailout plan totaling more than $50 billion in taxpayer money to ensure that the Wall Street banks and investment houses would recover their money. Critics of the bailout noted that not a penny of this money would go to the millions of poor and middle-class Mexicans who are bearing the major burden of the crisis.[24]

Neither the bailout nor interest rates as high as 92 percent on Mexican government securities had stemmed the peso's continuing decline by mid-March 1995.[25] Austerity measures imposed by the Mexican government were expected to put 750,000 Mexicans out of work during the first four months of 1995, and interest rates of 90 percent or more on mortgages, credit cards, and car loans would push many families into insolvency.[26] Estimates of the number of U.S. jobs that would be lost due to the related drop in exports to Mexico ran as high as 500,000.[27]

Shock waves from the Mexican crisis reverberated throughout the world's interlinked financial markets as speculators scurried to move their money to safer havens. When the Mexican stock market bubble burst, speculators with holdings in other Latin American countries got nervous and quickly pulled out their money, resulting in a fall of more than 30 percent in one month in the per-share value of the leading Latin American stock funds.[28] When the U.S. bailout linked the dollar to the falling peso, wary currency speculators sold dollars to buy German marks and Japanese yen, further weakening the dollar in international currency markets.[29]

How did this look to the Stratos dwellers from high above the clouds? I happened to be flying from New York to San Francisco in the midst of the Mexican peso debacle. The March 1995 issue of the United Airlines magazine *Hemispheres*, placed in every seat pocket, featured an article praising the success of the NAFTA and calling for its extension to the rest of the Western hemisphere.[30]

The ability to move massive amounts of money instantly between markets has given speculators a weapon by which to hold public policy hostage to their interests, and they are increasingly open about calling attention to this fact. Economist Paul Craig Roberts of the Cato Institute, a Washington, D.C., think tank devoted to the propagation of corporate libertarianism, lectured President Clinton in a *Business Week* op-ed piece:

> The dollar is also under pressure because investors have realized that Clinton favors big government "solutions," while other parts of the world, especially Asia and Latin America, are curtailing the scope of government and growing rapidly as a result. Equity investors have developed a global perspective, and they prefer markets where government is downsizing and the prospects for economic growth are

good. . . . It would also help if Congress were to repeal hundreds of ill-considered laws that benefit special interests at the expense of the overall performance of the economy, and if thousands of counterproductive rules in the Code of Federal Regulations were removed.[31]

The process is simple. If the speculators who are shuffling hundreds of billions of dollars around the world decide that the policies of a government give preference to "special interests"—by which they mean groups such as environmentalists, working people, or the poor—over the interests of financial speculators, they take their money elsewhere, creating economic havoc in the process. In their minds, the resulting economic disruption only confirms their thesis that the policies of the offending government were unsound. The view expressed to the *Washington Post* by a New York foreign exchange analyst is typical: "A lot of central banks love to blame it on the speculators. I think it's more a question of their gross incompetence in managing their monetary policy than a speculative attack."[32]

The financial press continues to describe what is happening in terms of global investors and international capital flows, as though we were still living in a world in which those who have savings commit them to productive uses beneficial to society with the expectation of steady, long-term returns. The reality that the Stratos dwellers are loath to acknowledge is that financial institutions once dedicated to mobilizing funds for productive investment have transmogrified into a predatory, risk-creating, speculation-driven, global financial system engaged in the unproductive extraction of wealth from taxpayers and the productive economy. This system is inherently unstable and is spiraling out of control, spreading economic, social, and environmental devastation and endangering the well-being of every person on the planet. Among its more specific sins, the transmogrified financial system is cannibalizing the corporations that once functioned as good local citizens, making socially responsible management virtually impossible and forcing the productive economy to discard people as costly impediments to economic efficiency.

15

CORPORATE CANNIBALISM

Mergers, acquisitions, and leveraged buyouts completed in 1988 cost a staggering $266 billion. . . . None of this . . . paid for as much as a single connecting bolt in a new machine . . . for an ounce of new fertilizer nor a single seed for a new crop. . . . A corporation that takes the long view of its profits and the broad view of its social responsibilities is in great danger of being acquired by an investors group that can gain financially by taking over the corporation and turning it to the pursuit of more immediate profit.

—William M. Dugger[1]

FINDING WAYS TO CREATE NEW VALUE in a sophisticated modern economy is seldom easy. Finding ways to create new value that will produce returns in the amount and with the speed demanded by a predatory financial system many times larger than the productive economy is virtually impossible.[2] The quickest way to make the kind of profit the system demands is to capture and cannibalize existing values from a weaker market player. In a free market, the "weaker" player is often the firm that is committed to investing in the future; providing employees with secure, well-paying jobs; paying a fair share of local taxes; paying into a fully funded retirement trust fund; managing environmental resources responsibly; and otherwise managing for the long-term human interest. Such companies are a valuable community asset, and in a healthy economy, they pay their shareholders solid and reliable—but not extravagant—dividends over the long term. They do not, however, yield the instant shareholder gains that computerized trading portfolios demand.

As Joel Kurtzman points out, by current market logic such firms should sell their assets and pay out the proceeds to shareholders.

Companies dismembering themselves look good on the computerized maps in the investors' nose cones. They pay rich rewards, their stock prices remain high, and they have virtually no investment in the future in research and development. This sort of company would be all payoff, and the computers would fight one another to buy it.[3]

When responsible managers are disinclined to cannibalize their own companies, the financial system stands eager to fund a buyout by those who will. In consequence, a predatory financial system teams up with a predatory market to declare responsible managers "inefficient" and purge them from the system, making the socially responsible corporation an endangered species.

RAIDING THE "INEFFICIENT" CORPORATION

A special breed of extractive investor, the corporate raider, specializes in preying on established corporations. The basic process is elegantly simple and profitable, though the details are complex and the power struggles often nasty. The raider identifies a company traded on a public stock exchange that has a "breakup" value in excess of the current market price of its shares. Sometimes they are troubled companies. More often, they are well-managed, fiscally sound companies that are being good citizens and looking to the long term. They may have substantial cash reserves to cushion against an economic downturn and may have natural resources holdings that they are managing on a sustainable yield basis. Often the raider is looking specifically for companies with reserves and long-term assets that can be sold off and that have costs that can be externalized onto the community.

Once such a company is identified, the prospective raider may form a new corporation as a receptacle for the acquired company. Often the receptacle corporation is financed almost entirely with debt and has little or no equity. The borrowed funds are used to quietly buy shares of the target company on the public stock exchanges at the prevailing market price up to the maximum allowed by law. An offer is then tendered to the company's board of directors to buy the outstanding shares of the company's stock at a price above the going market price, but below its breakup value. If the takeover bid is successful, the acquiring company consolidates the purchased company into itself, thus passing to the acquired company the debt that was used to buy it. Through a bit of financial sleight of hand, the acquired company has been purchased by using its own assets to secure the loans used to buy it.

Those who organize the deal ensure virtually risk-free gains for themselves by collecting large fees for their "services" in putting the deal together. Since the deals are financed mostly with money from banks or investment funds, the risks are borne largely by others, including the public that insures the bank deposits and gives up tax revenues to subsidize interest payments on the loan financing, and the small investors and pensioners whose money is at stake.

The "new" company now has considerable additional debt. To pay off that debt, the new management may draw down its cash reserves and pension funds, sell off profitable units for quick cash returns, bargain down wages, move production facilities abroad, strip natural resource holdings, and cut back maintenance and research expenditures to increase short-term gain—generally at the expense of long-term viability. Nearly 2,000 cases have been identified in which the new owners have virtually stolen a total of $21 billion from company pension accounts, which they often declare to be "excess" funding, to apply to debt repayment.[4]

Once the debt is paid down and the company is reporting rapid growth in annual profits, the firm may be sold back to the public through a stock offering at a significant premium. The raider congratulates himself or herself for "increasing economic efficiency" and "adding value" to the economy and seeks another target. These are the essentials of the leveraged buyout, a form of corporate cannibalism.

The key to the leveraged buyout is the ability to assemble the financing package. One might think that responsible bankers and investment brokers would shun such deals, which involve making huge unsecured loans to newly formed companies with no assets. To the contrary, since the deal makers offer unusually high interest rates to offset the lack of collateral, banks and investment houses often compete with one another for the opportunity to participate. During the 1980s, some large banks, awash in the same petrodollars that they were lavishing on indebted Southern countries in the 1970s, sought out the deal makers with offers of financing at the first rumor of a new takeover strike. Normally, the final financing package involves a combination of bank loans and funds realized from the sale of high-interest bonds, commonly called "junk bonds" because they are issued by shell corporations with no assets.

All this is played out with a chilling sense of moral detachment. In the words of Dennis Levine, a Wall Street high-flyer who was imprisoned for insider trading:

We had a phenomenal enterprise going on Wall Street, and it was easy to forget that the billions of dollars we threw around had any material impact upon the jobs and, thus, the daily lives of millions of Americans. All too often the Street seemed to be a giant Monopoly board, and this game-like attitude was clearly evident in our terminology. When a company was identified as an acquisition target, we declared that it was "in play." We designated the playing pieces and strategies in whimsical terms: white knight, target, shark repellent, the Pac-Man defense, poison pill, greenmail, the golden parachute. Keeping a scorecard was easy—the winner was the one who finalized the most deals and took home the most money.[5]

What happens all too often after the buyout is complete is illustrated by the acquisition of the Pacific Lumber Company and its holdings of ancient redwoods on the California coast by corporate raider Charles Hurwitz. Before Hurwitz acquired it in a hostile takeover, the family-run Pacific Lumber Company was known as one of the most economically and environmentally sound timber companies in the United States. It was exemplary in its pioneering development and use of sustainable logging practices on its substantial holdings of ancient redwood timber stands, was generous in the benefits it provided to its employees, overfunded its pension fund to ensure that it could meet its commitments, and maintained a no-layoffs policy even during downturns in the timber market.[6] These practices made it a prime takeover target.

After establishing control of the company, Hurwitz immediately doubled the cutting rate of the company's thousand-year-old trees. According to *Time*, "In 1990, the company reamed a broad, mile-and-a-half corridor into the middle of the Headwaters forest and called it, with a wink and a snicker, 'our wildlife-biologist study trail.'"[7] On a visit to Pacific's mills at Scotia, Hurwitz told the employees, "There's a story about the golden rule. He who has the gold rules." With that pronouncement, he drained $55 million from the company's $93 million pension fund.[8] The remaining $38 million was invested in annuities of the Executive Life Insurance Company that had financed the junk bonds used to make the purchase—and which subsequently failed.[9]

The hypocrisy of some corporate raiders is even more outrageous than their actions. To justify his role in the mass firings and wage cuts that followed the takeover of the Safeway supermarket chain, investor George Roberts told the *Wall Street Journal* that the supermarket chains employees "are now being held accountable. . . . They have to produce up to plan, if they are going to be competitive with the rest of the world. It's high time we did that."[10]

Roberts and his principal partner, each of whom is worth more than $450 million, had taken over Safeway along with three other partners. Together, the group put up roughly $2 million of their personal money to complete the deal. *Forbes* magazine heralded it in a headline as "The Buyout That Saved Safeway" by freeing the company "from the albatross of uncompetitive stores and surly unions."[11] The pay of Safeway workers in Denver was cut by 15 percent, and truck drivers complained of being forced to work sixteen-hour shifts. Some $500 million was shifted from taxes to interest payments, and the hundreds of millions in taxes formerly paid by tens of thousands of Safeway employees simply evaporated. For their contribution to making America more competitive by stemming the greedy impulses of Safeway's stock clerks, the five partners reaped a profit of more than $200 million.[12]

The fact that interest payments are tax deductible helps make all this possible. Since operating profits that would have been taxable are turned into deductible interest payments, the public subsidizes the cannibalizing of the nation's productive corporate assets. The effect on the U.S. taxpayer is far from trivial. During the 1950s, American corporations paid out $4 in taxes for every $1 in interest. During the 1980s, the increase in debt financing reversed the ratio, with corporations paying out $3 in interest for every $1 in taxes. One study concluded that $92 billion a year was thus shifted from taxes to interest payments. Whereas corporations paid 39 percent of all taxes collected in the United States in the 1950s, they paid only 17 percent in the 1980s. The share paid by individuals rose from 61 percent to 83 percent. Many corporations even collected refunds on taxes paid in the years before a takeover![13]

Corporate raiding and other forms of predatory extractive investment have become a source of handsome rewards for those with the stomach for it. In 1982, making the *Forbes* magazine list of the 400 wealthiest Americans required assets of $100 million. Only nineteen of those who made the 1982 list had made their fortunes in finance. Just five years later, in 1987, the smallest fortune that qualified for the list was $225 million, and sixty-nine of the 400 who qualified were from finance—most of them having cashed in on the wave of corporate takeovers.[14]

The corporate raiders boldly assert that they are performing an important service to the American economy by eliminating inefficiency and restoring American competitiveness in the global economy. A compliant press dutifully reports their claims with minimal challenge. "The twisted logic of the robber barons of the Reagan era," writes Jonathan Greenberg, a financial journalist, "is that the living wage of middle America had decimated our economy." As Greenberg concludes, "The truth of the era of corporate takeovers has little to do with economic competitiveness. It's this simple: we've been robbed."[15]

WEEDING OUT SOCIAL RESPONSIBILITY

Members of the corporate establishment insist that the problems of corporate excess can be dealt with through self-regulation without the need for public oversight or enforcement. This is rather like recommending that police departments and the courts be disbanded in favor of calling on compulsive street criminals to police themselves.

Others argue that the socially responsible action is usually the more profitable and therefore the logical choice purely on economic grounds. They overlook the fact that while responsible action may be the more profitable over the long-term, financial markets demand instant returns and corporate raiders are standing by to trash any company that isn't responding.

Still others argue that corporations are simply collections of people and that raising their awareness of the social and environmental consequences of their actions will correct any problems. They overlook the fact that there are a great many socially and environmentally conscious managers. The problem is that they work within a predatory system that demands they ask not "What is the right thing to do?" but rather "What is the most immediately profitable thing to do?" This creates a terrible dilemma for managers with a true social vision of the corporation's role in society. They must either compromise their vision or risk being expelled by the system.

The Stride Rite Corporation, a shoe company, provides an example.[16] In addition to its generous contributions to charitable causes, it became known for its policy of locating plants and distribution facilities in some of America's most depressed inner cities and rural communities to revitalize them and provide secure, well-paying jobs for minorities. The policy was a strong personal commitment of Arnold Hiatt, Stride Rite's chief executive officer, who believed that business could and should contribute more to community life than simply profits to its stockholders. As CEO, Hiatt was able to hold his board of directors in line behind this policy until 1984.

In that year, a 68 percent drop in income, the first drop in thirteen years, convinced the company's directors that the firm's survival depended on moving production abroad. They were concerned, among other things, that if they did not make that move, the company would become a takeover target. Hiatt fought the board of directors on this policy for as long as he could and ultimately resigned. According to Myles Slosberg, a director and former executive vice president of Stride Rite, the pursuit of low-cost labor bargains has since become something of a "Holy Grail" for the company. The systemic forces bearing on Stride Rite were enormous. Its U.S. workers averaged $1,200 to

$1,400 a month for wages alone, plus fringe benefits. The skilled workers in China who are hired by contractors to produce Stride Rite's shoes earn $100 to $150 a month, working fifty to sixty hours a week. In addition to moving its plants abroad, Stride Rite moved its national distribution center in the United States from Massachusetts to Louisville, Kentucky, to take advantage of lower-cost U.S. labor there and an offer of tax abatements from the state valued at $24 million over ten years.

Stride Rite sales doubled, and the price of its stock increased sixfold, making it a favorite on the New York Stock Exchange, including among socially conscious investors impressed by its record of corporate giving. According to Ervin Shames, Stride Rite's current chairman, "Putting jobs into places where it doesn't make economic sense is a dilution of corporate and community wealth.[17]

The Stride Rite experience presents a chilling example of the inexorable workings of a predatory global economy. Through a combination of the bidding down of Stride Rite's share of the public tax burden and the shifting of jobs from well- to poorly-paid workers, Stride Rite's management participated in a massive exercise in wealth redistribution from working people to its shareholders—from those who produce value through their skills and physical exertion to those who contribute only the use of surplus money. Yet Stride Rite's management cannot be blamed for this move.

If Hiatt, as Stride Rite's CEO, had carried the day, stuck to his convictions, and refused to move production abroad, a hovering group of investment bankers most certainly would have noted this "breech of fiduciary responsibility" to the firm's shareholders. They would have acquired the company through a hostile takeover, fired Stride Rite's socially concerned management, and moved the production abroad far more abruptly and with even worse consequences for the workers and the community.

Some investment funds specialize in buying and selling companies in labor-intensive industries that have resisted moving to low-wage countries. The AmeriMax Maquiladora Fund, a group of U.S. and Mexican investors initially backed by Nafinsa, Mexico's largest national development bank, was formed specifically to target U.S. companies that have resisted the move abroad. According to its prospectus:

> The Fund will purchase established domestic United States companies suitable for maquiladora acquisitions, wherein a part or all of the manufacturing operations will be relocated to Mexico to take advantage of the cost of labor. The Fund will seek to acquire companies

where labor is a significant component of a company's cost of goods sold. It is anticipated that within six to 18 months after a company has been acquired by the Fund, the designated portion of the company's manufacturing operations will be relocated to Mexico to take advantage of reduced labor costs.

We anticipate that manufacturing companies that experience fully loaded, gross labor costs in the $7–$10 per hour range in the U.S. may be able to utilize labor in a Mexican maquiladora at a fully loaded, gross labor cost of $1.15-$1.50 per hour. Though each situation may vary, it is estimated that this could translate into annual savings of $10,000–$17,000 per employee involved in the relocated manufacturing operations. It is anticipated that most investments will be retained for three to eight years.[18]

The potential profits from reselling such relocated companies are substantial. At a savings of $17,000 per employee, shifting 1,000 jobs from the United States to Mexico creates a potential increase of $17 million in annual profits. Assuming that the company's stock normally sells for ten times the company's annual earnings, this translates to an increase of $170 million in the market value of the company's stock.[19] Clearly those who invest in such schemes are not doing so from a desire to provide secure and well-paying jobs to needy Mexican workers.

A rogue financial system is actively cannibalizing the productive corporate sector. In the name of economic efficiency, it is rendering responsible management ever more difficult. Those who call on corporate managers to exercise greater social responsibility miss this basic point. Corporate managers live and work in a system that is virtually feeding on the socially responsible. That system is transforming itself into a two-tiered structure, creating a world that is deeply divided between the privileged and the dispossessed, between those who have the power to place themselves beyond the prevailing market forces and those who have become sacrificial offerings on the altar of global competition.

16

MANAGED COMPETITION

The business system is increasingly taking the form of lean and mean core firms, connected ... to networks of other large and small organizations, including firms, governments, and communities ... [These] networked forms of industrial organization ... exhibit a tendency to reinforce, and perhaps to worsen, the historic stratification of jobs and earnings.

—Bennett Harrison[1]

The recent quantum leap in the ability of transnational corporations to relocate their facilities around the world in effect makes all workers, communities and countries competitors for these corporations' favor. The consequence is a "race to the bottom" in which wages and social conditions tend to fall to the level of the most desperate.

—Jeremy Brecher[2]

ON SEPTEMBER 14, 1993, E. I. DU PONT de Nemours & Company announced it would dismiss 4,500 employees in its U.S.-based chemical business by mid-1994 to cut costs. While 4,500 families struggled to adjust to the fact that the economy had labeled their breadwinner a redundant burden, the money markets cheered. This layoff was part of a larger cutback of 9,000 people from du Pont's total worldwide workforce of 133,000—all part of a plan intended to cut the company's costs by $3 billion a year.[3] The price of a share of du Pont stock jumped $1.75 on the day of the announcement. Such announcements have become daily fare in the financial press. Clearly, important changes are occurring in the structure of industry. According to *The Economist*:

The biggest change coming over the world of business is that firms are getting smaller. The trend of a century is being reversed.... Now it is the big firms that are shrinking and small ones that are on the rise. The trend is unmistakable—and businessmen and policy makers will ignore it at their peril.[4]

It is a widespread perception that the massive corporate giants have become too large and bureaucratic to compete against the more nimble and innovative smaller firms that we are told are rapidly gaining the advantage in highly competitive global markets. Proponents of this view point to the fact that large firms are shedding employees by the hundreds of thousands. To back their claim they cite statistics showing that the new employment and technological innovations are being generated primarily by more competitive small and medium-sized firms. Although employment growth and innovation do generally come from the smaller firms, to claim that smaller firms have the advantage in global markets is highly misleading.

INTEGRATION AND COOPERATION AT THE CENTER

For all their praise of free-market competition, most corporations seek to avoid it for themselves at every opportunity. As Adam Smith observed in 1776, "People of the same trade seldom meet together, even for merriment and diversion, but the conversation ends in a conspiracy against the public, or in some contrivance to raise prices."[5] Such cooperation need not be born of evil motives. Competition creates turbulence, which is embraced as opportunity by speculators. But for those who manage productive enterprises, the resulting uncertainty makes investment planning inherently difficult, disrupts the orderly function of the firm, and can result in serious economic inefficiency. The desire to increase control and predictability by reducing competition might be considered one of the natural laws of the market.

Firms try to reduce competition in the global economy by the same means they have always used, by increasing their control over capital, markets, technology, and competitors. However, the combination of a globalized economy and modern information technologies lets firms consolidate that control on a scale never before possible. The competitive tactics are also familiar. Weaker competitors are absorbed, colonized, or crushed. Accommodation is sought with stronger competitors through strategic alliances, mergers, acquisitions, and interlocking boards of directors.

A favorite corporate libertarian argument for globalization is that opening national markets introduces greater competition and leads to increased efficiency. This neglects the larger reality that when markets are global, the forces of monopoly transcend national borders to consolidate at a global level. As soon as borders are opened, the pressure mounts to allow domestic firms to merge into ever more powerful combinations in order to be "competitive" in the global marketplace. When a Philip Morris acquires a Kraft and a General Foods, as it did in the 1980s to create the United States' largest food company, it does not make U.S. markets more competitive. Rather it creates a strengthened platform from which to create and project monopoly power on a global scale.

As a rule of thumb, economists consider a domestic market to be monopolistic when the four top firms account for 40 percent or more of sales. Through a series of mergers and consolidations, the top four major appliance corporations in the United States (Whirlpool, General Electric, Electrolux/WCI, and Maytag) controlled 92 percent of the U.S. appliance market as of 1990, and four airlines (United, American, Delta, and Northwest) accounted for 66 percent of U.S. revenue passenger miles. Four computer software companies (Microsoft, Lotus, Novell/Digital, and WordPerfect) controlled 55 percent of the U.S. software market in 1990, and two of them (Novell and WordPerfect) merged on June 27, 1994.[6]

When five firms control more than half of a global market, that market is considered to be *highly* monopolistic. *The Economist* recently reported five-firm concentration ratios for twelve global industries. The greatest concentration was found in consumer durables, where the top five firms control nearly 70 percent of the entire world market in their industry. In the automotive, airline, aerospace, electronic components, electrical and electronics, and steel industries, the top five firms control more than 50 percent of the global market, placing them in the monopolistic category. In the oil, personal computers, and media industries, the top five firms control more than 40 percent of sales, which shows strong monopolistic tendencies.[7]

The argument that globalization increases competition is simply false. To the contrary, it strengthens tendencies toward global-scale monopoly.

Agriculture has been a major subject in trade negotiations, with U.S. trade negotiators making a strong appeal for reducing barriers to free trade in agricultural commodities and eliminating protection for small farmers in Europe and Japan. The story of U.S. agriculture reveals why U.S. agribusiness corporations are so enthusiastically calling for the "freeing" of agricultural markets. It is part of the process of restructuring global agriculture into a two-tiered system controlled by the agribusiness giants.

From 1935 to 1989, the number of small farms in the United States declined from 6.8 million to under 2.1 million; a period during which the U.S. population roughly doubled. As farmers have gone out of business, so too have the local suppliers, implement dealers, and other small businesses that once supported them. Entire rural communities have disappeared. Meanwhile, the major U.S. agribusiness corporations have grown and consolidated their power. The top ten "farms" in the United States are now international agribusiness corporations with names like Tyson Foods, ConAgra, Gold Kist, Continental Grain, Perdue Farms, Pilgrims Pride, and Cargill—each with annual farm products sales ranging from $310 million to $1.7 billion.

Two grain companies—Cargill and ConAgra—control 50 percent of U.S. grain exports. Three companies—Iowa Beef Processors (IBP), Cargill, and ConAgra—slaughter nearly 80 percent of U.S. beef. One company— Campbell's—controls nearly 70 percent of the U.S. soup market. Four companies—Kellogg, General Mills, Philip Morris, and Quaker Oats—control nearly 85 percent of the U.S. cold cereal market. Four companies—ConAgra, ADM Milling, Cargill, and Pillsbury—mill nearly 60 percent of U.S. flour. This concentration is in part the consequence of 4,100 food industry mergers and leveraged buyouts in the United States between 1982 and 1990—and the consolidation process continues.[8]

The public is encouraged to believe that the corporate titans of Japan, North America, and Europe are battling it out toe-to-toe in international markets. This image is increasingly a fiction that obscures the extent to which a few core corporations are strengthening their collective monopoly market power through joint ventures and strategic alliances with their major rivals. Through these arrangements, firms share access to special expertise, technology, production facilities, and markets; spread the costs and risks of research and new product development; and manage relationships with their major rivals.

For example, American computer giants IBM, Apple Computer, and Motorola formed an interfirm alliance to develop the operating system and microprocessor for the next generation of computers. In 1991, Apple Computer turned to the Sony Corporation to manufacture the cheapest version of its PowerBook notebook computer.[9]

Toyota struck a deal with General Motors to produce Toyota cars in the United States for sale in Japan. General Motors now owns 37.5 percent of the Japanese auto manufacturer Isuzu, which produces automobiles for sale under the GM and Opel brand labels. Chrysler has had an ownership stake in Mitsubishi, Maserati, and Fiat. Ford Motor Company has a 25 percent stake in

Mazda and names three outside directors to the Mazda board. Ford and Mazda jointly own a dealer network in Japan, cooperate in new product design, and share production techniques.[10] *The Economist* suggests the following exercise:

> Take a really big international industry such as cars, in which the products are complicated and fairly expensive. Write down all the manufacturers' names (there are more than 20 large ones for cars) along the four sides of a square. Now draw lines connecting manufacturers that have joint ventures or alliances with one another, whether in design, research, components, full assembly, distribution or marketing, for one product or for several, anywhere in the world. Pretty soon, the drawing becomes an incomprehensible tangle; just about everyone seems to be allied with everyone else. And the car industry is not an exception. It is a similar story in computer hardware, computer software, aerospace, drugs, telecommunications, defense and many others.[11]

Cyrus Friedheim, vice-chairman of Booz, Allen & Hamilton, a management consulting firm, foresees an economic future dominated by what he calls "the relationship-enterprise," a network of strategic alliances among firms spanning different industries and countries that acts almost as a single firm. He points to the discussions among Boeing, members of the Airbus consortium, McDonnell Douglas, Mitsubishi, Kawasaki, and Fuji about cooperating on the joint development of a new super-jumbo jet and to the group formed by the world's major telecommunications firms to provide a worldwide network of fiber-optic underwater cables. According to Friedheim, these corporate juggernauts will dwarf existing global corporate giants, with individual relationship enterprises reaching total combined revenues approaching $1 trillion by early next century, making them larger than all but the six largest national economies.[12]

The world's corporate giants are creating a system of managed competition by which they actively limit competition among themselves while encouraging intensive competition among the smaller firms and localities that constitute their periphery. The process forces the periphery to absorb more of the costs of the "value added" so that the core can produce greater profits for its own insatiable master, the global financial system.

CENTRALLY MANAGED ECONOMIES

The scale of the concentration of economic power that is occurring is revealed in the statistic that of the world's hundred largest economies, fifty are economies internal to corporations.[13] The aggregate sales of the world's ten largest corporations in 1991 exceeded the aggregate GNP of the world's hundred smallest countries.[14] General Motors' 1992 sales revenues (133 billion) roughly equaled the combined GNP of Tanzania, Ethiopia, Nepal, Bangladesh, Zaire, Uganda, Nigeria, Kenya, and Pakistan. Five hundred fifty million people inhabit these countries, a tenth of the world's population.

The world's 200 largest industrial corporations, which employ only one-third of one percent of the world's population, control 28.3 percent of the world's economic output.[15] The top 300 transnationals, excluding financial institutions, own some 25 percent of the world's productive assets.[16] The combined assets of the world's fifty largest commercial banks and diversified financial companies amount to nearly 60 percent of *The Economist*'s estimate of a $20 trillion global stock of productive capital.[17] The global trend is clearly toward greater concentration of the control of markets and productive assets in the hands of a few firms that make a minuscule contribution to total global employment. The giants are shedding people but not control over money, markets, or technology.

This concentration of economic power in relatively few corporations raises an interesting contradiction. Corporate libertarians regularly proclaim that central economic planning is grossly inefficient and unresponsive to consumer preferences. Yet successful corporations maintain more control over the economies defined by their product networks than the central planners in Moscow ever achieved over the Soviet economy. Central management buys, sells, dismantles, or closes component units as it chooses, hires and fires people at the stroke of a pen, moves production units around the world at will, decides what revenues will be given up by subordinate units to the parent corporation, appoints and fires managers of subsidiaries, sets transfer prices and other terms governing transactions among the firm's component organizations, and decides whether individual units can make purchases and sales on the open market or must do business only with other units of the firm. Unless top management chooses to invite dissenting views, its decisions on such matters are seldom open to question or review by any subordinate person or unit.

Although no global corporation yet manages a planned economy on the scale of the former Soviet economy, they are coming closer. The 1991 sales of the world's five largest diversified service companies (all of which happen to be Japanese) were roughly equivalent to the entire 1988 gross domestic product (GDP) of the former Soviet Union. Cuba, with a GDP of $26.1 billion, now ranks seventy-second among the world's centrally managed economies; the first seventy-one are all global corporations. Tiny North Korea doesn't even make the list of the world's 500 largest centrally managed economies.

It is far from incidental that, in its internal governance structures, the corporation is among the most authoritarian of organizations and can be as repressive as any totalitarian state. Those who work for corporations spend the better portion of their waking hours living under a rule that dictates their dress, their speech, their values, their behavior, and their levels of income—with limited opportunity for appeal. With few exceptions, the corporation's employees can be dismissed without recourse on almost momentary notice. The current "lean and mean" transformation of the corporation seeks to extend this authoritarian rule beyond the boundaries of the corporation itself over far larger networks of organizations in ways that allow the corporation to consolidate its control while reducing its responsibility for the well-being of any member of the network.

SHEDDING JOBS AND CONCENTRATING POWER

Although there are regional variations, the world's most successful transnational corporations—whether Japanese, European, or American—are engaged in a process of transforming themselves and the structures of global capitalism to further consolidate their power through complex networking forms of organization. Bennett Harrison, author of *Lean and Mean: The Changing Landscape of Corporate Power in the Age of Flexibility*, calls it, "concentration without centralization." Four elements of that transformation are of particular relevance to our analysis.[18]

Downsizing Staff and Contracting Out   Drastic cuts in personnel are the most visible aspect of downsizing, but they are in most instances only one part of a larger organizational strategy. The larger scheme is to trim the firm's in-house operations down to its "core competencies," generally the finance, marketing, and proprietary technology functions that represent the firm's primary sources of economic power. The staffing of these functions is reduced to the bare minimum and consolidated within the corporate headquarters.

Peripheral functions, including much of the manufacturing activity, are farmed out to networks of relatively small outside contractors, often in low-wage countries. Employment shifts from the corporate core to peripheral contractor organizations that form part of a production network of firms that depend on the markets and technology controlled by the corporate core. Peripheral activities that are not contracted out and cannot be automated may be located far away from corporate headquarters. These are, for example, the "back offices" of the big insurance companies and banks, which are generally staffed with poorly paid female clerical workers.

Using Computers and Automation to Reduce Staff and Inventory   The core corporation brings the full capabilities of computers and automation to bear in whatever manufacturing functions it retains and in the management information systems by which it flexibly coordinates the product network's far-flung activities. Automation has two key purposes. One is to pare down the number of workers to an absolute minimum, such as in AT&T's plans to replace thousands of telephone operators with computerized voice-recognition systems.[19] The second is to minimize inventories by linking dispersed suppliers with marketing outlets using "just-in-time" delivery of parts and supplies.

Mergers, Acquisitions, and Strategic Alliances to Reduce Competitive Pressures   The corporations that occupy the core positions in major networks pursue a variety of strategies to manage the potentially destructive competition among themselves. One is to meld through mergers and acquisitions. Another is to construct strategic alliances through which they share technology, production facilities, and markets and engage in joint research.

Investment in Headquarters Teamwork and Morale to Maintain Loyalty and Performance   Those who work in the core are well compensated, with full benefits and attractive working conditions to assure their loyalty and commitment. Their job is to protect, control, and expand the various sources of the corporation's monopoly power, including its logo, image, brand names, intellectual property rights, financial and political assets, and strategic alliances.

The peripheral functions—farmed out either to subordinate units within the corporation or to outside suppliers dependent on the firm's business—are performed by low-paid, often temporary or part-time "contingent" employees who receive few or no benefits and to whom the corporation has no commitment. The result is a two-tiered structure that is highly differentiated with regard to competitive pressures. There is considerable, if uneasy, cooperation among the corporations that control the cores of major networks to maintain their collective monopoly control over markets and technology. The peripheral units, even those that remain within the firm, function as independent small contractors pitted in intense competition with one another for the firm's continuing business. They are thus forced to cut their own costs to the bone. This dualistic structure is an important part of the explanation for the growing income gap found in the United States and many other countries.

According to Harrison, "It is the strategic downsizing of the big firms that is responsible for driving down the average size of business organizations in the current era, *not* some spectacular growth of the small firms sector, per se."[20] The largest 1,000 companies in America account for over 60 percent of the gross national product, leaving the balance to 11 million small businesses.[21] The contracting-out process does create new opportunities for smaller firms, but the power remains right where it has been all along—with the corporate giants. Lacking independent access to the market, the smaller firms that orbit core corporations function more as dependent appendages than as independent businesses.

This explains why, when the world's largest corporations unceremoniously shed well educated, loyal, and hardworking employees, they are actually increasing their economic power. From 1980 to 1993, the Fortune 500 industrial firms shed nearly 4.4 million jobs, more than one out of four that they previously provided. During that same period, their sales increased by 1.4 times and assets by 2.3 times. The average annual chief executive officer compensation at the largest corporations increased by 6.1 times to $3.8 million.[22]

Although some corporations have been forced into downsizing by weak markets and lax management, others have downsized from a position of considerable strength. GTE announced plans on January 13, 1994, to lay off more than 17,000 employees in the face of a strong market and a steady growth in operating income. Other companies enjoying growth in markets and profits that announced significant layoffs at the end of 1993 or the beginning of 1994 include: Gillette (2,000 employees), Arco (1,300), Pacific Telesis (10,000), and Xerox (10,000). Some cut real fat from the payrolls. Other cuts were part of the shift to outsourcing. Many were made possible by new technologies. Major job cuts often accompany mergers and acquisitions, which are usually aimed at strengthening and consolidating market share while reducing employment costs. After Chevron merged with Gulf in 1984, it reduced the combined workforce by nearly half, to about 50,000 people. It cut another 6,500 people in 1992–93.[23]

General Electric shed 100,000 employees over eleven years to bring total employment down to 268,000 in 1992. During that same period, its sales went up from $27 billion to $62 billion, and net income increased from $1.5 billion to $4.7 billion.[24] GE became smaller only in terms of the number of employees who shared the benefits of its growth in profits and market share. It mainly shed its commitment to provide productive and well-remunerated employment for 100,000 people and their families. It did not shed its technical, financial, or market power.

Some of the more vivid examples of a two-tiered structure are found in the agriculture sector. Large agribusiness corporations commonly reduce their own risks, while increasing their profits, by contracting out production to smaller farms. The owners of the small farms provide the major capital investment and bear the risks of crop failure. Since the corporate giant controls the market, the small farmer has little choice but to accept the terms it dictates—including production methods, the price of the inputs it requires the farmer to buy, and the price it will pay for the crop. The only choice left to farmers is to accept the terms, go out of business, or find another crop whose market is not yet controlled by a core corporation. This restructuring of agriculture has contributed to decreasing the farmers' share of consumers' food dollars from 41 percent in 1910 to 9 percent in 1990.[25]

Figures compiled in 1980 by the U.S. Department of Agriculture revealed that production and marketing contracts covered the production of 98 percent of sugar beets, 95 percent of fluid-grade milk, 89 percent of chicken broilers, 85 percent of processed vegetables, and 80 percent of all seed crops. When a contractor firm controls the market, producers are at its mercy. When Del Monte decided, for example, to transfer the bulk of its peach procurement from northern California to Italy and South Africa, most of its contract farmers saw their market vanish for reasons that had nothing to do with the local appetite for peaches.[26]

Such conditions mock Adam Smith's notion of a competitive market comprised of small buyers and sellers. The farmer receives a lower price and the consumer pays a higher price than either would have obtained under conditions of true competition.[27] The world's major agribusiness corporations are rapidly extending this system to the world.

BRAND POWER VS. RETAIL POWER

Within this restructuring drama, we see a secondary drama being played out in a major contest between the manufacturing giants and the retailing giants for control of the core network positions. The growing success of the retailing giants is revealed by the growing rate of bankruptcy among retailers in the United States. Since 1991, retail firms have been going bankrupt at a rate of more than 17,000 a year, up from approximately 11,000 in 1989. Many of them have been driven out of business by the mega-retailers.[28] According to *Business Week*:

> A vast consolidation in U.S. retailing has produced giant "power retailers" that use sophisticated inventory management, finely tuned selections, and above all, competitive pricing to crowd out weaker players and attract more of the shopper's dollar. . . . They're telling even the mightiest of manufacturers what goods to make, in what colors and sizes, how much to ship and when. . . . Leading the pack, of course, is Wal-Mart Stores. The nation's No. 1 retailer is expected to grow 25% this year, to some $55 billion in sales, at a time when retailers as a whole will be lucky to grow 4%.[29]

When Wal-Mart grows at a rate of 25 percent in an industry that is growing at no more than 4 percent, its growth is clearly at the expense of rivals that lack comparable clout. The smaller retailers that used to be the commercial core of and major employers in most towns and cities have been hit particularly hard. Analysts predicted that retailers accounting for half of all sales in the United States in 1992 would disappear by the year 2000. Systems analyst and syndicated columnist Donella Meadows describes what happens when a Wal-Mart comes to town:

> In Iowa the average Wal-Mart grosses $13 million a year and increases total area sales by $4 million, which means it takes $9 million worth of business from existing stores. Within three or four years of a Wal-Mart's arrival, retail sales within a 20-mile radius go down by 25 percent; 20 to 50 miles away, sales go down 10 percent.
>
> A Massachusetts study says a typical Wal-Mart adds 140 jobs and destroys 230 higher-paying jobs. . . . Despite public investments in restoring downtown business districts, vacancies increase. Rents drop,

and the remaining enterprises pay lower wages and taxes. Competing chain stores in existing malls leave and are not replaced.[30]

The mass retailing superpowers—Wal-Mart, Kmart, Toys 'R' Us, Home Depot, Circuit City Stores, Dillard Department Stores, Target Stores, and Costco, among others—are core firms in vast consumer goods networks. The mega-retailers are notorious for playing suppliers against one another and for abruptly shifting their sourcing from domestic firms to low-labor-cost countries such as China or Bangladesh. Many small manufacturers have suddenly found themselves in bankruptcy when the major part of their market evaporated. Even the manufacturing giants, such as Procter & Gamble, that lack their own retail outlets are under intense pressure from the retailing giants to cut their prices and profit margins.

As the big retailers grow, they tend to favor larger suppliers that have the resources and sophistication to meet their demands for customized products and packages, computer linkups, and special delivery schedules. This contributes to further consolidation on the manufacturing side. Only a decade ago, no single toy maker controlled more than 5 percent of the market.[31] Now, in a toy industry dominated by Toys 'R' Us and general discounting giants such as Wal-Mart, Kmart, and Target Stores, the manufacturing side is dominated by just six companies.

While basically applauding this as a move toward greater efficiency, even *Business Week* sounds a cautionary note: "what if the growing clout of power retailers stifles too many small companies and forces too many large ones to dodge risks? The close ties between retailers and their surviving suppliers could ultimately end up raising consumer prices and reducing innovation."[32]

RACE TO THE BOTTOM

While competition is being weakened at the core, it is intensifying among smaller businesses, workers, and localities at the periphery as they become pitted against one another in a desperate struggle for survival. What the corporate libertarians call "becoming more globally competitive" is more accurately described as a race to the bottom. With each passing day it becomes more difficult to obtain contracts from one of the mega-retailers without hiring child labor, cheating workers on overtime pay, imposing merciless quotas, and operating unsafe facilities. If one contractor does not do it, his or her prices will be higher than those of another who does. With hundreds of millions of people desperate for any kind of job the global economy may offer, there will always be willing competitors. Pressed to maximize their own margins, the core corporations close their eyes to the infractions and insist that they have no responsibility for working conditions in the factories of their contractors.

Descriptions of the working conditions of millions of workers, even in the "modern and affluent" North, sound like a throwback to the days of the early industrial revolution. Consider this description of conditions at contract clothing shops in modern, affluent San Francisco:

> Many of them are dark, cramped and windowless. . . . Twelve-hour days with no days off and a break only for lunch are not uncommon. And in this wealthy, cosmopolitan city, many shops enforce draconian rules reminiscent of the nineteenth century. "The workers were not allowed to talk to each other and they didn't allow us to go to the bathroom," says one Asian garment worker. . . . Aware of manufacturers' zeal for bargain-basement prices, the nearly 600 sewing contractors in the Bay Area engage in cutthroat competition—often a kind of Darwinian drive to the bottom. . . . Manufacturers have another powerful chip to keep bids down. Katie Quan, a manager of the International Ladies Garment Workers Union in San Francisco, explains, "They say, 'If you don't take it, we'll just ship it overseas, and you won't get work and your workers will go hungry.'"
>
> In 1992 a [Department of Labor] investigation of garment shops on the U.S. protectorate of Saipan found conditions akin to indentured servitude: Chinese workers whose passports had been confiscated, putting in eighty-four-hour weeks at subminimum wages.[33]

The line between conditions in the South and the North as defined by geography becomes ever more blurred. Dorka Diaz, a twenty-year-old textile worker who formerly produced clothing in Honduras for Leslie Fay, a U.S.-based transnational, testified before the Subcommittee on Labor-Management Relations of the U.S. House of Representatives that she worked for Leslie Fay in Honduras alongside twelve- and thirteen-year-old girls locked inside a factory where the temperature often hit 100 degrees and there was no clean drinking water. For a fifty-four-hour week, she was paid a little over $20. She and her three-year-old son lived at the edge of starvation. In April 1994, she was fired for trying to organize a union.[34]

China has become a favorite of foreign investors and corporations seeking cheap labor and outsourcing for offshore procurement at rock-bottom prices. *Business Week* described the prevailing conditions of Chinese factory workers:

> In foreign-funded factories, which employ about 6 million Chinese in the coastal provinces, accidents abound. In some factories, workers are chastised, beaten, strip-searched, and even forbidden to use the bathroom during work hours. At a foreign-owned company in the Fujian province city of Ziamen, 40 workers—or one-tenth of the work force—have had their fingers crushed by obsolete machines. According to official reports, there were 45,000 industrial accidents in Guangdong last year, claiming more than 8,700 lives. . . . Last month . . . 76 workers died in a Guangdong factory accident.[35]

In India, an estimated 55 million children work in various conditions of servitude, many as bonded laborers—virtual slaves—under the most appalling conditions. Some are paying off the debts of their impoverished parents or have been sold into bondage by parents unable to feed them. Others have been kidnaped. The unfortunate ones are paid nothing at all. Former Indian Chief Justice P. M. Bhagwati has publicly testified to observing examples of boys working fourteen to twenty hours a day: "They are beaten up, branded [with red-hot iron rods] and even hung from trees upside down."

More than 300,000 of India's child laborers work in India's carpet industry, which exports $300 million worth of carpets a year to the global economy, mainly to the United States and Germany. They work fourteen to sixteen hours a day, seven days a week, fifty-two weeks a year. India's carpet manufacturers argue that they must have child laborers to be able to survive in competition with the carpet industries of Pakistan, Nepal, Morocco, and elsewhere that also use child laborers.[36]

Those who heed the call to become globally competitive should bear in mind what it takes to stay ahead of the pack in the race to a bottom with no finish line.

According to conventional wisdom the wonder of the marketplace is the way in which it disciplines firms to maintain overall economic efficiency. In the global economy, however, the largest corporations have learned how to manage competition to minimize it for themselves while maximizing it for others—using it as one more management tool to pass more of their own costs onto people and communities.

The underlying patterns of the institutional transformation being wrought by economic globalization persistently move power away from people and communities to concentrate it in mega-corporations that have slipped the bonds of human accountability and delinked from the human interest. We have become captives of the tyranny of a rogue system that is running on autopilot into the face of a great mountain. Driven by its own imperatives, that system has gained control over many of the most important aspects of our lives, constantly demanding that we give ourselves over totally to its purpose—making money. We now face an even more ominous prospect. Having gained control of the institutions that once served our needs and intent on eliminating inefficiency to increase profits, the system has found that people are the primary source of inefficiency.

17

NO PLACE FOR PEOPLE

We are entering a new phase in human history—one in which fewer and fewer workers will be needed to produce the goods and services for the global population.

—*Jeremy Rifkin*[1]

In the corporate economies of the contemporary West, the market is a passive institution. The active institution is the corporation . . . an inherently narrow and short-sighted organization. . . . The corporation has evolved to serve the interests of whomever controls it, at the expense of whomever does not.

—*William M. Dugger*[2]

WE SEE A PATTERN REPEATED at all levels of society and in every corner of the world. In the name of increasing efficiency hundreds of millions of people are being discarded by a global economy that has no need for them. In Mexico, small farmers are displaced to make way for mechanized agriculture. In India, they are forced off their lands by massive new dams needed to produce electricity so that factory workers can be replaced by more efficient machines. On Wall Street, the human traders who key decisions into computer terminals to execute trades in global money markets are replaced by more efficient computer programs. Small-town merchants are driven out by superstores run by mega-retailers, who in turn are threatened by dot-com retailers. Voice-recognition devices and automated answering devices replace telephone operators. Multimedia education replaces teachers. Corporate downsizing is eliminating redundant workers and middle managers. Corporate mergers and consolidation eliminate middle, and even top, managers. There is no end in sight.

FIRST THE MUSCLE, NOW THE BRAIN

We are crossing the threshold into the second industrial revolution. The first industrial revolution exploited a newfound human mastery of energy to give machines enormous muscle power and greatly reduced the demand for physical human labor. Machines, however, could not calculate, reason, discriminate visual patterns, or recognize and interpret human speech. Thus, every machine required a human operator to provide it with a brain and a human intermediary to serve as its eyes and ears. The greater the number of machines, the greater the number of people needed to tend them. The more sophisticated the machines, the greater the skills their operators required and the higher the wages skilled operators could command. The second industrial revolution is exploiting major advances in information technology that use computers and electronic sensors to give machines eyes, ears, and brains to see and hear, interpret, and act on their own.

Economists with secure, tenured positions at leading universities assure us that we have no need to worry. The increases in productivity will spur economic growth, and growth will mean more jobs, they tell us, just as happened in the first industrial revolution. They fail to note that when the British textile industry was mechanized during the first industrial revolution, Britain shifted much of the resulting unemployment to India. It placed prohibitive tariffs on textiles imported from India to Britain, while British colonial administrators in India virtually eliminated the tariff on British textiles imported to India and levied taxes on Indian cloth produced domestically for domestic sale and on household spinning wheels.[3] The colonies also absorbed many migrants who were surplus to the European economy. Exported to the colonies, they commandeered the best lands to grow export crops, such as cotton, to feed the mother-country industries.

The second industrial revolution, based on a process of colonization defined more by class than by geography, is forcing ever more of the world's population into the ranks of the colonized.

Efficiency is about producing a greater output with less input. When we increase productive output per hour of human labor, we speak of increasing productivity. In the simplified examples of the sort favored by economics texts, it seems quite a good thing.

A farmer who buys a small tractor can cultivate more acres to provide more food and income for her family or devote fewer hours to toiling in the fields. Either way the farmer gains, no one loses, and the society is enriched in a variety of ways.

Unfortunately, the real world isn't like such simplified textbook examples. Note that in our example, the manager, the owner, and the laborer are one and the same person—she makes the decision, bears the costs, and decides whether the productivity gain will go toward increasing production or reducing work time. In the real world, the decision is likely to be made by an agribusiness corporation based solely on profitability. A few favored workers will be required to increase their output; the remainder will lose their jobs, with few alternative prospects.

It seems that the only certain beneficiaries of productivity increases in a nonunionized, labor-surplus world are the owners of capital. Yet, as management analyst William Dugger suggests, we may be on the way to displacing them as well:

> The corporation is a true Frankenstein's monster—an artificial person run amok, responsible only to its own soulless self. Some fascinating possibilities present themselves. Corporations have already begun to buy up their own stock, holding it in their treasury. Taken to the logical conclusion, when 100 percent of the stock is treasury stock the corporation will own itself. It will have dispensed entirely with shareholders from the species Homo sapiens. To whom or to what would it then be responsible? Take these speculations about organized irresponsibility a bit further. . . . Could a corporation entirely dispense with not only human ownership but also human workers and managers? . . . What would it be then? . . . It would exist physically as a network of machines that buy, process, and sell commodities, monitored by a network of computers. Its purpose would be to grow ever larger through acquiring more machines and to become ever more powerful through acquiring more computers to monitor the new machines. It would be responsible to no one but itself in its mechanical drive for power and profit. It would represent capitalism at its very purest, completely unconcerned with anything save profit and power.[4]

Perhaps one day, if allowed sufficient freedom to follow its own unrestrained tendencies, a global corporation will achieve the ultimate in productive efficiency, an entity made up solely of computers and machines busily engaged in the replication of money. We might call it the perfectly efficient corporation. Although this is surely not what anyone intends, we are acting as though this is the world we seek to create.

PAIN AT THE TOP

Behind their bold public defense of an economic system in an advanced stage of self-destruction, there are growing reports of unease and concern even among the most elite of the Stratos dwellers. In 1980–82, 79 percent of managers reported that their job security was "good" or "very good." By 1992–94, that figure had fallen to 55 percent.[5] It is not simply that their own positions are increasingly at risk. It is a sense that something simply isn't right, that they are leaving their children a deeply troubled world. Many corporate managers face growing conflicts between their personal values and what their corporate positions demand of them.

When justifying outrageous executive salaries, the press commonly notes the importance of such rewards in motivating the heads of corporations to exert their best efforts. When William A. Anders, the chairman of General Dynamics Corporation, was granted a $1.6 million bonus for having kept his company's stock price above $45 for ten days, a company spokesperson told the *Washington Post* that the bonus plan was needed to give top executives the incentive to change the company's business strategy and focus on maximizing returns to shareholders.[6] It is an extraordinary claim that the most privileged and well-paid professionals in the world require million-dollar bonuses to motivate them to do their jobs.

Derek Bok, the former president of Harvard University, offers a telling explanation. He suggests that top corporate executives must be paid such outrageous sums to ensure that they place the short-term interests of shareholders above all other interests that they might otherwise be tempted to consider—such as those of employees, the community, and even the corporation's own long-term viability.[7] In short, top executives have to be paid outrageous salaries to motivate them not to yield to their instincts toward social responsibility. Viewed from this perspective, these salaries indicate how distasteful the job of top corporate managers has become in the era of corporate downsizing.

With no end to the bloodletting in sight, a growing number of managers are losing their enthusiasm for their jobs, as *Fortune* reported in its July 25, 1994, cover story, "Burned-Out Bosses":

> [M]anagers who were trained to build are now being paid to tear down. They don't hire; they fire. They don't like the new mandate, but most have come to understand that it's not going to change. That realization makes the daily routine different: Work no longer energizes; it drains.

Under the circumstances it seems almost immoral to take much joy in work. So they become morose and cautious, worrying that they will be washed away in the next wave of discharges. Meanwhile, they work harder and longer to make up for the toil of those who have left. Fatigue and resentment begin to build.[8]

Unlike the financial speculators who move billions of dollars around the world from computer terminals detached from human reality, the managers of companies that produce real things deal every day with flesh-and-blood humans. They are the ones who must respond to the demands of the money managers for greater "efficiency" by imposing on their former friends and colleagues an experience almost as devastating as the loss of a loved one. As one CEO related to *Fortune*, "You get through firing people the first time around, accepting it as part of business. The second time I began wondering, 'How many miscarriages is this causing? How many divorces, how many suicides?' I worked harder so that I wouldn't have to think about it."[9]

An executive recruiter reported visiting a manager who had just gone through several rounds of firing immediate subordinates. Previously a strong, take-charge executive, he was now smoking, had lost weight, was unable to look the recruiter in the eye, and seemed extremely nervous. For another executive who had previously eliminated thousands of jobs, the need to put several thousand more former colleagues out on the street resulted in a loss of appetite and difficulty sleeping. He began breaking out in spontaneous fits of crying and one day couldn't get out of bed.

Those who achieve the pinnacles of financial and professional success in America seldom lack for physical comforts. They are learning, however, that no amount of money can buy peace of mind, a strong and loving family, caring friends, and a feeling that one is doing meaningful and important work.

The world is changing even for managers who were once at the pinnacle of power and prestige within their industries. Richard W. Snyder, one of the best known and most powerful figures in the publishing business, had a key role during his thirty-three-year career in building Simon and Schuster into a major U.S. communications firm with an annual gross income of $2 billion. On June 14, 1994, he was abruptly and summarily sacked as chairman and CEO during a five-minute meeting with the CEO of Viacom, Inc., which had recently taken over Simon and Schuster's parent company Paramount Communications. The reason given was simply "a difference in styles."[10]

Under the leadership of its chairman Kay R. Whitmore, Eastman Kodak reported 1992 profits of $1.14 billion—a margin of roughly 5 percent on sales.

On August 6, 1993, he was fired by the company's outside directors on the grounds that he was moving too slowly on cost reduction. He had announced 1992 layoffs of only 3,000 of Kodak's 132,000 employees. Institutional share-holders were clamoring for cuts of at least 20,000. Financial analysts heralded his firing as clear evidence that the outside directors were committed to plac-ing the interests of investors ahead of those of management and employees. Kodak stock closed up $3.25 at the end of the day.[11]

No one is immune. There is no longer security at any level of the pyramid. *The Economist* recently noted:

> Being the boss of a big American firm has been one of the safest and most richly rewarded jobs in the world. Until recently, that is. Last week the bosses of IBM, Westinghouse and American Express lost their jobs. A few months earlier Robert Stempel was unceremoniously re-moved as chairman of General Motors. . . . Now those at the top of big companies are wondering who will be next.[12]

The Economist attributes the phenomenon to a shift of shareholder power from the individual investor to performance-oriented investment funds that are flex-ing their muscles to kick out top managers of corporations that they consider to be "underperforming." There is the need for takeover battles as fund manag-ers realize they can simply fire managers whose performance is lagging.

LIMITING COMMITMENT

Corporate restructuring is not simply about the drastic elimination of jobs; it is also about downgrading those that remain. The white-collar labor market is becoming more like the labor exchanges where jobless day laborers gather, hoping to hire out for the day. The "just-in-time" inventory concept now ap-plies to people too.

The number of workers employed by temporary agencies has increased 240 percent in ten years. Manpower, the largest of 7,000 U.S. temp agencies with 600,000 temporary workers on its rolls, is now America's largest private employer. Although some workers are part-time or temporary by choice, in 1993 nearly a third of the 21 million part-time workers in the United States said that they would prefer full-time jobs. Many displaced workers become self-employed, contracting out individually for temporary work. Most of these have suffered sharp declines in income. Although much of the evidence is anecdotal, Census Bureau statistics reveal that from 1989 to 1992, the real median income of Americans who worked for themselves fell 12.6 percent to $18,544. Many of the newly self-employed workers are earning well below $18,000 a year—a level that makes supporting a family in the present American economy difficult, if not impossible.[13]

Young professionals are now actively counseled to plan career paths independently of their companies, to build their resumes and their outside contacts so that they are ready to move on when a new opportunity arises or when their companies abandon them. The advice to young people starting their careers: treat every job as though you are self-employed.[14]

Not so long ago, the firm for which a person worked was almost like family. It was a primary support system in an otherwise often impersonal and transient world. A good job was far more than an income. It was a source of identity and of valued and enduring relationships. Those days are no more, placing yet more stress on the family itself. In the present job market, the distinction between white-collar and blue-collar workers is less significant than the distinction between those who have permanent jobs and those who don't. The system nurtures an attitude of get what you can from the system while you can. Look out for yourself, because no one else will.

A SPREADING CANCER

Rather like the spread of a malignant cancer, the dysfunctional values and dynamics that characterize U.S. corporations and financial markets are spreading to Europe and Japan where corporations have traditionally been known for their sense of responsibility to their workers and the interests of the communities in which they are located. By May 1994, a binge of corporate restructuring in Europe, similar to that in the United States, had pushed Europe's unemployment rate to 10.9 percent.[15] Even these rates, high as they are, may mask a much deeper dysfunction. In Belgium, unemployment was 8.5 percent in 1992, but 25 percent of the workforce was living on public assistance.[16] Persistent joblessness is resulting in growing social unrest, exacerbating racial tensions, and sparking a vicious backlash against immigrants. Joblessness is especially acute among youth, whose unemployment rate is twice that of the general population and still rising. On March 25, 1994, 50,000 students marched down a Paris boulevard, "taunting police and chanting slogans demanding jobs." A survey of 3,000 European teenagers found them "confused, vulnerable, obsessed with their economic futures."[17]

The onslaught is strongly supported by the propaganda machinery of the corporate media establishment, which is quick to turn every injustice created by the excesses of corporate globalization into justification for yet more excess. Pointing out that the unemployment rate in Europe has averaged about 3 percentage points higher than in the United States, *The Economist* cautioned, "no trade barrier will keep out the technological changes that are revolutionizing work in the rich world; and a trade war is sure to destroy more jobs than it saves."[18] It counseled Europe to emulate the United States by reducing social safety nets that "give the unemployed little incentive to seek work," minimum wages that "cost young workers their jobs," employer social security contributions that reduce demand for labor, and "strict employment-protection rules" that discourage firms from hiring by making "it hard, if not impossible, to lay off workers once they are on the payroll." To those who point out that the quality of jobs in America has deteriorated as a consequence of such policies, *The Economist* has a ready answer:

> Too many [of the jobs being created in America], say the merchants of gloom, are part-time, temporary and badly paid. The real wages of low-skilled workers have fallen over the past decade. Yet in comparison with Europe, this should be seen as a sign of success—an example of a well-functioning labour market—not a failure. As manufacturing has declined, America and Europe have both faced shrinking demand for low-skilled labour. In America, the relative pay of these workers was allowed to fall, so fewer jobs were lost. European workers, by contrast, have resisted the inevitable and so priced themselves out of work.[19]

In short, according to the corporate press, Europe's unemployment problem is a result of overpaying the poor, taxing the rich, and imposing regulations that limit the ability of European firms to get on with serious downsizing. *The Economist* editorial pointed to moves by various European countries to reduce minimum wages, cut payroll taxes, and loosen employment-protection laws as signs of hope.[20] *Business Week* offered similar counsel:

> To ensure it remains competitive once the down-cycle wanes, Europe must be willing to see more of its low-value-added manufacturing jobs move to Eastern Europe and elsewhere. . . . And it must reduce farm subsidies while continuing to hammer away at high wages and corporate taxes, short working hours, labor immobility, and luxuri-

ous social programs. If Europeans don't follow these prescriptions, this recession may be doomed to be more than just a cyclical one. . . . Putting up trade barriers will only insulate Europeans from the discipline they need to maintain.[21]

Although running a bit behind the United States, the evidence suggests that European companies and governments are increasingly heeding this advice, which means that the unemployment, racial tension, and social unrest currently plaguing Europe are almost certain to spiral upward. We may presume that *The Economist* will then praise Europe for its success.

The dream of the corporate empire builders is rapidly being realized. The global system is harmonizing standards across country after country—ever downward toward the lowest common denominator. Driven by the imperatives of global financial markets, the global system values only money. People, with their incessant special-interest demands for living wages, prosperous communities, and healthy environments, are an unwelcome economic burden—a meddlesome source of inefficiency to be eliminated.

Human well-being will never be secured by the kind of economic growth demanded by a rogue financial system that values people, planet, and the civilizing bonds of culture and community only for their current market price. It comes down to a question of how we want to live. If we want societies that value life more than money, we must re-create our institutions accordingly.

Part V

RECLAIMING OUR POWER

18

THE ECOLOGICAL REVOLUTION

By deliberately changing the internal image of reality, people can change the world.

—Willis Harman[1]

I believe that the world has moved closer to oneness and more people see each other as one with the other. . . . It is possible to have new thoughts and new common values for humans and all other forms of life.
—Wangari Maathai, coordinator, Kenya Green Belt Movement[2]

NO SANE PERSON SEEKS A WORLD divided between billions of excluded people living in absolute deprivation and a tiny elite guarding their wealth and luxury behind fortress walls. No one rejoices at the prospect of life in a world of collapsing social and ecological systems. Yet we continue to place human civilization and even the survival of our species at risk mainly to allow a few million people to accumulate money beyond any conceivable need. We continue to go boldly where no one wants to go.

We are now coming to see that economic globalization has come at a heavy price. In the name of modernity we are creating dysfunctional societies that are breeding pathological behavior—violence, extreme competitiveness, suicide, drug abuse, greed, and environmental degradation—at every hand. Such behavior is an inevitable consequence when a society fails to meet the needs of its members for social bonding, trust, affection, and a shared sacred meaning.[3] The threefold crisis of deepening poverty, environmental destruction, and social disintegration manifests this dysfunction.

The collective madness of pursuing policies that deepen the dysfunction is not inevitable. The idea that we are caught in the grip of irresistible historical forces and inherent, irreversible human imperfections to which we must adapt is pure fabrication. Corporate globalization is being advanced by the conscious choices of those who see the world through the lens of the corporate interest. Human alternatives do exist, and those who view the world through the lens of the human interest have both the right and the power to choose them.

Healthy societies depend on healthy, empowered local communities that build caring relationships among people and help us connect to a particular piece of the living earth with which our lives are intertwined. Such societies must be built through local-level action, household by household and community by community. Instead we have created an institutional and cultural context that disempowers the local and makes such action difficult, if not impossible.

To correct the dysfunction, we must shed the illusions of our collective cultural trance, reclaim the power we have yielded to failing institutions, take back responsibility for our lives, and reweave the basic fabric of caring families and communities to create places for people and other living things. These actions are within our means but will require transforming the dominant belief systems, values, and institutions of our societies—an Ecological Revolution comparable to the Copernican Revolution that ushered in the scientific-industrial era. The parallels are instructive.

COMPETING VISIONS OF REALITY

The Copernican Revolution was grounded in a basic change in the prevailing perception of the nature of reality. The issues involved bear examination, because they go to the root of our present crisis and help define the challenge of the Ecological Revolution.[4]

Transcendental monism (the view that consciousness or spirit gives rise to matter) has formed the philosophical foundation of many Eastern cultures, at least until the recent onslaught of Western science, industrialization, global competition, and consumerism. Adherents of this tradition believe that consciousness is the primary reality and that matter is a creation of consciousness or spiritual energy. Based on the belief that all consciousness, as well as the material manifestation of consciousness, originates from the same underlying unity, transcendental monism considers inner wisdom, accessed through our spiritual connection with the infinite, to be the primary source of valid knowing. This tradition had commonly been associated with a denial of things material, a fatalistic acceptance of one's material condition, a strong sense of community, and a deep reverence for nature.

In the West, the Judeo-Christian tradition took quite a different course, personifying God as a being who lives in a distant and separate realm and whose attention is centered on earth and its human inhabitants. In this tradition, God's will and wisdom were revealed through prophets, such as Moses, or through his incarnation as Jesus. The earth was believed to be the center of the universe, with the sun, stars, and planets revolving around it. These beliefs remained the foundation of scientific thought and moral and political authority in Europe until as recently as 500 years ago.

Then in 1543, Nicholas Copernicus published *Revolution of the Celestial Spheres,* setting forth the thesis that the earth is only one among the planets that revolve around the sun, itself one of countless such stars of the cosmos. This led to a historic confrontation between science and the church as to whether scientific observation or divine revelation is the more valid source of human knowledge. Materialistic monism (the view that matter gives rise to consciousness or spirit) became the image of reality embraced by science and unleashed what historians refer to as the Copernican Revolution. Adherents to this tradition believe that matter is the primary reality, physical measurement is the one valid source of knowledge, and the experience of consciousness is only a manifestation of the material complexity of the physical brain. For this tradition it is inconceivable that any form of consciousness exists independently of a physical presence. Materialistic monism has been the foundation of Western scientific training and culture throughout most of the scientific-industrial era. It has commonly been associated with a denial of the spiritual and an emphasis on materialism, individualism, and the exploitation of nature.

According to historian Edward McNall Burns, the significance of the Copernican Revolution is found in the fact that "No longer need the philosopher pay homage to revelation as a source of truth; reason was now held to be the solitary fount of knowledge, while the whole idea of spiritual meaning in the universe was cast aside like a worn-out garment."[5] The intellectual and moral authority of the church was greatly weakened.

The idea that only those things that can be measured are suitable subjects for scientific study and acceptable as causal explanations has helped science distinguish "scientific explanations from such prescientific interpretations as the whims of the gods or the intervention of divine grace."[6] However, it also meant that consciousness, values, aesthetics, and other aspects of human experience were excluded from consideration in scientific inquiry. By rejecting free will and moral choice as acceptable explanations for behavior, science effectively exempted itself from moral responsibility for the application of scientific knowledge.

Seventeenth-century philosopher Thomas Hobbes took materialistic monism to its ultimate extreme. He maintained that absolutely nothing exists except matter. If there is a God, he must have a physical body. In Hobbes's view, good is merely that which gives us pleasure, evil that which brings pain, and the only meaningful purpose in life is to pursue pleasure[7]—a value system that now serves as the implicit moral premise of corporate globalization.

The institutions of religion and science—each with its own view of reality—henceforth competed for the soul of Western societies. Dualism (the view that matter and spirit are two distinct and independent aspects of reality) provided the basis for an uneasy accommodation between religious and scientific worldviews. While the church ministered to a constricted spiritual life, secular society came to embrace the material world as the primary reality, materialism as the dominant value, and ultimately economic growth as the primary human purpose.

As a philosophy of science, materialistic monism made possible the scientific and technological accomplishments of the scientific-industrial era. As a philosophy of life deeply embedded in modern culture, it has led us to the brink of self-destruction, because it leads so naturally to the embrace of Hobbesian values that alienate us from any higher meaning or purpose. Having embraced material self-indulgence as our purpose, an appeal to limit indulgence in the interest of economic justice or concern for future generations becomes a call to sacrifice the only thing that gives life meaning. It follows, as corporate libertarians sometimes maintain, that it is most rational for those who have the financial means to continue to enjoy the party for as long as it lasts. If they sacrifice these pleasures and the environmentalists are ultimately proved wrong, they will have sacrificed their reason for living to no end. If the environmentalists are proved right and the party ends in self-destruction, then at least they enjoyed it while they could.

Materialistic monism also prepared the way for an economics that, intent on achieving the status of a true science, embraced market prices, which can be observed and measured, as the sole arbiter of human values. It is impossible to understand or explain more than purely habitual human behavior without addressing the values, loyalties, aspirations, love, psychological conflicts, altruism, spirituality, conscience, and even metaphysical beliefs that inform them. Although central to our experience and well-being, they are often difficult to observe, let alone measure. Thus, as science defines itself, the term *social science* is a contradiction, because we lack the means to directly observe or measure many of the most important "causes" of social behavior.

This presses the social scientist to either redefine the prescriptions of scientific inquiry to fit the human reality or strip human beings of the qualities that make us truly human. Intent on achieving the stature of a science, economists chose the latter by postulating a hypothetical, economic man who mechanistically seeks only his own pleasure, defined in terms of measurable economic gain. Whenever a model requires a human decision maker—irrespective of gender—the economist thus substitutes the imaginary, decidedly nonhuman, economic man, who evaluates every choice on the basis of its financial return.

Having eliminated the human, economists then eliminated the behavior. Finding the interactions among people too hopelessly complex and difficult to measure, economists chose to observe the behavior of markets rather than the behavior of people. Market behavior involves prices and flows of money, which are more easily observed and measured.

Since a science must be objective and value-free, economics chose to reduce all values to market values as revealed in market price. Thus air, water, and other essentials of life provided freely by nature are treated as valueless, until scarcity and privatization render them marketable. By contrast, gold and diamonds, which have almost no use in sustaining life, are valued highly. The value of a human life is arrived at by calculating a person's lifetime earning potential or "economic contribution." As a cynic once accurately noted, "Economists know the price of everything and the value of nothing."

Contemporary philosopher Jacob Needleman suggests that, "In other times and places, not everyone has wanted *money* above all else; people have desired salvation, beauty, power, strength, pleasure, propriety, explanations, food, adventure, conquest, comfort. But now and here, *money*—is what everyone wants."[8] Why does modern society choose to define itself and its values solely in terms of a quest for money—a simple number of no intrinsic value? At first it seems one of the most curious puzzles of our time, until the realization dawns that in a modern monetized society survival itself depends on having money. In the words of Joe Dominguez and Vicki Robin, in their *New York Times* best-seller *Your Money or Your Life,* money becomes "something we all too often don't have, which we struggle to get, and on which we [come to] pin our hopes of power, happiness, security, acceptance, success, fulfillment, achievement and personal worth."[9]

Having accepted our dependence on money to meet our survival needs and constantly bombarded by advertising messages, we easily slip into a pattern of looking to money to provide us with a sense of achievement, identity, acceptance, worth, and meaning—forgetting the simple reality that only forgeries of the real thing are up for sale. The real thing must be earned by investing ourselves in loving relationships, being good friends and neighbors, living by ethical principles, and developing and engaging our abilities in ways that contribute to the life of the community.

But marketing experts surround us with a different cultural message. They don't sell laundry soap, they sell acceptance, achievement, and personal worth. They don't sell automobiles, they sell power, freedom, and success—the opportunity to feel alive, connected, and free—that which we really want. To buy what the marketers offer, we need money. As Dominguez and Robin explain:

> Money is something we choose to trade our life energy for. . . . Our allotment of time here on earth, the hours of precious life available to us. When we go to our jobs, we are trading our life energy for money. This truth, while simple, is profound.[10]

Money is not an ordinary number after all. It is our ticket to the same things that people have wanted in other times and places. It is a measure of the life energies expended in its acquisition. It has become our answer to the question "What am I worth?" and the measure of our collective worth and accomplishment as a nation. Professional charities have even made money the measure of our compassion: "Make a difference. Send us your check today." Defining ourselves in terms of money, we become trapped in a downward spiral of increasing alienation from living, from our own spiritual nature (see Figure 18.1).

Rather than teaching us that the path to fulfillment is to experience living to the fullest through our relationships with family, community, nature, and the living cosmos, the corporate media continuously repeat a false promise: whatever our longings, the market is the path to their instant gratification. Our purpose is to consume—we are born to shop. Entranced by the siren song of the market, we consistently undervalue the life energy that we put into obtaining money and overvalue the expected life energy gains from spending it. The more we give our life energies over to money, the more power we yield to the institutions that control our access to money and to the things it will buy. Yielding such power serves the corporate interest well, because corporations are creatures of money but serves our human interest poorly, because we are creatures of nature and spirit.

Forced to reexamine who we are by the limits of the planet's ability to accommodate our greed, we find ourselves confronted with a beautiful truth.

Figure 18.1: Downward Spiral of Deepening Alienation

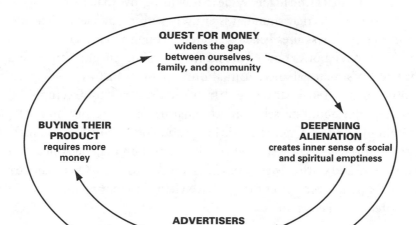

Whereas our pursuit of material abundance has created material scarcity, our pursuit of life may bring a new sense of social, spiritual, and even material abundance.

People who experience an abundance of love in their lives rarely seek solace in compulsive, exclusionary personal acquisition. For the emotionally deprived, no extreme of materialistic indulgence can ever be enough, and the material world becomes insufficient to our wants. A world starved of love becomes one of material scarcity. In contrast, a world of love is also one of material abundance. When we are spiritually whole and experience the caring support of community, thrift is a natural part of a full and disciplined life. That which is sufficient to one's needs brings a fulfilling sense of nature's abundance.

The implications are profound. Our seemingly insatiable quest for money and material consumption is in fact a quest to fill a void in our lives created by a lack of love. It is a consequence of dysfunctional societies in which money has displaced our sense of spiritual connection as the foundation of our cultural values and relationships. The result is a world of material scarcity, massive inequality, overtaxed environmental systems, and social disintegration. As long as we embrace money-making as our collective purpose and structure our institutions to give this goal precedence over all others, the void in our lives will grow and the human crisis will deepen. There is an obvious solution: create societies that give a higher value to nurturing love than to making money.

Idealistic as this may sound, it is entirely within our means. The key is a shift in consciousness already being created through an emerging synthesis of scientific and religious knowledge that embraces the integral connection between reality's material and spiritual dimensions.[11] Just as the Copernican Revolution ushered in the scientific-industrial era by freeing us from misperceptions about ourselves and the nature of our reality, an Ecological Revolution, based on a more holistic integration of the spiritual and material, may usher in an ecological era that will open as yet unimagined opportunities for our social and spiritual development. However, to realize this goal, we must reclaim for people the power that we have yielded to money and a corporate-dominated global economy.

LOCALIZING ECONOMIES, GLOBALIZING CONSCIOUSNESS

We humans have a distinctive ability to anticipate the consequences of our individual actions for our collective future and to change our behavior accordingly. We also have the capacity to discern repeating patterns in evolutionary processes and to distill from those patterns insights into how to maximize our own evolutionary potentials. One such regularly repeated pattern in the self-organizing growth and evolution of crystals, biological organisms, social organizations, and consciousness is a persistent advance toward higher orders of complexity.[12] Systems with the highest evolutionary potential are those able to nurture a rich diversity within a coherent unifying structure. The greater the diversity, the greater the evolutionary potential—if the unifying structure is maintained.

Arnold Toynbee found this pattern in his epic study of the growth and decline of the world's greatest civilizations. Civilizations in decline were consistently characterized by a "tendency toward standardization and uniformity." This pattern contrasted sharply with "the tendency toward differentiation and diversity" during the growth stage of civilizations.[13] It appears to be a near-universal truth that diversity is the foundation of developmental progress in complex systems, and uniformity is the foundation of stagnation and decay.

Standardization and uniformity seem to be almost inevitable outcomes of a globalized economy dominated by massive globe-spanning corporations geared to mass production and marketing in a culturally homogenized world.

It is difficult to imagine a civilization moving more totally toward standardization and uniformity than one unified by Coca-Cola and MTV. The processes of corporate globalization are not only spreading mass poverty, environmental devastation, and social disintegration, they are also weakening our capacity for constructive social and cultural innovation at a time when such innovation is needed as never before. Corporate globalization is leading us to an evolutionary dead end.

By contrast, economic systems composed of locally rooted, self-reliant economies create in each locality the political, economic, and cultural spaces within which people can find a path to the future consistent with their distinctive aspirations, history, culture, and ecosystems. A global system composed of local economies can accomplish what a single global economy cannot—encourage the rich and flourishing diversity of robust local cultures and generate the variety of experience and learning that is essential to the enrichment of the whole.

Economic globalization deepens the dependence of localities on detached global institutions that concentrate power, colonize local resources, and have no loyalty to any place. The greater a locality's external dependence, the less its ability to find within its own borders satisfactory solutions to its own problems. Although advocates of economic globalization commonly argue that globalization creates interdependence and shared interests, the argument is a misrepresentation. What actually happens is a growing dependence of people and localities on global corporations and financial markets. The consequence of this dependence is to pit people and localities against one another in a self-destructive competition for economic survival, yielding ever more power to the center (see Figure 18.2).

The power of the center stems from a number of interrelated sources: its power to create money, its ownership of the productive assets on which each locality depends, and its control of the institutional mechanisms that mediate relationships among localities. This power resides increasingly in global financial markets and corporations, which have established themselves as the de facto governance institutions of the planet. The more global the economy, the greater the dependence of the local and the greater the power of central institutions.

A globalized economic system delinked from place has an inherent bias in favor of the large, the global, the competitive, the resource-extractive, the short-term, and the wants of those with money. Our challenge is to create a locally rooted planetary system biased toward the small, the local, the cooperative, the resource-conserving, the long-term, and the needs of everyone—a system

Figure 18.2: Disempowering the Local

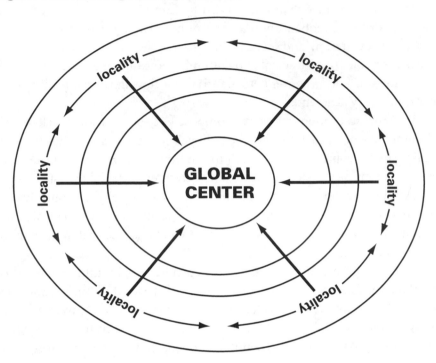

that empowers all people to create a good living in balance with nature. The goal is not to wall each community off from the world but rather to create zones of local accountability and responsibility within which people can reclaim the power that is rightly theirs to manage their economies in the common interest. It is a fundamental paradox of our time that in the name of market competition we have created a system that unifies corporations while dividing people and forcing them to compete for corporate favor. The human purpose is better served by a system that divides corporations and forces them to compete for the favor of people, in the true spirit of a competitive market. Let corporations compete to earn their profits. Let people and communities cooperate to create a good living for all.

In the world of the ecological age, people will be unified not by the mutual insecurity of global competition, but by a global consciousness that we share the same planet and a common destiny. This consciousness is already emerging and has three elements unique in human history. First, the formative ideas are the intellectual creations of popular movements involving millions of ordinary people who live and work outside the corridors of elite power. Second, the participation is truly global, bringing together people from virtually every nation, culture, and linguistic group. Third, the new consciousness is rapidly evolving, adapting, and taking on increasing definition as local groups meld into global alliances, ideas are shared, and consensus positions are forged in meetings and via the Internet, phone, and fax.

This process is creating a growing web of understanding, shared interests, and mutual compassion that is the proper foundation of a global community of people. The strength and vitality of this web arise because its members—unlike the Stratos dwellers who live in splendid, wealthy isolation—are rooted in real-world communities of place. They experience directly the consequences of the spreading crisis. Their experience is real, and they are naturally inclined to the human rather than the corporate interest.

By participating in the social movements that are the driving force of the Ecological Revolution, growing numbers of citizens are committing themselves to rebuilding their local communities and reaching out to others engaged in similar efforts. They actively recognize the need to act cooperatively in the global human interest through voluntary processes based on consensus and shared power.

These efforts are building the foundations of new human societies for the ecological age based on local economies and a global consciousness.

GUIDING PRINCIPLES

The formative ideas of the Copernican Revolution were produced by the scientific observation of physical bodies and can be traced to a handful of prominent scholars from the physical sciences. In contrast, the formative ideas of the Ecological Revolution are products of the collective human experience and the study of both living and nonliving systems. These ideas are articulated in countless consensus documents and declarations of citizen movements. They find theoretical grounding in the intellectual treatises of scholars from diverse academic disciplines, including history, sociology, ecology, economics, biology, physics, general systems theory, and ecological economics. These ideas may be distilled into a number of guiding principles for the creation of healthy twenty-first-century societies.

The Principle of Environmental Sustainability   Healthy societies are environmentally sustainable, which means their economies must satisfy three conditions.[14]

1. Rates of renewable resource use do not exceed the rates at which the ecosystem can regenerate them.
2. Rates of consumption or irretrievable disposal of nonrenewable resources do not exceed the rates at which renewable substitutes are developed and phased into use.
3. Rates of pollution emission into the environment do not exceed the rates of the ecosystem's natural assimilative capacity.

Any use of environmental resources or sink capacities greater than these rates is by definition unsustainable and compromises the opportunities available to future generations. The principle of environmental sustainability thus defines a collective property right of future generations that takes natural precedence over the individual property rights of the current generation.

The Principle of Economic Justice   Healthy societies provide all their members, present and future, with the essentials for a healthy, secure, productive, and fulfilling life. There is nothing wrong with additional rewards for those who contribute more, but only if everyone's basic needs are met, the options of future generations are not impaired, and there are strict limits on the concentration of economic power.

The Principle of Biological and Cultural Diversity   Healthy societies nurture the biological and cultural diversity of the planet. Diversity is the foundation of evolutionary potential. Nurturing biological and cultural diversity is fundamental to our constructive participation in the evolutionary process.

The Principle of People's Sovereignty (also known as the Principle of Subsidiarity)   In healthy societies, sovereignty resides in people. The purpose of the human economy is to meet human needs—not the needs of money, nor of corporations, nor of governments. The sovereign right of the people to decide what uses of the earth best nourish their bodies and their spirit within the limits of the first three principles is inalienable. People are best able to exercise this right when:

- Ownership and control of productive assets is locally rooted, thus increasing the likelihood that important decisions are made by those who will live with the consequences.
- Governance authority and responsibility are located in the smallest, most local system unit possible to maximize opportunity for direct, participatory democracy.
- More central system levels define their roles as serving and supporting the local in achieving self-defined goals.

The Principle of Intrinsic Responsibility   Healthy societies assign the full costs of resource allocation decisions to those who participate in making them—an essential requirement for efficiency in a self-regulating economic system. This principle applies to individual persons, enterprises, and political jurisdictions. No entity has the right to externalize the costs of its consumption to another. The goal is to structure economic relationships so as to encourage each locality to live within its sustainable environmental means. Much as a global economic system offers maximum scope in privatizing economic gains while externalizing the costs, a more local economic system of self-reliant local economies encourages internalizing costs, because both the consequences of cost externalization and the power to require that these costs be internalized come together in the same locality and even the same persons.

The Principle of Common Heritage   Healthy societies recognize that the planet's environmental resources and the accumulated knowledge of the human species are common heritage resources, and it is the right of every person—indeed every living being both present and future—to share in their beneficial use. No one has the right to monopolize or use common heritage resources in ways contrary to the broader interest of present and future generations. Indeed, it is the rightful responsibility of any who own environmental resources to serve as trustees in the interest of future generations and of those who possess special knowledge to share it with all who might benefit.

Healthy social function depends on giving the rights and responsibilities defined by these principles precedence over all other rights, including the property rights of individuals, corporations, and governments. Being people- and life-centered rather than corporate-centered, these principles offer a clear alternative to corporate libertarianism's prescription for social dysfunction.

Healthy societies seek balance in all things. They recognize a role for both government and locally accountable businesses, while resisting domination

Figure 18.3: Nested Economies

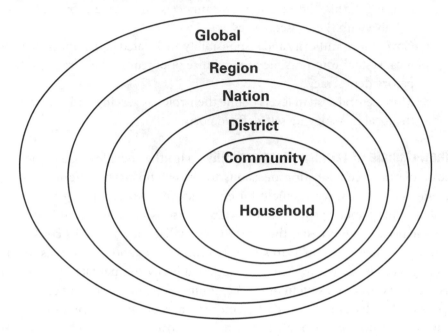

by powerful distant governments and corporations. Similarly, they seek local self-reliance while freely sharing information and technology, avoiding both external dependence and local isolation.

The appropriate organizational form for the ecological era is likely to be a multilevel system of nested economies with the household as the basic economic unit, up through successive geographical aggregations to localities, districts, nations, and regions (see Figure 18.3).[15] Embodying the principle of intrinsic responsibility, each level would seek to function, to the extent that it is reasonably able, as an integrated, self-reliant, self-managing political, economic, and ecological community. Starting from the base unit, each system level would seek to achieve the optimal feasible ecological self-reliance, especially in meeting basic needs.

To compensate for imbalances in environmental service endowments, units at each level would engage in selective exchanges with other units within their cluster, keeping those exchanges as balanced as possible. Households would exchange with households in their locality, localities with other localities in their district, and so on. The smaller the system unit, the greater the need for exchange. Thus, a substantial amount of household economic activity would necessarily involve external exchange. Although many households might grow some of their own food, it would be rare for a household to be self-sufficient. Community eco-economies would be somewhat more self-reliant, and so on, with regions being largely self-reliant.

Organizing to meet economic needs as close to the local level as feasible would enable the application of the principle of subsidiarity, which maintains that governance authority and responsibility should be vested in the smallest, most local unit possible. This would make it possible to maintain a market system in which market power is balanced with political power at each level. Local firms would enjoy a natural advantage, and there would be less long-haul movement of people and goods.

Less trade and greater local self-reliance may mean less consumer choice. In the Northern climates, we would eat winter or preserved vegetables and might put apples rather than bananas on our cereal. People in forested areas would construct their houses of wood, and those in hot, dry climates would build houses of earthen materials. Some prices might be higher. Overall, the sacrifices would be small compared with the prospects of greater economic security, caring communities in which people can walk the streets at night without fear, improved environmental quality, the survival of our species, and the creation of new evolutionary potentials.

As we reorganize ourselves into a multilevel system, it is likely that we will continue the present process of redrawing national boundaries. Countries that have grown too large and complex to be manageable may break up into smaller countries, as happened with the U.S.S.R. and has been debated in Canada. The present political movement in the United States toward greater local authority and autonomy is in part a response to the United States having reached an unmanageable size and complexity—even without the North American Free Trade Agreement, the Asia Pacific Economic Community, and the General Agreement on Tariffs and Trade. It makes good sense to devolve to the individual states more of the powers once lodged at the national level, including the power to regulate commerce and trade. Conversely, many smaller countries may find that they are too small to be viable and decide to undertake some form of merger. In the not too distant future, we may look back on the present, almost frantic press to form ever larger economic blocks through regional and global trade agreements as the last desperate gasp of a dying era.

The principles of the Ecological Revolution point toward a global system of local economies that distributes both power and responsibility, creates places for people, encourages the nurturing of life in all its diversity, and limits the opportunity for one group to externalize the social and environmental costs of its consumption onto others. Instead of forcing localities into international competition as a condition of their survival, a localized global system encourages self-reliance in meeting local needs. Instead of monopolizing knowledge for private gain, it encourages sharing knowledge and information. Instead of promoting a homogeneous globalized consumer culture, it nurtures cultural diversity. Instead of measuring success in terms of money, it encourages measuring success in terms of healthy social function.

IN THE HUMAN INTEREST

Although issues of class and political power figure prominently in its agenda, the Ecological Revolution is less a class struggle than a struggle of people against a rogue economic system that diminishes our humanity and threatens our collective survival. It is in the larger interest of all people, including the Stratos dwellers, that this system be transformed through a social learning process grounded in four truths.

1. Sovereignty resides only in people—all people, real people who need fresh air to breathe, clean water to drink, nutritious food to eat, and livelihoods that allow them to earn their keep. Neither governments nor corporations can usurp that sovereignty unless we choose to yield it.

2. Corporations have no natural or inalienable rights. The corporation is a public body created by a public act through issuing a public charter to serve a public purpose. We, the sovereign people, have the inalienable right to determine whether the intended public purpose is being served and to establish legal processes to amend or withdraw a corporate charter at any time we so choose. We need only decide.

3. The problem is the system. Incremental changes within individual corporations or political institutions cannot provide an adequate solution. The whole system of institutional power must be transformed.

4. The Ecological Revolution is a revolution of ideas, not guns. The Ecological Revolution is inclusive and invites the participation of all who seek to create healthy societies in which life may flourish. The human interest is not the corporate interest, but it is the interest of all people.

19

GOOD LIVING

*Our village was prosperous. . . . The real foundation of our prosperity . . .
was the deep and enduring sense of community that enabled us to make
the best use of these resources. . . . We had all the things we needed—
well-crafted, beautiful things that lasted a long time—but we did not do
much "consuming."*

—Eknath Easwaran[1]

*We were taught to see the world as a great machine. But then we could
find nothing human in it. Our thinking grew even stranger—we turned
this world-image back on ourselves and believed that we too were machines. . . . But the world is not a machine. . . . As we change our images
of the world, as we leave behind the machine, we welcome ourselves back.*

—Margaret J. Wheatley and Myron Kellner-Rogers[2]

By organizing societies around the pursuit of material gratification, we
have made a virtue of social dysfunction and diminished the quality of our
living. Humans are complex creatures. We have a demonstrated capacity for
hatred, violence, competition, and greed. We have as well a demonstrated capacity for love, tenderness, cooperation, and compassion. Healthy societies
nurture the latter and in so doing create an abundance of those things that are
most important to the quality of our living. Dysfunctional societies nurture
the former and in so doing create scarcity and deprivation. A healthy society
makes it easy to live in balance with one another and nature, whereas a dysfunctional society makes it nearly impossible.

Whether we organize our societies for social and environmental health or
for dysfunction is our choice. To a considerable degree, it is a choice between

organizing for the human interest and organizing for the corporate interest. By devoting ourselves to creating societies that enhance the *quality of our living* rather than the *quantity of our consumption*, we move simultaneously toward sustainability *and* a better life for nearly everyone. In this chapter we explore the possibilities.

CARING FAMILIES AND COMMUNITIES

Although a competitive instinct forms an important part of our nature, there is substantial evidence that competition is a subtheme to the more dominant theme of bonding, caring, and cooperation. As with all species that depend on social bonding for their survival, humans evolved to belong and cooperate as well as to compete. According to cultural anthropologist Mary Clark:

> The early human species could not have survived without the expanded social bonding beyond parent and offspring needed to protect helpless human infants—a job that mothers alone could not accomplish. Social bonding to one's group was a biological necessity—for adults as well as infants.[3]

Things haven't really changed so much. Social bonding is as essential to the healthy functioning of a modern society as it was to more traditional or tribal societies. Harvard University political scientist Robert Putnam refers to the bonding that characterizes a strong civil society as "social capital" and has shown its importance in a study of local government effectiveness in Italy.

Beginning in 1970, Italy created twenty regional governments. Their formal structures were identical. There were dramatic differences, however, in the social, economic, political, and cultural context in which these structures were planted. The localities ranged "from the pre-industrial to the post-industrial, from the devoutly Catholic to the ardently Communist, from the inertly feudal to the frenetically modern." In some localities, the new government structures were "inefficient, lethargic, and corrupt." In others, they were dynamic and effective, "creating innovative day care programs and job training centers, promoting investment and economic development, pioneering environmental standards and family clinics."[4]

Putnam found only one set of indicators that consistently differentiated those localities in which the government worked from those in which it didn't. These were indicators of a strong and active civil society, as measured by "voter turnout, newspaper readership, membership in choral societies and literary clubs, Lions Clubs and soccer clubs." Localities high on these indicators had what Putnam called a highly developed "social capital." Rich networks of nonmarket relationships built a general sense of trust and reciprocity that increased the efficiency of human relationships.[5]

We have given too little attention to the importance of social capital to the healthy functioning of societies and rarely consider the impact of economic structures and policies on its formation or depletion. How about your community? Does it contain small local shops run by merchants you know by name, or only mega-shopping malls and large retail chain outlets that send their profits elsewhere? Is there a thriving farmers' market where you can get to know the people who produce your food, or only a supermarket selling food imported from thousands of miles away? Are farms small, individually owned, and family operated, or are they controlled by huge corporate enterprises and worked mainly by itinerant landless laborers? Do people devote their free time to Little League baseball, community gardens, local theater, community choirs, community centers, and school boards, or to watching commercial TV? Are there credit cooperatives and local banks committed to supporting local enterprises, or only branches of large urban banks that package local deposits into loans to international hedge funds? Do residents consider the area their permanent home, or are working and professional people largely itinerant? Are productive assets owned locally or by distant corporations? Are local forests harvested selectively and sustainably by local firms to provide materials for local industry? Or are they being stripped bare by huge global corporations that export the raw timber to distant lands?

The answers to such questions are powerful predictors of the sense of dignity, freedom, responsibility, prosperity, and security of local people and the extent to which relationships are characterized by trust, sharing, and cooperation.

UNDEVELOPING THE SUSTAINERS

Some 80 percent of environmental damage is caused by 20 percent of the world's population—1.1 billion overconsumers. As Alan Durning points out in *How Much Is Enough*, these are the people who organize their lives around cars, meat-based diets, and the use of prepackaged and disposable products.[6] Meanwhile, another 20 percent of the world's people live in absolute depriva-

Table 19.1: Earth's Three Sociological Classes

OVERCONSUMERS 1.1 billion >US$7,500 per capita (Cars, Meat, Disposables)	SUSTAINERS 3.3 billion US$700–7,500 per capita (Living Lightly)	EXCLUDED 1.1 billion <US$700 per capita (Absolute Deprivation)
Travel by car and air	Travel by bicycle and public surface transport	Travel by foot or donkey
Eat high-fat, high-calorie, meat-based diets	Eat healthy diets of grains, vegetables, and some meat	Eat nutritionally inadequate diets
Drink bottled water and soft drinks	Drink clean water plus some tea and coffee	Drink contaminated water
Use throwaway products and discard substantial wastes	Use unpackaged goods and recycle wastes	Use local biomass and produce negligible wastes
Live in spacious, climate-controlled, single-family homes	Live in modest, naturally ventilated homes, with extended or multiple families	Live in rudimentary shelters or in the open; usually lack secure tenure
Maintain image-conscious wardrobes	Wear functional clothing	Wear secondhand clothing or scraps

tion. Durning makes another important point, however, that is generally neglected: roughly 60 percent of the world's people are presently meeting most of their basic needs in relatively sustainable ways (see Table 19.1). As members of the world's sustainer class, they travel by bicycle and public surface transport; eat healthy diets of grains, vegetables, and some meat; buy few prepackaged goods; and recycle most of their wastes. Although their lifestyles do not correspond to our vision of consumer affluence, neither do they evoke a vision of hardship, and in a properly organized society such lifestyles can be richly satisfying.

Consider, for example, the difference between living in a community organized around walking, bicycling, and public transportation compared to living where public spaces are dominated by automobiles and freeways. An environmentally friendly, low-meat, low-fat diet based on natural foods may result in better health and increased mental and physical vitality than a diet high in animal fats. A life free from fashion fads, impulse buying, junk foods, useless gadgets, and the long hours of work required to buy them is a life free from much of what alienates us from the life of family, community, and nature.

Herein lies the tragedy of nearly fifty years of economic growth and national development. Rather than building societies that create a good life for sustainers and bring the deprived into the sustainer class, we have followed the path of encouraging overconsumers to consume more, converting sustainers into overconsumers, and pushing many of those in the sustainer class into the excluded class. In the process, we have often made life more difficult for those who remain in the sustainer class by displacing the production systems that once met their needs and by giving priority to public facilities—such as highways and shopping malls—that serve overconsumers rather than those that serve sustainers—such as public transit, bike lanes, and public markets.

FROM OVERCONSUMPTION TO SUSTAINABLE COMMUNITY

We commonly assume that moving from an overconsumer to a sustainer lifestyle requires giving up the things that make our lives comfortable and satisfying. There is another, more attractive, possibility: organize our living spaces and production systems so that we improve the quality of our living while simultaneously eliminating the excessive burdens we now place on the environment. The move that Fran (my spouse) and I made to New York City in 1992 helped us see the possibilities. Although New York is deeply afflicted with crime, poverty, and other manifestations of the inequities of modern economic life, we did not experience the cold, impersonal city we had expected. Instead, we found a city of ethnically diverse local neighborhoods and small family shops that throbs with a human energy and vitality we have rarely experienced elsewhere. New York is far from a model of sustainability and has much that detracts from the quality of life, but we came to appreciate living in New York in ways we had not anticipated.

With a high residential population density—an average of 5,000 people per square block, housed in multifamily dwellings—a functioning subway system, and shopping facilities within walking distance of most residences, New York's per capita energy consumption is half the average for the United States as a whole. For the first time in forty years, Fran and I did not have a car. My office was in our apartment, and Fran commuted to work on the subway. More than 90 percent of our shopping needs were met within a three-block radius of our apartment door: pharmacy, hardware, electronics, books, groceries, clothing, housewares—all in abundant selection. For my office needs, there was an ecologically conscious printing shop directly across the street, a software store around the corner, and two office supply stores within a five-minute walk.

Similarly, we had a vast array of restaurants of every conceivable ethnicity and price range, jazz clubs, theater, opera, dance, art galleries, museums, free public concerts, and health clubs—easily accessible by walking or subway. An extraordinary system of parks and botanical gardens made nature accessible even within the city boundaries. When we needed to get out of the city, we took the train or rented a car from a neighborhood agency. Rather than feeling deprived by our lack of a car, we felt liberated—no commutes in heavy traffic, parking problems, insurance hassles, or auto repair ripoffs. The thousands of dollars we saved each year helped make it possible for me to devote my life to the things I wanted to do, like write this book.

We especially enjoyed the Union Square farmers' market, just half a block from our front door. Here, four days a week, people who operated neighboring small farms, dairies, cottage wineries, and kitchen bakeries sold their wares—eggs and poultry from free-range chickens, milk from cows not given to bovine growth hormone injections, organically grown fruits and vegetables, fresh meat and fish all free of additives and artificial hormones. Most of the year, I prepared our meals mainly from what was available at the market. Eating nutritious, flavorful, unprocessed, chemical-free foods, we found ourselves feeling healthier and more vital, sleeping better, and thinking more clearly. We enjoyed getting to know the farmers and were pleased that our food purchases were supporting environmentally responsible, local family farms.

Carrying home fresh unpackaged foods from the market in our own shopping bag meant that we had little packaging waste. The city recycled cans, glass, plastic, and newspapers. At the Saturday and Wednesday markets, a local voluntary organization collected organic wastes for composting. We sent very little garbage to the landfill.

On the whole, we were leading healthier, happier, and more environmentally responsible lives than we ever had before—not because we were being heroically virtuous, but because the place where we lived was organized in a way that made it easy and enjoyable to do so. This experience helped us see the impact of the way communities are organized on the quality of social and environmental relationships and thereby of our living. Many things could be done to make New York City more livable and sustainable—starting with banning personal automobiles from Manhattan—but there is a lot on which to build.

A major part of the burden we overconsumers place on the planet comes from our use of automobiles, airplanes, and throwaway products that come in unnecessary packaging, and our consumption of unhealthy foods produced by methods that destroy the earth and leave what we eat poisoned with toxic residues. Few of us would find it a burden to give up long commutes on crowded freeways, constant noise, job insecurity, gadgets we never use, clothes we seldom wear, unhealthy fatty diets, chemically contaminated fruits and vegetables, products that don't last, useless packaging, tiring business trips, and drafty energy-inefficient homes and buildings. By learning to resolve our disputes by nonmilitary means, we would eliminate the approximately 30 percent of all global environmental degradation that results from military operations.[7]

Individual choices can make a difference. We can reduce the amount of meat in our diets. We can buy a water filter to reduce our dependence on bottled water and soft drinks. We can buy fewer clothes or a more gas-efficient car. There are countless such positive choices to be made. However, we must also organize our societies to make the responsible choices easy and economical. Let's look at how properly organized human communities and societies could improve the quality of our lives while at the same time making three major systems—urban space and transportation, food and agriculture, and materials—more sustainable.

Urban Space and Transport

In *Reclaiming Our Cities and Towns*, David Engwicht reminds us that people invented cities as places devoted to human interaction. The purpose of cities is to "facilitate exchange of information, friendship, material goods, culture, knowledge, insight, [and] skills" with little need for travel.[8] Cities once consisted primarily of exchange spaces for people—places such as shops, schools, residences, and public buildings. The pathways that connected exchange spaces were also places to meet and reaffirm relationships with neighbors.

The automobile has changed our cities in fundamental ways, colonizing ever more of the spaces that were once devoted to human exchange and transforming them into systems of parking lots connected by highways. Thus, many of the spaces that once brought us together have been converted into noisy, congested, polluting places that isolate us from one another and destroy the quality of city life. The faster and more densely the traffic flows through our neighborhood, the less we feel at home there and the less likely we are to relate to and befriend our neighbors.[9]

The automobile is not only one of our least energy-efficient modes of transportation, it is also one of our least space efficient. When we take into account the multiple parking spaces that each car must have at home, office, shopping center, church, recreational facilities, and school, plus the amount of road space required for its movement, the total space required by each family car is typically three times greater than the space occupied by the average family home.[10]

One reason people flee to the suburbs is to escape the environmental and social consequences of giving cities over to automobiles. When productive agricultural lands are paved over, we become separated from nature and one another by even greater distances, our dependence on automobiles increases, and per capita energy consumption skyrockets, both for transportation and to heat and cool the detached, single-family dwellings in which suburbanites live. There is sound foundation for the conclusion of urban ecologists William Rees and Mark Roseland that "sprawling suburbs are arguably the most economically, environmentally, and socially costly pattern of residential development humans have ever devised."[11]

Automobile companies sell their products as tickets to freedom, defined in many auto ads as the escape by automobile from city and suburbs to the unspoiled countryside. It is ironic, because the automobile has been perhaps the single greatest contributor to making our urban areas unlivable, turning our countryside into sprawling suburbs and strip malls, and making us more dependent on cars to survive the consequences of this affliction.

In 1950, the average American drove some 3,800 kilometers (2,356 miles). That figure had risen to 9,700 kilometers (6,014 miles) by 1990. Greater freedom? Roughly half of the miles Americans drive involve commuting to work on congested roadways. Between 1969 and 1990, the number of miles traveled to work by the average American household increased 16 percent. The second major use of cars is shopping. The average distance traveled for shopping increased by 88 percent. A third use is for matters such as business travel, delivering children to and from school, doctor visits, and church attendance—up 135 percent. Social and recreational travel actually declined by 1 percent, perhaps because we had less time left for it. It is estimated that in the largest U.S. urban areas, 1 billion to 2 billion hours a year are wasted due to traffic congestion. In Bangkok, the average worker loses the equivalent of forty-four working days a year sitting in traffic.[12]

It is not difficult to figure out who benefits from this damage to the quality of our living. In terms of sales, the three largest corporations in America are General Motors Corporation (cars), Exxon Corporation (oil), and Ford Motor Company (cars). Mobil Corporation (oil) is number seven.

In 1992 Groiningen, a Dutch city of 170,000 people, dug up its city-center highways and took a variety of steps to make the bicycle the main form of transportation. As a consequence, business has improved, rents have increased, and the flow of people out of the city has been reversed. Local businesses that once fought any restraint on the automobile are now clamoring for more restraint.[13]

It is a step that many more cities should take. Few measures would do more to improve the quality of our living and the health of our environment than organizing living spaces to reduce our dependence on the automobile. Other actions to help accomplish this include planning and controlling the use of urban space to increase urban density and the proximity of work, home, and recreation; restricting parking facilities; increasing taxes on gasoline; and investing in public transit and facilities for pedestrians and cyclists.

"Hold on," says the corporate libertarian. "What about the impact on the economy? One job in six in the United States is linked to the auto industry. In Australia, it is one in ten.[14] Unemployment would skyrocket and stock prices would plummet if we were to reorganize space to do away with the automobile. It would be an economic disaster."

This important point is best answered with another question. Is it rational to structure an economy so that investors profit from socially harmful investments and the only employment people can find involves doing things that reduce our quality of life? An intelligent species can surely find a better way to provide people with a means of livelihood. We will return to this issue in a moment.

Food and Agriculture

Our food and agriculture system is similarly designed to generate profits for giant chemical and agribusiness corporations with little regard for the health of people and the ecosystem. This system features chemical-intensive, mechanized production; long-distance shipping; captive contract producers; migrant laborers paid bare subsistence wages; and large government subsidies paid to giant corporations. The system is suited to the profitable mass production of standardized food products, but comes at the cost of depleting soils and aquifers, contaminating water with chemical runoff, and driving out the small family farms that were for many years the backbone of strong rural communities. This system delivers to the consumer highly processed, wastefully packaged foods of dubious nutritional value contaminated with chemical residues. Although the system abundantly fills supermarkets, it features misleading nutritional claims; strongly resists any effort to inform consumers about additives, synthetic hormones, genetically modified organisms, and toxic residues they may be ingesting; and gives consumers little option of choosing organically grown, unprocessed foods produced by local farmers. Our food choices have largely been reduced to whatever big corporations find it most profitable to offer.

Even as adults intent on exercising healthful and responsible choice, we seldom have any way of knowing whether the piece of fish we are about to buy was caught by a massive foreign factory trawler sweeping the ocean bare with fine mesh drift nets or harvested by a local fisherman using environmentally responsible gear. We have no way of knowing whether a piece of meat is from an animal raised on properly managed, natural rangelands or from one raised on unstable lands from which tropical forests were recently cleared and fattened in feedlots on grain that might otherwise have fed hungry people. There is no way to tell whether the cows that supply our milk have been injected with artificial hormones, because under pressure from the Monsanto corporation, the government prohibits the labeling that would tell us.

If our goal is to provide a good living for people, we need to transform our food and agriculture system much as we must transform our habitats and transportation systems. Our goal must be to optimize the use of land and water resources to meet an expanding population's needs for a nutritionally adequate diet, fiber, and livelihoods. And we must do it in an environmentally sustainable way.

An appropriate system would most likely be composed of tens of thousands of intensively managed, small, family farms producing a diverse range of food, fiber, livestock, and energy products for local markets. Farming practices would use bio-dynamic methods to maintain soil fertility, retain water, and control pests. The food system would be designed to limit, contain, and recycle contaminants—including recycling human wastes—and would depend primarily on renewable solar-generated energy sources—including animal power and biogas—for preparation, production, processing, storage, and transport.[15] Steps toward such a system would include carrying out agrarian reform to break up large corporate agricultural holdings, providing adequate credit facilities for small farmers, creating farmer-based research and extension systems oriented to bio-intensive methods, requiring full and accurate labeling of food products, eliminating financial and environmental subsidies for agricultural chemicals, increasing the costs of food transport by eliminating energy and other transportation subsidies, and creating locally accountable watershed management authorities to coordinate measures for soil and water protection.

Although moving toward more localized food and agriculture systems and healthier, less fatty diets would require adjustments in our eating habits, this is not a vision of sacrifice and deprivation. Rather, it is a vision of a fertile earth and of vibrant and secure human communities populated by people with healthy bodies and minds nourished by wholesome, uncontaminated foods. The elements of this vision are technically and socially feasible. They simply require restructuring the relevant systems in line with the human rather than the corporate interest.

Materials

To achieve true sustainability, we must reduce our "garbage index"—that which we permanently throw away into the environment that will not be naturally recycled for reuse—to near zero. Productive activities must be organized as closed systems. Minerals and other nonbiodegradable resources, once taken from the ground, must become a part of society's permanent capital stock and be recycled in perpetuity. Organic materials may be disposed into the natural ecosystems, but only in ways that assure that they are absorbed back into the natural production system.

Individual consumers are regularly urged to sort and recycle discards—an important but insufficient measure. Many of the most important decisions are out of our hands, and much of the garbage related to our individual consumption is created and discarded long before any product reaches us. The market rarely offers us a choice of a daily newspaper printed on recycled paper using nontoxic, biodegradable ink. Nor can we ensure that the dutifully bundled newspapers we place at curbside for recycling will indeed be recycled. Such decisions lie in the hands of publishers, paper manufacturers, politicians, and government bureaucrats.

Over a twenty-year period, assuming current levels of recycling, the typical American household "consumes" the equivalent of roughly 100 trees in the form of newsprint. Sixty to 65 percent of that newsprint is devoted to advertisements.[16] Even though we may never read and have no interest in the ads, we are not given the option of subscribing to a paper without them.

According to the Worldwatch Institute, "most materials used today are discarded after one use—roughly two thirds of all aluminum, three fourths of all steel and paper, and an even higher share of plastic."[17] The physical environment is disrupted to extract the materials involved, vast amounts of garbage are generated, we work extra hours to earn the money to keep replacing what is discarded, and we become beasts of burden endlessly toting replacements from the store to our homes and then out to the garbage. This may be good for the economy, corporate profits, and executive salaries; but it degrades the quality of our living.

Recycling not only reduces the environmental costs of resource extraction, it saves energy as well. Producing steel from scrap requires only a third as much energy as producing it from ore, reduces air pollution by 85 percent, reduces water pollution by 76 percent, and eliminates mining wastes. Making newsprint from recycled paper takes 25 to 60 percent less energy than producing it from virgin wood pulp, while reducing the release of air pollutants by 74 percent and water pollutants by 35 percent. Reuse produces even more dramatic gains. Recycling the glass in a bottle reduces energy consumption by a third, while cleaning and reusing the bottle itself can save as much as 90 percent of the energy required to make a new bottle.[18]

Germany has pioneered the idea of life-cycle product planning and responsibility. Government-mandated programs encourage manufacturers of automobiles and household appliances to assume responsibility for the disassembly, reuse, and recycling of their products. Besides being environmentally sound, this practice relieves the consumer of the burden of disposing of those items at the end of their useful lives.[19] Life-cycle management can be carried out through lease arrangements in which the ownership of the item remains with the manufacturer, which becomes responsible for both maintenance and disposal and thus has an incentive to design products for maximum durability and ease of recycling.

Governments can encourage producers to design their products and packaging to limit disposal by charging them a fee to cover the estimated public cost of eventual disposal. Governments can also require that multisized and odd-shaped beverage and other containers be replaced with standardized, durable, glass containers that can be reused many times simply by washing and relabeling.[20]

SUSTAINABLE LIVELIHOODS

An important part of the demand for economic growth comes from the carefully cultivated myth that the only way we can keep people employed is to expand aggregate consumption to create jobs at a rate faster than corporations invest in labor-saving technology to eliminate them. We neglect an important alternative—to redefine the problem and concentrate on creating livelihoods rather than jobs.

A job is defined by *Webster's New World Dictionary* as "a specific piece of work, as in one's trade, or done by agreement for pay; anything one has to do; task; chore; duty."[21] A livelihood is defined as "a means of living or of supporting life."[22] A job is a source of money. A livelihood is a means of living. Speaking of jobs evokes images of people working in the factories and fast-food outlets of the world's largest corporations. Speaking of sustainable livelihoods evokes images of people and communities engaged in meeting individual and collective needs in environmentally responsible ways—the vision of a local system of self-managing communities.

We could be using advances in technology to give everyone more options for good, sustainable living. If we so choose, instead of demanding that those fortunate enough to have jobs sacrifice their family and community lives on the altar of competition while others languish in the ranks of the unemployed, we could be organizing our societies around a twenty- to thirty-hour work-week to assure secure and adequately compensated employment for almost every adult who wants a job. The time thus freed could be devoted to the social economy in activities that meet unmet needs and rebuild a badly tattered social fabric.

The possibilities are extraordinary once we acknowledge that many existing jobs not only are unsatisfying but also involve producing goods and services that are either unnecessary or cause major harm to society and to the environment. This includes a great many of the jobs in the automobile, chemical, packaging, and petroleum industries; most advertising and marketing jobs; the brokers and financial portfolio managers engaged in speculative and other extractive forms of investment; ambulance-chasing lawyers; 14 million arms industry workers worldwide; and the 30 million people employed by the world's military forces.[23]

This leads to a startling fact. Societies would be better off if, instead of paying hundreds of millions of people sometimes outrageous amounts to do work that is harmful to the quality of our living, we gave them the same pay to sit home and do nothing. Although far from an optimal solution, it would make more sense than the wholly irrational practice of organizing societies to pay people to do things that result in a net reduction in real wealth and well-being. Why not organize to support them instead to do activities that are socially beneficial and environmentally benign, such as providing loving care and attention to children and the elderly, operating community markets and senior citizen centers, educating our young people, counseling drug addicts, providing proper care for the mentally ill, maintaining parks and commons, participating in community crime watch, organizing community social and cultural events, registering voters, cleaning up the environment, replanting forests, doing public-interest political advocacy, caring for community gardens, organizing community recycling programs, and retrofitting homes for energy conservation. Similarly, many of us could use more time for recreation, quiet solitude, and family life and to practice the disciplines and hobbies that keep us physically, mentally, psychologically, and spiritually healthy.

Our problem is not too few jobs; it is an economic structure that creates too much dependence on paid employment and then pays people to do harmful things while neglecting so many activities that are essential to a healthy society. It is instructive to remember that until the last ten to twenty years, most adults—the majority women—served society productively in unpaid work in the social economy. In many instances, these societies had a stronger social fabric and offered their members a greater sense of personal security and fulfillment than does our own.

Although initiatives toward creating sustainable livelihood economies may evolve in different ways in response to different circumstances and aspirations, we may infer some of their features from the above principles and examples. For example, in urban areas, they would most likely be organized around local urban villages or neighborhoods that bring residential, work, recreation, and commercial facilities together around sustainable production to meet local needs with a substantial degree of self-reliance. They would feature green spaces and intensive human interaction and seek considerable self-reliance in energy, biomass, and materials production.

Human and environmental productive activities would be melded into local, closed-loop coproduction processes that recycle sewage, solid waste, and even air through fish ponds, gardens, and green areas to continuously regenerate their own resource inputs. Urban agriculture and aquaculture, repair and reuse, and intensive recycling would provide abundant livelihood opportunities in vocations that increase sustainability. Organizing these activities around neighborhoods that are also largely self-reliant in social services would help renew family and community ties, decentralize administration, and increase the sharing of family responsibilities between men and women. Needs for transporting people and goods would be reduced. Locally produced foods would be fresh and unpackaged or preserved in reusable containers.

We might find a wide range of traditional and electronic-age cottage industries, many involved in various kinds of recycling, existing side by side with urban agriculture. Family support services such as community-based day care, family counseling, schools, family health services, and multipurpose community centers could become integral neighborhood functions, engaging people in useful and meaningful work within easy walking distance of their homes. Many localities may issue their own local currency to facilitate local transactions and limit the flow of money out of the community. Most adults would divide their time between activities relating to the money economy and those relating to the social economy. We would see a return of the multifunctional home that serves as a center of family and community life and drastically reduces dependence on the automobile and other energy-intensive forms of transportation. We might line our byways with trees rather than billboards. We might limit advertising to product information that is available on demand, only when we want it.

On the path to true social efficiency, we would have ample time for other aspects of living, including recreation, cultural expression, intellectual and spiritual development, and political participation. We might travel to other localities for cultural exchanges. We might maintain friendships and collegial relations with others around the world by videophone. Or we might conference on computer networks to share exotic recipes, ideas on how to organize a local food co-op, or experiences in campaigning to improve public transit service. We might network internationally on citizen advocacy regarding proposed new trade rules. Or we might tune in to the news broadcasts from Russia, India, and Chile to see how people there are reacting to election results in South Africa.

We do have the option of creating healthy societies that allow us to live whole lives. It is time to reclaim our power and get on with that task.

20

AGENDA FOR CHANGE

*A political community cannot be healthy if it cannot exercise a signifi-
cant measure of control over its economic life.*
                                        —*Herman Daly and John Cobb Jr.*[1]

*I sympathize, therefore, with those who would minimize, rather than
with those who would maximize, economic entanglement between nations. Ideas, knowledge, art, hospitality, travel—these are the things which
should of their nature be international. But let goods be homespun whenever it is reasonably and conveniently possible, and above all, let finance
be primarily national.*
                                        —*John Maynard Keynes*[2]

FEW RIGHTS ARE MORE FUNDAMENTAL than the right of people to create caring, sustainable communities and to control their own resources, economies,
and means of livelihood. These rights in turn depend on their right to choose
what cultural values they will embrace, what values their children will be taught,
and with whom they will trade. A globalized economy denies these rights by
transferring the power to make the relevant choices to global corporations and
financial institutions. The question of whether people or corporations will chart
the course of the human future is a pivotal issue in the Ecological Revolution.

The guiding principles of the Ecological Revolution are actively probusiness
and promarket, but they are also strongly partial to locally owned businesses
that provide employment to local people, pay local taxes to maintain local
infrastructure and social services, meet local social and environmental standards, participate in the community, and compete fairly with similar businesses in markets that have no dominant players. If a global corporation wishes
to make the case that it can offer local people what local enterprise cannot, it

should be up to local people to judge the substance of its argument. If defending democracy, human values, economic justice, and livelihoods is protectionist, then let us all proudly proclaim ourselves to be protectionists.

This chapter deals with specific measures to transform governance to reclaim our colonized political and economic spaces and restore the rights of people. The aim is to limit the power and freedom of the largest corporations in order to restore democracy and the rights and freedoms of people and communities. This requires more than simple reforms.

RECLAIMING OUR POLITICAL SPACES

Political rights belong to people, not to artificial legal entities. The claim by corporations to the same constitutional rights as natural-born persons is a legal perversion without moral or logical foundation. As instruments of public policy, corporations should obey the laws decided by the citizenry, not write those laws. The corporate claim to First Amendment free speech protection, on which corporations base their right to lobby and carry out public campaigns on political issues, is particularly pernicious. As Paul Hawken observes, by invoking this right, "corporations achieve precisely what the Bill of Rights was intended to prevent: domination of public thought and discourse."[3]

We must give high priority to legislative and judicial action aimed at establishing the legal principle that corporations are public bodies created by issuing a public charter to serve public needs and have only those privileges specifically extended to them by their charters or the law. These privileges are properly subject to withdrawal or revision at any time through popular referendum or legislative action. If a corporation persistently seeks to exceed the privileges granted by its charter—such as knowingly selling defective products—or fails to honor its obligations under the law—such as consistently violating laws regarding toxic dumping—it is the right and responsibility of citizens, acting through their government, to disband it by withdrawing its charter. It is the same as their right to abolish any public body that, in their judgment, no longer serves the public interest.[4]

Shareholders, managers, employees, consumers, and others have every right in their capacity as private citizens to express their political views for or against the corporate interest. They also have the right to form and fund not-for-profit organizations to advance any cause they choose to support in their private capacities using their personal funds. Corporations have no such natural right. They simply do not belong in people's political spaces.

A first step toward removing corporations from the political sphere would be to eliminate all tax exemptions for corporate expenditures related to lobbying, public "education," public charities, or political organizations of any kind. The ultimate goal, however, is to prohibit the involvement of publicly traded corporations in any activity intended to influence the political process or to "educate" the public on issues of policy or the public interest. Furthermore, corporate officers should be prohibited by law from acting in their corporate capacities to solicit political contributions or political advocacy efforts from employees, suppliers, or customers.

The increasingly aggressive use by corporations of not-for-profit organizations as fictitious citizen fronts for corporate political lobbying highlights how thin the line is that separates corporate involvement in public education and charitable giving from overt political involvement. Even corporate giving to true public charities and the arts has become increasingly suspect. For example, when New York City proposed a sweeping smoking ban in public places in the fall of 1994, the Philip Morris Corporation made known to the city's many arts organizations it had funded that it expected their support in opposing the ban.

A publicly traded corporation will almost inevitably align its charitable giving with its own financial interests. There is little other basis on which it can justify allocating shareholder profits for charitable purposes. If corporations truly care about the communities in which they reside, then let them provide good, secure jobs and safe products, maintain a clean environment, obey the law, and pay their rightful share of taxes. Let their managers, shareholders, and employees contribute to charitable and educational causes of their choice from their share of the corporation's distributed wages, salaries, and profits of the corporation.

Similarly, any nonprofit organization in which 50 percent or more of the trustees are senior officers of corporations with more than $500 million in total assets should be ineligible for tax-exempt status on the presumption that it is a front organization operated to advance the corporate interest. When nonprofit organizations with corporate boards raise public monies, issue public statements, or make presentations to public bodies, they should be required to identify themselves as such.

Removing corporations from political participation is an essential step toward reclaiming our political spaces. It is not, however, sufficient. *New York Times* columnist Russell Baker all too accurately described the 1994 U.S. congressional elections as an auction, more of a bidding war to outspend opponents on negative campaign ads than a contest of vision, issues, and competence.[5] This trend has left American voters increasingly disillusioned with democracy and outraged at a government controlled by big-money interests.

Politics in America has been reduced to a system of legalized bribery. If democracy is to survive, reforms must get corporations and bribery out of politics. The ability to spend millions of dollars to saturate the electronic media, especially television, with negative messages about one's opponent has become a key to winning elections. So long as winning an election is excessively expensive and the only sources of adequate funding are powerful financial interests, policy will favor financial interests over the public interest. Setting term limits or voting incumbents out of office will accomplish very little. Three deep and sweeping campaign reforms are necessary:

1. Public elections should be publicly funded. Political action committees should be abolished, and corporations should be prohibited from making any kind of political contribution or using corporate resources to favor any candidate or issue in a political campaign.

2. Total campaign expenditures should be limited. Let candidates concentrate on competing to get their messages out as effectively as possible within a set spending limit—a better measure of their ability to spend public funds responsibly.

3. In return for their right to use public airways, television and radio stations should be required to provide exposure for candidates for public office on issues-oriented interview programs and debates on an equal-time basis. Informing the public about the views and qualifications of candidates for office is one of the most basic responsibilities of the news media in a democracy, and they should be held accountable for fulfilling it.

With their dominance of the mass media and their growing infiltration of the classroom, corporations increasingly control and shape our primary institutions of cultural reproduction, constantly reinforcing the values of consumerism and the basic doctrines of corporate libertarianism in an effort to align mainstream culture with the corporate interest. To reclaim our colonized political spaces, we must reclaim our colonized cultural spaces. Three measures merit serious consideration:

1. *Media Antitrust.* Special antitrust legislation for the media should establish that it is prima facie evidence of monopolistic intent for a single corporation to own more than one major public media outlet, whether a newspaper, radio station, TV station, or home cable service. Furthermore, the operation of a media outlet should be the primary business of the corporation that owns it. This would ensure that the outlet is not used primarily as a means to advance other corporate interests. No individual should be allowed to have a majority holding in more than one such media corporation. This would enhance the free-speech rights of the public by limiting the ability of a few powerful individuals and corporations to dominate access to the major means of public communication.

2. *Advertising.* In classical market economics, the role of business is to respond to market demand, not to create it. Tax deductions for advertising provide a public subsidy for hundreds of billions of dollars a year in corporate advertising aimed at enticing people to buy things that they neither want nor need and creating a consumer culture detrimental to the health of society and the planet. Advertising, other than purely informative advertising based on verifiable facts regarding the uses, specifications, and availability of a product, is not in the public interest. At a minimum, the costs should not be deductible as a business expense. In addition, as a pollution control measure, a public fee might be assessed on advertising in outdoor or other public spaces with the proceeds used to fund public-interest consumer education. Factual product information might be provided on demand through product directories, including on-demand directories that are accessible through computer services and interactive TV.

3. *Schools.* Schools should be declared advertising-free zones, administration of public schools should remain a public-sector function, and corporate-sponsored teaching modules should be banned from classroom use under the ban on in-school advertising.

Reclaiming our political spaces goes hand in hand with reclaiming our economic spaces.

RECLAIMING OUR ECONOMIC SPACES

Both capitalism and communism acknowledge a basic truth expressed by the popular aphorism, "He who has the gold rules." Communist theory explicitly calls for worker ownership of the means of production. Adam Smith implicitly assumed worker ownership in his vision of an ideal market economy composed of small farmers and artisans, a circumstance in which owner, manager, and worker are commonly one and the same. In practice, both communism and capitalism have failed to live up to their ideal. Communism vested property rights in a distant state and denied the people any means of holding the state accountable for its exercise of those rights. Capitalism persistently transfers property rights to giant corporations and financial institutions that are largely unaccountable even to their owners.

There is an important structural alternative: a market economy composed primarily, though not exclusively, of family enterprises, small-scale co-ops, worker-owned firms, and neighborhood and municipal corporations. Malaysian consumer activist Bishan Singh calls it the community enterprise economy, as it melds the market forces of the money economy with the community forces of the social economy.[6] Historian and political economist Gar Alperovitz argues that just such a major restructuring of the American economy is already under way:

> [led] . . . by civic-minded entrepreneurs, innovative labor unions and
> effective local governments. . . . The number of firms now experi-
> menting with worker-ownership approaches 10,000, involving per-
> haps 12 million people—more than the entire membership of pri-
> vate-sector trade unions. There are also more than 30,000 co-ops, in-
> cluding 4,000 consumer goods co-ops, 13,000 credit unions, nearly
> 100 cooperative banks and more than 100 cooperative insurance com-
> panies. Add to this 1,200 rural utilities and nearly 5,000 housing co-
> ops, plus another 115 telecommunication and cable co-ops.[7]

A common element of these ownership innovations is that they establish local control of productive assets through institutions that are anchored in and accountable to the community.[8] This tends to make capital patient and rooted, an essential condition of stable, healthy communities. Such initiatives are thus vitally important in building the foundations of healthy societies, but they are seriously disadvantaged by economic policies and institutions that favor the large, the global, and the predatory. Reclaiming our economic spaces requires that we transform such policies and institutions to shift the advantage in favor of the small and the locally accountable. To do so, we will need to restore the integrity and proper function of our financial institutions and systems, shift the social and environmental costs of production to producers and the users of their products, eliminate subsidies to big business, localize markets, deconcentrate capital ownership, establish corporate accountability, and restore market competition. The term *transform* is used advisedly. If these measures seem to run counter to the current trend toward the big and the global, that is precisely the intent. The goal is to transform an undemocratic and rapacious capitalist economy into a democratic and socially efficient market economy.

Financial Transactions Tax   A small tax on the purchase and sale of financial instruments such as stocks, bonds, foreign currencies, and derivatives would be a disincentive to very short-term speculation and arbitraging and remove an important source of unearned financial profit.

Graduated Surtax on Short-Term Capital Gains   Capital gains on assets held only for a brief time are usually a form of unearned income and are appropriately taxed at a rate higher than the rate of tax on earned income. A surtax on net short-term capital gains above and beyond the normal income tax would make many forms of speculation unprofitable, stabilize financial markets, and lengthen investment perspectives without penalizing long-term productive investment. The capital gains surtax on the sale of an asset held less than a week might be as high as 80 percent on the otherwise untaxed portion, falling to 50 percent on assets held more than a week but less than six months, 35 percent on those held for more than six months but less than three years, 10 percent for assets held from three to six years, and 0 percent beyond that.[9]

One Hundred Percent Reserve Requirement on Demand Deposits   As far back as 1948, Henry C. Simmon, founder of the conservative University of Chicago school of economic monetarism, argued for a 100 percent reserve requirement on demand deposits to limit banks' ability to create money and to restore the money creation function to government. Many economists have since called for a similar measure.[10] The reserve requirement in the United States currently averages less than 10 percent. Phased in over several years to allow the financial system to adjust, this action would deflate the borrowing pyramid and help restore the connection between the creation of money and the creation of wealth.

Tight Regulation of Financial Derivatives   Many forms of derivatives are basically high-risk gambling instruments that serve primarily to generate fees for the investment houses that package and sell them while creating dangerous financial instability. Like any other form of gambling, their creation, sale, and purchase should be tightly regulated and heavily taxed. Pension funds and other funds managed as public trusts should be strictly prohibited from trading in instruments so classified and from investing in companies that do. All publicly held corporations that engage in derivatives trading should be required to include a full report each quarter on their derivatives trading activities, report their potential financial exposure on such instruments, and reveal the proportion of their financial assets held in derivatives.

Preferential Treatment of Community Banks   The U.S. banking system was once made up of unitary or community banks that collected local savings deposits, made loans to local businesses, and financed mortgages to expand local home ownership. Successive changes in banking regulations have allowed the former community banks to be colonized by gigantic money-center banks that channel local deposits into the global money system. If the banking system is to serve local economies, the system of community banks must be restored by requiring money-center banks to divest their branches and by tightening community investment laws to require that a substantial majority of the investment portfolio of any bank covered by federal deposit insurance be invested within its service area and that all its investments meet federally mandated standards. The large, global money-center banks that wish to speculate with their depositors' money in risky investments around the world should be required to obtain deposit insurance from private insurers, with the premiums determined by the risks involved. Federal insurance should be reserved for community banks that serve community needs and play by community rules.[11]

Rigorous Enforcement of Antitrust Laws   Vigorous legal action should be taken to break up concentrations of corporate power. There should be a legal presumption that any acquisition or merger reduces competition and is contrary to market principles and the public interest. The burden of proving otherwise to skeptical regulators should fall squarely on those presenting such proposals.

Worker and Community Buyout Options   In most instances, the human interest is best served by patient, rooted capital. To this end, worker and community buyouts of corporate assets should be supported by public policy. For example, before a major corporation is allowed to close a plant or undertake a sale or merger, the affected workers and community should have a legal right of first option to buy the assets on preferential terms. The terms should reflect the workers' years of personal investment of labor in the company and the local community's collective investment in public facilities that have made its local operations possible. In most businesses, there are many investors in addition to the formal shareholders, and this investment should be recognized in the law. Bankruptcy rules should be structured similarly to give employees and communities the option of taking possession, on preferential terms, of the corporation's remaining assets after bankruptcy proceedings. Similarly, when a company is required to divest parts of its operation under antitrust laws, employees or the community or both should have first option to buy the divested units. Rules governing company pension funds might allow their use by employees to purchase voting control of their firm's assets. Government oversight should structure worker and community buyouts so that workers and communities have real control—in contrast to many Employee Stock Ownership Plans (ESOP) that vest control in management.

Tax Shifting   One of the most basic, but often violated, principles of tax policy is that taxes should be assessed against activities that contribute to social and environmental dysfunction. Therefore, tax laws should be revised to reduce taxes on activities that benefit society, such as employment (including employer contributions to social security, health care, and workers' compensation). The lost revenue would be made up by taxing activities that contribute to social and environmental dysfunction, such as resource extraction, packaging, pollution, imports, corporate lobbying, and advertising. Such taxes would cascade up through the system to encourage more social and environmentally responsible behavior and discourage the use of harmful products. For example, a carbon emissions tax at the source on coal, oil, gas, and nuclear energy would increase end-user prices and encourage conservation and conversion to solar energy sources such as solar heating, wind, hydro, photovoltaic, and biomass. Resulting increases in transportation costs would provide a nondiscriminatory natural tariff to encourage the localization of markets. The added cost of automobile commuting would encourage investment in public transit and locating closer to one's work. A tax on pollution emissions would encourage pollution control. A tax on the extraction of virgin materials would encourage conversion to less polluting, less materials-intensive product designs and modes of production and a greater reliance on recycled materials. Assessing manufacturers an amount sufficient to cover estimated costs to dispose of their product packaging would discourage unnecessary packaging. Import tariffs would encourage economic self-reliance.

Annual Profit Payout   Instead of taxing corporate profits, corporations should be required to pay out their profits each year to their shareholders. Profits would thus be taxed as shareholder income at the shareholder's normal marginal rate—much like mutual fund earnings are now taxed. The double taxation of corporate profits—once to the corporation and once to the shareholder—would be eliminated, along with the deferral of shareholder taxes and the many distortions that the corporate income tax introduces into corporate decision making. If this were carried out universally, corporations would have no incentive to shift profits around the world to the jurisdiction with the lowest tax rate. Interest payments on debt financing would come directly out of profits rather than out of taxes, thus discouraging the use of debt and encouraging greater reliance on equity financing. Many leveraged buyouts that depend on the tax deductability of interest to make them profitable would be discouraged. Corporations would be taxed on specific activities that it is in society's interest to limit, such as the use of carbon fuels, resource extraction, and speculative financial transactions. Such taxes would be difficult to avoid. Corporate expansion would also become more difficult—a step toward keeping markets more competitive—because a company would not be able to grow simply because management decided to reinvest its profits rather than paying them out to shareholders. If a corporation wanted funds to expand, it would need to raise new money in the financial markets and make its case accordingly. Shareholders could, of course, be given the option of rolling over their dividends into additional stock, much like the current U.S. procedure on the taxation of earnings from mutual funds.

Corporate Welfare   Welfare reform should give top priority to getting dependent corporations off the welfare rolls. Corporate subsidies range from resource depletion allowances to subsidized grazing fees, export subsidies, and tax abatements. Such subsidies should be systematically identified and eliminated, with the possible exception of those needed to establish and nurture locally owned, community-based enterprises.

Intellectual Property   Information is the only resource we have that is nondepletable and can be freely shared without depriving anyone of its use. Every contemporary human invention necessarily builds on the common heritage of human knowledge accumulated over thousands of years and countless generations. This is the information commons of the species. The justifiable purpose of intellectual property right protection is to provide incentives for research and creative contribution, not to create protected information monopolies. Laws relating to intellectual property rights should be reformed to conform to this principle. Such rights should be defined and interpreted narrowly and granted only for the minimum time necessary to allow those who have invested in for-profit research to recover their costs and a reasonable profit. The patenting of life-forms or genetic processes, discoveries funded with public monies, or processes or technologies that give the holder effective monopoly control over a type of research or class of products should be precluded by law. As with any common heritage resource, when there is a conflict between an exclusive private interest and a community interest, the community interest should prevail.

As business is localized, it will be possible to localize government as well. As Paul Hawken notes, it is big business that creates the need for big government to control its excesses and clean up its messes. Similarly, it is the interference of big business that renders government ineffective. Hawken describes the dynamic:

> Business assumes the role of guardianship vis-á-vis the ecosystem and fails miserably in the task; government steps in to try to mitigate the damage; business tries to sabotage this regulatory process and nimbly sidesteps those regulations that are put on the books; government ups the ante and thereby becomes a hydra-headed bureaucratic monster choking off economic development while squandering money; business decries "interference in the marketplace" and sets out to redress its grievances by further corrupting the legislative and regulatory process in an attempt to become de facto guardian, if not de jure.[12]

The bigger our corporations, the greater their power to externalize costs and the greater the need for big government to protect the public interest and to clean up the consequent social and environmental messes. The more we cut our giant corporations down to human scale, the more we will be able to reduce the size of government.

Addressing extreme inequality in the distribution of economic power is also important to decolonizing economic spaces. As our current experience shows, justice and sustainability are virtually impossible to achieve in an unequal world. Extreme inequality enables the economically powerful to colonize the environmental resources of the weak and thus consume beyond their environmental means. This commonly deprives the economically weak of their basic means of livelihood and delinks the economically strong from the environmental consequences of their actions. The excluded poor respond to their resulting insecurity by having many children—the one thing they can call their own and their only prospective source of care in their hour of need. As the rich expand their consumption and the poor produce more children, the human burden on the planet grows.

A more just and sustainable society with an equitable distribution of income would limit overconsumption and reduce the incentive to seek security through having large families. Measures toward this end include the following:

Guaranteed Income   An idea long popular with both conservative and progressive economists, a guaranteed income merits serious consideration. It involves guaranteeing every person an income adequate to meet his or her basic needs. The amount would be lower for children than for adults but would be unaffected by a person's other income, wealth, work, gender, or marital status. It would replace social security and existing welfare programs. Since earned income would not reduce the guaranteed payment, there would be little disincentive to work for pay, though employers might have to pay more to attract workers to unpleasant, menial tasks.[13] If some choose not to work, this should not be considered a problem in a labor surplus world.

Such a scheme would be expensive but could be supported in most high-income countries by reducing military spending, corporate welfare, and existing entitlement programs and increasing taxes on unearned income and luxuries and user fees on pollution, resource extraction, and other activities a sustainable society seeks to discourage. Combined with an adequate program of universal publicly funded health insurance and merit-based public fellowships for higher education, a guaranteed income would greatly increase the personal financial security afforded by more modest incomes and provide greater scope for those who wish to do unpaid work in the social economy. In low-income countries, agrarian reform and other measures to assure equitable access to productive natural resources for livelihood production might appropriately substitute for a guaranteed income.

Progressive Income and Consumption Taxes   Taxes on incomes up to the level required to meet basic needs in a comfortable, satisfying, and responsible way should be eliminated, as should sales or value-added taxes on basic food, clothing, shelter, health, personal hygiene, educational, and entertainment or recreational expenditures needed to sustain good living. There should, however, be a sharply graduated tax on incomes above the guaranteed minimum—going as high as 90 percent on top income brackets. In addition to a tax of at least 50 percent on estates over a million dollars, inheritance or trust income should be taxed to the receiving individual the same as any other personal income. Appropriate exceptions may be provided for family farms and businesses.

There should be a substantial luxury tax on nonessential consumption items that are socially harmful or environmentally wasteful or destructive. Personal charitable contributions, including to family foundations, should be fully tax exempt, thus providing a substantial incentive for individuals with excess incomes to support a strong independent sector as a counter to the power of the state and the corporation. Such measures would move us toward more equitable and sustainable societies while maintaining incentives to do socially useful work.

Pay Equity   The performance of an effective organization depends on the productive contribution of all its members. It is perfectly reasonable that those who carry more responsibility and bring more to the organization be compensated accordingly. But how much more? What is a proper ratio between the compensation of the highest and lowest paid worker in an organization? Two to one? Ten to one? A hundred to one? A thousand to one? Ratios of well over a thousand to one are common in U.S. corporations, even if we limit the comparison to U.S. workers and CEOs. A healthy society must establish a reasonable balance between economic incentive and economic justice. Public policy should provide incentives to keep the ratio within a reasonable limit, say a ratio of no more than fifteen to one. If a company considers its lowest paid worker is worth $10,000, then it could pay its CEO $150,000. If it raised the lowest paid worker to $20,000 then the CEO's pay could go up to $300,000. If the top jobs in a corporation or other organization are so difficult or distasteful that qualified applicants cannot be attracted for such a sum, then perhaps the job needs to be restructured. If the job is too demanding because the corporation is simply too big, then perhaps the corporation should be broken up to make it more manageable. Society can easily learn to do without the services of those who require compensation packages in the millions of dollars to motivate them to perform their jobs effectively.

Equitable Allocation of Paid Employment   Access to opportunities for paid employment should also be allocated as fairly as possible through measures to reduce the workweek and assure equal employment opportunity regardless of gender, race, or other extraneous considerations.

Such measures can be phased in over time and adjusted to reflect experience. The idea here is not to provide a prescriptive blueprint but rather to illustrate the kinds of policies that would lead us toward healthier societies. Different approaches will surely be appropriate in different settings, and the administration and funding of such initiatives should be undertaken by the smallest and most local governance units possible. For example, in predominantly agrarian societies with equitable land distribution, a very small guaranteed minimum income might be adequate. The same might be true in stable egalitarian societies in which living costs are low and there are ample employment opportunities for all who wish to work. A guaranteed income is probably most necessary to correct imbalances in societies such as the United States, where living costs are high, there is extreme inequality, and jobs paying a wage adequate to maintain a decent living are scarce.

If we are to manage our economic spaces in the human interest, we will need accounting tools suited to this purpose. Sixto Roxas, an economist and former international bank executive from the Philippines, explains that conventional national income accounts do not meet this need, because they measure the costs and benefits of economic activity from the standpoint of the firm, not the community. The differences are fundamental. For example, the firm profits by employing the least possible number of workers at the lowest possible wage. The community profits by having its members fully employed at the highest possible wage. The firm may profit by depleting a local forest or mineral resource and then moving elsewhere, while the community is left devastated.

Roxas and his colleagues are developing community-based accounting systems that assess economic costs and benefits in terms of their consequences for the health of households, communities, and ecosystems.[14] They also record how much of the value generated from local economic activity remains in the community and how much flows out. Thus, if local forests are being clear-cut and the timber and profits are being exported while the community is left with a barren landscape, this shows up as a net loss rather than the net gain recorded by conventional economic accounting. Significant attention is needed to developing and applying such systems as economic management tools.

LOCALIZING THE GLOBAL SYSTEM

Transnational corporations have for decades used global institutions and international agreements to circumvent democratic processes, force open national economies, and transfer control over markets, finance, resources, and productive assets to themselves. Any agenda to reclaim economic and political spaces for people must address the need to replace this predatory system of global governance with a system that:

- Empowers people and institutions at national and local levels to control and manage their economic resources to their own benefit;
- Makes it difficult for any locality to externalize its production or consumption costs beyond its borders; and
- Encourages cooperation among localities in the search for solutions to shared problems.

These objectives are strongly supported by the application of sound market principles. As we have already seen, to function in the public interest, markets must operation within a framework of enforceable rules that maintain the conditions of socially efficient market allocation. Otherwise productive investment is driven out by predatory speculation, cost internalizing firms are put out of business by cost externalizers, and the market becomes dominated by centrally planned corporate monopolies. It is therefore important for global institutions to support national and local governments in their efforts to implement sound market rules. Normally, such rules will favor local producers that use local resources to meet local needs and will protect local markets and resources from colonization by economic predators. At the same time, the people of a country must have the freedom to decide the extent to which they wish to integrate their national economy with the national economies of other willing partners. Whatever its level of integration, a primary obligation of the individual country to the international system is to keep its exports and imports with the rest of the world roughly in balance.

Currently, global governance functions related to economic, social, and environmental affairs are divided between the United Nations system—comprised of the United Nations secretariate; its specialized agencies such as the World Health Organization, the International Labour Organization, the Food and Agriculture Organization; and its various development assistance funds such as UNDP, UNFPA, UNICEF, and UNIFEM—and the Bretton Woods system—comprised of The World Bank, the IMF, and the World Trade Organization. The Bretton Woods institutions dominate the economic policy arena, yet accept no accountability for the social and environmental consequences of their policies. The under funded United Nations has virtually no influence over economic policies, but is left with the task of cleaning up the social and environmental messes the flawed policies of the Bretton Woods three leave in their wake.

The founders of the United Nations intended that coordination of international economic, social, cultural, educational, health, and related affairs, including oversight of the Bretton Woods institutions, would rest with the United Nations Economic and Social Council (ECOSOC). Although the World Bank, IMF, and WTO are officially designated specialized agencies of the United Nations, they have become far more powerful than the other specialized UN agencies and reject any UN effort to coordinate or oversee their activities.

Dividing the governance of the global affairs of one world between two competing governmental systems has not been a workable arrangement. A choice must ultimately be made between the Bretton Woods system and the UN system. The UN system has been only marginally effective—in part because of under-funding, neglect, and lack of ability to influence the economic policies of the Bretton Woods institutions—but has by far the broader mandate, is more open and democratic, is generally respectful of national sovereignty, and gives serious attention to human, social, and environmental priorities. The more secretive and undemocratic Bretton Woods institutions have greater professional competence and enforcement power, but generally take a narrowly economistic view of the world, run roughshod over national sovereignty and democratic processes, encourage competition among nations, and consistently place financial and corporate interests ahead of human and planetary interests.

Some would argue that the choice should favor the Bretton Woods institutions because of their ability to get things done. Given that the things they do most effectively are destructive and that their coercive methods consistently disregard the will and interests of those who bear the consequences this seems a poor choice. The United Nations has been less effective, but its more open and democratic decision processes and its greater responsiveness to the will of the people effected have generally resulted in more consensual agendas aligned with human and planetary interests. Since the underlying goal is to strengthen democracy and give social and environmental goals priority over corporate profits, the more sensible choice is to reaffirm the mandate of the United Nations, invest in building its capacity to fulfill it, and decommission the Bretton Woods institutions.

Under its reaffirmed economic mandate the United Nations would work with member countries to regain control of their economies, establish necessary regulatory regimes, and orient their economies toward domestic priorities. In addition to strengthening the mandates and capacities of existing UN agencies in international economic affairs, three new UN agencies are proposed, each with a role nearly the opposite of that of the Bretton Woods institution it will replace.[17]

UN International Insolvency Court (UNIIC)   Whereas the World Bank has led low-income countries ever more deeply into the debt bondage that holds their economies and resources hostage to the predators of the global economy, the primary responsibility of the proposed UNIIC will be to help countries free themselves from this burden. A debtor government that determines its debt obligations have reached a critical level and cannot be repaid without impairing the well-being of its citizens would voluntarily initiate the insolvency procedure by presenting its case to the court. After a preliminary assessment the debtor country would be granted a stay on its repayments for a period sufficient to complete the court's review and decision process. In the meantime it would also agree to incur no new debt.

An assessment process would determine how much a country owes and is able to pay over time without compromising its ability to perform essential governmental functions, including the delivery of necessary social services. The Court would also review the country's debt portfolio to identify odious debts that were not legitimately contracted—which would include many World Bank and IMF loans—or were used for purposes that yielded no public benefit—such as World Bank designed projects that failed to produce projected benefits due to faulty design or negligent oversight. The UNIIC would sanction the repudiation of such odious debts on the basis of international legal precedents.[15] Repudiation of World Bank and IMF loans would force them to call the guarantees from their member countries to cover their own debts, which would in turn build political support to decommission them.

A negotiated debt relief plan would provide for the rescheduling, reduction, and cancellation of the remaining debt on terms that would allow the indebted government to continue necessary functions, including the delivery of essential social services. Such plans would ideally take into account the implicit debt owed to the debtor country by creditor countries in the North for wealth previously extracted without proper compensation. Debt relief plans should include a schedule for freeing the country of international debt and putting in place mechanisms henceforth to keep its international accounts in balance.

UN International Finance Organization (UNIFO)   Whereas, the International Monetary Fund has forced countries to deregulate the flow of money and goods across their borders and to bear the consequences of resulting trade imbalances, international indebtedness, exploitation, and financial instability, the proposed UNIFO would work with UN member countries to achieve and maintain balance and stability in international financial relationships, free national and global finance from the distortions of international debt and debt-based money, promote productive domestic investment and domestic ownership of productive resources, and take such actions as necessary at the international level to support nations and localities in creating equitable, productive, sustainable livelihoods for all. Lacking either lending capacity or enforcement powers its functions would be limited to maintaining a central data base on international accounts, flagging problem situations, and facilitating negotiations among trading partners to correct imbalances. The UNIFO would also provide advisory services on request. Among its other functions it would facilitate the negotiation and implementation of international agreements that support joint action by national governments to prevent the use of offshore banks and tax havens for money laundering and tax evasion.

UN Organization for Corporate Accountability (UNOCA)   Whereas, the World Trade Organization regulates national and local governments to prohibit them from regulating transnational corporations, trade, and finance in the public interest, the UNOCA will assist governments in establishing sensible and appropriate regulatory regimes to assure the public accountability of international corporations and finance. To this end it will provide information and advisory services, facilitate the negotiation of relevant international agreements, and coordinate actions by national governments to break up concentrations of corporate power (especially in banking, media, and agribusiness), prevent unfair competitive practices, decharter corporations with a history of regulatory violations and repeat convictions for criminal behavior, enable persons harmed by a corporate subsidiary in one country to sue the parent company for damages in another, eliminate corporate subsidies, and prohibit corporations from attempting to influence political processes. To facilitate the process of rolling back international agreements that guarantee corporate rights at the expense of the rights of people, the UNOCA will facilitate the negotiation of international agreements that guarantee the right of countries and localities to: maintain balanced and mutually beneficial trading relationships with other countries; set rules and standards for businesses—including international corporations—operating in their jurisdictions;[16] prohibit the patenting of genetic materials, life forms and processes, and indigenous knowledge; and access beneficial information and technologies from other countries on reasonable terms.

Specialized Agencies   Responsibility for trade-related labor, health, food, and environmental standards properly falls with the jurisdiction of the United Nations agency with the relevant mandate and expertise, such as the International Labour Organization, the World Health Organization, the Food and Agriculture Organization, and the UN Environment Programme (UNEP). UNEP for example, might take the lead in developing environmental information systems that call attention to the cross border shifting of environmental burdens from one nation to another through environmental discharges or imbalances in the trading of environmental resources and toxic wastes. With an appropriate strengthening of its mandate and technical capacities, UNEP might coordinate the development and use of appropriate statistical and accounting methods and facilitate the negotiation of international agreements on standards, monitoring, and dispute adjudication relating to regional and national environmental cost internalization. Monitoring functions should be decentralized so far as possible, with each locality, district, nation, and region maintaining its own monitoring capability and accounts. When disputes regarding the cross border externalization of environmental burdens cannot be resolved directly through bilateral negotiations, they should be adjudicated by the appropriate judicial bodies, including the International Court of Justice.

To be effective and credible in carrying out the proposed functions with regard to international economic affairs, it will be important to keep the United Nations relatively free from corporate influence—an issue elaborated in Chapter 21.

The decisions that shape humanity's future are being made by a small but powerful corporate elite that has circumvented and corrupted the institutions of democracy to advance a narrow special interest agenda without regard to the consequences for others. The reforms outlined in this chapter all serve a common purpose: to restore the democratic accountability of political and economic decision making to the majority who bear the consequences. In Part VI we will review key events of the period 1995 through 2000 to see what they tell us of the prospects for such reforms and the path to their realization.

As the institutions of corporate globalization tighten their grip over the world's economic resources and deepen the corruption of the institutions of democracy, their excesses become ever more visible and direct our attention to some crucial questions. For example: Will life or money be humanity's defining value? Will people or corporations determine the path to our collective future? Is there sufficient spiritual awareness and political will within the human polity to achieve the necessary reforms to restore the democratic accountability of our institutions before the social and environmental devastation wrought by corporate globalization becomes irreversible? There are signs of hope, even in the growing excesses of the corporate world, because the more obvious and arrogant the excess, the faster the spiritual and political awakening of the world's people unfolds.

Part VI

FROM CORPORATE RULE TO CIVIL SOCIETY

21

MAKING MONEY, GROWING POORER

No one said, "Wouldn't it be cool to have a juggernaut economy that destroys the capacity of every living system on Earth."
—Paul Hawken, political activist and founder, Smith and Hawken[1]

The new nomadic capital never sets down roots, never builds communities. It leaves behind toxic wastes, embittered workers and indigenous communities driven out of existence.
—Anita Roddick, political activist and founder, The Body Shop[2]

FAST FORWARD TO THE BEGINNING of the Third Millennium. Seattle '99 is the icon of a now boisterously visible global movement engaging the struggle for life and democracy. The elites who once gathered in peaceful, secluded elegance to chart the course of the corporate global economy now meet behind police barricades with a backdrop of mass protests. The lines have been drawn, and a substantial group of committed activists has been awakened.

Previous chapters document the progress and consequences of corporate globalization up to early 1995. The destructive trends have since continued on an ever more alarming downward path. The global financial system has become even more short-sighted and unstable. The pressure on corporations to keep their share prices rising at all costs continues to grow. And the corruption of the political process has become so intolerable in the United States that people have started taking to the streets in mass protests demanding sweeping structural reforms.

From Asia, Latin America, Western and Eastern Europe, Africa, and North America the reports are all much the same. Civilization is being dismantled as a trade barrier and the commons is for sale to the highest bidder. Social and environmental standards are being rolled back. Safety nets for the poor are being phased out in favor of increased welfare for dependent global corporations. Small farms, shops, and factories continue to be displaced by global corporations and subsidized imports. Pollution, foreign debt, environmental destruction and inequality continue to grow in response to public policies put in place by the World Bank, IMF, and WTO or by governments acting at the behest of corporations and other wealthy interests.

Everything seems to be on the auction block—from water, air, information, indigenous knowledge, prisons, seeds and genetic codes, to social security, health care, and schools—turning public services available to everyone into private services available only to those who can pay and common heritages resources into private property. As ecological economist Herman Daly has noted, it is as if humanity has decided to hold a final going out of business sale.

This is the reality behind the growing citizen protest movements. The following are some highlights of events since *When Corporations Rule the World* was originally published.

CASINOS IN CYBERSPACE

The link between money making and value creation has become even more tenuous. From $1.5 to $2 trillion dollars now change hands daily in the world's foreign exchange markets. Only some 2 percent is related to trade in real goods and services. In January 2000, before a market correction brought many high tech stocks back down near earth, 170 Internet firms that had gone public since 1995 had a combined stock market valuation of $600 billion on total revenues of only $8 billion.[3]

In its April 3, 2000, cover story on "Wall Street's Hype Machine," *Business Week* observed that there is no longer any pretense of objectivity in television reporting on the financial markets. "Most analysts, for example, no longer act as information providers, but as stock promoters."[4] Commentators pushed stocks and hyped the bubble—buy recommendations outnumbered sell recommendations by 72 to 1. At least until the onset of a market correction in late 2000, value investing—buying stocks for the long term on the basis of the underlying value of the company—was out. Momentum investing—quickly buying and then selling a stock exhibiting short-term upward momentum—

was in. A decade earlier, investors held a NASDAQ stock on average for two years. By 2000 the average was five months. In 1999 Wall Street spent $1.2 billion on advertising—three times what they spent five years earlier.[5]

From 1990 to 1999, the market value of world output (GDP) increased by 129 percent from $31.4 to $40.5 trillion (in constant 1998 dollars).[6] During the same period the total capitalization (market value) of global stock markets rose by 293 percent from $9.4 trillion to $27.5 trillion.[7] The fact that the value of financial assets, claims on real wealth, grew so much faster than growth in real output reflects the distortions of stock markets fueled by hype and debt. From March 1995 to March 2000 margin debt in the United States— money borrowed from brokers to finance stock purchases—increased by 463 percent: $60.2 billion to $278.5 billion.[8] From 1995 to the first quarter of 2000, the debts of U.S. financial sector institutions increased by 81 percent to $7.7 trillion. The institutions in the business of pure money, using money to make money for those who have money, held more debt than any other sector, including government, households, and nonfinancial businesses.[9]

Recall from Chapter 13 how the banking system creates money out of nothing by issuing loans. The picture emerges here of a system in which banks lend to one another to create a growing debt pyramid that inflates the financial assets they have available among themselves to buy and sell countries and companies and to finance mega-mergers and acquisitions. A 1999 study found that the top five investment banks in America—banks that hold equity positions in other corporations—were leveraged on a ratio of 27 to 1.[10]

The extreme instability of an unregulated global financial system built on mountains of debt was revealed by the financial collapse that spread through Asia, Russia, and Latin America in 1997 and 1998. Typically, growth in the affected countries had been fueled by rapid inflows of foreign money attracted by high interest rates and rapidly inflating stock bubbles. Little, if any, of this money went into real investments to expand productive capacity. Rather it simply fueled the inflation of stock and real estate prices, creating great fortunes out of hot air.

Speculation became so much more profitable than true investment that the owners of real industrial and agricultural assets diverted the cash flow from their enterprises to play in the markets rather than maintain or upgrade their existing facilities. The faster new "investment" flowed in, the faster real productive capacity was decapitalized. Domestic production and exports declined as the import of foreign-made luxury goods—paid for with the borrowed foreign exchange—increased. It was much like a person with no real income or assets briefly adopting an extravagant lifestyle by accepting and maxing out all the credit cards that arrive in the mail.

As each "miracle" economy became hopelessly overextended to foreign creditors, the more savvy speculators pulled out their money, the value of the domestic currency crashed, the economy collapsed, and the International Monetary Fund stepped in with publicly guaranteed loans to bail out the private international banks left holding uncollectible loans.[11] Unemployment in the affected Asian countries doubled and in Latin America it reached its highest level in 15 years.[12]

The September 1998 collapse of a U.S.-based hedge fund, Long-Term Capital Management, gave the public a rare glimpse into the secretive world of high stakes financial speculation that fuels this instability. Leveraged at a ratio of $25 in loans for every dollar of equity, Long-Term Capital Management made huge, risky bets in the world's financial markets. When they went bad, the threat posed to the U.S. and world financial system compelled the U.S. Federal Reserve to step in to arrange a private bailout. There are an estimated 4,000 hedge funds in the world and some are reportedly leveraged by as much as 100 to one. An unregulated global financial market with the power to create money from nothing to finance high stakes financial speculation—with an expectation that government will step in with bailouts when things go bad—is an invitation to financial disaster.

DEMOCRACY FOR SALE

There was a time when government regulators played a role in limiting such excess. Now they facilitate it. Data on U.S. political contributions compiled by the Center for Responsive Politics make the reason all too clear. For the 1990 through 2000 election cycles the Finance Insurance/Real Estate industry reported total contributions of $811 million to the Democratic and Republican parties, consistently exceeding the contributions of all other industry categories by a substantial margin. For the 2000 U.S. election cycle, they reported a single election cycle industry record of $249 million in contributions.[13]

The Federal Elections Commission projected that candidates for federal office would spend a total of $3 billion in the 2000 campaigns, an increase of about $800 million from four years earlier. Opulent parties sponsored by corporations courting political favor were the central feature of the 2000 Republican and Democratic political conventions. The need for serious campaign finance reform to get bribery out of politics grows by the day.

Rampant political corruption, most of it legal, has put the public interest on the auction block and turned democracy in the United States into a meaningless charade. The more unequal the distribution of wealth the more dominant the voice of big money interests in the political process and the more the rules are skewed to further favor the wealthy. In the U.S. 2000 presidential election it made relatively little difference to big money which of the two major party candidates—Al Gore or George W. Bush—won. Both were Yale-educated, white-male, conservative-corporate-globalists from political-elite families and were owned by big money interests.

A poll commissioned by *The Nation* magazine and the Institute for Policy Studies, a Washington, D.C., based think tank found deep concern among a majority of Americans for issues mentioned only rarely or not at all by either of the two major party candidates, including the gap between rich and poor (91%) and the lack of health insurance for the poor (74%). On other issues, both candidates took positions sharply at odds with the majority of the electorate. For example, both candidates expressed their commitment to increasing international trade. A large majority of respondents (83%) favored protection for workers, the environment, and human rights even if it meant slowing trade and the economy. Both candidates called for an increase in defense expenditures. A strong majority (63%) of the electorate favored a reduction in defense spending to increase funding for education, Social Security, and paying down the national debt. When third party presidential candidates, including Green Party candidate Ralph Nader, called for action on these issues their voices were shut out by the corporate media and excluded from the corporate sponsored televised debates.

Bush ultimately claimed the White House in perhaps the most tainted election in U.S. history. In the swing state of Florida, where Bush's brother was governor and the co-chair of the Bush campaign supervised the election process, there was substantial evidence of serious election irregularities, including intentional efforts to disenfranchise thousands of African-American voters. An extended dispute over the irregularities was ended when five right-wing Supreme Court justices intervened to stop the counting of legitimate ballots rejected by defective machines located mostly in low-income precincts where the voters favored Gore—a decision most independent legal scholars denounced as blatantly partisan and legally indefensible.

More concerned with maintaining public confidence in a flawed system than with playing watchdog, corporate media pundits played down events that might raise doubts about the integrity of the process and dismissed those who complained as poor losers—advising them to accept the result and get on with their lives. Consequently, those who relied for their information solely on the corporate media had little idea of either the seriousness or the systematic nature of the many irregularities. Even so, a *Washington Post*-ABC News poll conducted the week before Bush was installed in the White House found that 40 percent of those interviewed were sufficiently informed to conclude that Bush had not been legitimately elected.

Thanks to the Lobbying Disclosure Act of 1995 it is now possible to track what various corporations and interest groups spend on professional lobbyists to influence the U.S. federal government. Reported lobbying expenditures for 1998 totaled $1.42 billion, up 13 percent over 1997. The number of registered lobbyists swelled from 14,946 on September 30, 1997 to 20,512 on June 15, 1999. *In 1998 there were more than 38 registered lobbyists and $2.7 million in lobbying expenditures for each member of the U.S. Congress.*[14]

For many large corporations, campaign contributions have become the highest return investment they can make. For example, by investing $1.2 million in campaign contributions the Glaxo Smith Kline pharmaceutical corporation won a nineteen-month patent extension on the drug Zantac that was estimated to be worth $1 billion, a net return of 83,333 percent. Eight million in campaign contributions preserved a logging road subsidy worth $458 million to the logging industry—a 5,725 percent return. For a mere $5 million the broadcasting industry secured free digital TV licenses worth $70 billion for a 1,400,000 percent return on their investment.[15]

Along with the overt lobbying, covert political strategies have also intensified. Expertly orchestrated campaigns are carried out by industry associations and public relation firms to obscure issues in the public mind and block important reforms that might limit corporations' ability to externalize their costs onto the public. Pursue a public interest cause relating to food safety, auto safety, fuel efficiency, genetic engineering, environmental protection, Internet privacy, gun control, health-care reform, teen smoking, water purity, the minimum wage, violence on television, recycling—you name the issue. If your proposal might cut into corporate profits a corporate coalition will put millions of dollars behind a campaign to sink it. They will hire "experts" to support their position, place op-eds and "news" stories that seek to discredit you, cut off your public or foundation funding, question your science, raise concerns about the cost of corrective action, and dismiss you as a greedy opportunist pursuing a narrow special interest. Your opponents will generally present themselves as representatives of grassroots citizen groups, but their funding will be corporate and their address is likely that of a corporate public relations firm. Activists call them "Astroturf" lobbies.[16]

Corporations have also stepped up their spending on glossy advertising campaigns professing their deep social and environmental commitment. Shell Corporation's advertisement in the October 1999 *National Geographic*, featuring full color pictures of pristine rainforests and touting Shell's commitment to working with indigenous peoples, is an especially cynical example.

> Time and time again at Shell we're discovering the rewards of respecting the environment when doing business. If we're exploring for oil and gas reserves in sensitive areas of the world, we consult widely with the different local and global interest groups. Working together our goal is to ensure that bio-diversity in each location is preserved. We also try to encourage these groups to monitor our progress so that we can review and improve the ways in which we work.

Shell should know that glossy ads will not erase the memory of the Ogoni leaders hanged in Nigeria for their role in protesting the Shell corporation's devastation of their homelands. One can only wonder how different the world might be if the money spent on such corporate greenwash was devoted instead to cleaning up production operations and improving the lives of people in the impacted areas.

UN Secretary General Kofi Annan proposed to corporate leaders at the World Economic Forum summit in Davos in January 1999 that the United Nations and the world's largest corporations join in partnership to strengthen human rights, raise labor standards, and protect the environment. He set forth a bold vision "to unite the powers of markets with the authority of universal ideals. Let us choose to reconcile the creative forces of private entrepreneurship with the needs of the disadvantaged and the requirements of the future generations."

A number of corporations eager to hide their social and environmental sins under the cover of the UN logo quickly signed on. Civil society organizations that want to see the United Nations take the lead in international efforts to hold global corporations accountable for their misdeeds raised their voices in protest, pointing out that UN partnerships with ethically challenged corporations are more likely to damage the UN's credibility than to improve corporate behavior.[17]

It seems that the Secretary General, who saw the initiative as a way for the cash starved United Nations to enlist the aid of organizations with vast resources in the UN's cause, did not fully appreciate the fact that corporations are not philanthropic organizations and that their interests rarely align with the interests of those seeking protection for human rights, labor, and the environment. Among the first participants in the UN Global Compact, the centerpiece of his initiative, were corporations such as Nike, Shell, and Rio Tinto that the public has come to see as international symbols of corporate greed, human rights abuse, and environmental destruction. Other notorious corporate participants include Novartis and Aventis (leaders in the effort to force consumers to accept transgenic foods without proper testing or labeling), Bayer, BASF, and DuPont (leaders in ozone depletion), and Daimler Chrysler (a market leader in gas guzzling SUV's). A number of business associations have also joined, including the International Chamber of Commerce and the World Business Council on Sustainable Development, both known for their vigorous efforts to pre-empt any attempt by the United Nations to hold transnational corporations to enforceable international standards.

Companies interested in participating in the Global Compact need only send the UN a statement expressing their support for the idea of the Compact and its nine principles relating to human rights, employment, and environmental standards. Once a year member companies are invited to send the UN a report describing their "best practices" in each of these areas for posting on the UN's Global Compact website. There is no provision to screen applicants or monitor the performance of members. Indeed, there is no expectation that members will abide by the principles. Maria Livianos Cattui, secretary general of the International Chamber of Commerce, made clear when the Compact was proposed that "business would look askance at any suggestion involving external assessment of corporate performance, whether by special interest groups or by UN agencies. The Global Compact is a joint commitment to shared values, not a qualification to be met. It must not become a vehicle for governments to burden business with prescriptive regulations."[18]

Most people accept the need for police and courts to enforce democratically determined laws essential to the peace, security, and well-being of society. Corporations are strong advocates of such laws for others, but take offense at the merest suggestion they be held to some public standard as burdensome meddling in their private affairs. It is sad that the UN Secretary General so easily accepted, and thus tacitly endorsed, this hypocrisy at the expense of the UN's reputation and legitimacy.

Buying special subsidies and regulatory exemptions politician-by-politician and country-by-country is expensive and time consuming. Corporations have learned that it is much more efficient to use international agreements to cir-cumvent national and local governments altogether. To this end the World Trade Organization (WTO) was established on January 1, 1995, with an an-nounced mandate to establish and enforce the trade rules essential to prevent trade wars and protect the interests of poor nations.

As demonstrated by its practice, the real function of the WTO is to block new regulatory initiatives by national and local governments that conflict with the interest of global corporations and financiers and to roll back existing rules regulating trade, corporations, and finance. For example, the WTO told Japan that its tax on bourbon whiskey produced in the United States was too high. Canada was told it could not protect its culture by taxing U.S. magazines. India was told it could not provide its people with inexpensive generic drugs because this would be unfair to foreign drug companies that profit handsomely from branded products. The United States was told its law banning the import of tuna fish caught with methods harmful to dolphins would have to be changed.

Europeans were told they could not give an import preference to bananas produced by small farmers in the Carribean. They were also told that until they provided conclusive scientific proof that they are harmful they could not restrict the import of beef treated with growth hormones or genetically modi-fied food products. Concern that they may pose risks to human and environ-mental health was not sufficient justification. The WTO further reserved to itself the right to determine whether Europeans, and others, could require the labeling of genetically modified foods. In each case the WTO sought to over-turn rules enacted by democratically elected governments in the interests of their citizens. To the WTO, democracy and human rights are trade barriers to be eliminated in the defense of corporate rights.

Proposals up for consideration at the aborted Seattle WTO meeting in 1999 would have placed further restrictions on governmental action to favor local over foreign investors (including in banking, media, and other service sectors), preserve national food security by protecting local farmers from preda-tory foreign competition, protect forest and water resources from expropria-tion by foreign corporations, or regulate speculative movements of interna-tional money. Other proposals would have required countries to clear the way for privatization of public services such as schools, health care, and municipal water. After the Seattle debacle, the corporate globalists immediately began regrouping to move these proposals ahead in future WTO gatherings and through other international forums.

In addition to their Seattle WTO defeat, America's corporate globalists had been stunned by two earlier setbacks at the hands of civil society. In 1997,

President Clinton was forced to shelve his request for usually routine Congressional action to renew the Fast Track authority that allows the Executive Branch to negotiate trade agreements and then push approval through the Congress with no amendments and minimal debate. They suffered another setback when in December 1998 the OECD announced the termination of negotiations on the Multilateral Agreement on Investment, which would have precluded virtually any governmental regulation of the free international flow of speculative money or foreign ownership of domestic assets. It would further have required governments to compensate foreign investors for any loss of expected profits resulting from the introduction of new environmental, health, or safety regulations and would have prevented governments from giving any preference to local over foreign firms in procurement or other forms of public support. A massive public outcry mobilized by concerned citizen groups forced the termination of negotiations.

America's corporate globalists intensified their lobbying efforts to reestablish their hold on the political process and quickly won a string of victories over the opposition of labor, environment, and other public interest groups. On May 11, 2000, the U.S. Senate approved the African/Carribean trade bill. Then came the passage of a bill establishing permanent trading relations with China, followed in July 2000 by passage of a Vietnam trade bill. All were touted as measures to assist poor countries, normalize trade relations, and open foreign markets to U.S. exports. The day after the China agreement was signed into law by President Clinton *The Wall Street Journal* noted the real reason the corporate establishment put its full lobbying weight behind the China trade bill: to guarantee that U.S. companies could safely move more production to China with assured access to U.S. markets.[19] That, of course, is what the Africa/Carribean and Vietnam bills were about as well.

I was recently asked by a writer for a business publication what corporate leaders could do to protect their corporations from the growing backlash of "special interest groups." The very framing of the question revealed the myopia of the corporate establishment. First, it equates the corporate interest with the public interest and dismisses those who act on behalf of life and democracy as special interests. Second, it identifies the problem as the protesters, rather than the social and environmental wrongs for which the protesters seek remedies.

Next time you hear a corporation touting its commitment to people and the environment, find out how much it is spending through industry associations, campaign contributions, professional lobbyists, and public relations firms like Hill & Knowlton, Burson-Marsteller, Shandwick, or Ketchum PR to roll back social and environmental regulations, win new trade agreements, extract subsidies from government, defeat citizen-led, public-interest campaigns, and paint a green happy face on its misdeeds.[20]

The first responsibility of a corporate leader who truly cares about the well-being of people and planet is to acknowledge that for a market to work in the larger public interest there must be enforceable rules set through an open democratic process that involves not just powerholders, but all whose interests are at stake. There must also be borders—not walls, but speed bumps—to protect those who play by local rules from those who don't. Any corporation that works actively to defeat the efforts of citizen groups to establish enforceable rules of corporate accountability, bribes politicians—legally or illegally—or otherwise seeks special political favor at the expense of an open and equitable democratic process cannot rightfully claim to be a responsible citizen.

The second responsibility of a concerned corporate leader is to recognize that the right to determine the rules of the market properly resides in real people not in corporations—not even corporations that believe they are acting with the best interests of the society in mind. They are not elected bodies and they have no special expertise in representing interests other than their own. Because of their enormous power and resources their political involvement inevitably distorts the democratic process. The only responsible political involvement for a corporation is to work for rules that get corporations out of politics and restore the integrity of the democratic process. Beyond that the socially responsible corporation obeys the law and stays out of politics. Period.

Corporate executives who wish to do more toward the creation of a truly just, sustainable, and compassionate world in their personal capacities as individual citizens are quite another matter. Their experience and expertise make them welcome partners in working with citizen movements working to establish enforceable market rules that serve the interests of all—not just those of the cloud minders who already are doing very well.

LIFE ON STRATOS

Financial bubbles continued to lift the fortunes of Stratos dwellers further into the heavens as the Troglytes working the mines below struggled harder to get by on stagnant or declining incomes. By 1998 the assets of the world's top three billionaires totaled more than the combined GNP of all the least developed countries and their 600 million people.[21] Of the world's 6 billion people, 2.8 billion—nearly half—were living on less than $2 a day. Some 1.2 billion lived on less than a dollar a day.[22] Average growth in per capita income from 1990–98 was negative in 50 countries—often a direct result of corporate libertarian policies imposed by the IMF and World Bank under structural adjustment.

From 1973 to 1998 productivity in the United States increased by 33 percent,[23] but the wage of the worker in the middle of the heap—the *median* wage—declined in constant dollars.[24] To make ends meet, the typical family household worked longer hours, sent additional family members into the workforce, and went deeper into debt. In 1999, U.S. household debt reached a total $6.5 trillion, 98 percent of total disposable annual income.[25]

Virtually all of the benefit of America's productivity gains went to those least in need, mostly to the wealthiest 10 percent who now own almost 90 percent of all business equity, 88.5 percent of bonds, and 89.3 percent of stocks.[26] In 1999 the total compensation of U.S. corporate CEOs averaged $12.4 million, 475 times the average production worker's pay—up from a ratio of 141 to one in 1995.[27] In 1998, 29 percent of all U.S. workers were in jobs paying poverty-level wages, defined as an hourly wage too low, given a standard work week, to pull a family of four above the poverty line.[28] From 1995 to 1998 the average net worth of families earning $100,000 and up rose 22 percent, to more than $1.7 million. That of families earning $10,000 to $25,000 a year dropped by 20 percent as they fell more deeply into debt.[29]

This maldistribution of productivity gains was no accident. Whenever the cloud minders feared that falling unemployment might push up wages, the Federal Reserve—run by the nation's top bankers—stepped in with an interest rate increase to cool the economy. Meanwhile, corporations stepped up their efforts to downsize, move jobs to low-wage countries, and import temporary workers from abroad who must accept whatever wages and working conditions the employer offers or return home.

Despite talk of forgiveness, the indebtedness of Southern countries increased from $2.1 trillion in 1994 to $2.5 trillion in 1998 (1998 dollars).[30] In 1996, sub-Saharan Africa paid $2.5 billion more in debt service than it received in new long-term loans and credits. Africa spends four times more on debt service than on health care.[31]

Corporate mergers and acquisitions continued the process of eliminating competition and consolidating power at the core. In 1994, the worldwide total value of mergers and acquisitions was $560.3 billion. It reached $2.5 trillion in 1998 and $3.4 trillion in 1999.[32] Once constrained by a taboo against hostile takeovers, Europe joined the feeding frenzy. The value of European mergers and acquisitions reached $988 billion in 1998, leapt by 66 percent to $1.5 trillion in 1999, and was expected to reach $2 trillion in 2000.[33]

Aside from the highly publicized antitrust case brought against Microsoft Corporation, the growing political influence of the largest corporations seems to have all but eliminated concern within the U.S. political establishment about the concentration of economic power. In 1998, when the two biggest remaining parts of the fabled Rockefeller Empire, Exxon and Mobil, recombined in the largest merger in history up to that time, the politicians were silent. The Glass-Steagall Act passed in 1934, to reduce the risk of bank failure, expressly prohibited banks from engaging in the insurance business. When the Citicorp banking corporation and the Travelers Group insurance corporation announced their intent to merge and form the world's largest financial institution, a Republican Congress and the Democratic Clinton administration joined in a remarkable display of bipartisanship to eliminate the legal barrier to this marriage by repealing Glass-Steagall. A few days later Deutsche Bank bought the Bankers Trust Corporation to form a financial institution even larger than the new Citigroup. A similar silence greeted America Online's January 10, 2000, announcement of its $185 billion deal to buy Time Warner, setting yet another new record as the largest merger in history.[34]

In the grand tradition of Orwellian doublespeak, we are told in each case that the resulting combination will increase efficiency, enhance competition, and benefit consumers.[35] As it turns out, the only certain winners are the deal makers who receive the commissions and the top managers of the merged companies who generally use the occasion to reward themselves with additional bonuses and stock options. In many instances both shareholders and consumers end up losing.[34]

By conventional financial indicators—episodes of extreme instability notwithstanding—the corporate global economy continues to create unprecedented financial wealth. It is, however, for the most part a false prosperity built on illusions and financial bubbles, and it comes at an increasingly intolerable cost.

ENVIRONMENTAL COSTS

There was much talk at the end of the past century of a dematerialized economy. As the stocks of Internet start-ups soared into the stratosphere, pundits hailed the miracle of a new "Information Economy" in which wealth was being created with pure information, creating a new economic reality delinked from the constraints of economic cycles and environmental limits. It was true that the stock bubbles on which many dot-com multimillionaires built their fortunes had no direct environmental impact. However, the lifestyles their fortunes make possible—which run toward oversized, gas-guzzling SUVs, trophy mansions, mountain vacation homes, private jets, exotic vacations in distant lands, and feasting from the top of the food chain—are quite another matter.

There is nothing new about making money out of nothing. Banks do it every time they make a loan. When people spend money, however, they expect real value in return. There is also the dirty little secret that information technology depends on sophisticated hardware that requires massive amounts of toxic chemicals to manufacture. Silicon Valley (Santa Clara County, California) has twenty-nine toxic Superfund sites—more than any other county in America—and 80 percent of the waste is from electronics manufacturing.

Internet or no, the "new" economy looks very much like a continuation of the old economy in its impact on the earth's climate, forests, coral reefs and fisheries, soils, and fresh water. Worldwide losses related to storms, floods, and other severe weather events attributable in part to human-caused global warming exceeded $430 billion (1998 dollars) in the 1990s, more than five times the cost of such natural disturbances in the 1980s.[37] Even in the information age, each person living in a high-income country consumes on average from 45 to 85 tons of natural resources annually, including their total share of soil erosion, mining wastes, and other ancillary materials. Industrial economies require about 300 kilograms of natural resources to generate each US$100 in income.[38]

The World Wide Fund for Nature has compiled a Living Planet Index that shows a drop of 30 percent in the health of the living wealth of earth's forests and waters over a single generation from 1970 to 1995. When the index reaches zero bacteria and cockroaches may still be here, but there will be few humans around to marvel at how much money we have left behind in our bank accounts.

A joint study released in September 2000 by the United Nations Development Programme (UNDP), the UN Environment Programme (UNEP), the

World Bank and the World Resources Institute assesses five ecosystem types (agricultural, coastal, forest, freshwater, and grasslands) in relation to five eco- system services (food and fiber production, water quantity, air quality, biodiversity, and carbon storage). It found that sixteen of the twenty-five eco- system/service combinations had declining trends. Only one—food and fiber production by forest ecosystems—presented a positive trend, which was due to expanding industrial forest monocropping at the expense of species diver- sity.[39] These declines are all a consequence of human economic activity. Bio- invasion, the second greatest threat to biodiversity after habitat loss, now threat- ens some 20 percent of the world's endangered vertebrate species. It is a direct result of the introduction, through expanded trade, of exotic invasive species into ecosystems that have no defenses against them.[40]

By 1995 we had already learned a lot about the costs to humanity of the reckless chemical and radioactive contamination of our soils and waters. Yet only in 1996, when Theo Colborn and her research team published *Our Stolen Future*, did the public become aware of the full implications of the 70,000 synthetic chemicals now dispersed in the human environment.[41] Thousands of these chemicals mimic the action of hormones in humans and other living creatures and are responsible for declining sperm counts, reproductive fail- ures, a high incidence of deformities in frogs, fish, and birds, and the impaired intellectual and behavioral development of human children.

A newly recognized hazard of the nuclear era is the use of depleted ura- nium (DU), a waste product of the nuclear arms and energy industries that is used to harden military munitions. When used in combat the uranium in the round ignites on impact and combines with oxygen to form a cloud of ura- nium dust that is persistent and highly toxic to those who breathe or ingest it, causing disability and/or death. From 300 to 800 tons of DU munitions were fired in Iraq and northern Kuwait during the Gulf War leaving vast areas con- taminated with the deadly toxic material with a radioactive half-life of 4 to 5 billion years—the present age of the earth. DU has become a prime suspect as a source of the Gulf War Syndrome that afflicts as many as 90,000 of the 697,000 U.S. troops who served in the Gulf, even though the military steadfastly de- nies any possible link. Similar munitions were used by NATO troops in Kosovo, posing a considerable risk not only to NATO troops, but to the returning refu- gees who will suffer the consequences for generations to come.[42] The contin- ued production and use of such munitions reveals the extent to which a nar- row focus on the immediate utility of a technology can result in a callous disregard of the longer-term consequences.

Two new pollution threats have come to public attention since 1995: electromagnetic radiation and transgenic organisms. Health authorities have noted recent sharp increases in asthma, sleep disorders, hypertension, tinnitis, memory loss, and influenza and flu-like illnesses. The increase began in the United States in November 1996, at the same time that digital cell phone service was first introduced into a number of U.S. cities. Pulsed radio-frequency and microwave radiation levels have since increased by up to 100,000-fold in some large cities. The 1996 Telecommunications Act mandated universal wireless services and banned state and local governments from regulating transmission facilities on environmental grounds.[43] Major increases in wireless communication devices and related radiation are projected.

The rapid and wide-scale commercialization and dissemination of transgenic organisms is also a post-1995 phenomenon. Conventional plant breeding, which involves selective cross breeding between plants of the same or closely related species, simulates natural processes. Genetically engineered plants are by contrast commonly transgenic, meaning they are created by moving genetic material across nature's carefully erected species barriers and inserting them into the cells of a wholly alien species, even crossing the boundaries between bacteria, plants, and animals. Bacterial genes may be inserted into corn or fish genes into tomatoes. Harmful as they are, at least nuclear and chemical wastes do not self-reproduce. Transgenic organisms do. They also mutate and interact with other species—and once released into the environment they may prove impossible to recall or isolate.[44]

Under pressure to rapidly achieve dominant market positions, biotech companies have rushed transgenic organisms to the market with minimal testing, government oversight, or regard for potential health and environmental consequences. By 1999 100 million acres were planted in transgenic crops, primarily in the United States, Argentina, and Canada.[45] Faced with a growing public outcry from citizen groups alerted to biotech corporations playing Russian roulette for profit with the living systems of the planet, seven major biotech corporations formed the Council for Biotechnology Information to carry out a $50 million public relations campaign to assure the public that their products are both beneficial and harmless.[46]

Rapidly expanding technological frontiers now give humanity god-like capacities to manipulate the basic building blocks of matter, life, and the electromagnetic spectrum. Corporations with billions of dollars at stake insist that they should be allowed to move ahead with commercializing and disseminating products based on these technologies until others provide conclusive proof that they are harmful. But our understanding of the implications of such technologies for our own bodies and the earth's living systems remains minuscule. We are like a child with a box of matches sitting next to an open container of gasoline armed only with the knowledge that striking a match will produce a pretty flame. The consequences of letting corporations make for us such basic decisions about altering the chemical, electromagnetic, and genetic environment of the planet—in some instances permanently and irreversibly—purely on the basis of what is possible and profitable at the moment is becoming increasingly foolhardy.

SOCIAL COSTS

The health and security of people and nature is the only true measure of prosperity. We can rejoice that there have been gratifying improvements in selected social indicators over the past several decades in some low-income countries, including increases in life expectancy, primary and secondary school enrollment ratios, and access to safe water. Yet worldwide some 90 million children remain out of school at the primary level. Some 100 million children are living or working on the streets. Three hundred thousand children were soldiers during the 1990s and 6 million were injured in armed conflict.[47] In 2000 the number of international refugees and internally displaced persons was estimated to be upwards of 57 million.[48] Over a thirty-year period in Canada and the United Kingdom, divorce rates increased by 500 percent and births to unmarried women by 600 percent.[49]

According to a report prepared for the United Nations Development Programme, "Since 1989 the countries of Eastern Europe and the former Soviet Union have suffered severe setbacks in human development and poverty to an extent unprecedented in industrial countries during peacetime."[50] In Russia, life expectancy has plunged to less than sixty years for men. Some 75 percent of Russians now live below or barely above the poverty line, while 50 to 80 percent of Russia's school-age children are classified as having a physical or mental disability.[51]

As of the end of 1999, nearly 34 million people worldwide were infected with HIV, including 23 million in sub-Saharan Africa where it is erasing the significant gains in life expectancy achieved in the 1970s.[52] Financially strapped health services are ill equipped to respond.

Abandoning their tradition of lifetime employment, Japanese corporations have joined their American counterparts in placing profits before people. Corporate downsizing increased Japan's unemployment rate to 4.9 percent in

April 2000 from its historic level of virtually zero.[53] Increased pressure and longer hours for the workers who remain have made death from the stress of overwork a national issue. According to Japan's National Police Agency there was a 62 percent increase in work-related suicides between 1997 and 1998, from 4,786 to 7,935.[54] Rising unemployment has also been accompanied by rising crime.

Rosy economic statistics and much celebration of America's booming economy notwithstanding, America is also plagued by some disturbing social trends. A major Fordham University study on the social health of America found significant positive improvements from 1970 to 1996 in indicators of infant mortality, life expectancy at age 65, poverty among those 65 and older, and high school dropouts. At the same time it found alarming increases in youth suicide, violent crime, child poverty, inequality and child abuse, along with a decline in wages and health care coverage.[55]

As of the end of 1999, 6.3 million Americans were under some form of judicial supervision—on probation, in jail or prison, or on parole. This was 3.1% of all U.S. adult residents, up 250 percent from 1.8 million in 1980, the first year for which data are available.[56] Two million of these under supervision were imprisoned, giving America—land of the free—the highest rate of imprisonment of any country in the world, with the possible exception of Russia. More than 55 percent of those in prison were African-Americans, many for relatively minor, nonviolent drug offenses.[57] It seems our deeply troubled society has chosen imprisonment as the primary solution to its social ills.

For all the current focus on criminal justice in the United States, it is striking that no official statistics are compiled on corporate crime, although it is flourishing on a scale that makes most street crime seem petty by comparison. On a single day, June 15, 2000, *The New York Times* reported the following:

- "Top executives of the New York Life Insurance Company were accused in a racketeering lawsuit yesterday of enriching themselves by charging tens of millions of dollars in excess fees to the retirement plans that the insurer maintains for its workers and agents."[58]
- "In an indictment filed in Federal District Court in Manhattan, prosecutors charged 21 people with conducting a racketeering enterprise based at DMN [Capital Investments]."[59]
- "Three former executives of CUC International [now Cendant Corporation] pleaded guilty to federal charges in what the authorities said was the largest and longest accounting fraud in history, continuing at least 12 years and costing investors $19 billion."[60]

Include the illness, physical injury and death from dangerous, defective, and mislabeled products, dangerous workplace conditions, and the release of toxic pollutants and the human and financial costs of organized corporate crime become truly staggering. Corporations also profit from facilitating crimes, for example the money laundering facilities provided by major banking corporations to drug dealers, tax cheats, and other criminals[61] and the facilitation of cigarette smuggling by major tobacco companies. Yet, unlike the harsh mandatory sentences imposed on street criminals even for petty crimes, the persons responsible for corporate crime rarely suffer personal fines or imprisonment.

Corporations profit not only from committing and facilitating crime, they also profit from punishing street criminals. Prison operators such as Corrections Corporation of America, Wackenhut Corrections Corporation, and Sodexho SA aggressively promote prison privatization globally.[62] J.C. Penney, Victoria's Secret, IBM, Toys 'R' Us, and TWA are among the U.S. corporations that have augmented their profits by employing prisoners who reportedly earn as little as 11 cents an hour with no benefits—a rate competitive with the worst of China's sweatshops.[63] Under a new law that took effect in July 2000, Kentucky prisons began billing prisoners up to $50 a day for room and board. Other states were expected to follow.[64] Combine long mandatory sentences for minor drug offenses, a strong racial bias, prisons run by corporations for profit, the sale of convict labor to corporations at sweatshop rates, and a charge for prison room and board and you have a modern system of bonded labor, a social condition otherwise known as slavery.

It may all be summed up by the punch line from the story of the surgeon who announced to the family of the patient on whom he had just operated. "I have good news and bad news," he said. The good news is the operation was a success. The bad news is the patient died."

The good news of the 1990s was a robust economy and booming stock market that corporate pundits joyously applauded as an economic miracle of the modern age. The bad news was that it was a false prosperity built largely on the illusions of financial bubbles. The robust economy that swelled the bank balances of the few was killing the life of society and the planet at an accelerating pace—and most corporate power holders remained in deep denial.

Fortunately, the last half of the decade of the 1990s also provided some truly good news, signs of a stirring in the human soul—an awakening of popular consciousness to the reality of corporate globalization. It was most visible in massive protests throughout the world against the World Bank, IMF, WTO, and other institutions of global corporate rule. It was, and is, also finding expression in a new politics, a search for spiritual renewal, and the emerging leadership of a new generation of creative and sophisticated young activists committed to creating a world of justice for all. Some call it the global movement for a living democracy. It is a source of hope for the future of humanity.

22

THE LIVING DEMOCRACY
MOVEMENT

*And we are determined here in Montgomery—to work and fight until
justice runs down like water, and righteousness like a mighty stream.*
—Martin Luther King Jr.

*We, the people of the world, will mobilize the forces of transnational civil
society behind a widely shared agenda that bonds our many social movements in pursuit of just, sustainable, and participatory human societies.
In so doing we are forging our own instruments and processes for redefining the nature and meaning of human progress and for transforming
those institutions that no longer respond to our needs.*
—The People's Earth Declaration, UNCED NGO Forum 1992

THE GLOBAL MOVEMENT FOR A LIVING DEMOCRACY announced itself to the
world on November 30, 1999 in Seattle, Washington. Its deep historical roots
extend back at least to December 16, 1773 when a brave band of patriots took
possession of a sailing ship in Boston harbor and dumped its cargo of tea into
the sea to protest taxation without representation and the trading monopoly
of the powerful British East India Company. Now celebrated as the Boston
Tea Party, this bold act of nonviolent civil disobedience led the way to the
American Revolution that liberated thirteen North American settlements from
British colonial rule and gave birth to the United States of America.

Other historic antecedents include the labor movement and its long
struggle to protect the rights and lives of working people from corporate abuse.
They include India's independence movement led by Mahatma Gandhi to end

centuries of British rule that began in 1600 when the British East India Company established its first trading post on Indian soil.

The global movement for a living democracy also builds on the national democracy movements that played crucial roles in the overthrow of the Marcos regime in the Philippines, the breakup of the Soviet empire, and the fall of apartheid in South Africa. The civil rights, environmental, peace, women's, and gay rights movements all contributed to preparing the way for its current expression in the United States. Each of these antecedents was largely decentralized and democratic in its mode of organization and sought transformative justice through nonviolent means.

THE CHANGING FACE OF RESISTANCE

A desire to rid the world of economic injustice, which many now recognize to be inseparable from ending corporate rule, gave birth to the forces of communism and socialism that played a major role in defining twentieth-century politics up until the dissolution of the Soviet Union in 1991. Neither communism nor socialism, however, attempted to end the concentration of economic power embodied in the corporation. Rather they socialized that power to make it an instrument of state control. Both honored materialism and financial values over life values.

By contrast, the predominant call of the living democracy movement, as reflected in the themes of its protest actions, is not to socialize the corporation, but rather to exclude or dismantle it. The movement is also truly international in its conception and execution. This results partly from necessity—the offending corporations and Bretton Woods institutions are global in scale and operation—and partly from opportunity—the recent advances in telephone, fax, and Internet communication that make possible the global self-organization of highly decentralized popular movements.

Seattle '99 was only the visible tip of a very large iceberg. The following are but a few of the many important demonstrations that prepared the way.

- On July 13, 1993, several hundred Indian farmers gathered at the site of a Cargill Corporation seed preparation plant north of Bangalore and demolished the partially completed structure with their bare hands in a call to expel Cargill from India.
- On January 1, 1994, the inaugural day of the North American Free Trade Agreement (NAFTA), 4,000 Indians in the Mexican state of Chiapas

launched an armed rebellion against corporate globalization. Mexican political analyst Gustavo Esteva called it the "first revolution of the twenty-first century," because it redefined the terms of popular struggle. The Chiapas people did not call on their fellow Mexicans to take up arms against the state, but rather to join them in a broad social movement to liberate local spaces from colonization by alien political and economic forces.

- In July 1995, 10,000 Papua New Guineans protested against structural adjustment prescriptions being imposed on their country by the World Bank that would deepen the exploitation of their lands and resources by transnational corporations.

- On December 15, 1995, more than 15,000 environmentalists, trade unionists, and members of Third World solidarity, anti-racist, and women's groups demonstrated against corporate rule in Madrid at the bi-annual Summit of the European heads of state.

- Thirteen thousand Thai farmers camped outside their prime minister's office in Bangkok throughout most of April 1996 to protest the take-over of their lands by foreign corporate interests for dams and eucalyptus plantations.

- From February 23–25, 1998, representatives of peoples' movements from all the continents met in Geneva to launch a loosely organized global alliance called the Peoples' Global Action against "Free" Trade and the World Trade Organization (PGA) to coordinate national and international protests. Committed to nonviolent civil disobedience, decentralization, and the construction by people of local alternatives to global corporate rule, the PGA is a pure networking structure with no membership or legal identity.

- In May 1998, the PGA launched its first action, timed to coincide with the May 8–9 meeting of G-8 foreign and finance ministers in London, the May 15–17 Summit of the G-8 heads of state in Birmingham, UK, and the May 18–20 Second Inter-Ministerial Conference of the WTO in Geneva. The action began when hundreds of thousands took to the streets in Delhi on April 28 and in Hyderabad on May 2 calling for a rejection of the World Trade Organization. Throughout the month, Days of Action against "Free Trade and the WTO" were held in more than 26 countries, including a demonstration involving 50,000 people in Brazilia on May 20. The focal point of the PGA action was May 16 when 10,000 people joined a bicycle and tractor caravan that converged on Geneva from three locations in Germany. On the same day 60,000 demonstrators formed a human chain around the G-8 meeting site in Birmingham, UK, demanding an end to Third World debt. Protest actions continued throughout the week in Geneva in the face of violent police repression.

- The night of June 3, 1998, activists in the UK destroyed seven separate test plot crops of transgenic rapeseed, bringing to nineteen the total number of known genetic field "decontaminations" in that country. The goal was not to socialize the corporations promoting transgenic foods, but rather to bar the entry of their products into Europe.
- On November 28, 1998, members of the ten million-strong Karnataka State Farmers Association uprooted and burned a Monsanto test crop of transgenic cotton plants in India. Three other Monsanto test sites were similarly destroyed in Karnataka and Andha Pradesh. More than 10,000 Indians signed "Quit India" postcards and mailed them to Monsanto headquarters.
- The June 18, 1999, global day of action called "Carnival Against Capital" was timed to coincide with the G-8 meeting in Cologne, Germany. The focus was on financial centers, banking districts, and the headquarters of major transnational corporations. Mass demonstrations in London temporarily stopped trading at the London International Futures and Options Exchange and, by the end of the day, London's financial district looked like a battle zone. Cars were set ablaze and a building was damaged. In Port Harcourt, Nigeria, 10,000 people braved military repression to march to the gates of Shell Oil for a speech by Owens Wiwa, brother of Ken Saro-Wiwa, the former Ogoni leader who was hanged by Nigeria's military government for his role in earlier protests against Shell devastation of the Ogoni homelands. Other street actions were held in Minsk, Montevideo, Toronto, Los Angeles, Madrid, Prague, Zurich, Amsterdam, Barcelona, Los Angeles, New York, and other cities. Most focused squarely on the institutions of transnational capital.
- The week before Seattle, protesters occupied the WTO headquarters in Geneva to unfurl banners and send out communiques to the world on the WTO fax machines. In New Delhi 300 indigenous people occupied the local World Bank premises, covering it with posters, slogans, and cow dung.

On the same day that 50,000 protestors took to the streets in Seattle, 9,000 members of the longshoreman's union—workers whose jobs depend entirely on international trade—temporarily shut down all the ports on the West Coast of the United States in solidarity. In addition to concurrent demonstrations in other U.S. cities, an estimated 75,000 people were involved in parallel protests throughout France. Thousands more took to city streets in England, India, Canada, Australia, Philippines, Netherlands, Germany, Switzerland, and other countries throughout the world.

The massive citizen opposition in Seattle and beyond emboldened official delegates to the WTO meeting from a number of Southern countries belonging to the Group of 77, a grouping of 120 of the world's poorest countries, to resist the heavy-handed effort of the U.S. government to gain endorsement for its corporate agenda. This resistance, plus the general disruption caused by the demonstrators who blocked access to the meeting site, precluded agreement on new WTO initiatives. This sent out an empowering message to millions of people and shook the corporate establishment. The institutions of corporate power no longer seemed invincible.

TAKING THE FUN OUT OF SECRET DEAL MAKING

After Seattle, virtually everywhere the power elites met to circumvent democracy and make deals to advance the corporate agenda, they were forced to gather behind police barricades surrounded by thousands of protestors.

On April 16, 2000, 15,000 demonstrators took to the streets of Washington, D.C., calling for the decommissioning of the World Bank and the International Monetary Fund (IMF) and the cancellation of Third World debt. Although battalions of police thwarted the effort to shut down the official meetings, the actual outcome was far grander. To secure the meeting and rebuff the demonstrators, the police blocked off all access to a major part of the city, effectively shutting down the regular operations not only of the IMF and the Bank, but also much of the U.S. government for an entire day. The city was thus divided between the vacant streets controlled by the police and the streets alive with the colors, banners, and puppets of protestors chanting, "This is what democracy looks like." It provided a powerful visual image of the stark contrast between a living democracy and a lifeless police state that I will not soon forget.

Spokespersons from the IMF and the Bank attempted to portray the protestors as spoiled children of privilege who were acting out of ignorance to deny the world's poor the benefits of IMF and Bank programs. Ignorance and privilege, however, resided with those speaking on behalf of the IMF and the Bank who seemed to be unaware that millions of poor people around the world have for years been taking to the streets to protest the destruction of their lives and livelihoods by IMF and the Bank programs and policies. The UK-based World Development Movement documented fifty separate episodes of civil unrest in opposition to the IMF and its policies in low-income countries between December 1999 and September 2000. Together these protests involved more than a million people in Argentina, Bolivia, Brazil, Colombia, Costa Rica, Ecuador, Honduras, Kenya, Malawi, Nigeria, Paraguay, South Africa, and Zambia.[1] In the end the D.C. protestors won the war of finger pointing when a spokesperson for the G-77, which was at that moment holding its heads of state meeting in Cuba, issued a statement supporting the demonstrators and their cause.

That same month Mexican dairy farmers made their own statement about corporate globalization by dumping rancid milk on the streets of Mexico City. They were protesting the subsidized milk powder being imported from the United States under NAFTA that was driving domestic milk prices below the costs of production and threatening to put them out of business.[2]

Soon after the Washington, DC protests, delegates to the June 2–6, 2000 meeting of the Organization of American States in Windsor, Canada, were met by thousands of protestors, as were representatives to the World Petroleum Congress in Canada, June 11–15, 2000. On July 21, 2000, the heads of state of the G-8 (the G-7 plus Russia) met on the remote and heavily fortified Japanese island of Okinawa at the U.S. Kadena Air Base. Twenty-seven thousand protestors surrounded the base to call for an end to the U.S. military presence.[3]

An estimated 20 million people participated in a nationwide strike in India against liberalization and privatization on May 11, 2000. Both houses of the parliament had to be adjourned.

On June 30, 2000, José Bové, spokesperson and founder of the French Peasant Confederation, went on trial in Millau, France (population 20,000) with ten of his colleagues on charges of dismantling a McDonald's restaurant. Fifty thousand supporters from France and around the world converged in Millau in solidarity. High-profile international activists who testified as expert witnesses turned the hearings into a trial against corporate globalization.[4]

The meeting of IMF and World Bank directors in Prague on September 26–28, 2000, opened normally on the first day, but when it was time to return to their hotels, delegates found their way blocked by lines of police and protestors. The next day few delegates showed up. Announcing they had finished their business early, officials cancelled the third and final day. In January 2001 the WTO announced its Fall 2001 meeting would be held in Qatar, a tiny, remote Middle Eastern monarchy known for its suppression of human rights and its strict prohibition on civil dissent.

There can be no mistaking the global nature of the movement, nor the growing sense of solidarity among people of all nationalities who are joining in resistance to a system that would have us each compete to the death with our neighbor as the price of our individual survival. It brings to mind the movie *Gladiator*. Captives of the Roman Empire were sent into the arena where their only choice was to kill or be killed—until the gladiators realized that by banding together to defy the emperor, they all might live.

Facing a challenge to its authority, the corporate establishment responded to the popular resistance in the classic fashion of authoritarian rulers throughout history. It mobilized its police powers to brutalize the protestors and its captive media to portray the protestors as hot-headed, ill-informed, antisocial, isolationist, rock-throwing vandals engaged in disrupting legitimate democratic processes, who merit no respect or hearing and by inference deserve to be beaten, gassed, and shot by police and military units to preserve the peace and order for decent people.

With the exception of a few fringe misfits and vandals, the vast majority of the protestors have been nonviolent and well-informed. They were on the streets only because a corrupted political system and a captive media left them few alternatives. Furthermore, for every person on the streets, there were tens of thousands of sympathizers who were there in spirit. For each consequential demonstration there were hundreds of teach-ins, seminars, and study groups through which people educated one another on the issues and mobilized to work for change. For every corporate media outlet that missed the point of the demonstrations, there were hundreds of independent newsletters, magazines, e-mail listserves, audio and video streaming Internet sites, and microradio transmitters communicating the real story.

In the end the corporate establishment's disinformation campaigns and police brutality served only to strengthen the movement. The corporate media further damaged their credibility as sources of reliable information. Television shots of police battalions in Darth Vader costumes ruthlessly beating, gassing, and shooting those engaged in the nonviolent expression of their right to speech and assembly created a public sense of living under an oppressive police state. Such images awaken public outrage, deepen the will to resist, and bring new recruits to the movement. It has a particularly strong educational impact on those on the receiving end of the police violence.

For many of the educated, white Americans who participated, the experience of being beaten and gassed by police, arrested on trumped-up charges, handcuffed, thrown in jail, and denied basic rights to legal counsel and needs like food, water, medicines, and bathroom facilities awakened a consciousness of the daily experience of people of color in America in their relations with the "justice" system. It is no coincidence that judicial and prison reform is moving rapidly toward the top of the movement's agenda, along with a commitment to bridge the racial divide and build a truly inclusive movement dedicated to eliminating all forms of oppression and achieving justice and democracy for all.

REACHING OUT, REDEFINING ISSUES

Those who were paying attention in Seattle saw evidence of a profound political shift emerging in America. Recall that Seattle '99 brought together peoples of diverse races, religions, ages, economic classes, sexual orientation, and nationalities concerned with a vast array of issues. There were people of faith, union members, youth, environmentalists, gays and lesbians, indigenous peoples, peace and human-rights activists, small farmers, organic food advocates, small-business owners, independent media representatives, and many others. Teenagers marched with octogenarians, millionaires with the homeless.

Each had come to realize that whatever their concern, it was at risk under a regime of corporate rule. Their shared quarrel was not with trade, but with the use of trade rules to strengthen corporate rights and power at the expense of people and planet. Underlying the cacophony of voices was a unifying commitment to democracy and life born of a realization that unless they joined in common cause to build a truly democratic world that works for all, they would find themselves living in a world that works for no one. It was an important step in a grand convergence of social forces aligned behind identity and single-issue politics to form a politics of the whole. It reflected a deepening of consciousness that is being expressed not only in efforts to broaden alliances, but also to expand the perspectives of each of the participating constituencies.

Consider the four major groups with lead roles in Seattle '99: people of faith, labor unions, environmentalists, and youth. Participation by people of faith centered on the Jubilee 2000 campaign for debt forgiveness, which expressed a growing consciousness within many Christian churches about the centrality of social and economic justice in Christ's teaching. This reaffirmation of the original foundation of the Christian faith is bringing new vitality to a growing number of Christian denominations and congregations, drawing inspiration from leading Christian theologians such as Thomas Berry, Marcus Borg, Walter Wink, and Matthew Fox.

Labor unions expressed their commitment to international labor solidarity, recognizing that in a borderless world of high unemployment, the rights and wages of every working person are at risk unless they are guaranteed for all. There were also the historic path-breaking alliances between labor and environmentalists. Union members had come to realize there will be no jobs without a healthy environment. Environmentalists realized that unless people have secure jobs and labor rights the environment will be destroyed in the desperate struggle for survival. Both recognized that they gain strength against corporate abuse by standing together.

Most inspiring of all were the youth who led the direct action efforts in Seattle and put their bodies on the line to bring the WTO meeting to a standstill. Tired of being manipulated and lied to for profit by a system that is stealing their future, the world's youth are awakening to the need for deep transformative change and the fact that its realization will depend on their leadership. They spent months training one another in the principles and methods of nonviolent direct action and decentralized, consensus-based, self-organization that model the values and processes of the radically democratic societies they seek to build. Included among their ranks were university students who have led antisweatshop campaigns and protested the growing corporate presence on their college campuses, and secondary school students mobilized against the intrusion of commercial television into their classrooms.

As each of these elements of the larger convergence redefines itself and reaches out to other constituencies in common cause, the prospects for transformative change seem ever more real and immediate.

SLOWING THE DAMAGE

The building momentum for transformative change is not limited to the streets. Since 1995 the movement has in a number of ways made itself felt in the corridors of power. As noted in Chapter 21, its members successfully blocked the extension of President Clinton's authority to negotiate trade agreements under Fast Track rules and forced an end to negotiation of the draconian Multilateral Agreement on Investment. At the same time they played a significant role in negotiating landmark international agreements on land mines and biodiversity. Domestically, U.S. groups blocked an effort by the Clinton administration to degrade the labeling standards for organic foods.

All across the United States civil society groups are working with local governments on initiatives to limit corporate rights and revoke the charters of habitual corporate criminals.[5] Most are largely symbolic gestures, but they are a start and play an important role in public education and consciousness raising.

Early lawsuits seeking to hold tobacco companies liable for the health consequences of using misleading advertising to sell harmful products once seemed equally symbolic—and futile—until 1998 when the industry agreed to pay $246 billion to state governments in compensation for health costs due to smoking. On July 14, 2000, a jury in Miami-Dade county made the largest damage award in history, ordering the tobacco industry to pay $144.8 billion in punitive damages to 500,000 Florida smokers.[6]

Little notice was taken of the fact that a few corporations were quietly convincing farmers to convert to genetically modified seeds in the United States and other countries—until citizen groups made the potential health and environmental risks of genetically modified organisms (GMOs) a major issue in Europe. A subsequent European ban on the import of genetically modified seeds and agricultural products sent shock waves through the U.S. food and agriculture sector. A number of corporations, including McDonald's, Frito-Lay and Gerber quickly agreed to eliminate or reduce their use of genetically modified foods.

In July 2000 a coalition of U.S. citizen groups announced a major program targeted at other well-known food companies, starting with Campbell Soup Company, urging them to stop using genetically modified foods until more testing is done.[7] Concerned about market resistance to their crops, American farmers began cutting back on the percentage of their corn, soybean, and cotton fields planted with genetically altered seeds, not only halting but reversing a rapid growth trend.[8]

Even though such victories are partial and temporary, they demonstrate that even with their massive financial, media, and lobbying resources the forces of corporate globalization are far from invincible when the people decide they have had enough. Each victory helps to slow the damage, to build public awareness of what is at stake, and demonstrate that ordinary people with little more than truth, determination, and the public interest on their side can make a difference.

BUILDING ALTERNATIVES

Less visible are the countless positive initiatives being undertaken by people around the world who are no longer waiting for governments and corporations to save humanity from its own excesses. With the support of a committee headed by Steven Rockefeller, thousands of people around the world have participated in drafting an Earth Charter that articulates a broadly shared vision of the world that can be. It surely has been the most extraordinary consensus building process in human history.[9]

Global Action Plan has created sustainable living support groups in fifteen countries involving 50,000 households and 125,000 people in making their households and consumption patterns more environmentally friendly. Millions have embraced voluntary simplicity in their personal lives, thus reducing their dependence on the institutions of money. If voluntary simplicity is the fastest growing movement in America, as some claim, then socially responsible investing cannot be far behind. As of 1999, $2.16 trillion in investment funds—roughly 13 percent of all investments under professional management in the United States—were socially screened, involved in shareholder advocacy, and/or directed to community investment. This was a remarkable increase of 82 percent over 1997 levels.[10]

America's Green Party began to take hold as a national political force when consumer advocate Ralph Nader launched an aggressive 2000 campaign for president under its banner. Nader's super rallies in Portland, Seattle, Minneapolis, Boston, Oakland, and New York drew crowds of 10,000 to 15,000 enthusiastic supporters, by far the largest political rallies of the 2000 presidential election cycle. Nader's message focused attention on the extent to which the two major U.S. parties, the Democrats and the Republicans, represent two versions of the same corporate agenda. His campaign articulated alternatives that virtually defined the political agenda of the living democracy movement in the United States.

The corruption of the 2000 U.S. presidential election, including the intentional and systematic disenfranchisement of thousands of African-Americans in Florida, pushed the limits of tolerance for a great many Americans and rekindled the flame of the civil rights movement in the form of a national pro-democracy movement. The call went up for a sweeping structural reform of American politics to secure the franchise of all citizens, get bribery out of politics, and remove barriers to third-party participation. The proposed reforms include updating voting technology, creating uniform election standards and same day voter registration, abolishing the electoral college, full public funding of elections, proportional representation, instant run-off voting, free access to the public airwaves and political debates for qualified third party candidates, and strict conflict of interest rules for elected representatives with corporate ties or funding.

It is encouraging to note what the election revealed of the mood of the U.S. electorate. The election's mind numbing campaign and ignoble outcome notwithstanding, the voters favored Gore, the more socially progressive of the two major party candidates. Bush won much of his support by campaigning on a rhetoric of compassion that obscured his record of meanness. And though viciously attacked by the corporate press for his anti-corporate message, Green Party candidate Ralph Nader made the strongest showing of any third party candidate.

It was only after the Supreme Court five stepped in to stop the vote count and handed him the presidency, that Bush fully revealed his uncompassionate intent by naming right wing extremists to a number of key cabinet posts and pushing forcefully ahead with a legislative agenda that featured tax breaks for the rich, the militarization of space, increasing corporate welfare, opening public lands to private exploitation, turning social security over to Wall Street bankers, and regimenting education with standardized testing. If the Bush administration holds to an agenda so starkly at odds with the more compassionate mood of the electorate, the potential for backlash may create an extraordinary mobilizing opportunity for those who seek to create a truly compassionate and democratic political alternative.

As political and economic elites compete to win the spoils of a corrupt system, citizens who live and work outside the corridors of institutional power are taking on the toughest problems facing humanity and demonstrating successful alternatives in their personal lives and in local communities and national initiatives.

Environmental justice groups are taking the lead in initiatives to rebuild urban and rural areas to bring them into balance with nature and secure fair access to available services and resources for all races and cultural communities.[11] Citizens are restoring degraded lands to vibrant health, rebuilding local economies, using biological methods to treat sewage and other wastes, finding alternatives to prisons, taking on roles as peace makers within their communities and between countries, working to save family farms, and developing and promoting energy saving technologies to counter global warming. *YES! A Journal of Positive Futures* is a rich source of information on such initiatives and how to become involved.[12]

Major national movements in Canada (The Council of Canadians), Chile (RENACE), and the Philippines have mobilized thousands of organizations representing millions of people in the cause of articulating and advancing national visions of democratic, life-centered societies. These are true grassroots movements seeking to redefine society and transform national politics from the bottom up.[13]

Initiatives throughout America are seeking to counter the trend toward corporate control and ownership. Some 3,000 community development corporations across the country support local business development. More than a thousand family farms in the U.S. and Canada have contracts with local residents to provide fresh produce.[14] The Boulder Independent Business Alliance is one of many local business initiatives that provide a mutual support system for local independent businesses and educate community members about the benefits of building a healthy, stable local economy based on local, independent businesses.

These and countless related initiatives are the proactive side of the living democracy movement, demonstrating the possibilities of local democratic control within a framework of commitment to creating healthy, ecologically sound communities that work for all. They are also a manifestation of the same awakening of cultural consciousness that drives the protests.

IT'S THE CULTURE

If the economy was the key to understanding the old politics, culture is the key to understanding the new politics. In their new book *The Cultural Creatives*, values researcher Paul Ray and feminist author Sherry Anderson draw on extensive survey data to describe a deep awakening of cultural consciousness in America revealed in a changing balance in the distribution of adult Americans among three cultural groupings.[15]

1. *The Modernists.* At 93 million (48 percent of adult Americans), Modernists are the largest cultural group in America. They accept the commercialized urban-industrial world as the obvious right way to live. They focus on material progress and want their children to be better off materially than they were themselves. To these ends they honor the drive to acquire money and property. In their pursuit of material success they tend to spend beyond their means, take a cynical view of idealism and value winners. To them, living responsibly means taking care of self and family. They are the leaders of America's most powerful corporate and political institutions and are the leading champions of corporate globalization.

    Modernists see themselves as defenders of rationality, technological advance, prosperity, and individual freedom against the traditionalists,

New Agers, and religious mystics who resist or question material progress. They look to global corporations and financial markets as powerful engines of wealth creation engaged in converting the otherwise idle resources of the planet into usable products to the ultimate benefit of all. If on occasion these institutions do harm, that is a necessary price of progress toward realizing the larger common good. The Modernist's numbers are relatively stable.

2. *The Traditionals* reject the materialistic values of modernism and call for a return to more traditional values and gender roles. They believe in community, family, helping others, volunteering, creating and maintaining caring relationships, and working to create a society based on traditional values. They tend toward religious conservatism and seek to build stable relationships, often through their religious congregation. They have a tendency toward fundamentalism and religious, racial, and ethnic scapegoating. About 50 percent of the U.S. adult population around the time of World War II, the Traditionals have since declined to about 25 percent (48 million adult Americans) and are in continuing decline in both absolute and percentage terms.

3. *The Cultural Creatives.* Less than 5 percent of adult Americans as recently as the early 1960s, Cultural Creatives now comprise 26 percent (50 million) of the adult population and are growing both in numbers and as a percentage of the whole. They share with Modernists a receptivity to change, but reject materialistic hedonism, the cynicism of the corporate media, and the greed and individualism of the consumer/ corporate culture. They share with Traditionals a concern for human relationships, volunteerism, and contributing to society, but reject the Traditionalists' tendencies toward survivorism, sexism, exclusion, and belief in the right of humans to dominate nature. Sixty percent of Cultural Creatives are women.

    Generally optimistic about human possibilities, Cultural Creatives look beyond both modernism and traditionalism to the possibility of creating inclusive, life-affirming societies that work for all. They are at the forefront of contemporary social and environmental activism. Indeed, an individual Cultural Creative is commonly involved in as many as four to six different groups working for social and environmental change. They provide the leadership for the movements and initiatives that are giving birth to the living democracy movement and they formed the core of the Seattle WTO protest.

A variety of international surveys reveal that the cultural shift identified in America by Ray and Anderson is part of a larger global trend toward a loss of confidence in hierarchical institutions—including those of government, business, and religion—and a growing trust in a personal inner sense of the appropriate. This trend is accompanied by a declining interest in economic gain and a growing desire for meaningful work and sense of purpose in life.[16]

Leadership among the Cultural Creatives generally comes from a subgroup composed of those who combine their outward commitment to family, community, the environment, and internationalism with attention to the development of an inner spiritual life. They align with the values of what some have called an integral culture, meaning they honor life in all its dimensions, both inner and outer. These "Core" Cultural Creatives, as Ray and Anderson characterize them, are about 12 percent of the adult American population. Their social consciousness is grounded in an inner spiritual consciousness of life's underlying unity. They are at the forefront of efforts to craft a new ecological and spiritual worldview, a new literature of social concerns, and a new problem agenda for humanity.

The cultural groupings described by Ray and Anderson bring into focus the cultural foundation of the struggle between the forces of corporate globalization and the forces of global civil society. Modernists are the architects and cheerleaders of corporate globalization. They define the so-called political center in the United States. The Republican and Democratic parties both vie for their vote. The Cultural Creatives are the driving force behind the living democracy movement and the emergence of America's Green Party.

Many Traditionals have significant doubts about both corporate globalization and the living democracy movement. They share with Cultural Creatives a rejection of the materialistic and hedonistic values that corporate globalization shares with modernism, and they dislike the exploitation of the people who live in small towns and rural communities. But they also reject many of the liberal social and environmental values that the Cultural Creatives enthusiastically embrace. Militantly patriotic, they are alarmed by the loss of national sovereignty that comes with corporate globalization. At the same time they take pride in the global projection of America's economic and military power. They are also inclined to believe that God gave the earth to humans to exploit for their own ends, and that commercial success is a sign of the individual's righteousness in God's eyes.

FROM CULTURAL CONSCIOUSNESS TO POLITICAL ACTION

Educator Parker Palmer provides a simple map of the process by which the seemingly soft path of a cultural awakening translates into a hard path of political and institutional transformation. The process begins with the awakening of the individual consciousness to the ways in which perceptions and behaviors are shaped by the unexamined assumptions and values of the prevailing culture. It is rather like awakening from a cultural trace. Once the trance is broken the individual experiences an increasingly painful disconnect between the more examined or authentic values of their awakened consciousness and the realities of family, work, and community life grounded in the values of the old culture.

Eventually the individual decides, in Parker's words, "to live divided no more." He or she finds that the sense of isolation that results from attempting to live by authentic values in an inauthentic culture can be broken only by joining with like-minded persons to form communities of congruence. Initially small and isolated, these communities eventually meld into larger alliances as the individual's sphere of identification with the larger community of life grows. Step by step, authentic cultural spaces are created and expanded. As alliances grow they gradually achieve the power to transform the logic and reward systems of society's political and economic institutions.[17]

Ray and Anderson present a similar analysis, tracing the dynamic growth in the population of Cultural Creatives in the United States to the civil rights movement. They note that before the civil rights movement both blacks and whites tended to accept the prevailing cultural code defining the relations among the races as the natural order of things. The civil rights movement raised the consciousness of peoples of all races that this code was simply a belief system that served certain interests, but had nothing to do with any natural order. Having learned to recognize the difference between the natural order and an unexamined belief system in reference to race relations, it became easier to see how similar cultural codes artificially defined the relations between men and women, people and the environment, straights and gays, people and corporations, and people and the economy.

As each successive cultural trance is broken, the individual is able to live more freely and consciously in coherent relationship with the life of community and planet. In turn the alliances that form around the new cultural awareness grow more holistic in their defining story and their vision of the society that might be. Gradually they take on more significant challenges. Previously modest experiments with new ways of addressing social and environmental needs move to scale. Step by step the way is prepared to create the public culture and institutions of a truly civil society.

The political history of the human species during the last half of the twentieth century was largely defined by the contest for state power between two extremist ideologies: communism and capitalism. One emphasized community to the exclusion of the individual. The other emphasized the individual to the exclusion of community. Both uncritically embraced the materialistic values of cultural modernism and measured their performance by the material output of their respective economies, a realm in which capitalism easily and inevitably triumphed. Communism died unmourned. Its former opponent vanquished, capitalism has stepped up its assault on life, equity, and democracy.

The emerging struggle of the twenty-first century centers less on ideology and class than on culture. The living democracy movement, capitalism's new challenger, measures progress not by increases in the aggregate consumption of the few, but by the quality of life of everyone. It seeks not to capture state power, but rather to reduce and democratize it. It seeks not to eliminate the market, but rather to restore it. It is driven not by the love of money, but by a love of life. Its source of power is the awakening of a new cultural consciousness. Its defining goal is a civil society.

23

A CIVIL SOCIETY

What's so beautiful about being alive at this moment is that we are reawakening to the sacredness of life itself, in the soil and air and water, in our brothers and sisters of other species, and in our own bodies. . . . People are sick and tired of being pitted against each other when there's already so much suffering and the Earth itself is under assault. They're ready to reconnect and honor the life we share.
— Joanna Macy, "The Great Turning," YES! *magazine*[1]

When activists reframe a significant cultural context, they're like the child who shouts that the emperor is wearing no clothes. They expose a whole belief system for what it is—a belief system, not the natural order of things, not reality. . . . Then people who never before doubted the status quo, who took it as God-given and utterly legitimate, start to ask their own questions.
— *Paul Ray and Sherry Anderson,* The Cultural Creatives[2]

AFTER MONTHS OF PREPARATION and anticipation and a full calendar of commitments to speak at the many teach-ins and seminars planned for Seattle '99, missing the "Protest of the Century" was one of the great disappointments of my life. A persistent nosebleed that precluded air travel reduced me to watching the unfolding events on television from 3,000 miles away.

Although television cameras concentrated on the violence, even a continent away I could feel the incredible life energy of those who gathered in Seattle in nonviolent direct action to challenge the World Trade Organization's assault on life and democracy. For weeks after Seattle '99 friends told me what it felt like to join so many people in a shared commitment to life and democracy. One after another repeated the phrase, "It made me feel so alive." More than anything, that is what the Seattle protests were about—experiencing the deep sense of meaning and connection that comes when we feel our personal life energy aligned with the life energy of thousands of others representing humanity's wondrous diversity, acting together in mutual love and respect to create a world that works for all. It was an important moment of awakening that touched the consciousness of millions of people.

AWAKENING CONSCIOUSNESS

A few months before Seattle '99, the Positive Futures Network, which I serve as Board Chair, had held a retreat in Port Townsend, Washington, where 40 leaders from a diverse range of social movements across America came together for three days of reflection and sharing on "The State of the Possible." It was a time to build relationships and find common purpose. Toward the end of our gathering our attention turned to the possibility that we might find a defining idea— an organizing principle—that would help our various movements converge toward creating a transformative force greater than the sum of its parts. As expressed by Sarah van Gelder, the executive editor of *YES!* magazine, the unifying idea that emerged is that "We are working toward a shift from a society centered on the love of money to one centered on the love of life." For me, this simple but powerful idea defines the great work of our time.[3]

A year later, the Positive Futures Network organized a similar retreat with another group of movement leaders to reflect on the meaning of Seattle '99 in relation to the lessons of other important social movements of the twentieth century. As before, we sought to build relationships and common language that would help us meld our diverse interests and commitments into a movement of the whole. Early on, the group turned from the more abstract discussion of movements, institutions, and social change to a more deeply personal exchange that touched us all in ways we had not anticipated. It began when Belvie Rooks, an African-American writer and educator, called us to recognize that the distinctive experience of race by people of color in America leads to a different sense of priorities than those that drive most white-led movements. "Most of my passionate conversations with people in the African-American community are not about saving the planet," she said. "They are about saving our children."[4]

Later, Robert Jeffrey, pastor of an inner-city church in Seattle told us how he was sick of conducting funerals for kids killed in shootings, tired of being angry.

My anger grows out of my despair over the sewer that I must walk through each day. It's a world where brilliant people that you know personally are hopelessly strung out on drugs, a world where most of your high school friends are already dead or in prison. It's a world where you daily see teenage children spread-eagled face down in the street because their country is at war with them. A world where you bank with institutions that launder the money of corporate criminals that provide the drugs to your children and then refuse to give loans to the community-based businesses that could create the jobs that they so desperately crave.[5]

As one after another of the people of color in our group shared their stories of the pain that a racist society inflicts on their lives, we formed a talking circle, one after another sharing stories of the pain that flows from the disconnect between the injustice we needlessly inflict on one another and the vision of a world that could be. Our sharing created a new level of trust and understanding—a sense of the oneness of life and the meaning of community—that deepened our common commitment to work to create a world that works for all.

Such experiences are part of the awakening and deepening of consciousness that is the foundation of the growing movement, each step building and focusing the flow of social energy toward what writer and Buddhist scholar Joanna Macy calls the "Great Turning." Macy sees three dimensions of the Great Turning. The first involves resistance, holding actions like the WTO protests that slow the destruction. The second involves creating new social and economic structures. The third is spiritual awakening. As Macy explains,

New coalitions and new ways of production and distribution are not enough for the Great Turning. They will shrivel and die unless they are rooted in deeply held values—in our sense of who we are, who we want to be, and how we relate to each other and the living body of Earth. That amounts to a shift in consciousness, which is actually happening now at a rapid rate. This is the third dimension of the Great Turning, and it is, at root, a spiritual revolution, awakening perceptions and values that are both very new and very ancient, linking back to rivers of ancestral wisdom.[6]

With the awakening comes a deepening of our love for all beings and a growing potential to create a society that nurtures and rejoices in the love of life.

LIFE'S GUIDING PRINCIPLES

To awaken to life is in part to awaken to life's incredible capacities and to learn to honor its ways in our own relationships and institutions. We may thus discover potential in ourselves that we have long denied. The following are a few of life's guiding principles as they are coming to be understood and articulated by a new breed of biologists such as Mae-Wan Ho, Elisabet Sahtouris, Janine Benyus, Dorion Sagan, and Lynne Margulis who have broken free of the mechanistic, reductionist models of conventional science to observe and understand life on its own terms.[7] They tell us that:

Life Is Self-Organizing and Cooperative   Life's organizing mechanisms are highly decentralized and self-regulating right down to the level of the individual cell—with each healthy living entity, each cell and organism, constantly adapting and balancing its own needs against those of the larger whole on which its own well-being depends. Much of the decision making essential to maintaining our own bodily functions takes place at the cellular level through processes that suggest each cell has a sense of both its own identity and its function within the whole. The regulatory processes of biological communities are even more radically self-organizing, with no functional equivalent of a brain or central nervous system. Furthermore, the new biologists are finding that the successful species within such communities are not the largest, strongest, and most brutal competitors. Rather they are the species that find opportunities to meet their own needs in ways that contribute to the life of the whole, as with the honeybee that pollinates the flower in exchange for its nectar. Life is predominantly a cooperative enterprise.

Life Is Bounded by Managed, Permeable Borders   To sustain itself, life must be open to exchange with its environment. Yet to maintain its internal coherence, it must manage these exchanges. Life thus depends on permeable, managed boundaries. If the wall of the cell is breached, the cell's matter and energy instantly mix with the matter and energy of the environment and it dies. Multicelled organisms cannot survive without a skin or other protective covering. The oceans, mountains, and climatic zones that bound biological communities or ecosystems serve to exclude invasive species. Even the biosphere of our planet depends on the earth's gravitational field to hold in place an atmosphere and ozone layer that control the exchange of radiation with the larger universe to maintain the conditions necessary to planetary life.

Life Is Local and Adapted to Place   Each living community adapts itself to the most intricate details of its particular physical locale, in turn modifying the physical landscape by creating and holding soil; capturing, storing, and releasing water; and creating microclimates. Life thus creates conditions suited to increasing its variety and the conversion of more of the inert matter of the planet into living matter with the capacity for creative choice.

Life Is Abundant, Frugal, and Sharing   Biological communities are highly efficient in energy capture and recycling, living exemplars of the motto "Waste not, want not." Energy and materials are continuously recycled for use and reuse within and between cells, organisms, and species with a minimum of loss, as the wastes of one become the resources of another. Frugality and sharing are the secret of life's rich abundance, a product of its ability to capture, use, store, and share available material and energy with extraordinary efficiency.

Life Is Diverse and Creative   Life does not exist either in monoculture or in isolation from other life. Life's rich diversity of species and cultures gives the biocommunity resilience in times of crisis and provides the building blocks for life's incredible capacity to adapt, learn, innovate, and freely share knowledge toward realizing new potentials.

These appear to be among the fundamental organizing principles of all healthy living systems—including healthy human economies and societies. They point to the possibility of creating truly democratic, self-organizing societies made up of strong, place-based communities with permeable, managed borders, each adapted to a diverse and vibrant local ecosystem abundant with life, engaged in the creative, cooperative exchange of information, technology, and resources with its neighbors to assure every person an adequate and satisfying means of living. There is nothing radical or exotic about such a concept. Think of it as a society based on a combination of participatory democracy, a life-affirming ethical culture, and market economies composed of responsibly managed, human-scale, locally owned enterprises.

We are, after all, living beings. We should not therefore be surprised to find that the principles that guide the healthy function of all living systems are also relevant design principles for the organization of healthy human societies.

CIVIL-IZING SOCIETY

The term civil society, now closely identified with the global democracy movement, came into contemporary use with the emergence of the pro-democracy movements in Eastern Europe. In its most common use, civil society is synonymous with the nonprofit, nongovernmental sector. Originally, however, it had a far more powerful meaning.

Aristotle (551-479 B.C.), the ancient Greek philosopher, used the term *politika koinonia* (political society/community) to express the idea of a civil or civil-ized society of free and equal citizens who act in their civic roles with a mindful consciousness of the needs of both the individual and the whole. Aristotle's term was later translated into Latin as *societas civilis*, or civil society.

The goals of the living democracy movement are remarkably aligned with Aristotle's vision of the *politika koinonia*. Used in this sense, the larger goal of the living democracy movement is to create a radically democratic global civil society of free and equal, civically conscious citizens. It is in this sense, that the term is used here.

If we are to transform the present decidedly uncivil global capitalist society into a global civil society, we must deepen our understanding of their defining differences. Figure 23.1 illustrates these differences based on critical insights from Nicanor Perlas and his book *Shaping Globalization: Civil Society, Cultural Power and Threefolding*.[8]

In the civil society, the cultural sphere is the dominant sphere of public life and is a product of the active community life of free, culturally aware people whose personal identity is grounded in a deep sense of the spiritual unity of the whole of life. Such a culture is authentically life affirming. Its values, symbols, and beliefs serve as the foundation on which the members of a civil society create and formalize the institutions of polity (governance) and economy.

The life-affirming values of authentic cultures lead naturally to the creation of authentically democratic polities based on a deep commitment to open, active, and equitable participation in political discourse and decision making. They also lead naturally to the creation of authentic market economies comprised of local enterprises that provide productive, satisfying livelihoods for all and vest in each individual an ownership share in the productive assets on which their livelihood depends. This creates the possibility for the society to be radically self-organizing and predominantly cooperative in the manner of all healthy living systems, and to maximize the opportunity for each individual to develop and express their full creative potential in service to the life of the

Figure 23.1: Civil or Capitalist Society?

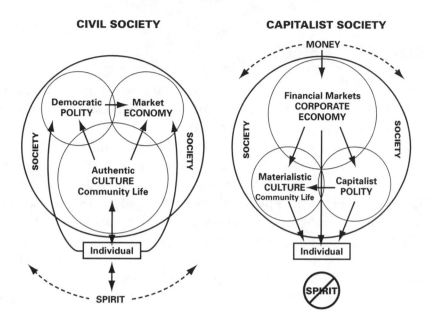

CIVIL OR CAPITALIST?

whole. The power and values that define the civil society flow upward from the living spirit through people to culture and then to institutions.

In the capitalist society, the economy is the dominant sector. Here power and values flow from money to economic institutions that in turn shape the institutions of government and culture to align society's rules, values, and symbols with financial interests. The key to capitalism's power over society is its ability to maintain a materialistic culture that denies the spirit and constantly reinforces the idea that humanity's capacity for greed, competition, and violence exceeds its capacity for sharing, cooperation, and love. Capitalism's dependence on an inauthentic and unexamined culture is also its key vulnerability, as such a culture is contrary to what most people know deep within their being to be true. An inauthentic culture cannot survive an awakening of consciousness.

The living democracy movement appropriately works simultaneously on many different fronts, including protest, education, policy advocacy, political mobilization, and practical initiatives to rebuild community, local economies, and ecosystems. In the midst of so many wonderfully diverse initiatives it is easy to lose sight of the deeper reality that the movement is born of a cultural awakening and its most immediate work is primarily cultural. Its most effective political strategy therefore is likely to be one that advances a cultural awakening and a consolidation of the social energies thereby released. [9]

CULTURAL STRATEGY

During the Vietnam War, I served an eleven-month tour as an instructor at the Special Air Warfare School at Eglin Air Force Base in Florida. According to the official doctrine, to win the Vietnam War American military forces would need to win the hearts and minds of the people of Vietnam. To this end, the training for U.S. Air Force personnel heading to Vietnam included a unit on how to package and eject propaganda leaflets out of the back of a military transport plane so they would scatter properly. The leaflets told the Vietnamese about how America cared about them and was seeking to bring them freedom and democracy. But American bombs and napalm spoke louder than the pamphlets. The world's most powerful military force lost the hearts and the minds—and the war—to a peasant army of a people fighting for their freedom.

The current contest between the forces of corporate globalization and those of the movement for a living democracy is by conventional calculations similarly mismatched. Corporate globalization has the money and the guns. But the exercise of raw power against an awakened populace almost always proves to be self-defeating. The more aggressively the institutions of global capitalism use their money, media control, and police powers to suppress the struggle for life and democracy, the more quickly they expose the illusions on which their power rests, thus accelerating the awakening and hastening their own fall.

Isolation Breaking

As noted in the previous chapter, 50 million adult Americans—the Cultural Creatives—now embrace the values that are the foundation of the living democracy movement. Already the Cultural Creatives are the country's second largest cultural grouping, and their numbers are growing rapidly. Because they are ignored by the media and unrepresented by either the Republican or Democratic parties, they remain largely invisible to themselves and the establishment. Consequently, most feel culturally isolated, out of step with the mainstream, and politically disempowered. This, however, could change with surprising speed.

The Seattle WTO protests contributed substantially to breaking this sense of isolation and advancing the process of alliance building around the value of an awakened consciousness. So have other protests, teach-ins and seminars, the programs and publications of the independent media, and independent political movements like the Green Party.[10]

Myth Busting

Capitalism builds its legitimacy on a foundation of cultural myths. Expose the myths and its legitimacy crumbles. Myth busting therefore becomes a simple, but powerful cultural strategy. It requires nothing more than speaking truths that resonate with the wisdom that resides in every human heart—truths of such self-evident validity that they require no special expertise or eloquence to articulate and defend. The following are examples:

- Life is more valuable than money.
- Life is the source of all true wealth.
- Destroying life to make money is a social pathology.
- Democracy is an obvious alternative to corporate rule.
- A market economy is an obvious alternative to both capitalism and socialism.
- True prosperity means every person has an adequate and fulfilling means of living.
- Most people are by nature cooperative and compassionate.
- Natural rights reside only in living beings.
- It is the right of all people to participate in the decisions that shape their lives.
- Political democracy is inseparable from economic democracy.
- Human institutions have only the power we choose to yield to them.
- Laws made by people can be changed by people.

By sharing our truths we find and connect with one another, build communities of congruence, and reclaim the cultural sphere.

Culture Jamming

Advertisers seek to build positive associations with their logos and brand names and encourage us to embrace them as our symbols of meaning and identity. Nike, for example, hopes that when you wear the Nike Swoosh logo you will feel as though you are sailing effortlessly through the air to score the winning point. The corporate media wants us to associate the word capitalism with democracy, market freedom, and lavish material prosperity for all.

Culture jamming or ad busting is the art of parodying logos, brand names, and advertising slogans to shock people into a new awareness and turn the power of the advertiser's message back upon itself.[11] For example, culture jammers may build an association between the Nike Swoosh and images of sweatshop laborers in Indonesia. To an ad showing two Marlboro cowboys riding on horseback, they add the caption, "Bob, I had to have a lung removed." Or they may circulate a picture of a body hanging by a noose from the Shell standard to bring to mind the image of Ken Saro-Wiwa, hanged for protesting Shell's drilling operation in Nigeria.

Canadian journalist Naomi Klein points out in her book *No Logo*, that for many multibillion dollar companies, their primary asset is their logo. Nike, for example, has no factories of its own. It outsources production of all its shoes and apparel. In 1997, it spent half a billion dollars on advertising to build its brand image. Anything that devalues that logo threatens the company at its roots, because the logo is its major asset. This creates an extraordinary vulnerability, as successful student-led, antisweatshop campaigns against Nike, the Gap, Disney, and other brand name consumer companies that follow the Nike strategy have demonstrated.[12]

Right Language

Determining the language of the public discourse is another key to an effective cultural strategy. Here the corporate globalists have seriously outmaneuvered the movement. For example, by defining themselves as free traders, corporate globalists at once claim the public's positive associations with both trade and freedom—instantly implying their opponents are negative antitrade, antifreedom extremists. Also, by focusing on trade they deflect attention away from the real issue, which is corporate rule, and direct it to trade, which for most people is not an issue. Protestors countered that they favor fair trade, not free trade—a distinction that is important, but has little meaning beyond activist circles.

The movement made another tactical error with regard to the term globalization. To most people globalization means that global communication and interdependence among people are increasing along with a greater sharing of resources and technology to spread material prosperity. Harvard economist and Nobel Laureate in Economics Amartya Sen sums up the popular conception.

Opponents of globalization may see it as a new folly, but it is neither particularly new, nor, in general a folly. It is largely an intensification of the processes of interaction involving travel, trade, migration, and dissemination of knowledge that have shaped the progress of the world over millennia. The polar opposite of globalization is persistent separatism and relentless autarky.[13]

When corporate globalists say globalization is beneficial and inevitable, most people nod their heads and say "of course." When protestors say they are against globalization they sound like marginal xenophobic crazies to those who, like Sen, aren't aware that globalization is a code word for global corporate rule at the expense of democracy, people, and planet. The resulting miscommunication is a dream come true for corporate spin doctors.

In truth, most members of the living democracy movement rejoice at the increasing interaction of people through travel, trade, migration, and dissemination of knowledge. Indeed, this is arguably the most truly international movement in history, built on deep and enduring international friendships and alliances and a sense of responsibility to the whole of the planet and the human community. Many now speak more precisely of their opposition to *corporate* globalization. The next step is for the movement to embrace a name that conveys a sense of its positive vision of a world that works for all.[14]

■ ■ ■

Entranced by promises of a material paradise of limitless luxury, humanity has too long ignored the mismatch between the imperatives of our existence as living beings on a finite planet and the imperatives of the institutions of money that chart our path to the future. Created to build colonial empires in service to kings, global corporations are ill suited to the task of building just, sustainable, and compassionate civil societies that nurture sufficiency, partnership, and respect for the whole of life. Corporate globalists and the corporate empires they serve may be at the cutting edge of technological innovation, but socially and environmentally they are relics of a bygone era of imperial colonial rule, elite privilege, and state-sanctioned plunder.

Life and democracy are defining values of the Ecological Revolution and the citizen movement that is bringing it into reality. The pursuit of short-term financial values is as incompatible with the healthy living function of people and planet as corporate rule is incompatible with democracy. The task ahead is to transform a world ruled by corporations dedicated to the love of money to a world ruled by people dedicated to the love of life.

So great is the power of the institutions aligned against this transformation that we may fail to notice the blinding speed with which life-affirming changes are unfolding around us. Consider how fundamentally the civil rights, environment, peace, women's, and gay rights movements have transformed many of our collective perceptions and values regarding human and environmental relationships in a mere 40 years. Though much remains to be done, each has made its contribution to replacing the materialistic dominator culture of the global capitalist society with the spiritually grounded partnership cultures of civil societies.

Experience teaches that often the underlying forces for powerful social change build silently and invisibly over decades, even centuries, until at a moment of dramatic breakthrough the seemingly impossible dreams of millions of people become a new social reality. We have seen it, for example, in the collapse of the Soviet Union and in South Africa in the sudden dissolution of apartheid and the peaceful election of Nelson Mandela to the presidency. As late as 1988 no one was even considering the possibility that by 1991 the Soviet Union would peacefully dissolve itself, Germany would be reunited, the Berlin Wall would be gone, and the leadership of the former "evil empire" would invite the United States to help dismantle its nuclear arsenal. The extraordinary events in South Africa were similarly unanticipated as little as three years before they occurred. Born of a confluence of necessity and possibility, similar forces are now building toward the civil-izing of global society.

As a species we now find ourselves confronted with a choice either to take the step to a new level of understanding and function in service to the whole of life—to consciously and intentionally reinvent human society—or to risk our own extinction. We have the knowledge, the technology, and the necessity to rethink and intentionally recreate humanity's economic, political, and cultural institutions to achieve peace, justice, and prosperity for all as a collective creative act. This powerful combination of imperative and opportunity presents us with the most compelling creative challenge in all of human history—an unprecedented opportunity to create the truly civil society of which philosophers, religious prophets, and countless millions of others have dreamed for millennia.

The great struggle between humanity and its institutions—between a culture of life and a culture of money—is far from resolved. Nor is the outcome foreordained. We may find hope and inspiration, however, in a grand story—a story of creation—that melds spiritual insight with scientific knowledge to give deeper meaning and purpose to our existence and the challenge before us.

EPILOGUE:
A STORY FOR OUR TIME

Without a global revolution in the sphere of human consciousness, nothing will change for the better . . . and the catastrophe toward which this world is headed, whether it be ecological, social, demographic or a general breakdown of civilization, will be unavoidable.

—Václav Havel

I wonder if we wouldn't become more gracefully productive by recognizing that we are all living cells within living organisms like cities, bioregions, continents, and the earth itself. Could we lessen our stress, become healthier and more whole, if we saw our work as simply helping these organisms realize their own living wholeness?
—Daniel Kemmis, Mayor of Missoula, Montana[1]

THE ADVANCING HUMAN CRISIS has deep spiritual roots. Economic life divorced from spiritual meaning and identity treats life simply as a commodity to be sold to the highest bidder. A civil society, in contrast, rests on a foundation of authentic meaning and purpose. Thomas Berry, in *The Dream of the Earth*, proposes that our survival as a species may depend on discovering a new story that gives a sense of meaning and purpose to our existence and the challenge ahead. Berry and others, including Brian Swimme, Joanna Macy, Mae-Wan Ho, Elisabet Sahtouris, Lynn Margulies, Matthew Fox, and Duane Elgin, have since drawn from many sources, including astrophysics, quantum physics, the new biology, and the wisdom of the world's many religious traditions, to craft the outlines of such a story. It is a contemporary story of cosmic creation that reveals the epic significance of the choices now before us.

LIFE'S JOURNEY OF DISCOVERY

The story begins as much as 15 billion years ago when a new universe flared into being in a massive burst that dispersed minute energy particles, the stuff of creation, across the vastness of space. With the passing of time these particles self-organized into atoms, which swirled into great clouds that coalesced into galaxies of countless stars that grew, died, and were reborn as new stars, star systems, and planets. The cataclysmic energies unleashed by the births and deaths of billions of suns converted simple atoms into more complex atoms and melded atoms into even more complex molecules, each step opening new possibilities for the growth and evolution of the whole.

Each stage transcended the stage before in definition and capacity. It was as if a great intelligence had embarked on a grand quest to know itself through the discovery and realization of the possibilities of its being.

More than eleven billion years after the quest began, there was an extraordinary breakthrough on a planet orbiting one of the countless stars in an outer galaxy. Here the cosmos gave birth to living beings. Microscopic in size, they were simple, single-celled bacteria. Inconsequential though they seemed, they embodied an enormous creative potential and with time created the building blocks of living knowledge that made possible the incredible accomplishments that followed. They discovered the arts of fermentation, photosynthesis, and respiration fundamental to all complex life. They learned to exchange genetic material through their cell walls to share their discoveries with one another in a grand cooperative enterprise that created the planet's first global communication system. And they transformed and stabilized the chemical composition of the entire planet's atmosphere. As the fruits of life's learning multiplied, the variety, capacity, and potential of the planet's living cells grew apace.

In due course individual cells discovered the advantages of joining with one another in clusters to create multi-celled organisms of ever greater variety and potential. Step by step this extraordinary enterprise converted yet more of the inert matter of the planet into a splendid web of plant and animal life with growing capacity for innovation and choice. The new creatures that found a niche in which they could at once sustain themselves and contribute to the life of the whole survived. Those unable to find or create such a niche of service expired. Continuously experimenting, interrelating, creating, and building, the evolving web of life unfolded into a living tapestry of astonishing variety, beauty, awareness, and capacity for intelligent choice.

Then, a mere 2.6 million years ago, quite near the end of our 15 billion year story, there came the creation of a being with the capacity to reflect on its own consciousness; to experience with awe the beauty and mystery of creation; to articulate, communicate, and share learning; to reshape the material world to its own ends; and to anticipate and intentionally choose its own future. They called themselves "humans." They were the living spirit's most daring experiment.

Each of these human creatures was composed of 30 to 70 trillion individual, living, self-regulating, self-reproducing cells. More than half the dry weight of an individual human consisted of individual micro-organisms it needed to metabolize its food and create the vitamins essential to its survival. All these tiny living entities joined in an exquisitely balanced union to create each of these extraordinary creatures. It was a stunning cooperative achievement.

Humans were remarkably fast learners in the cosmic scheme of things. During their first two and a half million years they developed the capacity for speech, mastered the use of fire, produced and used sophisticated tools, engaged in artistic expression, learned to cultivate their food and to communicate in written form, established highly organized societies, and created organized systems of knowledge in botany, zoology, astronomy, and cosmology. As their scientific and organizational capabilities expanded, ever more impressive technical advances came at a rapidly accelerating rate—at each step increasing their ability to manipulate and control aspects of their material world.

CULTURAL CRISIS

Yet somewhere along the way something went terribly wrong, for the humans came to use their powerful technologies and institutions in ways that were increasingly destructive of life—and ultimately of themselves. Indeed, in a mere 100 years—between their years 1900 and 2000— they destroyed much of the living capital it had taken billions of years to create.

Some attribute this tragedy to a genetic flaw that doomed humans to the blind pursuit of greed and violence. Yet the earliest human civilizations were peaceful and cooperative and even during their most destructive periods the vast majority of humans were generous and caring.

Others saw the roots of the crisis as cultural, the consequence of a materialistic ideology, born of what humans called their Scientific Revolution.

The Scientific Revolution and the industrial and technological era that followed were in many respects the proudest period of human accomplishment. They freed a substantial portion of humanity from the deprivation, superstition, fear, and early death of peasant life and from often oppressive religious dogma. They produced humanity's most impressive technological accomplishments—including the means to eliminate physical toil, deprivation, and geographical barriers between people, to feed a rapidly growing population, and to greatly improve health and extend their life span. They created institutions of global governance and cooperation. And they established democracy and human rights as universal ideals.

Yet they also established a belief system that held matter to be the only reality and taught that the universe is best viewed as a giant clockwork set in motion at the beginning of creation and left to run down as the tension in its spring expired. They further taught that life is only an accidental outcome of material complexity and that consciousness is an illusion.

These beliefs became the foundation of a cultural system known as modernism that nurtured the pursuit of a narrow self-interest and absolved the individual of responsibility for the well-being of society and nature.

Never was human rejection of responsibility for society and nature greater than in the economic system humans called capitalism. Capitalists worshiped a god called the market. They believed the market had an invisible hand that miraculously turned acts of greed and ruthlessness to the benefit of the species. One of capitalism's defining features was a consumer culture. Capitalism cultivated this culture by saturating the communications media with the message that consumption of one or another advertised product would bring meaning and love to empty, lonely lives. Increasingly the creative energies of the species turned to building powerful institutions called corporations, which were dedicated to endlessly increasing consumption through a process called economic growth. Growth became such an obsession that few seemed to notice these corporations had taken over control of their lives and were destroying the life support system of the planet, the social fabric of the society, and the lives of billions of people.

AWAKENING

As the year 2000 approached there was evidence of an emerging culture shift. Millions of people around the world were awakening, as if from a deep trance, to the beauty, joy, and meaning of life. Many among them began to question consumerism. Others took to the streets by the hundreds of thousands, demanding a restoration of democracy, an end to corporate rule, and respect for the needs of all people and other living beings.

Yet others pondered the implications of a growing body of scientific evidence that matter, not consciousness, is the illusion—thus suggesting that conscious intelligence is the ground from which all else is manifest. A few began to rethink human possibilities in light of new evidence of life's creative capacity for cooperation and radical self-organization. Some who reflected on questions of human purpose came to see humans not as the end of creation's journey, but rather as instruments of its continued unfolding.

Those at the cutting edge of the culture shift—some called them the Cultural Creatives—suffered a deep sense of isolation from mainstream society, and their efforts to correct serious institutional pathologies were sometimes violently resisted by those who believed them to be misguided opponents of progress and prosperity. Thus an epic cultural struggle was engaged, a moment in time with deep implications not only for the future of humanity, but also for life's evolutionary course.

The story is our story. The choices are our choices. Our species, far beyond any other, has been engaged in a continuing process of intellectual, social, and technological evolution toward ever-greater species abilities. It is one of the great and mysterious wonders of the cosmos that as each of humanity's developmental stages has exhausted itself, it has left behind both the means and the imperative to break free from the familiar and take an uncertain step into the unknown. We now stand at the threshold of such a step.

A scientific paradigm that largely dismissed consciousness focused our life energies on the task of mastering the secrets of the physical world and on building technical capabilities. These capacities now open vast opportunities to build healthy societies devoted to advancing our social, intellectual, and spiritual growth. We have misused these capacities in many terrible ways and have yet to establish that we have achieved the maturity to use their power wisely. That same technology, however, gives us the ability to eliminate physical want and deprivation from the world; to give all human beings the freedom to devote a larger portion of their life energies to activities that are more fulfilling than the struggle for daily physical survival; and to bring ourselves into balance with nature.

Humanity's successes and failures during the era now passing can both be traced to distortions in our image of ourselves and of the cosmos. The Copernican Revolution divorced science from religion and focused our attention on mastering the secrets of the physical world. This opened the way to extraordinary technical accomplishments. We, humanity, have paid a heavy price, however, for our collective alienation from the deeper spiritual reality from which all life and consciousness flow. Our future now depends on graduating to a co-evolutionary perspective that recognizes the integral relationship between the spiritual and material aspects of our being and thereby allows us to recreate ourselves as whole persons, communities, and societies.

We are embarking on the most profound and exciting course change in human history—a challenge that calls us to awaken the full creative potential of our species, with the mutual caring and tolerance for diversity that are essential foundations of the healthy societies we hope to create. Engaged in a collective enterprise that requires the creative contribution of every individual, each of us must be prepared at any given moment to act as both courageous leader and humble follower—even at the same time. Engaged in an act of creation for which there is no blueprint, we must remember that we are each learners in an unfolding process that requires us to look with a critical eye and an open mind for the spark of goodness in each person and the kernel of truth in each idea.

NOTES

Introduction: Deepening Crisis—Cause for Hope

1. George Soros, *Open Society: Reforming Global Capitalism* (New York: Public Affairs, 2000), xi.
2. "Global Capitalism: Special Report," *Business Week*, November 6, 2000, 72–78, 74.
3. For a graphic, first-person account of the protests and the police response see Paul Hawken, "N30: WTO Showdown," *YES! A Journal of Positive Futures*, Spring 2000, 45–53. For the complete story of Seattle see Janet Thomas, *The Battle in Seattle: The Story Behind and Beyond the WTO Demonstrations* (Golden, Colo.: Fulcrum Publishing, 2000).
4. Aaron Bernstein, "Too Much Corporate Power?" *Business Week*, September 1, 2000, 145–158; and the related editorial "New Economy, New Social Contract," *Business Week*, September 1, 2000, 182.
5. Corporate libertarianism is an ideology that advocates total freedom for corporations from the restraints of regulation and national borders in the pursuit of profit. It is discussed at greater length in Chapter 5.

Prologue: A Personal Journey

1. On the occasion of the Liberty Medal Ceremony, Philadelphia, July 4, 1994.

Chapter 1: From Hope to Crisis

1. Jerry Mander, *In the Absence of the Sacred* (San Francisco: Sierra Club Books, 1991), 26.
2. United Nations Development Programme (UNDP), *Human Development Report 1993* (New York: Oxford University Press, 1993), 12.
3. Lester R. Brown, Michael Renner, and Brian Halwell (eds.), *Vital Signs 1999* (New York: W.W. Norton & Company, 1999), 65 & 69.
4. UNDP, *Human Development Report 1994* (New York: Oxford University Press, 1994), 31.
5. United Nations High Commissioner for Refugees, *The State of the World's Refugees* (New York: Penguin Books, 1993).
6. Gene Stephens, "The Global Crime Wave," *The Futurist*, July–August 1994, 22–28.
7. "Out-of-Wedlock Births up since '83, Report Indicates," *New York Times*, July 20, 1994, A-1, A-16.
8. UNDP, *Human Development Report 1994*, 31.
9. UNDP, *Human Development Report 1994*, 47.
10. United Nations High Commissioner for Refugees, *State of the World's Refugees.*
11. Lester R. Brown, Michael Renner, and Brian Halwell (eds.), *Vital Signs 2000* (New York:

W.W. Norton & Company, 2000), 98.

12. Gallup poll, June 2, 1990.

13. Harris poll, January 3, 1994.

14. "The New Deal: What Companies and Employees Owe One Another," *Fortune,* June 13, 1994, 44–52.

15. Poll result cited by Robert Reich, U.S. Secretary of Labor, in a presentation to the Democratic Leadership Council, Washington, D.C., November 22, 1994. The figure for those without college degrees is 68 percent.

16. Kettering Foundation, *Citizens and Politics: A View from Main Street America* (Dayton, Ohio: Kettering Foundation, 1991), iii-iv, as quoted in Stephen Craig, *The Malevolent Leaders: Popular Discontent in America* (Boulder, Colo.: Westview Press, 1993), 83.

17. Seymour Lipset and William Schneider, *The Confidence Gap: Business, Labor and Government in the Public Mind* (Baltimore: Johns Hopkins University Press, 1987), 410; Elizabeth Hann Hastings and Philip K. Hastings (eds.), *Index to International Public Opinion, 1992–1993* (Westport, Conn.: Greenwood Press, 1994).

Chapter 2: End of the Open Frontier

1. Royal Society of London and the U.S. National Academy of Sciences, *Population Growth, Resource Consumption, and a Sustainable World* (London and Washington, D.C.: Authors, 1992), as cited in Lester R. Brown, "A New Era Unfolds," in Brown, et al., *State of the World 1993* (New York: W. W. Norton, 1993), 3.

2. Herman E. Daly, "Sustainable Growth: An Impossibility Theorem," *Development,* no. 3/4 (1990): 45.

3. Originally published in Henry Jarrett (ed.), *Environmental Quality in a Growing Economy* (Baltimore: Johns Hopkins University Press, 1968), 3–14.

4. See the "Guiding Principles" enumerated in Chapter 18.

5. Lance Davis and Robert Huttenback, *Mammon and the Pursuit of Empire* (New York: Cambridge University Press, 1986), as cited in Richard Douthwaite, *The Growth Illusion* (Tulsa, Okla.: Council Oak Books, 1993), 46.

6. Davis and Huttenback, *Mammon and the Pursuit of Empire,* as cited in Douthwaite, 46.

7. These statistics were compiled by William E. Rees and Mathis Wackernagel, "Ecological Footprints and Appropriated Carrying Capacity: Measuring the Natural Capital Requirements of the Human Economy," in A-M Jannson, M. Hammer, C. Folke, and R. Costanza (eds.), *Investing in Natural Capital: The Ecological Economics Approach to Sustainability* (Washington, D.C.: Island Press, 1994), 380. Note that 1 hectare equals 2.47 acres. For further documentation of the thesis that human activities now exceed many of the natural limits of the ecosystem, see Robert Goodland, Herman E. Daly, and Salah El Serafy (eds.), *Population, Technology, and Lifestyle: The Transition to Sustainability* (Washington, D.C.: Island Press, 1992), 3–22; Donella H. Meadows, Dennis L. Meadows, and Jorgen Randers, *Beyond the Limits* (Post Mills, Vt.: Chelsea, Green Publishing, 1992); Gerald O. Barney, *Global 2000 Revisited* (Arlington, Va.: Millennium Institute, 1993); and Sandra Postel, "Carrying Capacity: Earth's Bottom Line," in Lester R. Brown et al., *State of the World 1994* (New York: W. W. Norton, 1994), 3–21.

8. Alan Durning, *How Much Is Enough? The Consumer Society and the Future of the Earth* (New York: W. W. Norton, 1992), 56.

9. Vandana Shiva, "Homeless in the 'Global Village,'" *Earth Ethics* 5, no. 4 (1994): 3.

10. "Aid for Profit: Japanese DDA in Leyte," *Kabalikat,* September 1990: 8–10.

11. "Pollution and the Poor," *The Economist,* February 15, 1992, 16–17.

12. Rees and Wackernagel, "Ecological Footprints," 382.

13. Rees and Wackernagel, "Ecological Footprints," 374.

14. Manus van Brakel and Maria Buitenkamp, *Sustainable Netherlands: A Perspective for Changing Northern Lifestyles* (Amsterdam: Friends of the Earth, 1992).
15. Alex Hittle, *The Dutch Challenge: A Look at How the United States' Consumption Must Change to Achieve Global Sustainability* (Washington, D.C.: Friends of the Earth, 1994).
16. van Brakel and Buitenkamp, *Sustainable Netherlands*, 6.
17. David Pimentel, Rebecca Harman, Matthew Pacenza, Jason Pecarsky, and Marcia Pimentel, "Natural Resources and an Optimal Human Population," *Population and Environment* 15, no. 5 (1994): 352.
18. Pimentel et al., "Natural Resources," 364.

Chapter 3: The Growth Illusion

1. Mahbub ul Haq, special advisor to the United Nations Development Programme's annual *Human Development Report*, in his Barbara Ward Lecture to the 21st World Conference of the Society for International Development, Mexico City, April 1994.
2. International Chamber of Commerce (ICC), *The Business Charter for Sustainable Development* (Paris: ICC, 1990), as quoted in Paul Ekins, "Sustainability First," in Paul Ekins and Manfred Max-Neef, *Real-Life Economics: Understanding Wealth Creation* (London: Routledge, 1992), 415.
3. Jan Tinbergen and Roefie Hueting, "GNP and Market Prices: Wrong Signals for Sustainable Economic Success That Mask Environmental Destruction," in Robert Goodland, Herman E. Daly, and Salah El Serafy (eds.), *Population, Technology, and Lifestyle: The Transition to Sustainability* (Washington, D.C.: Island Press, 1992), 52–62.
4. Tinbergen and Hueting, "GNP and Market Prices," 52–62.
5. Richard Douthwaite, "The Growth Illusion," in Jonathan Greenberg and William Kistler (eds.), *Buying America Back* (Tulsa, Okla.: Council Oak Books, 1992), 92–96.
6. Paul Ekins (ed.), *The Living Economy* (London: Routledge, 1986), 8.
7. Herman E. Daly and John B. Cobb Jr., *For the Common Good: Redirecting the Economy toward Community, the Environment, and a Sustainable Future* (Boston: Beacon Press, 1989), 401–55.
8. UNDP, *Human Development Report 1991* (New York: Oxford University Press, 1991).
9. Douthwaite, *The Growth Illusion*, 96–119.
10. Douthwaite, *The Growth Illusion*, 33–50.
11. Robin Broad and John Cavanagh, *Plundering Paradise* (Berkeley, Calif.: University of California Press, 1993), 24–31.
12. Broad and Cavanagh, *Plundering Paradise*, 24–31.
13. Eduardo A. Morato, "Far More Destructive Non-Events amidst Us," *Manila Chronicle*, June 18, 1991.
14. Broad and Cavanagh, *Plundering Paradise*, 61–72.
15. Morato, "Far More Destructive Non-Events amidst Us."
16. See John Young, "Mining the Earth," in Lester R. Brown et al., *State of the World 1992* (New York: W. W. Norton, 1992), 111.
17. Edgar Cahn and Jonathan Rowe, *Time Dollars* (Emmaus, Pa.: Rodale Press, 1992).
18. Clarence Shubert, "Creating People-Friendly Cities," *PCDForum Column* no. 72, April 5, 1994.
19. Douthwaite, *The Growth Illusion*, 33–50.
20. Edward McNall Burns, *Western Civilizations: Their History and Their Culture*, 5th ed. (New York: W. W. Norton, 1958), 659–60.
21. Douthwaite, *The Growth Illusion*, 50–56.
22. Bennett Harrison, *Lean and Mean: The Changing Landscape of Corporate Power in the Age of Flexibility* (New York: Basic Books, 1994), 191–92.

23. Robert Goodland, Herman E. Daly, and Salah El Serafy (eds.), *Population, Technology, and Lifestyle: The Transition to Sustainability* (Washington, D.C.: Island Press, 1992), xv.
24. Alicia Korten, "Cultivating Disaster: Structural Adjustment and Costa Rican Agriculture," *Multinational Monitor*, July/August 1993, 20–22.
25. Bruce Rich, *Mortgaging the Earth: The World Bank, Environmental Impoverishment, and the Crisis of Development* (Boston: Beacon Press, 1994), 155.
26. Clarence Maloney, "Environmental and Project Displacement of Population in India. Part I: Development and Deracination," *University Field Staff International Report*, no. 14 (Indianapolis, Ind.: University Field Staff International, 1990–91), 1.
27. Rich, *Mortgaging the Earth*, 156.
28. *Southeast Asia Regional Consultation on People's Participation in Environmentally Sustainable Development*, vol. 2, *National & Regional Reports* (Manila: Asian NGO Coalition, 1991), 1–2.
29. Walter Hook, "Paving over Bangkok: Development Bank-Funded Highways Will Displace Tens of Thousands," *Sustainable Transport*, no. 2 (September 1993): 7.

Chapter 4: Rise of Corporate Power in America

1. Richard L. Grossman and Frank T. Adams, *Taking Care of Business: Citizenship and the Charter of Incorporation* (Cambridge, Mass.: Charter, Ink., 1993), 6.
2. K. M. Panikkar, *Asia and Western Dominance* (Kuala Lumpur: The Other Press, 1993), 46; and "Dutch East India Company," *1998 Encyclopedia Britannica* (CD Edition).
3. K. M. Panikkar, *Asia and Western Dominance*, 48.
4. Edward McNall Burns, *Western Civilizations: Their History and Their Culture*, 5th ed. (New York: W. W. Norton and Company, 1958), 467; and "The British East India Company," *1998 Encyclopedia Britannica* (CD Edition).
5. "The Opium Wars," *1998 Encyclopedia Britannica* (CD Edition).
6. Douglas Dowd, *U.S. Capitalist Development since 1776: Of, by, and for Which People?* (Armonk, N.Y.: M. E. Sharpe, 1993), 10.
7. Leo Huberman, *We, the People: The Drama of America* (New York: Monthly Review Press, 1960), 50–52.
8. Adam Smith, *An Inquiry into the Nature and Causes of the Wealth of Nations* (1776; New York: Modern Library, 1937), 123.
9. Grossman and Adams, *Taking Care of Business*, 3.
10. Grossman and Adams, *Taking Care of Business*, 3.
11. Grossman and Adams, *Taking Care of Business*, 8–9.
12. Grossman and Adams, *Taking Care of Business*, 11–12.
13. As quoted in Edwin Merrick Dodd, *American Business Corporations until 1860* (Cambridge, Mass.: Harvard University Press, 1934), 130, as cited in Grossman and Adams, *Taking Care of Business*, 13.
14. Harvey Wasserman, *America Born & Reborn* (New York: Collier Books, 1983), 84.
15. As quoted in Wasserman, *America Born & Reborn*, 89–90.
16. Wasserman, *America Born & Reborn*, 90.
17. As quoted in Wasserman, *America Born & Reborn*, 291.
18. As quoted in Wasserman, *America Born & Reborn*, 92–93.
19. Wasserman, *America Born & Reborn*, 108.
20. Grossman and Adams, *Taking Care of Business*, 21.
21. Grossman and Adams, *Taking Care of Business*, 21.
22. Grossman and Adams, *Taking Care of Business*, 18–20.
23. Wasserman, *America Born & Reborn*, 110.
24. Grossman and Adams, *Taking Care of Business*, 18–20.

25. Paul Hawken, *The Ecology of Commerce* (New York: Harper Business, 1993), 108.
26. Wasserman, *America Born & Reborn*, 110.
27. Melvyn Dubofsky, *Industrialism and the American Worker, 1865–1920* (Arlington Heights, Ill.: Harlan Davidson, 1975), 87.
28. Wasserman, *America Born & Reborn*, 110–18; Dubofsky, *Industrialism and the American Worker*, 29–71.
29. Wasserman, *America Born & Reborn*, 110–18.
30. Wasserman, *America Born & Reborn*, 108.
31. Dubofsky, *Industrialism and the American Worker*, 72–108.
32. Wasserman, *America Born & Reborn*, 124; Dubofsky, *Industrialism and the American Worker*, 77–80.
33. Dowd, *U.S. Capitalist Development since 1776*, 157.
34. Robert L. Heilbroner, *The Worldly Philosophers* (New York: Simon and Schuster, 1992), 249–50.
35. Wasserman, *America Born & Reborn*, 140.
36. Wasserman, *America Born & Reborn*, 146–47.
37. Kevin Phillips, *The Politics of Rich and Poor* (New York: Harper Perennial, 1990), 241–42.
38. Walden Bello, with Shea Cunningham and Bill Rau, *Dark Victory: The United States, Structural Adjustment, and Global Poverty* (Oakland, Calif.: Institute for Food and Development Policy, 1994), 4–5.
39. Bello, *Dark Victory*, 3.
40. Bello, *Dark Victory*, 5.
41. Bello, *Dark Victory*, 5.
42. The 1978 figure is from Phillips, *Politics of Rich and Poor*, 239. The 1994 figure is from the survey of the world's billionaires by *Forbes*, July 18, 1994, 135.
43. *Forbes*, July 18, 1994, 135.
44. Bello, *Dark Victory*, 5–6.
45. Bello, *Dark Victory*, 3–4.
46. For further development of the autonomous purpose of corporations, see Jerry Mander, "Corporations as Machines," chap. 7 in *In the Absence of the Sacred* (San Francisco: Sierra Club Books, 1991).
47. William Greider, *Who Will Tell the People? The Betrayal of American Democracy* (New York: Simon and Schuster, 1992), 331.

Chapters 5: Assault of the Corporate Libertarians

1. "Is Free Trade Passe?" *Economic Perspectives 1*, no. 2 (1987): 131.
2. Gar Alperovitz, "Building a Living Democracy," *Sojourners*, July 1990, 16.
3. Michael Pusey, "Reclaiming the Middle Ground . . . From New Right 'Economic Rationalism,'" in Stephen King and Peter Lloyd (eds.), *Economic Rationalism: Dead End or Way Forward?* (New South Wales: Alien & Unwin, 1993), 18.
4. Michael Pusey, *Economic Rationalism in Canberra: A Nation-Building State Changes Its Mind* (Sydney: Cambridge University Press, 1991).
5. *Webster's New World Dictionary* (New York: Simon and Schuster, 1980), s.v. "rationalism."
6. David Boaz and Edward H. Crane, *Market Liberalism: A Paradigm for the 21st Century* (Washington, D.C.: Cato Institute, 1993), 23.
7. Adam Smith, *An Inquiry into the Nature and Causes of the Wealth of Nations* (1776; New York: Modern Library, 1937), 60–61.
8. Smith, *Wealth of Nations*, 674.
9. A. V. Krebs, *The Corporate Reapers: The Book of Agribusiness* (Washington, D.C.: Essential

Books, 1992); and an information sheet, "America's New 'Centrally Planned' Food Economy," prepared by A. V. Krebs and distributed by Prairie Fire Rural Action, Des Moines, Iowa.

10. Neva Goodwin, "Externalities and Economic Power," paper presented to session on "Is It the Economy or the Politics—Stupid?" at the fall retreat of the Environmental Grantmakers Association, Bretton Woods, New Hampshire, October 13–15, 1994, 2.

11. Smith, *Wealth of Nations*, 423.

12. Smith, *Wealth of Nations*, 700.

13. United Nations Centre for Transnational Corporations (UNCTC), E/C.IO/1993/2, March 3, 1993, 8; as reported by John Cavanagh in a May 1, 1993, memo.

14. These arguments are developed in detail by Herman E. Daly and John B. Cobb Jr., *For the Common Good: Redirecting the Economy toward Community, the Environment, and a Sustainable Future* (Boston; Beacon Press, 1989), 209–35.

15. Goodwin, "Externalities and Economic Power", 2.

16. James Stanford, "Continental Economic Integration: Modeling the Impact on Labor," *Annals of the American Academy of Political & Social Science 526* (March 1993): 92–110.

17. James Stanford, "Free Trade and the Imaginary Worlds of Economic Modelers," *PCDForum Column* no. 45, April 5, 1993.

18. Statistics cited by Richard J. Barnet, "Stateless Corporations: Lords of the Global Economy," *The Nation*, December 19, 1994, 754.

19. "Meet the World's Newest Billionaires," *Forbes*, July 5, 1993, 87.

20. "A Millionaire a Minute," *Business Week*, November 29, 1993, 100–102.

21. "21st Century Capitalism," *Business Week*, 1994 special issue, 13 & 16.

22. Lawrence Summers, internal World Bank memorandum dated December 12, 1991, 5. The relevant excerpts from this memo were quoted by *The Economist*, February 8, 1992, 62. Summers, a leading proponent of economic rationalism, responded to widespread public criticism of his argument by claiming that he had inserted it into the infamous memo as an ironic counterpoint rather than an actual proposal.

23. "Pollution and the Poor," *The Economist*, February 15, 1992, 16–17.

24. The call for the rich to consume more imports from poor countries is a regular theme in the World Bank's *World Development Report* series. See, for example, World Bank, *World Development Report 1992: Development and the Environment* (New York: Oxford University Press, 1992), 3.

Chapter 6: Decline of Democratic Pluralism

1. "Free Trade, up to a Point," *Times* (London), March 5, 1994, 18.

2. Susan George, Conference on Economic Sovereignty in a Globalising World, Bangkok, 24–26 March 1999, www.millennium-round.org/.

3. Francis Fukuyama, *The End of History and the Last Man* (New York: Avon Books, 1992).

4. The following points are drawn from Herman E. Daly and John B. Cobb Jr., *For the Common Good: Redirecting the Economy toward Community, the Environment, and a Sustainable Future* (Boston: Beacon Press, 1989), 49–60.

5. Based on personal correspondence from Marilyn Mehimann, Swedish Institute for Social Inventions, March 3, 1994.

6. Kenneth Hermele, "The End of the Middle Road: What Happened to the Swedish Model?" *Monthly Review*, March 1993, 14–24.

7. David Vail, "The Past and Future of Swedish Social Democracy: A Reply to Kenneth Hermele," *Monthly Review*, October 1993, 24–31.

8. Hermele, "The End of the Middle Road."

9. Hermele, "The End of the Middle Road."

10. Vail, "The Past and Future of Swedish Social Democracy."
11. Hermele, "The End of the Middle Road."
12. Hermele, "The End of the Middle Road."
13. Vail, "The Past and Future of Swedish Social Democracy."
14. Hermele, "The End of the Middle Road."
15. Hermele, "The End of the Middle Road."
16. Vail, "The Past and Future of Swedish Social Democracy."
17. This discussion of the three sectors or spheres of public life has been rewritten for the new edition based on a framework presented by Nicanor Perlas in *Shaping Globalization: Civil Society, Cultural Power and Threefolding* (Quezon City, Philippines: Center for Alternative Development Initiatives, 1999).
18. William M. Dugger, *Corporate Hegemony* (New York: Greenwood Press, 1989), 12–15.
19. Dugger, *Corporate Hegemony*, 15.
20. Dugger, *Corporate Hegemony*, 15.

Chapter 7: Illusions of the Cloud Minders

1. From "The Cloud Minders," *Star Trek*, episode 74, February 28, 1969.
2. Graham Hancock, *Lords of Poverty* (New York: Atlantic Monthly Press, 1989), 38–40.
3. Address by Barber B. Conable to the board of governors of the World Bank and International Finance Corporation, Washington, D.C., September 30, 1986, as quoted in Hancock, 38.
4. As reported in Nancy Scheper-Hughes, "The Madness of Hunger," *Why*, no. 14 (Fall 1993): 11.
5. Walter Hook, "Paving over Bangkok," *Sustainable Transport*, no. 2 (September 1993): 7.
6. Hook, "Paving over Bangkok," 6.
7. UNDP, *Human Development Report 1992* (New York: Oxford University Press, 1992).
8. U.S. data are for families and therefore are not directly comparable with the individual data used by UNDP.
9. Gar Alperovitz, "Building a Living Democracy," *Sojourners*, July 1990, 13.
10. "Executive Pay: The Party Ain't over Yet," *Business Week*, April 16, 1993, 56–64.
11. "Executive Pay."
12. "The Forbes Four Hundred," *Forbes*, October 18, 1993, 110–11.
13. Although net asset values are not directly comparable to gross national product, which is a measure of income, the orders of magnitude are revealing. GNP and population figures are from John W. Wright. *The Universal Almanac, 1994* (Kansas City, Mo.: Andrews and McMeel, 1993).
14. "The Forbes Four Hundred," 111.
15. Lawrence Mishel and Jared Bernstein, *The State of Working America: 1992–1993* (Armonk, N.Y.: M. E. Sharpe, 1993), 256.
16. Mishel and Berstein, *The State of Working America*, 46; based on data from the House of Representatives Ways and Means Committee, 1991. Figures are in 1992 dollars.
17. James M. Clash, "Reversal of Fortunates," *Forbes*, October 18, 1993, 105–6.
18. Eric Konigsberg, "No Hassles: The Ultimate Perk of the Ruling Class Is Freedom from Pesky Details," *Utne Reader*, September/October 1993, 76.
19. James Bennet. "New Ford Chief Hasn't Bought One. Lately." *New York Times*, October 7, 1993, D-l, D-15.
20. "CEO Disease: Egotism Can Breed Corporate Disaster—and the Malady Is Spreading," *Business Week*, April 1, 1991, 52–60.
21. Konigsberg, "No Hassles," 76.
22. Richard J. Barnet and John Cavanagh, *Global Dreams: Imperial Corporations and the New*

World Order (New York: Simon and Schuster, 1994), 325–29.

23. Barnet and Cavanagh, *Global Dreams*, 325–29. See also Cynthia Enloe, "Globetrotting Sneaker," *Ms.*, March/April 1995, 10–15.

24. "Eisner Pay Is 68% of Profit," *New York Times*, April 16, 1994, 48.

25. "The World's Wealthiest People," *Forbes*, July 5, 1993, 66–111; and "The Billionaires," *Forbes*, July 18, 1994, 134–219.

26. Robert B. Reich, *The Work of Nations* (New York: Alfred A. Knopf, 1991), 275.

27. Extensive documentation of this trend within the United States is provided by Reich, 268–81.

Chapter 8: Dreaming of Global Empires

1. "A Survey of Multinationals: Everybody's Favorite Monsters," *The Economist*, March 27, 1993, 7.

2. Richard J. Barnet and Ronald E. Muller, *Global Reach: The Power of the Multinational Corporation* (New York: Simon and Schuster, 1974), 13, 15–16, as cited in Howard M. Wachtel, *The Money Mandarins: The Making of a Supranational Economic Order* (Armonk, N.Y.: M. E. Sharpe, 1990), 6.

3. Akio Morita, "Toward a New World Economic Order," *Atlantic Monthly*, June 1993, 88.

4. Morita, "Toward a New World Economic Order," 92–93.

5. Morita, "Toward a New World Economic Order," 93.

6. Morita, "Toward a New World Economic Order," 94–95.

7. "Cosmocorp: The Importance of Being Stateless," *Columbia Journal of World Business 2*, no. 6 (November–December 1967), as quoted in Jeff Frieden, "The Trilateral Commission: Economics and Politics in the 1970s," in Holly Sklar (ed.), *Trilateralism: The Trilateral Commission and Elite Planning for World Management* (Boston: South End Press, 1980), 63–64.

8. *GATT—The Environment and the Third World, an Overview* (Berkeley, Calif.: Environmental News Network, 1992), 3, as cited in Paul Hawken, *The Ecology of Commerce: A Declaration of Sustainability* (New York: Harper Business, 1993), 101.

9. Rosabeth Moss Kanter, "Transcending Business Boundaries: 12,000 World Managers View Change," *Harvard Business Review*, May–June 1991, 151–65.

10. Calculated from global trade and output tables in Lester R. Brown, Hal Kane and Ed Ayres, *Vital Signs 1993: The Trends That Are Shaping Our Future* (New York: W. W. Norton, 1993).

11. "A Survey of Multinationals," 7.

12. "The Power of the Transnationals," *The Ecologist 22*, no. 4 (July/August 1992): 159.

13. United Nations, *World Investment Report* (New York: United Nations, 1993), 19, 22.

14. As quoted in Gerald Epstein, "Mortgaging America," *World Policy Journal 8*, no. 1 (Winter 1990–91): 29.

15. *Business Week*, May 14, 1990, 99.

16. Robert B. Reich, "Who Is Us?" *Harvard Business Review*, January–February 1990, 54.

17. Andrew Pollack, "G.M. to Make Toyota Cars for Sale in Japan," *New York Times*, April 16, 1993, D-l.

18. "The Stateless Corporation," *Business Week*, May 14, 1990, 98.

19. "The Stateless Corporation," 99–102.

20. Michael E. McGrath and Richard W. Hoole, "Manufacturing's New Economies of Scale," *Harvard Business Review*, May–June 1992, 94–102.

21. "A Survey of Multinationals," 8.

22. Office of Technology Assessment, U.S. Congress, *Multinationals and the National Interest: Playing by Different Rules* (Washington, D.C.: U.S. Government Printing Office, 1993),

1–4, 10.

23. Kenichi Ohmae, *The Borderless World: Power and Strategy in the Interlinked Economy* (London: HarperCollins, 1990), xii.

24. "U.S. Companies Use Affiliates Abroad to Skirt Sanctions," *New York Times*, December 27, 1993, A-l, D-3.

25. Ohmae, *The Borderless World*, x-xi.

26. Ohmae, *The Borderless World*, 19.

27. "Exports Will Fly High, but so Will Imports," *Fortune*, July 25, 1994, 64.

28. Andrew Cohen, "The Downside of 'Development,'" *The Nation*, November 4, 1991, 544–46.

29. This discussion is based on William Greider, *Who Will Tell the People? The Betrayal of American Democracy* (New York: Simon and Schuster, 1992), 378–87; Richard Rothstein, "Continental Drift: NAFTA and Its Aftershocks," *The American Prospect,* no. 12 (Winter 1993): 68–84; Ross Perot and Pat Choate, *Save Your Job, Save Our Country* (New York: Hyperion, 1993), 45–47; and Richard J. Barnet and John Cavanagh, "Creating a Level Playing Field," *Technology Review,* May/June 1994, 23–29.

30. As interviewed by and cited in Greider, 383.

31. "The Boom Belt: There's No Speed Limit on Growth along the South's I–85," *Business Week*, September 27, 1993, 98–104.

32. Robert Reich, *The Work of Nations* (New York: Alfred A. Knopf, 1991), 281.

33. Reported by Robert Reich in a presentation to the Democratic Leadership Conference televised on C-Span, November 29, 1994.

Chapter 9: Building Elite Consensus

1. As quoted in "Development as Enclosure," *The Ecologist* 22, no. 4 (1992): 131–47.

2. Felix Rohatyn, "World Capital: The Need and the Risks," *New York Review of Books,* July 14, 1994, 48.

3. Leonard Silk and Mark Silk, *The American Establishment* (New York: Basic Books, 1980), 183–90.

4. The discussion of these events is based on Laurence H. Shoup and William Minter, "Shaping a New World Order: The Council on Foreign Relations' Blueprint for World Hegemony," in Holly Sklar (ed.), *Trilateralism: The Trilateral Commission and Elite Planning for World Management* (Boston: South End Press, 1980), 135–56.

5. Silk and Silk, *The American Establishment*, 197–98.

6. Shoup and Minter, "Shaping a New World Order," 135–56.

7. Memorandum E-B32, April 17, 1941, Council on Foreign Relations, War-Peace Studies, NUL, as quoted in Shoup and Minter, 145–46.

8. From Memorandum E-B34, July 24, 1941, as quoted in Shoup and Minter, 141.

9. Shoup and Minter, "Shaping a New World Order," 141.

10. Bruce Rich, *Mortgaging the Earth* (Boston: Beacon Press, 1994), 49–56.

11. Thompson, "Bilderberg and the West," 157.

12. Statement by John Pomian (secretary to Joseph Retinger, who was a founder of Bilderberg and its first permanent secretary), as quoted in Thompson, 169.

13. Thompson, "Bilderberg and the West," 177.

14. As quoted in Thompson, "Bilderberg and the West," 177–78.

15. Sklar, *Trilateralism*.

16. From descriptive materials provided by the Trilateral Commission.

17. Thompson, "Bilderberg and the West," 176.

18. Thompson, "Bilderberg and the West," 177.

19. From an undated information sheet provided by the Trilateral Commission.

Chapter 10: Buying Out Democracy

1. As quoted in *Justice for Sale: Shortchanging the Public Interest for Private Gain* (Washington, D.C.: Alliance for Justice, 1993), 1.
2. As quoted in *Justice for Sale*, 10–11.
3. *Justice for Sale*, 11–12; Mark Megalli and Andy Friedman, *Masks of Deception: Corporate Front Groups in America* (Washington, D.C.: Essential Information, 1991), 153.
4. Megalli and Friedman, *Masks of Deception*, 153.
5. As quoted in *Justice for Sale*, 12.
6. *Justice for Sale*.
7. These and other cases are documented in Megalli and Friedman, *Masks of Deception*.
8. Rosemary Brown, "Unveiling Corporate Front Groups," *Co-op America Quarterly* (Winter 1994): 14. For a published directory of business-sponsored front groups, see Carl Deal, *The Greenpeace Guide to Anti-Environmental Organizations* (Berkeley, Calif.: Odonian Press, 1993); available from Odonian Press, Box 7776, Berkeley, CA 94707, for $5 per copy plus $2 handling per order.
9. William Greider, *Who Will Tell the People? The Betrayal of American Democracy* (New York: Simon and Schuster, 1992), 48.
10. *Justice for Sale*, 3.
11. Greider, *Who Will Tell the People?*
12. From a descriptive brochure provided by the Business Roundtable.
13. The ratio is based on the 1992 average annual compensation of $3.84 million for the CEOs of major U.S. corporations as reported by *Business Week,* April 16, 1993. Since the Roundtable members are the CEOs of the very largest U.S. corporations, we can presume that their average compensation is higher than the average reported by *Business Week.*
14. Sarah Anderson, John Cavanagh, and Sandra Gross, *NAFTA's Corporate Cadre: An Analysis of the USA*NAFTA State Captains* (Washington, D.C.: Institute for Policy Studies, 1993); available from IPS, 1601 Connecticut Ave. NW, Washington, D.C., 20009.
15. Greider, *Who Will Tell the People?*, 35.
16. John Stauber, "Countering the Flack Attack," *Co-op America Quarterly* (Winter 1994); 18.
17. Stauber, "Countering the Flack Attack," 18.
18. Greider, *Who Will Tell the People?*, 253–54.
19. Greider, *Who Will Tell the People?*, 270.
20. Pat Choate, "Political Advantage: Japan's Campaign for America," *Harvard Business Review*, September–October 1990, 87–103; "Is Japan 'Buying' U.S. Politics?" *Harvard Business Review*, November–December 1990, 184–98.

Chapter 11: Marketing the World

1. William Leach, *Land of Desire: Merchants, Power, and the Rise of a New American Culture* (New York: Pantheon Books, 1993), xiii.
2. Richard J. Barnet and John Cavanagh, "The Sound of Money," *Sojourners*, January 1994, 12.
3. Paul Hawken, *The Ecology of Commerce: A Declaration of Sustainability* (New York: Harper Business, 1993), 132.
4. Duane Elgin, *Voluntary Simplicity* (New York: William Morrow, 1993), 50–52.
5. Elgin, *Voluntary Simplicity*, 50–52.
6. Leach, *Land of Desire*, xv.
7. Leach, *Land of Desire*, 11–12.
8. The statistics and analysis of television are from Jerry Mander, *In the Absence of the Sacred: The Failure of Technology & the Survival of the Indian Nations* (San Francisco, Calif.:

Sierra Club Books, 1991), 75–82.

9. Mander, *In the Absence of the Sacred*, 97–98.

10. As cited in Richard J. Barnet and John Cavanagh, *Global Dreams: Imperial Corporations and the New World Order* (New York: Simon and Schuster, 1994), 171–72.

11. United Nations, *Report on the World Social Situation 1993* (New York: United Nations, 1993), 48.

12. Alan Thein Durning, "Can't Live Without It," *WorldWatch* 6, no. 3 (May–June 1993): 13.

13. Akio Morita, "Toward a New World Economic Order," *Atlantic Monthly*, June 1993.

14. As quoted in Barnet and Cavanagh, "The Sound of Money," 14.

15. Barnet and Cavanagh, "The Sound of Money," 14.

16. Sarah Ferguson, "The Comfort of Being Sad: Kurt Cobain and the Politics of Damage," *Utne Reader*, July/August 1994, 62.

17. *TV Nation*, produced by Michael Moore, NBC Television, August 2, 1994.

18. Except as otherwise referenced, information on corporate advertising in the classroom is from Alex Monar, "Corporations in the Classroom," *Co-op America Quarterly* (Winter 1994): 19–20.

19. As quoted in Robert Pear, "Senator, Promoting Student Nutrition, Battles Coca-Cola," *New York Times*, April 26, 1994, A-20.

20. "A, B, C, D, Economics," *New York Times*, May 26, 1992, A-23.

21. Donella Meadows, "Corporate-Run Schools Are a Threat to Our Way of Life," *Valley News*, October 3, 1992, 22; Monar, "Corporations in the Classroom," 20.

22. As quoted in Monar, "Corporations in the Classroom," 20.

23. Hawken, *The Ecology of Commerce*, 129.

24. "Empires of the 21ˢᵗ Century?" *Business Week*, February 21, 1994, 19.

Chapter 12: Eliminating the Public Interest

1. Presentation to eleven African heads of state, Libreville, Gabon, May 27, 1993.

2. The ad was placed by the Philippine government in 1975, as quoted in Elizabeth M. Krahmer and Donella H. Meadows, "Money Flows" (draft paper, March 29, 1994), 19.

3. Robin Broad, *Unequal Alliance 1979–1986: The World Bank, the International Monetary Fund, and the Philippines* (Berkeley, Calif.: University of California Press, 1988), 21.

4. Bruce Rich, "The Cuckoo in the Nest: Fifty Years of Political Meddling by the World Bank," *The Ecologist 24*, no. 1 (January/February 1994): 9.

5. Rich, "The Cuckoo in the Nest," 9.

6. *World Debt Tables 1992–93: External Finance for Developing Countries* (Washington, D.C.: World Bank, 1992), 212.

7. Frances Stewart, "The Many Faces of Adjustment," *World Development 19*, no. 12 (December 1991): 18–51.

8. *World Debt Tables 1992–93*, 208.

9. David C. Korten, *Getting to the 21st Century: Voluntary Action and the Global Agenda* (West Hartford, Conn.: Kumarian Press, 1990).

10. Reported by Pratap Chatterjee, "World Bank Failures Soar to 37.5% of Completed Projects in 1991," *Third World Economics*, December 16–31, 1992, 2.

11. Reported by Michael Cernea, "Farmer Organizations and Institution Building for Sustainable Development," *Regional Development Dialogue 8*, no. 2 I (Summer 1987): 1–19.

12. Paul Hawken, *The Ecology of Commerce: A Declaration of Sustainability* (New York: Harper Business, 1993), 99–100.

13. Information on the trade advisory committees is from Tom Hilliard, *Trade Advisory Committees: Privileged Access for Polluters* (Washington, D.C.: Public Citizen's Congress Watch, 1991).

14. U.S. Department of Commerce and Office of the U.S. Trade Representative, *Procedures and Rules for the Industry Advisory Committees for Trade Policy Matters,* (n.d.), 3, as cited in Hilliard, *Trade Advisory Committees,* 9.

15. Hilliard, *Trade Advisory Committees,* 7.

16. "Government Seeks Advice from Industry on U.S. Trade Policy," *Business America,* January 16, 1989, 9, as cited in Hilliard, 7.

17. Hilliard, *Trade Advisory Committees.*

18. As quoted in Mark Ritchie, "GATT, Agriculture and the Environment: The US Double Zero Plan," *The Ecologist 20,* no. 6 (November/December 1990): 217.

19. As cited in "Power: The Central Issue," *The Ecologist 22,* no. 4 (July/August 1992): 159.

20. Cited in Ritchie, "GATT," 216.

21. From a study by Tim Lang for the United Kingdom National Food Alliance, as reported in Tim Lang and Colin Hines, *The New Protectionism: Protecting the Future against Free Trade* (New York: New Press, 1993), 100–103.

22. In an April 24, 1993, interview with *New Scientist* magazine, cited in Natalie Avery, "How Companies Influence Global Food Standards," news release issued by *Third World Network Features,* 87 Cantonment Road, Penang, Malaysia, January 1994, 7.

23. Hope Shand, "Patenting the Planet," *Multinational Monitor,* June 1994, 9–13.

24. Shand, "Patenting the Planet," 9–13.

25. As quoted in Vandana Shiva, *Monocultures of the Mind: Perspectives on Biodiversity and Biotechnology* (London: Zed Press, 1993), 122.

26. Shiva, *Monocultures of the Mind,* 122.

27. *The Ecologist, Whose Common Future? Reclaiming the Commons* (Philadelphia: New Society Publishers, 1993), 55–56.

Chapter 13: The Money Game

1. "Hot Money," *Business Week,* March 20, 1995, 46.

2. The number of participants is an estimate noted by Representative Henry B. Gonzalez, chair of the House Banking Committee of the U.S. Congress, at a hearing on the derivatives market; cited in Thomas L. Friedman, "International Investors Bet Everything on Anything," *New York Times,* April 17, 1994, sec. 4, 1.

3. Diana B. Henriques, "Questions of Conflict Sting Mutual Funds," *New York Times,* August 7, 1994, 1.

4. "Another Year in 'Bank Heaven'?" *Business Week,* January 10, 1994, 103.

5. Pension fund figures are from Randy Barber and Teresa Ghilarducci, "Pension Funds, Capital Markets, and the Economic Future," in Gary A. Dymski, Gerald Epstein, and Robert Pollin (eds.), *Transforming the U.S. Financial System: Equity and Efficiency for the 21st Century* (Armonk, N.Y.: M. E. Sharpe, 1993), 288.

6. On an average day in July 1993, $1.087 trillion in dollar-based currency trades took place on the New York Clearing House Interbank Payments System alone. Jay Mathews, "Putting Currency on Trial," *Washington Post,* August 22, 1993, H-1.

7. Joel Kurtzman, *The Death of Money* (New York: Simon and Schuster, 1993), 64, 149.

8. For more detailed nontechnical discussions of the financial economy, see Kurtzman, *The Death of Money*; Howard M. Wachtel, *The Money Mandarins: The Making of a Supranational Economic Order* (Armonk, N.Y.: M. E. Sharpe, 1990); and Roy C. Smith, *The Money Wars: The Rise and Fall of the Great Buyout Boom of the 1980s* (Plume, N.Y.: Truman Talley Books, 1990).

9. The actual rate varies, depending on such things as the total assets of the bank, but it averages a little under 10 percent.

10. *Report of the Presidential Commission on Market Mechanisms* (Washington, D.C.: U.S.

Government Printing Office, 1988), 1–2, as cited in Wachtel, 251.

11. Kurtzman, *The Death of Money*, 98.
12. Kurtzman, *The Death of Money*, 161.

Chapter 14: Predatory Finance

1. The comment was made about a period of currency stability in March 1987, as quoted in Hobart Rowen, "Wielding Jawbone to Protect the Dollar," *Washington Post*, March 15, 1987, H-l, and cited in Howard M. Wachtel, *The Money Mandarins: The Making of a Supranational Economic Order* (Armonk, N.Y.: M. E. Sharpe, 1990), 269.
2. Joel Kurtzman, *The Death of Money* (New York: Simon and Schuster, 1993), 128.
3. Felix Rohatyn, "World Capital: The Need and the Risks," *New York Review of Books*, July 14, 1994, 53.
4. "A Survey of Multinationals: Everybody's Favourite Monsters," *The Economist*, March 27, 1993, 6.
5. Personal communication with J. T. Ross Jackson, president, Gaiacorp, Copenhagen, Denmark.
6. Carol J . Loomis, "Untangling the Derivatives Mess," *Fortune*, March 20, 1995, 50.
7. "Survey: Frontiers of Finance: On the Edge," *The Economist*, October 9, 1993, 4.
8. Saul Hansell, "A Primer on Hedge Funds: Hush-Hush and for the Rich," *New York Times*, April 13, 1994, A-l, D-15.
9. "Excerpts from Soros Testimony," *New York Times*, April 14, 1994, D-6.
10. Allen R. Myerson, "When Soros Speaks, World Markets Listen," *New York Times*, June 10, 1993, D-l.
11. "Big Winner from Plunge in Sterling," *New York Times*, October 27, 1992, D-9.
12. Elizabeth M. Krahmer and Donella H. Meadows, "Money Flows" (prepared for the annual meeting of the Environmental Grantmakers Association, March 24, 1994), 48.
13. Jay Mathews, "Putting Currency Trading on Trial," *Washington Post*, August 22, 1993, H-l, H-4.
14. Felix Rohatyn, "World Capital: The Need and the Risks," *New York Review of Books*, July 14, 1994, 51–52.
15. Saul Hansell, "A Bad Bet for P. & G.," *New York Times*, April 14, 1994, D-6.
16. Rohatyn, "World Capital," 52.
17. Susan Antilla, "A Concealed Danger for Funds," *New York Times*, April 17, 1994, 15.
18. "Today, Orange County: The Muni Mess on Wall Street: How Bad?" *Business Week*, December 19, 1994, 28–30.
19. Saul Ansell, "For Rogue Traders, Yet Another Victim," *New York Times*, February 28, 1995, Dl, D8; "The Lesson from Barings' Straits," *Business Week*, March 13, 1995, 30–32; Richard W. Stevenson, "Young Trader's $29 Billion Bet Brings Down a Venerable Firm," *New York Times*, February 28, 1995, A-l, D-9.
20. Sheryl WuDunn, "Tokyo Stocks Plunge on British Firm's Collapse," *New York Times*, February 27, 1995, D-l.
21. As cited in Joel Kurtzman, *The Death of Money* (New York: Simon and Schuster, 1993), 89–91.
22. Based on an interview with Christopher Whalen, chief financial officer for Legal Research International, by Russell Mokhiber of the *Corporate Crime Reporter*, January 19, 1995, distributed via Internet.
23. "The World's Wealthiest People," *Forbes*, July 5, 1993, 66; "The Billionaires," *Forbes*, July 18, 1994, 194–95.
24. "One Year Later: NAFTA Disaster!" Information package prepared and distributed by Public Citizen's Trade Program, Public Citizen, Washington, D.C., March 1995, 1.

25. "Austerity and Rates of 92% Fail to Perk Up the Peso," *New York Times*, March 16, 1995, D-8.
26. Anthony DePalma, "Mexicans Ask How Far Social Fabric Can Stretch," *New York Times*, March 12, 1995, A-l.
27. Allen R. Nyerson, "Peso's Plunge May Cost Thousands of U.S. Jobs," *New York Times*, January 30, 1995, D-4.
28. Anthony DePalma, "Crisis in Mexico Deepens Damage in Latin Markets," *New York Times*, January 11, 1995, A-l, D-2.
29. Ralph Nader, testimony on the bailout of the Mexican government before the Senate Banking Committee, U.S. Senate, Washington, D.C., March 9, 1995, 4; David E. Sanger, "Dollar Dips as the Peso Falls Again," *New York Times*, March 10, 1995, D-l.
30. Harvey D. Shapiro, "After NAFTA: Facing the New Global Economy," *Hemispheres*, March 1995, 74–79.
31. Paul Craig Roberts, "How Clinton Is Bashing the Buck," *Business Week*, August 8, 1994, 14.
32. Mathews, "Putting Currency Trading on Trial," H-4.

Chapter 15: Corporate Cannibalism

1. William M. Dugger, *Corporate Hegemony* (New York: Greenwood Press, 1989), x.
2. The meaning of the phrase "creating value" is commonly distorted by corporate libertarians to refer to anything that inflates a price or extracts a profit. I use the term here in reference to adding to the real value of the world's stock of goods, services, and productive assets.
3. Joel Kurtzman, *The Death of Money* (New York: Simon and Schuster, 1993), 164.
4. Data compiled by Donald L. Bartlett and James B. Steele, "America: What Went Wrong? Part 8: The Disappearing Pensions," *Philadelphia Inquirer*, October 27, 1991, 1-A, as cited in Jonathan Greenberg, "The Hidden Costs of Corporate Takeovers," in Jonathan Greenberg and William Kistler (eds.), *Buying America Back* (Tulsa, Okla.: Council Oak Books, 1992), 153.
5. As quoted in "The Power of the Transnationals," *The Ecologist 22*, no. 4 (July/August 1992): 159.
6. Ned Daly, "Ravaging the Redwoods; Charles Hurwitz, Michael Milken and the Cost of Greed," *Multinational Monitor*, September 1994, 12.
7. John Skow, "Redwoods: The Last Stand," *Time*, June 6, 1994, 59.
8. Skow, "Redwoods," 59.
9. Daly, "Ravaging the Redwoods," 13.
10. As quoted in Susan Faludi, "The Reckoning: Safeway LBO Yields Vast Profits But Exacts a Heavy Human Toll," *Wall Street Journal*, May 16, 1990, 1A, and cited in Greenburg, 159.
11. Gretchen Morgenson, "The Buyout That Saved Safeway," *Forbes*, November 12, 1990, 88, as cited in Greenberg, 155.
12. Greenberg, *Buying America Back*, 155.
13. Data compiled by Donald L. Bartlett and James B. Steele, "America: What Went Wrong? Part 3: Shifting Taxes from Them to You," *Philadelphia Inquirer*, October 22, 1991, 1–A, as cited in Greenberg, 152.
14. Greenberg, *Buying America Back*, 151.
15. Greenberg, *Buying America Back*, 159.
16. Based on Joseph Pereira, "Split Personality," as reprinted by *Utne Reader*, September/October 1993, 63–66, from the *Wall Street Journal*.
17. As quoted in Pereira, "Split Personality," 64.
18. As cited in Ross Perot and Pat Choate, *Save Your Job, Save Our Country: Why NAFTA*

Must Be Stopped—Now! (New York: Hyperion, 1993), 52–53.

19. Perot and Choate, *Save your Job*, 52–53.

Chapter 16: Managed Competition

1. Bennett Harrison, *Lean and Mean: The Changing Landscape of Corporate Power in the Age of Flexibility* (New York: Basic Books, 1993), 220.
2. Jeremy Brecher, "Global Village or Global Pillage?" *The Nation*, December 6, 1993, 685–88.
3. "Let the Good Times Roll—and a Few More Heads," *Business Week*, January 31, 1994, 28–29.
4. "The Rise and Rise of America's Small Firms," *The Economist*, January 21, 1989, 73.
5. Adam Smith, *An Inquiry into the Nature and Causes of the Wealth of Nations* (1776; New York: Modern Library, 1937), 128.
6. "The Age of Consolidation," *Business Week*, October 14, 1991, 86–94. "Making the Perfect Connection," *WordPerfect Report*, Summer/Fall 1994, 2.
7. These estimates are from "A Survey of Multinationals: Everybody's Favourite Monsters," *The Economist*, March 27, 1993 (special supplement), 17.
8. A. V. Krebs, *The Corporate Reapers: The Book of Agribusiness* (Washington, D.C.: Essential Books, 1992); A. V. Krebs, "America's New 'Centrally Planned' Food Economy" (information sheet distributed by Prairie Fire Rural Action, Des Moines, Iowa), 74, as quoted in Harrison, 13.
9. "The Virtual Corporation," *Business Week*, February 8, 1993, 100.
10. "The Partners," *Business Week*, February 10, 1992, 102–7.
11. "A Survey of Multinationals," 14.
12. *The Economist*, February 6, 1993, 69.
13. This compares 1991 GNP data for countries against total sales of the world' largest corporations for the same year. GNP data are from *The Universal Almanac*, 1994 (Kansas City, Mo.: Andrews and McMeel, 1993) supplemented by *The Economist, Book of Vital World Statistics* (New York: Random House, 1990). Aggregate sales data are from tables in *Hoover's Handbook of World Business 1993* (Austin, Tex.: Reference Press, 1993) for the world's 500 largest industrial corporations, the world's 50 largest utilities, the world's 50 largest retailing companies, and the world's 50 largest diversified service companies. Many sources indicate that only forty of the hundred largest economies are corporations. This smaller figure is based on the *Fortune* list of the world's hundred largest "industrial" corporations, which excludes nonindustrial corporations.
14. Paul Hawken, *The Ecology of Commerce* (New York: HarperCollins, 1993), 92.
15. Sarah Anderson and John Cavanagh, "The Top 200: The Rise of Global Corporate Power," Institute for Policy Studies, Washington, D.C., report released September 25, 1996, 2–3.
16. "A Survey of Multinationals," 6.
17. Asset figures for commercial banks and financial companies are from *Hoover's Handbook of World Business*, 68, 72.
18. Based on Harrison, *Lean and Mean*, 9–11.
19. "Let the Good Times Roll," 28–29.
20. Harrison, *Lean and Mean*, 18.
21. Hawken, *The Ecology of Commerce*, 8.
22. "Executive Pay: The Party Ain't Over Yet," *Business Week*, April 26, 1993, 56–62; "That Eye-Popping Executive Pay: Is Anybody Worth This Much?" *Business Week*, April 25, 1994, 52–58.
23. Brian O'Reilly, "The New Deal: What Companies and Employees Owe One Another," *Fortune*, June 13, 1994, 45.

24. John Naisbitt, *Global Paradox* (New York: William Morrow, 1994), 14.
25. Joan Dye Gussow, "A Nutrition Policy . . . That Leads to a Food Policy . . . That Leads to an Agricultural Policy," *WHY Magazine*, Summer 1993, 25.
26. Krebs, *The Corporate Reapers*, 102.
27. Krebs, *The Corporate Reapers*, 372–82.
28. "Learning to Survive in the '90s," *Business Week*, January 10, 1994, 95.
29. "Channeling Big Stores' Awesome Clout," *Business Week*, December 21, 1992, 98.
30. Donella Meadows, "Wal-Mart Should Come on Our Terms, Not at Our Expense," *Valley News*, June 12, 1993, 26.
31. "Clout! More and More, Retail Giants Rule the Marketplace," *Business Week*, December 21, 1992, 66–73; "Brawls in Toyland," *Business Week*, December 21, 1992, 36–37.
32. "Clout!" 73.
33. Laurie Udesky, "Sweatshops behind the Labels: The 'Social Responsibility' Gap," *The Nation*, May 16, 1994, 666–68.
34. Ms. Diaz's testimony before a hearing of the Subcommittee on Labor-Management Relations, Committee on Education and Labor, U.S. House of Representatives, Wilkes-Barre, Pa., June 7, 1994, as cited in an ad placed in the *New York Times*, June 19, 1994, A-23, by the International Ladies Garment Workers Union.
35. "Damping Labor's Fires," *Business Week*, August 1, 1994, 40–41.
36. Robert A. Senser, "Outlawing the Crime of Child Slavery," *Freedom Review*, November–December 1993, 29–35.

Chapter 17: No Place for People

1. Jeremy Rifkin, *The End of Work* (New York: G. P. Putnam's Sons, 1995), xiv.
2. William M. Dugger, *Corporate Hegemony* (New York: Greenwood Press, 1989), ix, xiii.
3. Richard Douthwaite, *The Growth Illusion* (Tulsa, Okla.: Council Oak Publishing, 1993), 24.
4. Dugger, *Corporate Hegemony*, 13.
5. Brian O'Reilly, "The New Deal: What Companies and Employees Owe One Another," *Fortune*, June 13, 1994, 50.
6. John Burgess, "Debate on Executive Pay Moves across the Atlantic," *International Herald Tribune*, October 24, 1991, Business/Finance section, 1.
7. Derek Bok, *The Cost of Talent: How Executives and Professionals Are Paid and How It Affects America* (New York: Free Press, 1993), 108–1.
8. Lee Smith, "Burned-Out Bosses," *Fortune*, July 25, 1994, 44–46.
9. Smith, "Burned-Out Bosses," 44–46.
10. Sarah Lyall, "Publishing Chief Is Out at Viacom," *New York Times*, June 15, 1994, D-1, D-16.
11. Alison Leigh Cowan and John Holusha, "Eastman Kodak Chief Is Ousted by Directors," *New York Times*, August 7, 1993, 49.
12. "Getting Rid of the Boss," *The Economist*, February 6, 1993, 13.
13. "The Contingency Work Force," *Fortune*, January 24, 1994, 31.
14. "Planning a Career in a World Without Managers," *Fortune*, March 20, 1995, 72–80.
15. "Slash and Earn on the Continent," *Business Week*, May 2, 1994, 45–46.
16. "Europe's Economic Agony," *Business Week*, February 15, 1993, 49.
17. "Rage in the Streets," *Business Week*, April 11, 1994, 46.
18. "Doleful," *The Economist*, October 9, 1993, 17.
19. "Doleful," 17.
20. "Doleful," 17.
21. "Europe's Economic Agony," 48–49.

Chapter 18: The Ecological Revolution

1. Willis Harman, *Global Mind Change: The Promise of the Last Years of the Twentieth Century* (Indianapolis, Ind.: Knowledge Systems, 1988).
2. Wangari Maathai, "All We Need Is Will," in *Can the Environment Be Saved without a Radical New Approach to World Development?* (Geneva: CONGO Planning Committee for UNCED, 1992), 27.
3. Mary E. Clark, "The Backward Ones," *PCDForum Column* no. 51, June 25, 1993.
4. The following discussion draws on Harman, 34–35; Duane Elgin, *Awakening Earth: Exploring the Evolution of Human Culture and Consciousness* (New York: William Morrow, 1993), 15–16; and personal communications with William Ellis.
5. Edward McNall Burns, *Western Civilizations: Their History and Their Culture*, 5th ed. (New York: W. W. Norton, 1958), 520.
6. Harman, *Global Mind Change*, 12.
7. Burns, *Western Civilizations*, 521.
8. Jacob Needleman, *Money and the Meaning of Life* (New York: Doubleday, 1991), 40–42.
9. Joe Dominguez and Vicki Robin, *Your Money or Your Life: Transforming Your Relationships with Money and Achieving Financial Independence* (New York: Viking, 1992), 54.
10. Dominguez and Robin, *Your Money or Your Life*, 54.
11. Fritjof Capra, *The Tao of Physics* (New York: Bantam Books, 1976); Gary Zukav, *The Dancing Wu Li Masters: An Overview of the New Physics* (New York: Bantam Books, 1979). Fritjof Capra, *The Turning Point: Science, Society, and the Rising Culture* (New York: Simon and Schuster, 1982), and Harman, *Global Mind Change*, deal specifically with the implications for society.
12. This thesis is developed in George T. Lockland, *Grow or Die: The Unifying Principle of Transformation* (New York: Dell, 1973).
13. Arnold Toynbee, *A Study of History*, abridgement of vols. 1–6 by D. D. Somerwell (New York: Oxford University Press, 1947), 555.
14. Herman Daly, "Toward Some Operational Principles of Sustainable Development," *Ecological Economics* 2 (1990): 1–6.
15. This scheme is based on James Robertson, *Future Wealth: A New Economics for the 21st Century* (London: Cassell Publishers Limited, 1989).

Chapter 19: Good Living

1. Eknath Easwaran, *The Compassionate Universe: The Power of the Individual to Heal the Environment* (Tomales, Calif.: Nilgiri Press, 1989), 73–74.
2. Margaret J. Wheatley and Myron Kellner-Rogers, *A Simpler Way of Life* (San Francisco: Berrett-Koehler Publishers, 1996), 6.
3. Mary E. Clark, "The Backward Ones," *PCDForum Column* no. 51, June 25, 1993.
4. Robert D. Putnam, "The Prosperous Community: Social Capital and Public Affairs," *The American Prospect* 13 (Spring 1993): 2.
5. Putnam, "The Prosperous Community," 2.
6. Alan Durning, *How Much Is Enough: The Consumer Society and the Future of the Earth* (New York: W. W. Norton, 1992). Durning's terms for the three socioecological classes are consumers, middle income, and poor.
7. Michael Renner, "Assessing the Military's War on the Environment," in Lester R. Brown et al., *State of the World 1991* (New York: W. W. Norton, 1991), 139.
8. David Engwicht, *Reclaiming Our Cities and Towns* (Philadelphia: New Society Publishers, 1993), 17.
9. Engwicht, *Reclaiming Our Cities*, 48–51.
10. Engwicht, *Reclaiming Our Cities*, 45.

11. William E. Rees and Mark Roseland, "From Urban Sprawl to Sustainable Human Communities," *PCDForum Column* no. 54, June 25, 1993.
12. Statistics are reported by Marcia D. Lowe, "Reinventing Transport," in Lester R. Brown et al., *State of the World* 1994 (New York: W. W. Norton, 1994), 82–84, from a study by the U.S. Federal Highway Commission. For further discussion, see Engwicht, 138–44.
13. Nicholas Albery, Matthew Mezey, and Peter Ratcliffe (eds.). *Social Innovations: A Compendium* (London: Institute for Social Innovations), 92–93.
14. Robyn Williams, foreword to *Reclaiming Our Cities and Towns*, by Engwicht.
15. Application of these concepts to villages in India is developed in detail in Anil Agarwal and Sunita Narain, *Towards Green Villages: A Strategy for Environmentally Sound and Participatory Rural Development* (New Delhi: Centre for Science & Environment, 1989).
16. Alan Thein Durning and Ed Ayres, "The Story of a Newspaper," *World Watch*, November/December 1994, 30–32.
17. Lester R. Brown, Christopher Flavin, and Sandra Postel, *Saving the Planet: How to Shape an Environmentally Sustainable Economy* (New York: W. W. Norton, 1991), 65.
18. Brown, Flavin, and Postel, *Saving the Planet*, 65.
19. Brown, Flavin, and Postel, *Saving the Planet*, 68.
20. Brown, Flavin, and Postel, *Saving the Planet*, 70.
21. *Webster's New World Dictionary*, 2d college ed. (New York: Simon and Schuster, 1980), s.v. "job."
22. *Webster's New World Dictionary*, s.v. "livelihood."
23. The armed forces and defense worker estimates are from UNDP, *Human Development Report 1994* (New York: Oxford University Press, 1994), 47, 60.

Chapter 20: Agenda for Change

1. Herman E. Daly and John B. Cobb Jr., *For the Common Good: Redirecting the Economy toward Community, the Environment, and a Sustainable Future* (Boston: Beacon Press, 1989), 174.
2. As cited in Daly and Cobb, *For the Common Good*, 209.
3. Paul Hawken, *The Ecology of Commerce: A Declaration of Sustainability* (New York: Harper Business, 1993), 108.
4. Hawken, *The Ecology of Commerce*, 120.
5. Russell Baker, "The Big Hog Wallow," *New York Times*, November 1, 1994, A27.
6. Bishan Singh, "A Social Economy: The Emerging Scenario for Change," in Tina Liamzon (ed.), *Civil Society and Sustainable Livelihoods Workshop Report* (Rome: Society for International Development, 1994), 29–37.
7. Gar Alperovitz, "Ameristroika Is the Answer," *Washington Post*, December 13, 1992, Cl.
8. For a partial inventory and assessment of this experience, see Jeff Shavelson, *A Third Way: A Sourcebook: Innovations in Community-Owned Enterprise* (Washington, D.C.: National Center for Economic Alternatives, 1990).
9. See Richard J. Barnet and John Cavanagh, *Global Dreams* (New York: Simon and Schuster, 1994), 416.
10. Herman E. Daly and John B. Cobb Jr., *For the Common Good: Redirecting the Economy toward Community, the Environment, and a Sustainable Future*, 2d. ed. (Boston: Beacon Press, 1994), 414–35.
11. See Barnet and Cavanagh, *Global Dreams*, 415–16.
12. Hawken, *The Ecology of Commerce*, 163.
13. James Robertson, *Benefits and Taxes: A Radical Strategy* (London: New Economics Foundation, March 1994), 12–17. A variant of the guaranteed income, a graduated positive income tax, is proposed by Daly and Cobb, *For the Common Good* (1989), 315–23. These

two sources discuss the history of such proposals and the support they have enjoyed from across the political spectrum.

14. Sixto K. Roxas, "Strategies for Community Economic and Social Transformation," in Liamzon, *Civil Societies and Sustainable Livelihoods*, 41–47.
15. Based on recommendations of a multiyear study on alternatives to corporate globalization to be released by the International Forum on Globalization in Spring 2001.
16. See Patricia Adams, *Odious Debts: Loose Lending, Corruption, and the Third World's Environmental Legacy* (London: Earthscan, 1991).
17. See Tim Lang and Colin Hines, *The New Protectionism: Protecting the Future against Free Trade* (New York: New Press, 1993), 127, for a discussion of positive approaches to protectionism.

Chapter 21: Making Money, Growing Poorer

1. Interview with Paul Hawken and David Korten by Sarah van Gelder, "Corporate Futures," *YES! A Journal of Positive Futures*, Summer 1999, 40.
2. Anita Roddick, *Business as Unusual: The Triumph of Anita Roddick* (London: Thorsons, 2000), 7.
3. Alan T. Saracevic, "Investors ponder if tech stocks can continue to pull the market," *The San Francisco Examiner*, January 3, 2000, B-1.
4. Marcia Vickers and Gary Weiss, "The Wall Street Hype Machine," *Business Week*, April 3, 2000, 168.
5. Vickers and Weiss, "Wall Street's Hype Machine," 113–127.
6. David Malin Roodman, *Vital Signs 2000* (Washington, D.C.: WorldWatch Institute, 2000), 75.
7. World Bank, *2000 World Development Indicators*, 264, www.worldbank.org/data/wdi2000.
8. Source: The Financial Markets Center. http://www.fmcenter.org.
9. *Flow of Funds Accounts of the United States* (Washington, D.C.: Board of Governors of the Federal Reserve System, June 9, 2000), 58.
10. Joseph Kahn, "More Scrutiny Is Sought for Firms That Run or Lend to Hedge Funds," *The New York Times*, April 29, 1999, *The New York Times* on the web, archives.
11. Walden Bello, "The Rise and Fall of Southeast Asia's Economy," *The Ecologist*, Vol. 28, No. 1, January/February 1998, 9–17; Walden Bello, "The End of the Asian Miracle," *The Nation*, January 12/19, 1998, 16–21; and Walden Bello, Shea Cunningham, and Li Kheng Poh, *A Siamese Tragedy: Development and Disintegration in Modern Thailand* (Oakland, Calif.: Food First, 1998).
12. UNRISD, *Visible Hands: Taking Responsibility for Social Development* (Geneva: UNRISD, 2000), 10.
13. Statistics reported by the Center for Response Politics, www.opensecrets.org.
14. "Influence, Inc.: The Bottom Line in Washington Lobbying," 1999 Edition, Washington, D.C.: The Center for Responsive Politics, www.opensecrets.org.
15. Don Van Natta Jr., "Campaign Fund-Raising Is at Record Pace," *The New York Times*, October 3, 1999, *The New York Times* on the web, archives.
16. For well documented cases see Sharon Beder, *Global Spin: The Corporate Assault on Enviornmentalism* (Dartington, U.K.: Green Books, Ltd., 1997); John Stauber and Sheldon Rampton, *Toxic Sludge Is Good for You! Lies, Damn Lies and the Public Relations Industry* (Monroe, ME: Common Courage Press, 1995); Jed Greer and Kenny Bruno, *Greenwash: The Reality Behind Corporate Environmentalism* (New York: The Apex Press, 1996); and *PR Watch Quarterly* published by the Center for Media & Democracy in Madison, Wisconsin, http://www.prwatch.org.
17. This account is based on the UN Global Compact website www.unglobal

compact.org and TRAC–Transnational Resource & Action Center, *Tangled Up In Blue: Corporate Partnerships at the United Nations* (San Francisco: TRAC, 2000). See also the TRAC website at www.corpwatch.org.

18. As quoted in TRAC, *Tangled Up in Blue*, 5.

19. Ian Urbina, "The Corporate PNTR Lobby: How Big Business Is Paying Millions to Gain Billions in China," *Multinational Monitor*, May 2000, 7–11 documents the intensive lobbying effort by U.S. corporations that pushed through a China trade bill strongly opposed by American labor unions and supported by only 18 percent of the U.S. public.

20. The website of the Center for Media & Democracy is a good place to start, www.prwatch.org. In addition to their own quarterly publication *PR Watch* they provide extensive links to other information sources.

21. UNDP, *Human Development Report 1999* (New York: Oxford University Press, 2000), 3.

22. World Bank, *World Development Report 2000/2001: Attacking Poverty* (New York: Oxford University Press, 2001), 3.

23. Chuck Collins and Felice Yeskel, *Economic Apartheid in America: A Primer on Economic Inequality & Insecurity* (New York: The New Press, 2000), 56.

24. The median wage is the pay of the worker in the middle. Fifty percent of workers earn more and fifty percent earn less. It gives a more accurate picture of the situation of the typical worker than does the average wage, which is biased sharply upward by exorbitant increases at the very top of the pay scale that are of no benefit to the average worker.

25. "Is the U.S. Building a Debt Bomb?" *Business Week*, November 1, 1999, 40–42; and Wells Capital Management, *National and Global Trends*, October 2000.

26. Collins and Yeskel, *Economic Apartheid in America*, 58–9.

27. "Executive Pay," *Business Week*, April 17, 2000, 100–11.

28. Economic Policy Institute, "Paycheck Economics: Wage and Income Trends—Up the Down Escalator," www.epinet.org.

29. Rich Miller, "All Get Richer—Except the Poor," *Business Week*, January 31, 2000, 47.

30. Sarah Porter, "Developing-Country Debt Increases," *Vital Signs 2000* (Washington, D.C.: WorldWatch Institute, 2000), 72.

31. The International Forum on Globalization, *Alternatives to Economic Globalization: A Citizen's Agenda*, draft report prepared by the Institute for Policy Studies, Washington, D.C., 2000.

32. Gretchen Morgenson, "Cautionary Note on Mergers: Bigger Does Not Mean Better," *The New York Times*, December 8, 1998, C-1 & C-23; and Michael Renner, "Corporate Mergers Skyrocket," in Lester R. Brown, Michael Renner, and Brian Halwell, *Vital Signs 2000: The Environmental Trends That Are Shaping Our Future* (New York: W.W. Norton, 2000), 142–143.

33. Stanley Reed and Carol Matlack, "The Big Grab: Deal Mania May Be Even Hotter in Europe This Year,"

34. "Welcome to the 21st Century: With one stunning stroke, AOL and Time Warner create a colossus and redefine the future," *Business Week*, January 24, 2000 (cover story).

35. Bryan Gruley, "Why Laissez Faire Is The Washington Line on Telecom Mergers: Even as the Big Get Bigger, Regulators Hope Deals will Boost Competition," *The New York Times*, May 10, 1999, A-1.

36. Gretchen Morgenson, "Cautionary Note on Mergers," C-1 & C-23.

37. Seth Dunn, "Weather Damages Drop," *Vital Signs 2000* (Washington, D.C.: WorldWatch Institute, 2000), 76.

38. World Resources Institute, Sustainable Development Information Service, "Global Trends," http://www.wri.org/index.html.

39. United Nations Development Programme, UN Environment Programme, World Bank,

and World Resources Institute, *World Resources 2000–2001: People and Ecosystems, The Fraying Web of Life* (Washington, D.C.: World Resources Institute, 2000).

40. World Resources Institute, Sustainable Development Information Service, "Global Trends," http://www.wri.org/index.html.

41. Theo Colborn, Dianne Dumanoski, and John Peterson Myers, *Our Stolen Future* (New York: Dutton, 1996). See also the series of articles on endocrine disrupters in *YES! A Journal of Positive Futures*, Summer 1998.

42. Jonathon Carr-Brown and Martin Meissonnier, "Tests Show Gulf War Victims Have Uranium Poisoning," *The Sunday Times: World*, September 3, 2000; Jonathon Carr-Brown, "One Man's Gulf War Threatens to Go Nuclear," *The Sunday Times: New Review*, September 10, 2000; Former U.S. Attorney General Ramsey Clark, "An International Appeal to Ban the Use of Depleted Uranium Weapons," www.iacenter.org/depleted/appeal.htm; and J. J. Richardson, "Depleted Uranium: The Invisible Threat," Mother Jones Wire, June 23, 1999, www.motherjones.com/total_coverage/kosovo/reality_check/du.html.

43. Arthur Firstenberg, "Radio Waves: Invisible Danger," *Earth Island Journal*, Winter 2000–2001, 25.

44. For a thorough and authoritative analysis of the dangers inherent in the indiscriminate modification of genetic materials for profit see Mae-Wan Ho, *Genetic Engineering: Dream or Nightmare?* (Bath, U.K.: Gateway Books, 1998).

45. Anthony DePalma with Simon Romero, "Crop Genetics On the Line In Brazil," *The New York Times*, May 16, 2000, *The New York Times* on the web, archives.

46. David Barboza, "Industry Moves to Defend Biotechnology," *The New York Times*, April 4, 2000, C-6.

47. UNDP, *Human Development Report 2000* (New York: Oxford University Press, 2000), 4.

48. Lester R. Brown, Michael Renner, and Brian Halwell, *Vital Signs 2000: The Environmental Trends That Are Shaping Our Future* (New York: W.W. Norton, 2000), 102.

49. June 21, 2000, ILO press release on the ILO World Labour Report 2000.

50. Ewa Ruminska-Zimny, "Human Poverty in Transition Economies: Regional Overview for HDR 1997," www.undp.org/hdro/oc22a.htm.

51. Stephen F. Cohen, "American Jouranlism and Russia's Tragedy," *The Nation*, October 2, 2000, 23.

52. Lester Brown, "Challenges of the New Century," in Lester Brown, et al., *State of the World 2000* (New York: W. W. Norton, 2000), 5.

53. Stephanie Strom, "Japanese Unemployment at Record High Ahead of Elections," *The New York Times*, April 1, 2000.

54. Darius Mehri, "Death by Overwork: Corporate Pressure on Employees Takes a Fatal Toll in Japan," *Multinational Monitor*, June 2000, 26–28.

55. Marc Miringoff and Marque-Luisa Miringoff, *The Social Health of the Nation: How America Is Really Doing* (New York: Oxford Press, 1999), 150–151. Although the rate of violent crime in America declined by 25 percent from 1991 to 1998, it was still up by 109 percent over 1970 according to figures from the Federal Bureau of Investigation, *Uniform Crime Reports*, from www.fbi.gov/ucr/ and Miringoff and Miringoff, 203.

56. Bureau of Justice Statistics, from www.ojp.usdoj.gov/bjs/correct.htm; and Miringoff and Miringoff, *The Social Health of the Nation*, 204.

57. Jerome G. Miller, "The American Gulag," *YES! A Journal of Positive Futures*, Fall 2000, 12–17.

58. David Cay Johnston and Joseph B. Treaster, "New York Life Sued Over Fees on Its Pensions," *The New York Times*, June 15, 2000, 8.

59. John Sullivan with Alex Berenson, "Brokers Charged With Crime Figures In Complex Fraud," *The New York Times*, June 15, 2000, A-1 & C27.

60. Floyd Norris and Diana B. Henriques, "3 Admit Guilt in Falsifying CUC's Books," *The New York Times*, June 15, 2000, C-1, C-8.

61. Ken Silverstein, "Trillion-Dollar Hideaway," *Mother Jones*, November/December 2000, 38–45.

62. Stephen Nathan, "The Prison Industry Goes Global," *YES! A Journal of Positive Futures*," Fall 2000, 34–35; and Henri E. Cauvin, "Wackenhut Set to Build New Prison in South Africa," *The New York Times*, August 12, 2000, *The New York Times* on the Web, archives.

63. Josh Levin, "The History of Prison Labor," *YES! A Journal of Positive Futures*," Fall 2000, 15.

64. Francis X. Clines, "Rooms Available in Gated Community: $20 a Day," *The New York Times*, July 10, 2000, A-14.

Chapter 22: The Living Democracy Movement

1. *States of Unrest: Resistance to IMF Policies in Poor Countries* (London: World Development Movement, 2000).

2. Dan Fineren, "Mexico Farmers Protest Cheap Imports from El Norte," *The New York Times*, April 18, 2000, C-4.

3. Calvin Sims, "Thousands Ring Okinawa Base in Demonstration Against U.S.," *The New York Times*, July 21, 2000, A-8.

4. Alun Griffiths, "Anti-Globalization Forces Rally in France," *YES! A Journal of Positive Futures*, Fall 2000, 7.

5. Paul Cienfuegos, "Sprouting Wings: A New Movement for Corporate Responsibility Takes Flight," *Business Ethics*, July/August 2000, 10–11.

6. Rick Bragg, "Jurors in Florida Give Record Award in Tobacco Case," *The New York Times*, A-1 & A-10; and Barry Meir, "Industry Crosses Troubling Line," *The New York Times*, July 15, 2000, A-10.

7. Andrew Pollack, "Food Companies Urged to End Use of Biotechnology Products," *The New York Times*, July 20, 2000, C-6.

8. David Barboza, "Farmers Are Scaling Back Genetically Altered Crops," *The New York Times,* April 1, 2000, A-6.

9. Jan Roberts, "The Earth Charter," *YES! A Journal of Positive Futures*, Winter 2001, 41. For more information go to www.earthcharterusa.org.

10. As reported by the Social Investment Forum, www.socialinvest.org/.

11. Tracy Rysavy, "Mothers for Eco-Justice," *YES! A Journal of Positive Futures*, Summer 1998, 25.

12. The *YES!* website, www.yesmagazine.org, is a rich source of stories and contact information.

13. These are discussed at greater length in *The Post-Corporate World: Life After Capitalism* (San Francisco: Berrett-Koehler Publishers; and West Hartford: Kumarian Press, 1999), 238–241, which also provides further documentation on the many citizen initiatives around the world to restore democracy and local communities and economies. It also includes a chapter on how to become involved. The Philippine movement and its underlying philosophy is described in more detail in Nicanor Perlas, *Shaping Globalization: Civil Society, Cultural Power and Threefolding* (Quezon City, Philippines: Center for Alternative Development Initiatives, 2000).

14. Ted Howard, "Ownership Matters," *YES! A Journal of Positive Futures*, Spring 1999, 24–27.

15. Paul H. Ray and Sherry Ruth Anderson, *The Cultural Creatives: How 50 Million People Are Changing the World* (New York: Harmony Books, 2000); and interview with Paul Ray and Sherry Anderson by Sarah Ruth van Gelder, "A New Culture Emerges," *YES! A Jour-

nal of Positive Futures, Winter 2001, 15–20.

16. Ronald Inglehart, *Modernization and Postmodernization: Cultural, Economic, and Political Change in 43 Societies* (Princeton, N.J.: Princeton University Press, 1997). For a summary report see Duane Elgin and Coleen LeDrew, "Global Paradigm Report: Tracking the Shift Underway," *Yes! A Journal of Positive Futures,* Winter 1997, 21; and Duane Elgin with Collen LeDrew, *Global Consciousness Change: Indicators of an Emerging Paradigm* (San Anselmo, Calif.: Millennium Project, 1997). For further information on Elgin's work visit his web site: www.awakeningearth.org.

17. Parker Palmer, "Integral Life, Integral Teacher," *YES! A Journal of Positive Futures,* Winter 1998/1999, 44–47.

Chapter 23: A Civil Society

1. Interview with Joanna Macy by Sarah Ruth van Gelder, "The Great Turning," *YES! A Journal of Positive Futures,* Spring 2000, 37.

2. Paul H. Ray and Sherry Ruth Anderson, *The Cultural Creatives: How 50 Million People Are Changing the World* (New York: Harmony Books, 2000), 122.

3. For a more complete report see Sarah Ruth van Gelder, "The Love of Life," *YES! A Journal of Positive Futures,* Fall 1999, 60–61.

4. Carol Estes, "White on Black," *YES! A Journal of Positive Futures,* Fall 2000, 59–60.

5. Robert Jeffrey, "Black on White," *YES! A Journal of Positive Futures,* Fall 2000, 61.

6. Interview with Joanna Macy, 34–37.

7. See David C. Korten, *The Post-Corporate World: Life After Capitalism* (San Francisco: Berrett-Koehler Publishers and West Hartford: Kumarian Press, 1999), chapters four through six for further development and documentation of these principles.

8. Nicanor Perlas, *Shaping Globalization: Civil Society, Cultural Power and Threefolding.* (Quezon City, Philippines: CADI, 2000), which is available from CADI, 110 South Rallos Street, Timog, Quezon City, 1103 Philippines, www.cadi.ph or GlobeNet3, 110 Spring Street, Saratoga Springs, NY 12866, U.S.A., www.globenet3.org.

9. In this regard, Ellen Schwartz and Suzanne Stoddard, *Taking Back Our Lives in the Age of Corporate Dominance,* is a wonderful book about how to subvert the system of global corporate rule through joyous, mindful living.

10. Helping to break the isolation is a key element of the mission of *YES! A Journal of Positive Futures,* which devoted its Fall 2000 issue to the cultural awakening and its implications, www.yesmagazine.org.

11. The concept of culture jamming has been developed and popularized by the creative media work of Kalle Lasn and the Adbusters Media Foundation in Vancouver, B.C., publishers of *Adbusters* magazine, www.adbusters.org. See Kalle Lasn, *Culture Jam: The Uncooling of America* (Eagle Book: William Morrow and Company, Inc).

12. Naomi Klein, *No Logo* (New York: Picador, 1999).

13. Amartya Sen, "Global Doubts," *Bridges Between Trade and Sustainable Development,* July–August 2000, 3.

14. As explained in the Introduction, the movement will ultimately name itself. I've chosen here to use the name *living democracy* by which the movement refers to itself in India.

Epilogue: A Choice for Life

1. Daniel Kemmis, "20 Questions," *Utne Reader,* January–February 1995, 79.

INDEX

ABOUT THE AUTHOR

Dr. David C. Korten has over thirty-five years' experience in preeminent business, academic, and international development institutions as well as in contemporary citizen action organizations. He is a co-founder and board chair of the Positive Futures Network, publisher of *YES! A Journal of Positive Futures*, founder and president of The People-Centered Development Forum, and an associate of the International Forum on Globalization.

Korten earned his M.B.A. and Ph.D. degrees at the Stanford University Graduate School of Business. Trained in economics, organization theory, and business strategy, his early career was devoted to setting up business schools in low income countries—starting with Ethiopia—in the hope that creating a new class of professional business entrepreneurs would be the key to ending poverty. He completed his military service during the Vietnam War as a captain in the U.S. Air Force, serving at the special Air warfare school and in the Air Force headquarters command and the Office of the Secretary of Defense.

Korten then served for five and a half years as a faculty member of the Harvard University Graduate School of Business where he taught students in Harvard's middle management and M.B.A. programs. He also served as academic director and Harvard advisor to the Nicaragua-based Central American Management Institute. He subsequently joined the staff of the Harvard Institute for International Development, where he headed a Ford Foundation–funded project to strengthen the organization and management of national family planning programs.

In the late 1970s, Korten left U.S. academia and moved to Southeast Asia, where he lived for nearly fifteen years, serving first as a Ford Foundation project specialist, and later as Asia regional advisor on development management to the U.S. Agency for International Development (USAID). His work there won him international recognition for his contributions to pioneering the development of powerful strategies for transforming public bureaucracies into responsive support systems dedicated to strengthening community control and management of land, water, and forestry resources.

Disillusioned by the evident inability of USAID and other large official aid donors to apply the approaches that had been proven effective by the nongovernmental Ford Foundation, Korten broke with the official aid system. His last five years in Asia were devoted to working with leaders of Asian nongovernmental organizations on identifying the root causes of development failure in the region and building the capacity of civil society organizations to function as strategic catalysts of national- and global-level change.

Korten came to realize that the crisis of deepening poverty, growing inequality, environmental devastation, and social disintegration he was observing in Asia was also being experienced in nearly every country in the world—including the United States and other "developed" countries. Furthermore he concluded that the United States was actively promoting—both at home and abroad—the very policies that were deepening the resulting global crisis. For the world to survive, the United States must change. Korten returned to the United States in 1992 and has since devoted his life to advancing that change.

Korten's publications are required reading in university courses around the world. He has authored or edited numerous books, including *When Corporations Rule the World* and *The Post-Corporate World: Life After Capitalism*, both published by Kumarian Press and Berrett-Koehler Publishers, and *Getting to the 21st Century: Voluntary Action and the Global Agenda* published by Kumarian Press. He contributes regularly to edited books and professional journals, and to a wide variety of periodical publications. He is also a popular international speaker and a regular guest on talk radio and television.

BK Selected Titles from Berrett-Koehler Publishers

What if Boomers Can't Retire?:
How to Build Real Security Not Phantom Wealth
Thorton Parker

Birth of the Chaordic Age
Dee Hock

Building a Win-Win World: Life Beyond Global Economic Warfare
Hazel Henderson

The Age of Participation:
New Governance for the Workplace and the World
Patricia McLagan and Christo Nel

Economic Insanity:
How Growth-Driven Capitalism is Devouring the American Dream
Roger Terry

A Higher Standard of Leadership: Lessons from the Life of Gandhi
Keshavan Nair

Stewardship: Choosing Service Over Self-Interest
Peter Bock

The New Management:
Bringing Democracy and Markets Inside of Organizations
William E. Halal

Tyranny of the Bottom Line:
Why Corporations Make Good People Do Bad Things
Ralph Estes

The Courageous Follower: Standing Up To and For Our Leaders
Ira Chaleff

EcoManagement:
The Elmwood Guide to Ecological Auditing and Sustainable Business
Ernest Callenbach, Fritjof Capra, Lenore Goldman, Rüdiger Lutz, and Sandra Marburg

Future Search: An Action Guide to Finding Common Ground in
Organizations and Communities
Marvin R. Weisbord and Sandra Janoff

Leadership and the New Science: Discovering Order in a Chaotic World
Revised and Expanded Edition
Margaret J. Wheatley

Send orders to: **Berrett-Koehler Publishers**
                        450 Sansome St., 12ᵗʰ Floor
                        San Francisco, CA 94111-3320 USA
                        Fax: (415) 362-2512
                        Website: www.bkconnection.com
                        Or order by phone: (800) 929-2929

What people are saying about

YES!

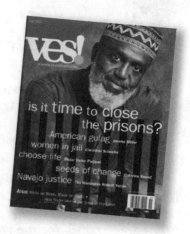

YES! is the best source I know for inspiration, information, connections, and stories for those of us who believe there is an alternative to a world torn apart by greed and violence—that for every "no" there is a "Yes".

David C. Korten, author of
When Corporations Rule the World

YES! is a joy to read—it does a beautiful job of telling the new story of what people are doing to create hope in a difficult world. It carries an unspoken spirituality where actions are valued and a longed for tomorrow seems a little closer than we realized.

Peter Block, author of *Stewardship*

YES! is . . . the bible of the sustainability movement.

The Seattle Weekly

YES! is published by the Positive Futures Network, an independent, non-profit organization based on Bainbridge Island, Washington in the United States. The organization was founded in 1996 by David Korten, YES! Editor Sarah van Gelder, and other visionaries concerned about the social, ecological, economic, and spiritual crises of our times. The Network's purpose is to illuminate and encourage the deep shifts in culture and institutions that lead to a more just, sustainable, and compassionate future.

The Positive Futures Network
P. O. Box 10818, Bainbridge Island, WA, 98110 USA
www.yesmagazine.org
www.futurenet.org

Stay in touch with the ideas that make a difference....

YES! —A Journal of Positive Futures is a quarterly magazine dedicated to tracking and encouraging the ideas and actions that can lead us all to a more just, sustainable, and compassionate future.

In each issue, the editorial team led by Sarah van Gelder brings you:

- **Practical ideas on steps you can take** to help shape the future such as creating a community money system or a supportive study circle, voicing your views on trade agreements or corporate charters, buying goods or investing in companies that fit your values, simplifying your life and nurturing your inner wisdom.

- Writers and visionaries such as **David Korten, Vandana Shiva, Donella Meadows, Juliet Schor, Naomi Wolf, Vicki Robin, Anita Roddick, Fritjof Capra, Rebecca Adamson, Archbishop Desmond Tutu, David Orr.**

- **Stories of emerging movements** for change—environmental justice, socially responsible investing, community-supported agriculture, nonviolence, voluntary simplicity, fair trade, and many more.

- **Resource guides** featuring publications, videos, web sites, organizations, and individuals that can tell you more about the topics covered in *YES!*

- **Reviews of leading-edge books** and videos on sustainable communities, alternative economics, spiritual growth, and much more.

Subscribe to *YES!*

(800) 937-4451 (International, call
1 (206) 842-0216)
Email: yes@futurenet.org

The Positive Futures Network
P. O. Box 10818,
Bainbridge Island, WA, 98110 USA
www.futurenet.org

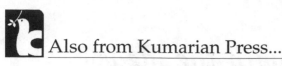 Also from Kumarian Press...

Globalization

The Post-Corporate World
David C. Korten

Beyond Globalization: Shaping a Sustainable Global Economy
Hazel Henderson

Bound: Living in the Globalized World
Scott Sernau

Capitalism and Justice: Envisioning Social and Economic Fairness
John Isbister

Globalization on Trial: The Human Condition and the Information Civilization
Farhang Rajaee

International Development, Environment, Conflict Resolution, Gender Studies, Global Issues

The Cuban Way: Capitalism, Communism and Confrontation
(Named 'Outstanding Academic Title' by CHOICE Magazine) Ana Julia Jatar-Hausman

Exploring the Gaps: Vital Links Between Trade, Environment and Culture
James R. Lee

Inequity in the Global Village: Recycled Rhetoric and Disposable People
Jan Knippers Black

Mainstreaming Microfinance:
How Lending to the Poor Began, Grew and Came of Age in Bolivia
Elisabeth Rhyne

Reconcilable Differences: Turning Points in Ethnopolitical Conflict
Edited by Sean Byrne and Cynthia L. Irvin

Transcending Neoliberalism: Community-Based Development in Latin America
Edited by Henry Veltmeyer and Anthony O'Malley

War's Offensive on Women:
The Humanitarian Challenge in Bosnia, Kosovo and Afghanistan
Julie A. Mertus for the Humanitarianism and War Project

Visit Kumarian Press at **www.kpbooks.com** or
call **toll-free 800.289.2664** for a complete catalog.

KUMARIAN PRESS